D1416285

001.642
R671 l

Logic and
Structured Design
for Computer Programmers

Harold J. Rood

Washburn University of Topeka

Prindle, Weber & Schmidt

PWS PUBLISHERS

Prindle, Weber & Schmidt • ♣ • Duxbury Press • ♠ • PWS Engineering • ⟁

Statler Office Building • 20 Park Plaza • Boston, Massachusetts 02116

Library,
I.U.P.
Indiana, Pa.

001.642   R671l

C.1

© Copyright 1985 by Harold J. Rood

All rights reserved. No part of this book may be reproduced or transmitted in any form or by any means, electronic or mechanical, including photocopying, recording, or any information storage and retrieval system, without permission, in writing, from the publisher.

PWS Publishers is a division of Wadsworth, Inc.

Printed in the United States of America

85 86 87 88 89 — 10 9 8 7 6 5 4 3 2 1

Library of Congress Cataloging in Publication Data

Rood, Harold J.
    Logic and structured design for computer programmers.

    Includes index.
    1. Electronic digital computers--Programming.
2. Structured programming. 3. Logic, Symbolic and
mathematical. I. Title.
QA76.6.R66 1985   001.64'2   85-533
ISBN 0-87150-869-9

ISBN 0-87150-869-9

Cover photograph © Copyright Peter Angelo Simon/Phototake

Interior design by Trisha Hanlon. Production handled by Debbie Schneider and Susan Graham. Typesetting by Caron LaVallie/PWS Composition Department. Cover designed by Susan Graham. Covers printed by New England Book Components. Text printed and bound by the Maple Vail Book Manufacturing Group.

Preface

This book is written as an introduction to the logic of data processing. It is intended for those who plan, but have not yet begun, to study programming – and especially for those with little background in mathematics or logic. Except for a brief consideration of alphanumeric literals, the book is free from particular languages. This gives the book wider applicability. It also isolates questions of logic from questions of language syntax so readers can concentrate on the logic of a problem without worrying about punctuation, column numbers, and so on. The book works through the logical problems common to many programming languages and provides the background in logic that many programming texts and courses presuppose.

The book is designed to be useful to the student who learns from examples as well as to the student who learns from explanations. The programming examples are designed to illustrate particular points rather than to serve as paradigms. Many aspects of program examples are deliberately oversimplified so that readers will be able to grasp the details of other aspects. Other aspects are oversimplified because the details vary too much from language to language. In other words, the examples were selected on the basis of usefulness as teaching tools; elegance and "real-world" applicability were only secondary considerations.

The design tools included in the text are flowcharts, structured flowcharts, Warnier/Orr diagrams, Nassi-Shneiderman diagrams, and pseudocode. Each of these tools could be used in either program design or systems analysis and design. With the exception of a short section covering systems flowcharts, the various tools are presented as program-design tools without mention of their systems-design capability.

The book presents tools and techniques in such a way that they may be understood by relatively unsophisticated students who will perfect their programming abilities later, as they learn the details of languages and systems and as they mature throughout their careers. The book is not intended as a final word on program design. It is not intended as a recommendation for industry standards or as a definitive statement concerning the programming tools presented.

The text begins by introducing flowcharts as a tool in discussing programming logic. Unstructured flowcharts are used because they are easiest to design at first. Chapter 4 introduces structured flowcharts, Chapter 6 introduces Warnier/Orr diagrams, and Chapter 7 introduces pseudocode and Nassi-Shneiderman diagrams. Each of these chapters invites readers to repeat earlier exercises using these structured program-design methods. By the end of Chapter 7, readers should have a good understanding of four current design/documentation tools: structured flowcharts, pseudocode, Nassi-Shneiderman diagrams, and Warnier/Orr diagrams.

Chapter 8 covers one- and two-dimensional arrays and provides moderately complicated (at the introductory level) problems for designing flowcharts and Warnier diagrams.

Chapter 9 introduces file processing. It covers file construction, including editing, file-extract programs, and file-update programs. Sequential processing was selected for detailed explanation because it presents the most interesting logic problems in file processing and because understanding sequential processing provides a good foundation for understanding file processing in general. ISAM and direct file processing are covered briefly for comparison.

Chapters 2, 3, and 5 deal with set theory and with truth functional logic. Chapters 2 and 3 serve three well-integrated purposes. They introduce set theory, including Venn diagrams, Boolean algebra, and the reduction of natural-language statements to set-theory statements. They suggest ways of using techniques from set theory to simplify programming problems. Finally, they use descriptions and statements from set theory to provide material for flowcharting problems that contain multiple decisions (nested if-thens). (However, Chapter 3 could be omitted without disrupting the flow of the text.) Chapter 5 introduces truth functional logic. It presents truth tables, decision tables, and equivalence rules in moderate detail. Perhaps this chapter's most important contribution is the section on the translation of English-language statements into truth functional statements. The chapters on set theory and truth functional logic both suggest ways of employing these logics to simplify programming problems. The book recognizes that the least complex solution is not always the most appropriate and also that many programmers are unfamiliar with these techniques. Nonetheless, these logics can be very helpful to program designers who understand them, know how to use them, and document them well.

Students who complete a course based on this text will have a good logical background, will be in a much better position to begin their computer language courses, and are more likely to succeed in them. Such students will understand the logic of programming in general and will be able to specify the logic for moderately complex programs. Consequently, when they begin computer language courses, they will be able to concentrate on the features of the particular language and on the application of that language to implement program solutions.

Including a course based on this text in the curriculum allows programming language courses to proceed at a more rapid pace. This course familiarizes students with topics that must otherwise be hurriedly covered at the beginning of (and to some extent throughout) each different language course.

Specific Course Suggestions

Logic and Structured Design for Computer Programmers is written to be useful in a variety of logic courses. It is easily adapted to courses emphasizing traditional logics, to those emphasizing programming logics, and to those emphasizing applications. Chapters 1, 2, and 4 provide a solid foundation for any of the subsequent chapters. The following tables suggest schedules for both semester-length and term-length courses with a variety of emphases.

Table for semester courses.

	Semester Courses 3-Hour				Semester Course 5-Hour
Week	Traditional Logic Emphasis Assignment	Programming Logic Emphasis Assignment	Applications Emphasis Assignment	Balanced Assignment	Assignment
1	1.1-1.4	1.1-1.4	1.1-1.4	1.1-1.4	1.1-1.5
2	1.5	1.5	1.5	1.5	1.6-1.10
3	1.6-1.9	1.6-1.10	1.6-1.10	1.6-1.9	2.1-2.6
4	2.1-2.6	2.1-2.6	2.1-2.6	2.1-2.6	2.7-2.8, 3.1
5	2.7-2.8	2.7-2.8	2.7-2.8	2.7-2.8	3.2-3.6
6	3.1-3.2	4.1-4.3	4.1-4.3	4.1-4.3	4.1-4.5
7	3.3-3.6	4.4	4.4	4.5	5.1-5.5
8	4.1-4.3	4.5	4.5	5.1-5.3	5.6-5.9
9	4.5	6.1-6.2	5.11-5.12	5.4-5.6	5.11-5.12
10	5.1-5.3	6.3-6.4	6.1-6.4, or 7.1 or 7.2	5.7-5.9	6.1-6.3
11	5.4-5.6	6.5-6.6	8.1-8.5	5.11-5.12	6.4-6.6
12	5.7-5.8	7.1	8.6-8.7	6.1-6.2	7.1-7.2
13	5.9-5.10	7.2	8.8-8.10	6.3-6.4	8.1-8.5
14	5.11-5.12	8.1-8.5	9.1-9.3	8.1-8.5	8.6-8.10
15	6.1-6.2	8.6-8.7	9.4	8.6-8.7	9.1-9.4
16	6.3-6.4	8.8-8.10	Appendix A	8.8-8.10	Appendix A

Table for term courses.

	Term Courses 3-Hour			Term Courses 5-Hour		
	Traditional Logic Emphasis	Programming Logic Emphasis	Applications Emphasis	Traditional Logic Emphasis	Programming Logic Emphasis	Applications Emphasis
Week	Assignment	Assignment	Assignment	Assignment	Assignment	Assignment
1	1.1-1.4	1.1-1.4	1.1-1.4	1.1-1.5	1.1-1.5	1.1-1.5
2	1.5	1.5	1.5	1.6-1.9	1.6-1.9	1.6-1.10
3	1.6-1.9	1.6.-1.9	1.6-1.10	2.1-2.6	2.1-2.6	2.1-2.6
4	2.1-2.6	2.1-2.6	2.1-2.6	2.7-8;3.3-4	2.7-8;4.1-3	2.7-8;4.1-3
5	2.7-2.8	2.7-2.8	2.7-2.8	3.5-6;4.1-3	4.4-4.5	4.4-4.5
6	3.3-3.6	4.1-4.3	4.1-4.3	4.5	6.1-6.3	5.11-12;6.1
7	4.1-4.3	4.5	4.5	5.1-5.5	6.4-6.6	6.2-6.4
8	5.1-5.3	6.1-6.2	5.11-5.12	5.6-5.9	7.1-7.2	8.1-8.5
9	5.4-5.7	6.3-6.4	8.1-8.5	5.11-5.12 6.1-4 or	8.1-8.5	8.6-8.10
10	5.11-5.12	7.1-7.2	8.6-8.7	7.1-2	8.6-8.10	9.1-9.4

These suggested courses reflect a pace that will allow beginning students to master the material. That is, they should be able to perform well on closed-book examinations over questions comparable to the assigned exercises. Students who have completed several programming courses will be able to proceed more quickly. Other students will find the material challenging and will proceed at a slower pace. The difficulty of the material can be controlled by assigning or not assigning the starred (*) sections and exercises. These parts of the text are the most difficult for beginning students.

Acknowledgments

I appreciate the assistance of a great many people who contributed to this work. There is room here to mention only a few.

Frank Severance first introduced me to Warnier Diagrams and provided many of the ideas used in their presentation. Frank and his course at the Lansing Community College inspired the first attempts to write this text. Although my work has now taken a different direction, it would have withered early without his support.

Professors A. Allan Riveland and Gary E. Schmidt at Washburn University and Larry E. Rinker, Training Coordinator, Santa Fe Railroad, read the first drafts of much of this material and provided the criticism and encouragement necessary to continue the project. Each continued to be of assistance throughout the project by answering what must have seemed an endless stream of questions about computer programming.

Professors Billy E. Milner and Don B. Mitchell of Washburn University and Robert G. Stoller, Manager of Systems and Programming at Washburn, helped with information about computers, programming languages, and documentation.

I appreciate the work of the publisher's reviewers who read and commented on earlier drafts of this work, including Lincoln Andrews, Miami Dade Community College; Albert R. Banocy, Sinclair Community College; Janis Bitely, Henry Ford Community College; Jonah Eng, Florida Junior College at Jacksonville; Gary Haggard, University of Maine; Lister Horn, Pensacola Junior College; Susumu Kasai, St. Louis Community College at Meramec; Edward L. Kosiewicz, Cuyahoga Community College; F.P. Mathur, California State Polytechnic; Edward Polhamus, Danville Community College; Richard K. Wiersba, Bentley College. Kasai's comments greatly helped to determine the direction taken in this text. The notes of Ed Kosiewicz enabled me to correct several misleading and erroneous passages. I wish to thank Al Banocy, Janis Bitely, David E. Schmidt of Fort Hays State University and Douglas P. Davis of St. Bonaventure University for using a preliminary draft of this material in their classes.

Because this material has been used in my own classes, it has undergone continued change and revision. I would especially like to thank Brigid L. Foster, Michelle D. Hubach, Kathleen Thompson, LuAnn J. Pickens, Jayne M. Wehking, and Tracy L. Stotts, who proofread and suggested corrections to one or more of the earlier drafts.

I appreciate the generous support of the Mary B. Sweet Sabbatical Fund of Washburn College, which made possible the study that gave rise to this work. I also thank Artcraft Display Co. Inc. for providing office space and equipment used in preparation of initial and revised drafts of this manuscript.

Finally, an enormous debt is owed to LaJean A. Rinker who prepared the several early versions of this manuscript for reproduction and use on campus and who prepared and proofread the final manuscript for publication.

– Harold J. Rood

Contents

Chapter 6 — *Warnier/Orr Diagrams for Program Design*

Chapter 7 — *Pseudocode and Nassi-Schneiderman Diagrams*

1. Computers and Flowcharts

1.1 Computers and Logic

Logic is the study of various principles or tools of correct reasoning and of the application of those tools in solving problems. This text is concerned with the application of logical tools to programming problems. We will consider two traditional branches of logic: set theory and truth functional logic; and four contemporary logical tools: flowcharts, Warnier diagrams, Nassi-Shneiderman diagrams, and pseudocode. These tools will be used to analyze various types of programming problems and to design solutions for them.

The nature of computer operations makes the use of correct reasoning a programming necessity. In spite of the so-called computer errors that one hears about, computers are very predictable and dependable. They accurately carry out the directions they are given. But, unlike humans, computers do not think; they are incapable of reasoning and can only follow their orders blindly. So, if a computer is to complete a task, all of the reasoning required to perform that task must be done by the programmer and entered into the computer in the form of a computer program. When a programmer has reasoned correctly and has accurately embodied that reasoning in a program, he or she can be sure of obtaining accurate results. On the other hand, the programmer who has not reasoned correctly can expect erroneous results, because computers do not correct even the most obvious programming errors. An erroneous program simply produces erroneous results. Hence, a good understanding of logic is valuable in helping the programmer to avoid programming errors and to produce programs that run as intended.

Most ''real-world'' programming problems are quite complex. The tools of logic are very helpful in **analyzing**, or breaking down, such problems into simple steps and simple instructions. This analysis is important because computers can understand only very simple instructions. The capacity of computers to perform complex tasks depends entirely on the ability of a programmer to analyze those tasks into a series of relatively simple instructions. The use of a programming language such as FORTRAN or COBOL enables the programmer to avoid talking about turning switches on and off, and it permits the programmer to give instructions to add numbers, read data, print names, retrieve information, and so on. But even when programming languages are used, the instructions must remain relatively simple. The greatest challenge of computer programming is the analysis of complicated tasks into a series of directions simple enough for the computer to follow. This analysis is greatly facilitated by the correct application of the tools of logic.

1.2 Algorithms

An **algorithm** is a set of rules or instructions for doing a task or solving a problem. It is a step-by-step series of instructions wherein each successive step is determined by the outcome of previous steps. A computer program is simply an algorithm for a computer that is written in a programming language. Although this book is not concerned with programming languages, it deals extensively with algorithms that could serve as bases for computer programs.

The first algorithm we shall examine is an algorithm for a person rather than for a computer. It is an algorithm for reviewing a sales receipt book, totaling the sales by using a calculator, and listing customers in three columns. Let's call it the ''sales report'' algorithm. Customers who spent more than $1000 are to be listed in column A, those who spent more than $100 but not more than $1000 are to be listed in column B, and all others are to be listed in column C. Because the receipts in the book were written in order, the task will be completed when the first blank receipt is reached. The following algorithm describes one method of completing this task.

1. Clear the calculator.
2. Read a receipt.
3. If the receipt is blank, write down the total on the calculator and stop; otherwise, continue.
4. Add the amount of the sale to the total on the calculator.
5. If the sale was greater than $1000, enter the buyer's name in column A and return to step (2); otherwise, continue.
6. If the sale was greater than $100, enter the buyer's name in column B and return to step (2); otherwise, continue.
7. Enter the buyer's name in column C and return to step (2).

This set of directions is an algorithm. It tells the person what to do and when to do it, including when to stop. It leaves no decisions for the person to make but, instead, specifies the action to be taken on the basis of what happened at previous steps.

In computer programming, algorithms are often designed through the use of special diagrams called flowcharts. Putting the "sales report" algorithm in the form of a flowchart, we obtain Figure 1.1. (The various shapes used in flowcharts will be explained in Section 1.3.)

Figure 1.1 Flowchart prepared for the "sales report" algorithm.

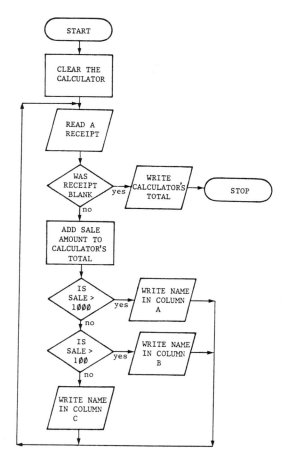

The "sales report" algorithm is fairly simple. It represents a job that is fairly simple. The jobs that you will want computers to do will be much more difficult. Nevertheless, the directions for each step must remain as simple as those given here.

1.3 Flowcharts

Historically, the primary logical tool of computer programmers has been the flowchart. **Flowcharts** are graphic representations of algorithms. In computer programming they form an intermediate step between human understanding of the task to be accomplished and the technical language that directs a computer to complete the various steps of the task. Moreover, in many cases, flowcharts or another comparable tool may be essential in developing and understanding the task. In programs of any appreciable complexity, the variables, contingencies, and logical relationships quickly exceed the ability of even excellent programmers to contemplate them all at once. Flowcharts are a means of considering one part of a problem, and for determining and recording a solution to that part, before going on to the next. Flowcharts are graphic representations, so the logic of the programs they represent is more readily accessible than the logic of the written programs. And flowcharts offer the additional advantage of enabling the programmer to work out the logic of a problem without becoming bogged down by the syntax of a particular language.

Some symbols used in flowcharts have become standard.

The **terminal symbol** indicates the beginning and the end of processing. It frequently contains the word START, STOP, or END.

The **input/output symbol** (or I/O symbol) indicates that the computer is to obtain new data or to record the results of computations. This symbol often contains directions to read records or to print report lines.

The **decision symbol** represents a branch in the flow of a program; it must contain directions that indicate which branch to follow. This symbol usually contains a question, and each of its branches is labeled with an answer.

The **process symbol** contains instructions that are not represented by other symbols. Process symbols usually contain directions for calculations.

Flow direction lines indicate the flow of the program. Arrowheads are drawn where flow direction lines join and where flow direction lines meet other symbols.

The **connector** is used to join areas of a flowchart. Connectors are used in sets that show the transfer of program flow (or control) from one point to another. All connectors in one set contain the same alpha-numeric character (letter or numeral). The connector is used only when points to be joined occur on the same page.

The **striped symbol** is used to represent a predefined process (or series of operations) when the flowcharts that define the process are included with the current set of flowcharts.

The **predefined process symbol** is used to represent a predefined process when the flowcharts that define the process are not included with the current set of flowcharts.

The many standard symbols and flow direction lines reveal considerable information about a program's logic, even when the symbols themselves contain no in-

Figure 1.2 Standard symbols and flow direction lines alone describe much of a program's logic.

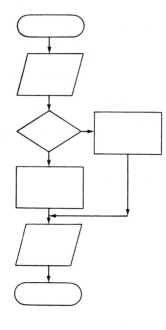

formation. Consider Figure 1.2. From the shape of the symbols and the flow direction lines, one would know that any program using this flowchart would

1. Start.
2. Read some information.[1]
3. Make a decision.
4. On the basis of that decision, do one process or the other.
5. Print a result in either case.
6. Stop.

One advantage of using a flowchart is that it enables us to consider the logic of a computer program without having to consider the program's content at the same time. When programs become complex, the ability to determine and understand logical structure without becoming confused by details is indispensable.

Figure 1.3 is a bit more complex. Examine it, and, before reading on, see whether you can determine what will happen on the basis of the type of symbols that you encounter.

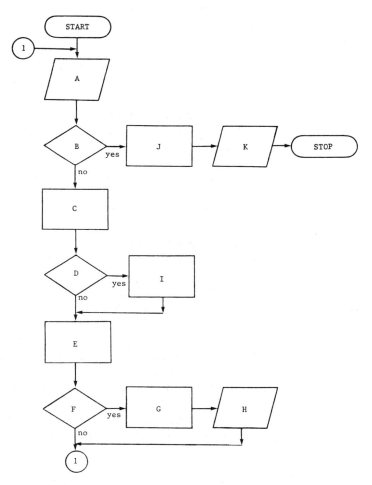

Figure 1.3 Determine what will happen as the program described by this flowchart is run.

This program will start, read information A[2], and then ask question B. If the answer to question B is negative, process C will be accomplished and question D will

---

[1] Because of its placement at the beginning of the flowchart, we assume that the I/O symbol represents the input of data to be processed.
[2] Because of its placement at the beginning of the flowchart, we assume that the I/O symbol represents the input of data to be processed.

be asked. If the answer to question D is affirmative, process I will be accomplished and, in either case, process E will be accomplished and question F will be asked. If the answer to question F is affirmative, process G will be accomplished and H will be printed. Control then passes to the top via connector 1. These steps will continue until an affirmative answer is given when question B is asked. When the answer to question B is affirmative, process J will be accomplished, K will be printed, and the program will stop.

The symbols that make up Figure 1.4 *do* contain directions. Study this flowchart and try to determine what will happen to the values of X and Y as the program runs.

Figure 1.4 Explain what will happen to the values of X and Y as the program described by this flowchart runs.

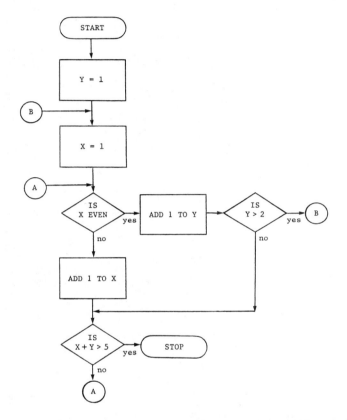

This program starts by setting X and Y both equal to 1. Then, because X is 1, it is not even and 1 is added to X, making it equal to 2. Then, because $X + Y = 3$, the second decision is negative and control is shifted by the connector to A at the top. X is now even, so 1 is added to Y, making $Y = 2$. Y is not greater than 2 and $X + Y$ is 4, so control is shifted to A at the top. X is still even, so 1 is added to Y, making $Y = 3$. Because Y is now greater then 2, control shifts via connector B to B at the top. X is reset to 1; X is not even; 1 is added to X, and control is shifted to A at the top. Continue to trace the steps of this program and verify that, when it stops, the values will be $X = 2$, $Y = 4$.

Attempting to follow even a simple flowchart can become confusing, particularly if one tries to keep track of values mentally. Following flowcharts is greatly facilitated by the use of a table to record values. To set up a **table of values**, construct a series of columns with one column for each different letter in the program. As you read the flowchart, record the value of each letter as it is established. When new values are established, cross out old values and record the new ones. When a value remains the same in two or more operations, it should be repeated on the chart. Table 1.1 was constructed for the flowchart shown in Figure 1.4.

Such a table helps us follow a program, and the numbers at the bottom of the table indicate the values stored in the computer when the program stops. It is impor-

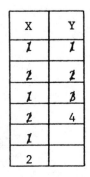

X	Y
1	1
2	2
1	3
2	4
1	
2	

Table 1.1 Table of values for the flowchart shown in Figure 1.4.

tant to realize that only the last entries in the table indicate corresponding values of X and Y. In Table 1.1, for example, the value of Y is not 1 at all times that X is 1. Completed tables do not provide answers to questions such as "What is the value of X when Y is 3?" Like answers can be obtained only by observing the changing values as tables are filled in. Even so, value tables are very helpful in elucidating the detail processing described by flowcharts.

On some occasions we may wish to keep track of how often certain decision symbols or process symbols are reached or what values have been printed. We keep track of these additional program features by expanding our table appropriately. Table 1.2 is also for the flowchart shown in Figure 1.4. It records the number of times that the first decision symbol is reached and the number of times 1 is added to X, in addition to the information recorded in Table 1.1.

Table 1.2 Expanded value table for the flowchart shown in Figure 1.4.

X	Y	First Decision	Add 1 to X
1	1	1	1
2	2	2	2
1	3	3	3
2	4	4	
1		5	
2		6	

Exercises 1.1–1.3

1. Examine the following flowchart, fill in the table of values, and answer the questions.

TABLE OF VALUES

Y	X	PRINT Y	SECOND DECISION

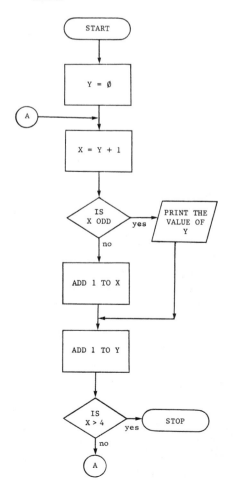

a. What numbers will be printed? (Use the PRINT Y column to record each value printed).
b. What values will X and Y have when the program ends?
c. How often will the second decision be reached?

2. Examine the following flowchart, fill in the table values, and answer the questions.

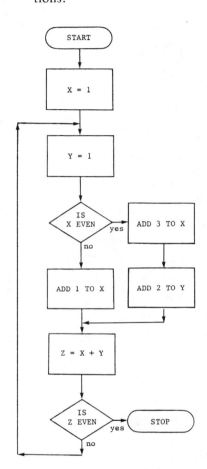

TABLE OF VALUES

X	Y	Z	FIRST DECISION

a. What will the values of X, Y, and Z be when this program ends?
b. How often will the first decision be reached?

1.4 Computers, Memory, and Input/Output

Fortunately, designing programs does not depend on a thorough knowledge of a computer's very complex architecture. A much simplified (perhaps oversimplified) picture of the computer is sufficient to support an understanding of programming logic. Computers can be viewed as consisting of three types of components: input devices, output devices, and the central processing unit or CPU.

As the name suggests, **input devices** are devices for entering programs or data into the computer. Input devices accept data in various forms (such as punched card or magnetic disk), convert that data into a form that is usable within the computer, and then transfer it to the computer's main memory.

The **central processing unit** (sometimes called the mainframe) is composed of a main memory unit, an arithmetic-logic unit, and a control unit. The **main memory unit** stores (1) data and programs that are made available by the input unit and (2) the results of computations carried out by particular programs. The **arithmetic-logic** unit carries out various simple computations as directed by the control unit. The **control unit** carries out the instructions of programs and directs the operation of the other units.

Output devices display or record the various results of a program. Output devices include printers and video screens to display results, and card punches and disk and tape drives to record results.

From the programmer's point of view, the control unit is invisible. Although it carries out the instructions of a program, it is not usually mentioned in them. The arithmetic-logic unit for the most part computes as one would expect it to compute, and few interesting logical considerations arise from it. By comparison, instructions involving the input device, output device, and main memory unit provide the substance for most logical considerations. For this reason, we shall consider computer instructions regarding these units in some detail.

Computer Memory

Nearly all of the instructions in a computer program refer to the computer's main memory. In fact, most of them involve storing something in the memory, altering something that is in the memory, or consulting the memory to determine items previously stored.

It is convenient to picture a computer's memory as consisting of a large number of locations in which data can be stored — similar to a series of mail boxes at an apartment complex. Each location can store exactly one piece of data. As the program is run, some of these locations are assigned names corresponding to the names that the programmer selects for use in the program. When those names occur in the program's instructions, items may be stored at the various locations and items that were stored before may be replaced.

Perhaps the simplest storage instruction directs the computer to store a particular piece of data at a particular location. Often these instructions are written as equations. The name of the storage location is written to the left of the equals sign; the data to be stored is written to the right. So, for example, NUMBER = 2 directs the computer to store the value 2 at the location that it is calling NUMBER.

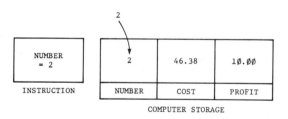

Other instructions alter data that has been stored. For example, ADD 1 TO NUMBER increases by 1 the value of the data that has been stored at NUMBER.

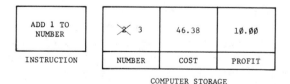

Some storage instructions mention more than one storage location. For example, NUMBER = COST mentions both a location called NUMBER and a location called COST. It directs the computer to take the value stored at COST and duplicate it at NUMBER so that both COST and NUMBER will store the value previously stored at COST.

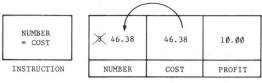

Each storage instruction mentions a unique location at which storage is to take place. That is, a single location name appears to the left of the equals sign. The expression to the right of the equals sign may, however, be more complex. For example, NUMBER = COST + PROFIT is a proper storage instruction. It directs the computer to add the value stored at COST to the value stored at PROFIT and then to store the result at NUMBER.

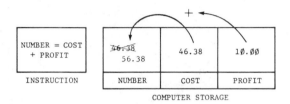

Storage commands involving arithmetic operations (addition, subtraction, and so on) direct the computer to complete the operations specified on the right of the equals sign and to store the result at the location named on the left.

A final variation in storage instructions involves the storage of particular words or symbols (called literals). To store a particular word, we enclose the word in either single or double quotation marks. If we want to store the word *yes* at a location that we were calling FLAG, we would use the instruction FLAG = ''YES''. This instruction would cause the word *yes* (without quotation marks) to be stored at FLAG.

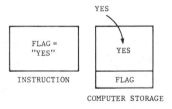

If we had instead written FLAG = YES, the computer would have tried to identify a storage location called YES and to duplicate the value stored at YES at the location called FLAG. This instruction would not usually get the word *yes* stored at FLAG. In general, an instruction with quotation marks placed around a word or a series of symbols concerns itself with that particular word or series of symbols, and that word is not interpreted as the name of a storage location.

Once data has been stored at a location, it will remain there until another instruction stores different data at that location. The data stored at any given memory location reflects the most recently executed storage instruction for that location.

The names of storage locations whose data will change during the execution of a program are called **variable names** or simply **variables**. The names of locations for data that remains constant during program execution are called **program constants**. Both variables and program constants may consist of single letters such as X and Y.

Or, depending on the programming language, they may consist of several letters, numerals, and other characters. When possible, it is good practice to select names that indicate the sorts of data to be stored (COST, then, is a good variable name for a location that will store a cost amount).

Figure 1.5 describes a portion of a computer's memory before and after a series of instructions is executed. Assume that data in the "before" table resulted from previous instructions.

Figure 1.5 (a) Flowchart. (b) "Before" data resulting from previous instructions. (c) Data in the computer's memory after a series of instructions is executed.

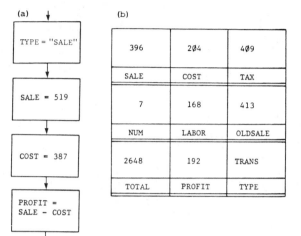

Flowcharts generally incorporate storage instructions within process symbols. These same expressions, particularly equations, are also used in decisions. An equation within a decision is to be interpreted not as an instruction, but as a question about stored values. Occurring within a decision, NUMBER = 5 asks whether the value 5 is stored at NUMBER; COST = GROSS + MARKUP asks whether the sum of the values at GROSS and MARKUP is equal to the value at COST. Answers to these questions, of course, depend on the most recent instructions to store values at the memory locations named.

Input/Output

Most computer operations require data to be entered and results to be printed, displayed, or recorded. Precise instructions and procedures for data input and output vary widely among programming languages. These differences have little effect on the logical design of programs, however, and we shall ignore them. Our early examples will confine input and output to reading records and printing reports.

Data for input may be conveniently divided into fields, records, and files. A **field** is usually a single unit of data (or the space on which a single unit of data could be recorded). A **record** is a collection of fields concerning a single person, thing, or event. A **file** is a collection of similar records concerning a particular group. A retail business might maintain a customer file with a record for each customer. Each record could contain a name field, an address field, and an age field. Figure 1.6 portrays two versions of such a file.

Figure 1.6 Two versions of a customer file.

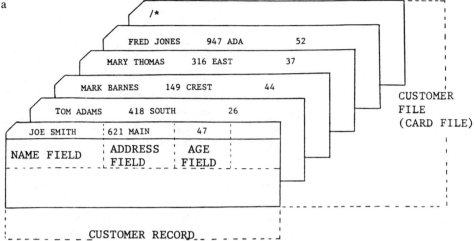

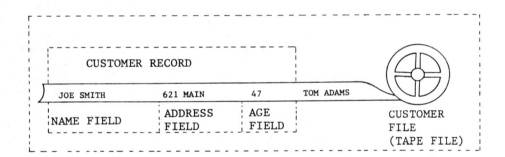

Files may be contained on punched cards, on magnetic tape, or on magnetic disks. The logical construction of elementary programs will not be affected by the method used.[3]

Before data from a file can be used, the file must be opened. We shall represent the instruction to open a file by the word OPEN, followed by the name of the file. The instruction OPEN CUSTOMER FILE prepares the customer file for processing. A companion instruction, CLOSE CUSTOMER FILE, is used after processing of that file is completed.

Once a file is opened, its individual records can be read. The process of reading a record is really a process of duplicating, in the computer's memory, the information on a particular record.

The instruction READ NAME directs the computer to store data from a particular field of the next record at the memory location called NAME. The instruction READ NAME, ADDRESS, AGE directs the computer to store data from three fields of the next record at three memory locations called NAME, ADDRESS, and AGE (see Figure 1.7).[4]

---

[3] However, disk storage provides considerable advantages for more sophisticated programs.

[4] Each language has its own way of designating which fields of the language are to be read.

Figure 1.7 (a) Instruction.
(b) Record.
(c) Computer storage.

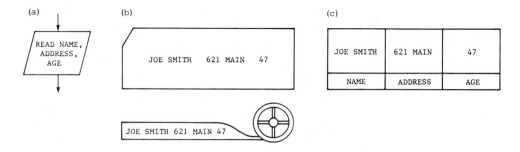

Once data is stored in memory, it remains until the instruction to read is executed again.[5] If the customer file of Figure 1.6 were being read, the second execution of READ NAME, ADDRESS, AGE would replace JOE SMITH with TOM ADAMS; 621 MAIN with 418 SOUTH; and 47 with 26. And this new data would remain available for use until READ NAME, ADDRESS, AGE was executed again.[5]

Diagrams that contain the READ instruction also usually contain an end-of-file or EOF decision. This decision transfers control to another part of the program after all data in a file has been read. The usual question within this decision is whether a special end-of-file marker has been reached. This end-of-file marker is inserted in the input file at the end of data to be processed. (Card files frequently use a card with /* as an end-of-file marker.) When this marker is read, the EOF decision directs control to another part of the program.

The end-of-file marker is not considered part of the data, and under ordinary circumstances it is not processed. And, even though the marker is read, it is not normally counted as one of the records read.

Figure 1.8 describes a simple program to read and process records. If the program described by this flowchart were using the customer record file, the records of Joe Smith through Fred Jones would be read and processed; the end-of-file marker (/*) would be read but not processed. With few exceptions, it is good practice to

Figure 1.8 A simple program to read and process records.

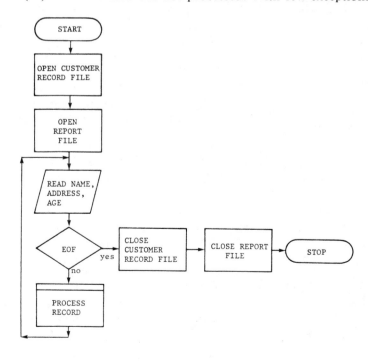

---

[5] Unless the items in storage are changed by some other instruction.

place the EOF decision immediately after the READ instruction. Placing it here helps ensure that the end-of-file marker will not be processed.

The output of information to tape or disk files also requires the opening and closing of files. Some languages require that output files be opened and closed, even though the output is to be a printed report. In such a language, a program to print a sales report would use the instruction OPEN SALES REPORT FILE before printing and the instruction CLOSE SALES REPORT FILE after the last output instruction.

To print a line on a report or a record in a file, we will use the instruction PRINT. The PRINT instruction directs the computer to print information stored at one or more of its memory locations. For example, PRINT NAME directs the computer to print whatever information is stored at the memory location called NAME.

Figure 1.9 (a) Instruction. (b) Computer storage. (c) Report.

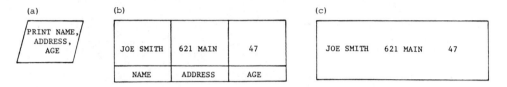

The instruction PRINT NAME, ADDRESS, AGE results in printing the content of three memory locations (see Figure 1.9).

In addition to data stored in memory, PRINT instructions may be used to print literals. The literal to be printed is enclosed in quotation marks following PRINT. The words or symbols within the quotation marks are printed verbatim (that is, word for word and symbol for symbol). For example, the instruction PRINT "NAME" would result in NAME.

Table 1.3 Given these instructions, Figure 1.9 prints these lines.

INSTRUCTION	LINE PRINTED
PRINT NAME	JOE SMITH
PRINT "NAME"	NAME
PRINT "NAME", NAME	NAME JOE SMITH
PRINT "NAME", NAME, "AGE", AGE	NAME JOE SMITH AGE 47
PRINT "MY NAME IS", NAME	MY NAME IS JOE SMITH
PRINT NAME, "IS", AGE, "."	JOE SMITH IS 47.

Table 1.3 shows what would be printed using Figure 1.9 and various print instructions.

In most of our examples, we assume that each PRINT instruction will advance the printer one line. That is, each PRINT instruction will start printing on a different line. When we want to print more than once (in different places) on the same line, we assume that the computer will handle this function without further instructions.

Figure 1.10 describes a program that will read the customer record file of Figure 1.6 and print a report containing the information from each record.

Figure 1.10 This flowchart will generate a report from the customer record file of Figure 1.6.

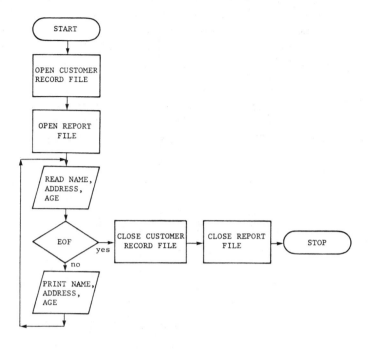

Open and Close, A Final Note

Files must be opened and closed. But, depending on programming language, OPEN and CLOSE instructions may not be required in programs themselves. In such cases, the opening and closing of files are handled along with other special instructions (called **job control**) before the program is executed, or they are handled automatically during program execution. Because OPEN and CLOSE instructions are not universally required – and especially because they pose no interesting problems in the logic of program design – we shall omit them from most of the forthcoming examples.

1.5 Routine Structures in Programs

Several routine structures are found in programs. Once these structures are understood, the logic of programs becomes more manageable.

Loops

The most important of the routine structures is the loop. **A loop** is a circular logical structure. It causes a series of steps to be continuously repeated until a decision passes control to some other part of the program. Loops are diagrammed in either of two ways:

1. By an upward flow direction line
2. By a connector that returns control to a previous point on the chart

Figures 1.11 and 1.12 are simple, logically identical, loops.

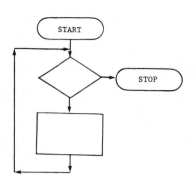

Figure 1.11 A simple loop.

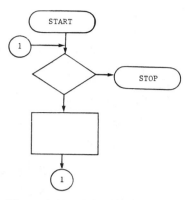

Figure 1.12 This simple loop is logically identical to Figure 1.11.

Perhaps the most important feature of any loop is the decision that allows control to exit the loop. We shall call this decision the **loop exit decision**. Without such a decision, a loop would cycle continuously and the program would never stop. Such undesirable loops are called **infinite loops**. Figures 1.11 and 1.12 both contain the all-important loop exit decision.

Figures 1.11 and 1.12 depict loops with a single process. But loops need not be this simple, nor need they be restricted to process symbols. Figures 1.13 and 1.14 represent more complicated programs that still contain only a single loop.

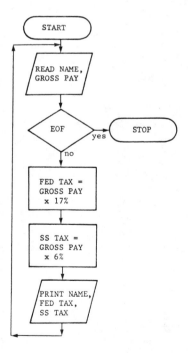

Figure 1.13 A single loop containing a variety of symbols.

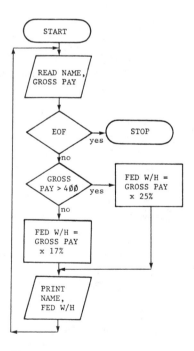

Figure 1.14 A single loop containing a variety of symbols.

Both Figures 1.13 and 1.14 contain the loop exit decision. Note, however, that here the loop exit decisions are in the middle of the loops, whereas in Figures 1.11 and 1.12 they were at the top. This decision may be placed at any location within the loop for unstructured flowcharts. When structured flowcharts are introduced in Chapter 4, greater restrictions will be placed on the location of loop exit decisions.

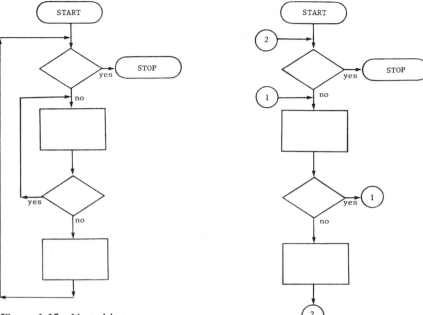

Figure 1.15   Nested loops.

Figure 1.16   Nested loops that are logically identical to those shown in Figure 1.15.

Loops can be (and often are) contained within other loops. In such cases, each loop has a separate loop exit decision. Figures 1.15 and 1.16 are examples of the loop-in-loop structure. Such loops are frequently called **nested loops**.

Figures 1.11 and 1.12 and Figures 1.15 and 1.16 are logically equivalent structures. That is, the members of each pair of charts describe identical processing. Some programmers prefer Figures 1.11 and 1.15, which make the logical structure easier to see, because the additional flow lines present a more detailed visual picture. Other programmers prefer Figures 1.12 and 1.16, because they want flow direction to be downward and to the right only. To ensure consistency, these programmers particularly want to avoid upward flow lines, and they use connectors to transfer control upward. In terms of the logic involved, this difference is primarily a matter of taste. However, in complicated programs, too many flow lines can obscure the program's logic. In such cases the use of connectors is essential.

We shall regard connectors, upward flow direction lines, and combinations of these features as appropriate for the construction of loops.

Counter

It is often desirable to maintain a count of the number of times a process within a loop has been completed. This is accomplished by inserting a **counter** into the flowchart. A counter consists of two elements:

1. A process that sets a variable equal to zero (or initializes the variable)
2. A process that adds 1 to (or increments) the variable each time the loop is completed

Figure 1.17 represents such a structure. In this flowchart, X will start at zero and will increase by 1 each time a loop is completed. When the decision is reached, X

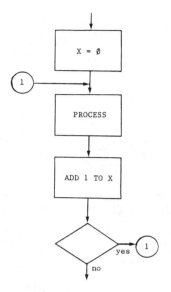

Figure 1.17 This flowchart contains a counter.

will be equal to the number of times the loop has been completed. The counter thereby counts the number of times the process has been accomplished.

An important detail in setting up a counter is that the variable must be initialized (set at zero) *before* the loop is entered. If the variable is initialized within the loop itself, its value will be reset at zero each time through the loop, and no counting will occur (see Figure 1.18). When control passes from this loop, the value of X will be 1 no matter how often the loop was repeated. This mistake most often occurs through careless placement of the return connector or flow direction line. The important thing to remember is to initialize the variable before starting the loop or (and this amounts to the same thing) to place the return arrow after the variable is set at zero, as shown in Figure 1.17.

Counters can be used with decisions to control the number of times a loop will be completed. The decision directs control out of the loop when the counter reaches a particular value. If X is the variable used in the counter, the question in the decision would be IS X = ___. When X equals the number specified, the loop is exited and the program continues (see Figure 1.19).

Note that the loop exit decision asked the question IS X $\geq$ 4 rather than IS X = 4. This is a safety measure. In a simple program, IS X = 4 would be safe enough, but in a complicated program that is poorly designed, the value of X may skip 4. Should this occur when the question reads IS X = 4, control would never leave the loop. By asking IS X $\geq$ 4, one assures that the program will be completed even if an error causes X to skip the value 4.

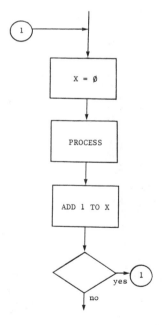

Figure 1.18 This flowchart illustrates the error of initializing the variable within the loop itself.

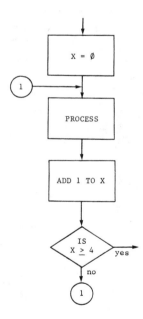

Figure 1.19 In this flowchart, the loop will be repeated four times before the program continues.

The flowchart shown in Figure 1.20 uses a counter (NUMBER) to limit the number of records that are processed. As written, the program anticipates that at least 25 records will be available. The EOF decision is included in case there are fewer than 25 records.

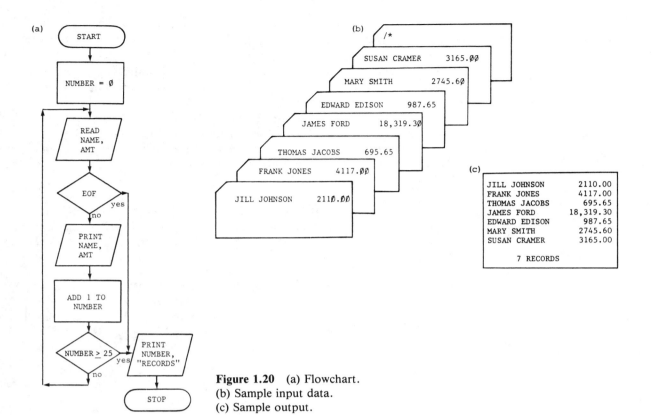

Figure 1.20   (a) Flowchart.
(b) Sample input data.
(c) Sample output.

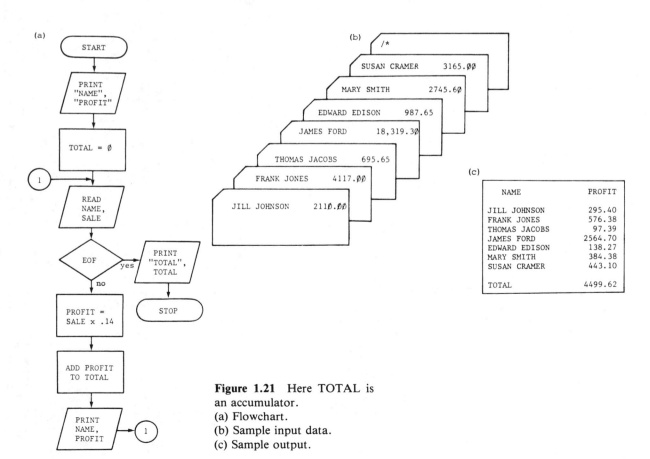

Figure 1.21   Here TOTAL is
an accumulator.
(a) Flowchart.
(b) Sample input data.
(c) Sample output.

Accumulator (Totals and Subtotals)

An **accumulator** is a structure that maintains a current total without affecting on-going calculations or processing. Accumulators are similar to counters in that both consist of a process that sets a variable equal to zero and another process that increments that variable. Accumulators differ from counters in that they are incremented by a variable amount rather than by 1. The variable amount used by accumulators results from data input or calculation. Accumulators are initialized before a loop and incremented within that loop. Their results are printed outside the loop.

The flowchart shown in Figure 1.21 represents a simple program that contains an accumulator called TOTAL. In this flowchart, the profit for each item is accumulated in TOTAL. When EOF is reached, this total is printed.

Note that accumulators are initialized before control enters the loop and are incremented within the loop, just as counters are. If a counter or accumulator is initialized within a loop in which it is incremented, it simply will not count or accumulate as anticipated.

Figure 1.22 represents a program that will read a series of sales figures, calculate, and print their average. Because an average is a total divided by a number of items, both a counter (NUM) and an accumulator (TOTAL) are used.

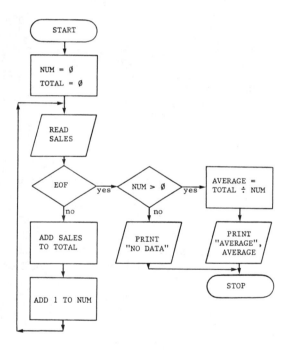

Figure 1.22 This flowchart uses both a counter and an accumulator to calculate an average.

The decision NUM > 0 is included to ensure that division by zero will not be attempted. Any instruction resulting in division by zero normally causes premature termination of a program. If this program were run without any data, it would take the affirmative path at EOF the first time READ was executed, and NUM and TOTAL would both be zero.

Figure 1.23 represents a program that will read a series of values and print the average of the odd-numbered values. To calculate that average, the program must accumulate the sum of the odd-numbered values and also count the number of odd-numbered values. In Figure 1.23, TOTAL is the accumulator for the odd-numbered values, and COUNT is the counter for the odd-numbered values. Both TOTAL and COUNT are initialized outside the loop and are incremented within it. NUM also acts like a counter and will count all of the cards read. But this program makes use

Figure 1.23 TOTAL is used as an accumulator, and both COUNT and NUM act as counters.

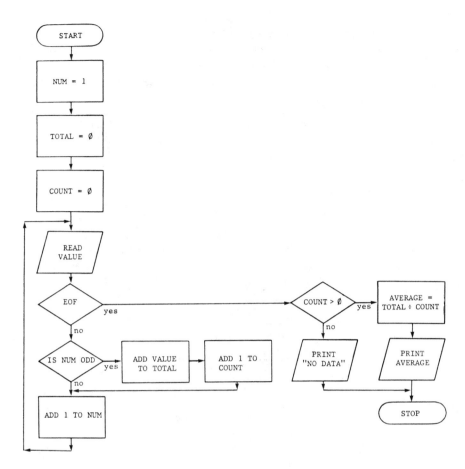

of NUM's value only to determine whether the most recent value read is odd- or even-numbered.

Indicators or Switches

Indicators, often called switches or flags, are used to record some event or circumstance within a program. An indicator consists of two elements:

1. A process that initializes a variable (sets that variable at a predetermined value)
2. A process that stores a different predetermined value when the particular event occurs.

Suppose, for example, that we wanted to update the program represented by Figure 1.21 so that a message would be printed to indicate whether or not any of the profits exceeded 1500. It would be necessary for the program to check each PROFIT after it is calculated and to record the fact if any are greater than 1500. It would also be necessary to add two input/output symbols and an appropriate decision to control the message to be printed. Figure 1.24 incorporates these features.

In this program we use FLAG as our indicator. FLAG is initialized with NO and is changed to YES if and when the PROFIT > 1500 decision sends control through the second part of the indicator. After all records have been read, a decision using the value stored at FLAG determines which message is to be printed. Note that, if even one PROFIT is greater than 1500, FLAG will be switched to YES and will remain at YES for the rest of the program (no provision was made to change it back to NO). But if no PROFIT is greater than 1500, FLAG will remain at NO

Figure 1.24 (a) Flowchart.
(b) Sample input data.
(c) Sample output.

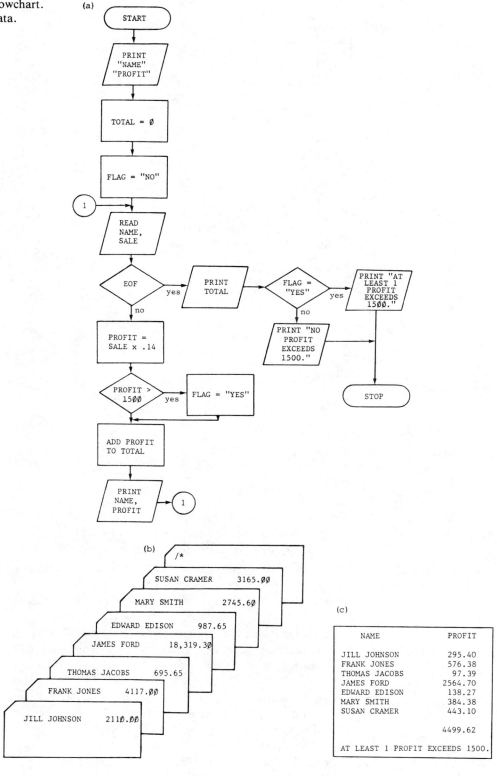

throughout the program. If more than one PROFIT is greater than 1500, the first one will change FLAG to YES. The others will simply leave YES stored at FLAG.

Any variable can be used in an indicator; usually a variable is chosen that will indicate the nature of the event or circumstance being recorded. In Figure 1.25,

Figure 1.25 Here NEGA-TIVE GRADE is an indicator.

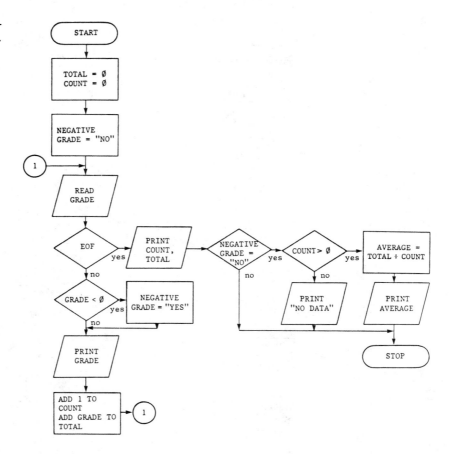

NEGATIVE GRADE is used to record whether any of the grades is negative. This indicator is used to avoid calculating and printing an average if any of the grades is negative.

Exercises 1.4–1.5

1. Design a flowchart for a program that will read SALES from each record, print each sales amount, and print the number of records read.

2. Design a flowchart for a program that will read SALES from each record, print each sales amount, and print the total of the amounts.

3. Design a flowchart for a program that will read SALES from each record and print the average of the sales amounts.

4. Design a flowchart for a program that will read NAME and SALES from each record and print the name and sales amount from each. It is to print the total of the amounts and a single message that indicates whether any amount exceeds 2000.

5. Design a flowchart for a program that will read NAME and SALES from each record and will print the name from each record whose sales were greater than 2000. The program is to print "NONE GREATER THAN 2000" if none of the sales exceeds 2000.

*6. Design a flowchart for a program that will read a name and a sales amount from exactly 10 records. Print each name and sales amount and the total of the sales amounts. Print a single message that indicates whether any of the sales amounts exceeded 2000.

*7. Design a flowchart for a program that will read names and sales amounts from 100 records or until EOF (whichever occurs first). Print the name of each individual whose sales amount exceeded 5000. Print the number of records read and a total of all sales greater than 5000.

*8. Design a flowchart for a program that will read names and sale amounts from up to 500 records. (That is, 500 will be read unless EOF is encountered.) Print the name and sales amount from each record on which the sales amount exceeds 1000. Print a single message that indicates whether any of the sales were less than 100.

*9. Read names and sales amounts from exactly 250 records. Print one message that indicates whether any of the sales amounts exceeded 1000 and another message that indicates whether any sales amount is less than 100. Also print the total of all amounts greater than 10.

1.6 Routine Structures, Continued

Control Breaks

Control breaks are decisions that temporarily interrupt "normal" processing so that some special process can be executed. They occur in programs that process sets of data in which there is more than one record for each item (whether the items are customers, agents, accounts, or spare parts). The records are sorted so that all records for a particular item follow one after the other. The control-break decision detects the transition from records of one item to records of another by comparing values in one record with stored values from a previous record. When this occurs, control is transferred for the special processing.

Figure 1.26 represents a program that will read names and values from a series of records that have been sorted by name. The program will print a grand total of the values and the number of different names read. OLDNAME will be the storage location (called the **compare field**) to be compared with the most recently read name (called the **control field**). After the first record is read, and after each control break, the value in NAME is stored at OLDNAME in preparation for remaining comparisons.

Figure 1.26 (a) Flowchart. (b) Sample input data. (c) Sample output.

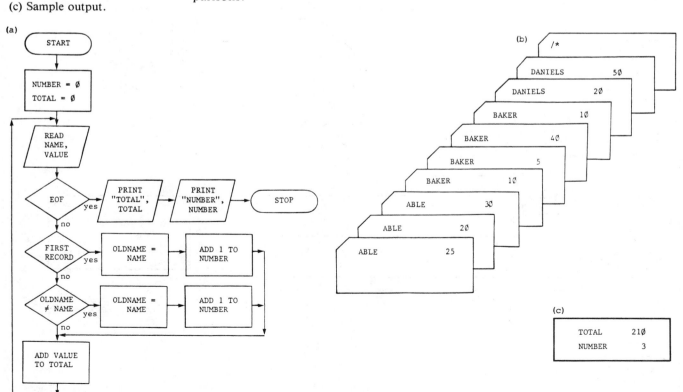

When the first record is read, its name is stored at NAME and also at OLDNAME. Each time a subsequent record is read, its name is compared with OLDNAME. So long as NAME and OLDNAME are not different, there is no control break. When there *is* a difference between NAME and OLDNAME, control-break processing is executed and the current name is stored at OLDNAME to be used in comparisons until another new name is encountered.

The FIRST RECORD decision is inserted into this program to establish the initial value of OLDNAME. On some systems, data that is "left over" from the last program could be stored at OLDNAME and cause a NO answer at the OLDNAME ≠ NAME decision for the first record. This would mean that the first record would not be counted.

Frequently, control breaks temporarily interrupt "normal" processing so that subtotals may be printed or stored. The first record for a new item signals the computer that it has processed all input for the previous item and that subtotals for the previous item can be printed or stored. Figure 1.27 is designed for a program to read names and amounts, to print each agent's name and total, and to print a grand total.

Figure 1.27 (a) Flowchart. (b) Sample input data. (c) Sample output.

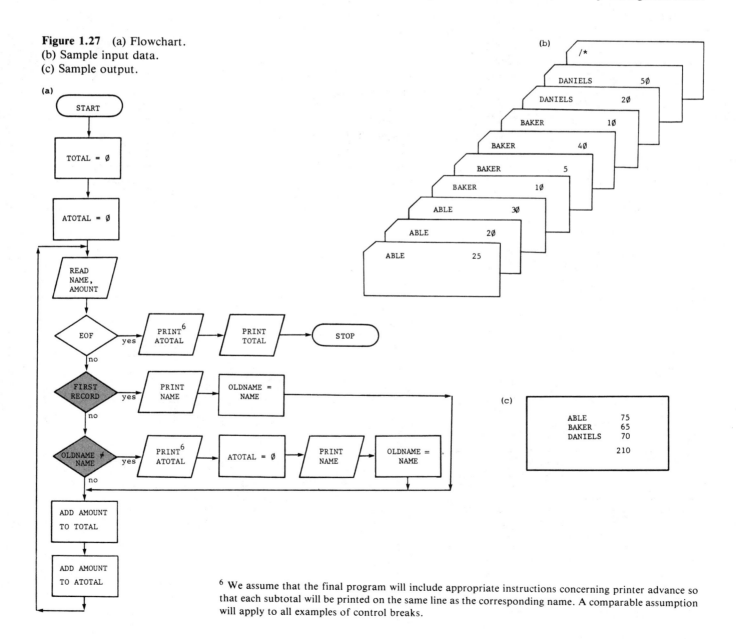

[6] We assume that the final program will include appropriate instructions concerning printer advance so that each subtotal will be printed on the same line as the corresponding name. A comparable assumption will apply to all examples of control breaks.

Library,
I.U.P.
Indiana, Pa.

001.642 R671l
c.1

It is expected that there will be several records with differing amounts for each agent but that the records have been presorted by agent name. (Hence, all records for one agent will be read before records for the next agent are read.)

The "normal" processing of the flowchart shown in Figure 1.27 includes reading a record, checking for EOF, and adding the amount to both TOTAL and ATOTAL. That routine is broken when a new name occurs and control is directed to PRINT ATOTAL, ATOTAL = 0, PRINT NAME, and OLDNAME = NAME. When executing this program, the computer will not "know" that it has finished with all of one agent's records until it encounters a new name. When a new agent's first record is read, the ATOTAL accumulator still contains the old agent's subtotal. So after the OLDNAME ≠ NAME decision is affirmative, ATOTAL (which still contains the old agent's subtotal) is printed and reset to 0. Then the new name is printed and "normal" processing resumes. "Normal" processing continues until another new agent or EOF is reached. After EOF, the program must print ATOTAL one additional time to include a subtotal for the last agent. Because an old agent's subtotal is printed after a new agent's record is read, it is important that the new agent's amount not be added to ATOTAL until after ATOTAL is printed and reset to zero. This means that the ADD AMOUNT TO ATOTAL instruction must occur after the control break.

In Figure 1.28 a new salesperson results in a control break that causes the total of the previous salesperson's sales to be added to the grand total, the salesperson's

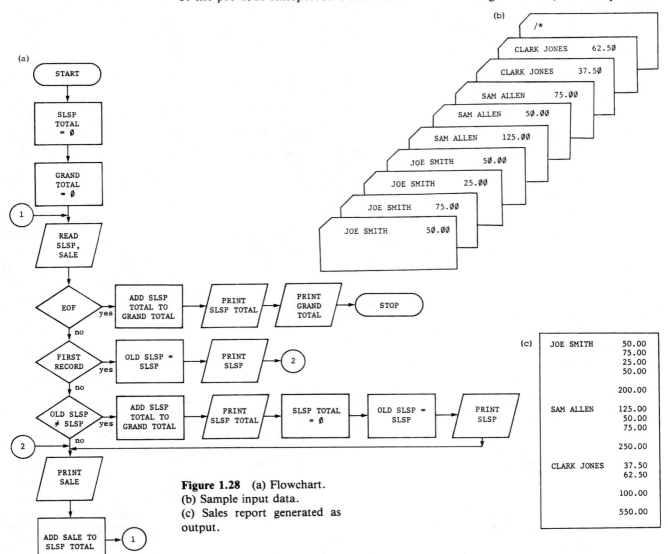

Figure 1.28 (a) Flowchart.
(b) Sample input data.
(c) Sales report generated as output.

Figure 1.29 (a) Flowchart. (b) Sample input data. (c) Sales report generated as output.

total to be printed, and then SLSP TOTAL to be reset to zero for the next salesperson's data. The sale for the new salesperson is not added until after SLSP TOTAL has been reset to zero.

The program represented by this flowchart also incorporates the FIRST RECORD decision. Without it, the first record might be treated as a new salesperson, and a SLSP TOTAL would be printed even though that total would be 0. Here the FIRST RECORD decision is used to avoid the control break for the first record.

The flowchart shown in Figure 1.29 is designed to read sales reports and to prepare a report with the name and total for each salesperson, along with a final total. SLSP TOTAL will be used to add the sales for each salesperson; SLSP TOTAL is reset to zero after each salesperson's total has been printed; AMOUNT is added to SLSP TOTAL after the control break.

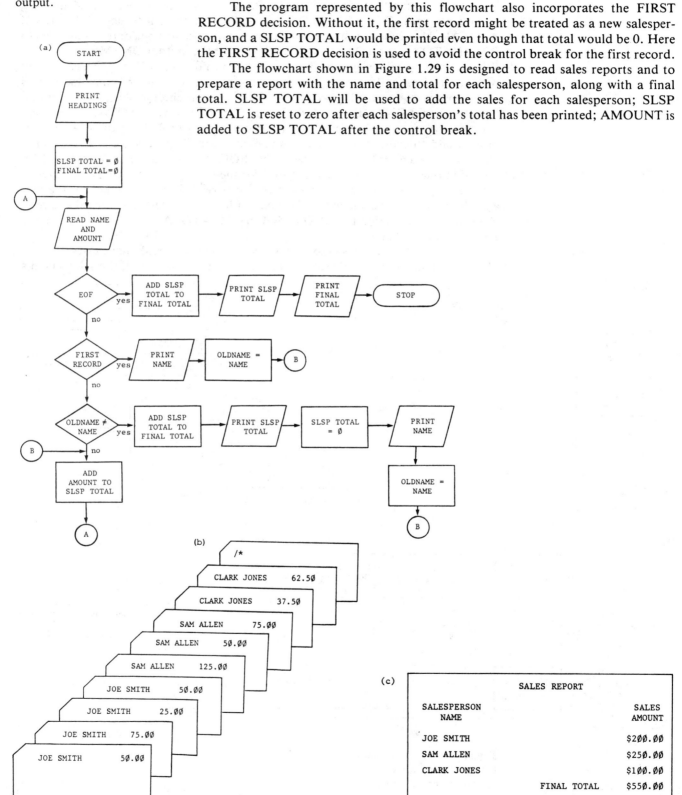

Exercises 1.6

1. Design a flowchart for a program that will read names and amounts from records that were sorted by name. Each name and each amount are to be printed once per record, and the number of different names is to be printed.

2. Design a flowchart for a program that will read names and amounts from records sorted by name. Each name and each amount are to be printed once per record, and the number of different names and the total of the amounts are to be printed.

3. Design a flowchart for a program that will read names and amounts from records sorted by name. Each name is to be printed once (even though it may occur on several records), and the total of all amounts is to be printed.

4. Design a flowchart for a program that will read names and amounts from records sorted by name. Each name is to be printed once (even though it may occur on several records). The total of the amounts and the number of different names are to be printed.

5. Design a flowchart for a program that will read names and amounts from records sorted by name. Each name is to be printed once, along with the total of that individual's amounts. The total of all amounts is to be printed.

6. Design a flowchart for a program that will read names and amounts from records sorted by name. Each name is to be printed once, along with the total of that individual's amounts. The total of all amounts and the number of different names are to be printed.

*7. Design a flowchart for a program that will read names and sales amounts from records that have been sorted by name. Each name is to be printed once. Sales amounts are to be printed once for each record, and a total of each person's amounts is to be printed. The number of individuals whose sales total is greater than 5000 is to be printed, along with an appropriate heading ("THE NUMBER OF INDIVIDUALS WITH SALES TOTALS GREATER THAN 5000 IS").

*8. Design a flowchart for a program that will read names and sales amounts from records that have been sorted by name. The program is to print each person's name, total, and commission. Commission is to be calculated as follows: no commission on total sales of less than 2000; a commission of 5% of total sales on sales from 2001 to 10,000; a commission of 7% of total sales on sales greater than 10,000. The program is to print the number of names, the number of records, total sales, and total commissions.

1.7 Universal Requirements for Flowcharts

Every flowchart must meet certain minimum requirements. Specifically, every flowchart must

1. Start somewhere
2. Stop somewhere
3. Unfailingly reach the stop

Meeting these requirements seems easy. But failing to meet them is equally easy. Two common failures are (1) creation of an endless loop and (2) creation of a branch that ends somewhere other than STOP. Figure 1.30 makes both of these errors. This flowchart fails to indicate what happens after FEDTAX is printed. It also contains an endless loop. No matter what answer is given at the FEDTAX > 1 decision, control goes back to 1. No new records are read, and EOF is never reached.

Figure 1.30   This flowchart illustrates two common errors in flowcharting.

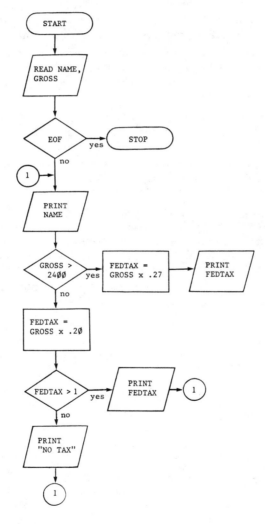

Not every loop or dead end is as obvious as these. But they all have unfortunate results. One reason why some endless loops are difficult to discover is that they result from the flowchart's content rather than its form. Figure 1.31 is an example of this sort of error.

Figure 1.31 This flowchart contains an endless loop that results from its content, not its form.

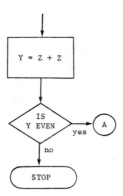

Assuming that Z is a whole number, Z + Z is always an even number and this program will never reach STOP. But that fact is not evident from the flowchart alone. This sort of error is more difficult to discover, because it involves the content of the program, not merely its logical structure. But practice in finding these errors in simple programs will help one spot them in "real-life" programs. The key to finding such errors lies in carefully checking a program by (1) tracing its logic on a flowchart and (2) creating a table of values and tracing the path of sample data to ensure that the program works. This technique may be helpful in debugging programs that run but nonetheless produce erroneous results.

1.8 Error Messages

Most programs are designed with the expectation that data to be used will be of a certain type, in a given amount, and usually within a given range. When the data used does not meet the programmer's expectations, the program may not run. Or, if it runs, it produces output that suggests a programming error. Erroneous data may be the result of careless data collection, data entry, or data manipulation by a previous program. An example of such an error is the entry of a minus sign in front of the cost of an item. Processing such an item would result in erroneous output, even though the processing itself was done correctly. Not every data error can be detected by a program. But errors that are outside the expected range of values (such as an item that costs less than nothing) can be detected and senseless output avoided.

Programs often test data after it is read and before it is processed to ensure that the data is within expected ranges. When data that lies outside expected ranges is encountered, the program prints an error message to alert the operator or other person reading the output that an error exists. Such a message might say, "A negative value was entered as the cost of item 231" or "127 hours worked was entered for John Smith during the week ending 3 January." Depending on the nature of the data error encountered, a program may be designed to do one of three things:

1. Print an error message and continue processing, including the unexpected entry.
2. Print an error message and continue processing all but the unexpected entry.
3. Print an error message and stop.

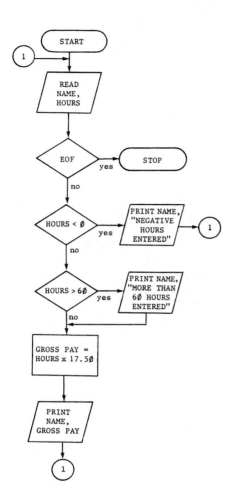

Figure 1.32 This flowchart provides for two error messages, but errors have very different effects on calculation and printing.

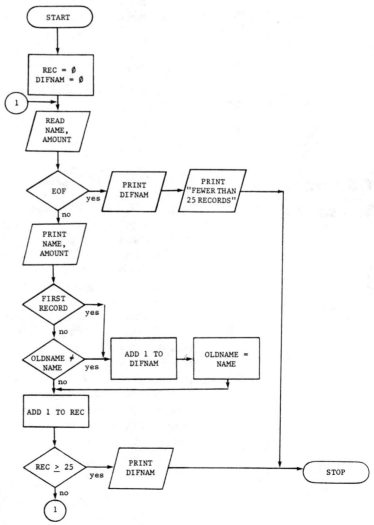

Figure 1.33 This flowchart provides an error message when data is insufficient.

Figure 1.32 will read a name and a number of hours worked from each record. It will also print the name and gross pay and will print an error message if the number of hours worked is less than zero or greater than 60. Figure 1.32 won't calculate or print a gross pay for anyone who worked fewer than zero hours, because such a figure could not possibly be correct. It will calculate and print a gross pay for someone who worked more than 60 hours, but it will print an error message (that number was unexpected but could be correct).

Another sort of unexpected data is the loading of too many or too few data records. For example, a program may be designed to process data from precisely 25 cards. But there is no guarantee that the computer operator will always load exactly 25 cards. To avoid problems similar to this, a program would maintain a count of records read and would print an error message whenever too few or too many were read.

Figure 1.33 will read the first 25 records and will print the name and amount on each record and the number of different names. An error message will be printed if fewer than 25 records are available. This flowchart will not reach EOF if at least 25 records are available. It will simply print and stop after the twenty-fifth record is processed.

Exercises
1.7–1.8

1. Find the errors in the following flowchart.

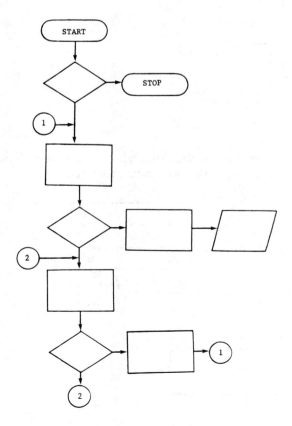

2. Find the errors in the following flowchart. This program was intended to read salespersons' names and sales and to print a report listing each salesperson's total sales and the number of salespersons.

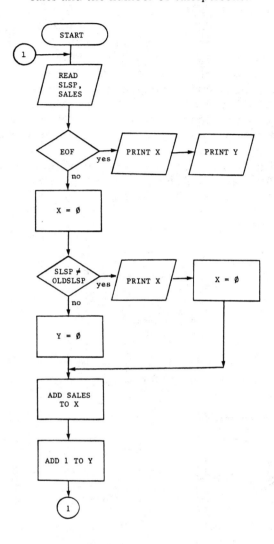

3. Follow the test data through the flowchart given in Exercise 2, and write the actual output that would be generated.

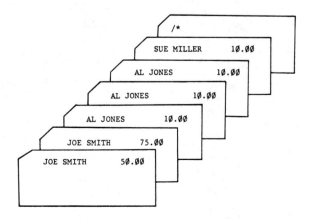

4. Design a flowchart for a program that will read names and grades. The program is to print each name and grade and to calculate and print the average of all grades. The program is to print one error message for every grade that is less than 0 and another for every grade that is greater than 100.

5. Design a flowchart for a program that will read names and grades. The program is to print each name and grade and to calculate and print the average of all grades from 0 to 100. An error message is to be printed for each grade that is less than 0 and for each grade that is greater than 100.

6. Design a flowchart for a program that will read names and grades from records that were sorted by name. Print each name once, along with the total of that person's grades. Also, for each individual, print an ERRONEOUS INPUT message if one or more of that individual's grades exceeds 100.

1.9 Program Design

The design of the programs in the early chapters of this text is simplified by the fact that these programs do not permanently store the information read from each record. Instead, they read a record, temporarily store its data, complete all computations for that record, and then read the next record. At any one time, the only data available for processing is data read from the last record. Programs of this sort can be analyzed into three parts: initial process, detail loop, and final process. The **initial process** consists of those things that must be done before data is read, such as initializing counters. The **detail loop** includes reading and processing individual records. It contains all those actions that must be taken for each record, such as printing a name or adding an amount to a total. The **final process** includes all those actions to be completed after all data has been read, such as printing totals. Table 1.4 summarizes the individual operations of each of these parts.

Table 1.4 The operation of the initial process, the detail loop, and the final process.

INITIAL PROCESS	OPEN FILES PRINT HEADINGS (TITLES AND DATES) INITIALIZE COUNTERS INITIALIZE ACCUMULATORS INITIALIZE INDICATORS	
DETAIL LOOP	READ AND LOOP EXIT INCREMENT COUNTERS INCREMENT ACCUMULATORS PERFORM CALCULATIONS PRINT DETAIL LINES (INDIVIDUAL NAMES, ETC.)	
	EXECUTE CONTROL BREAKS	PRINT SUBTOTALS INCREMENT COUNTERS INCREMENT ACCUMULATORS PERFORM CALCULATIONS RE-INITIALIZE COUNTERS, ETC.
FINAL PROCESS	PRINT SUBTOTALS PERFORM FINAL CALCULATIONS PRINT TOTALS CLOSE FILES	

Not all of the operations shown in Table 1.4 occur in every program, and they do not always occur in the order listed. But when they do occur, they are likely to be in the sections indicated.

The sections given in Table 1.4 provide some structure within which to work in designing simple programs. But actual program design begins with, and is determined by, the individual program's intended output. In each program, the output determines what input and processing are required. The availability of input may limit possible output, and the form of the input will bear on the type of processing to be done, but it is the output that determines most of a program's components. Consider the program represented by Figure 1.23. Its output requirement was to print an average of odd-numbered values. Calculating an average requires an accumulator, a counter, and a process symbol that contains the calculation. The average was to be of odd-numbered values only, so a decision was required to select those values. Finally, because the program was to read an indefinite number of records, a READ and EOF component was required. In designing this program, we would make a list of these components as follows:

1. Accumulator (for odd values)
2. Counter (for odd values)
3. Process to calculate the average
4. Odd-numbers decision
5. READ and EOF
6. Division-by-zero decision
7. Total print (Average)

Using this list in conjunction with Table 1.4 would result in Figure 1.34. This same method of program design is applied to Examples 1.1 and 1.2.

Figure 1.34 The flowchart from Figure 1.23 is annotated to highlight major program divisions.

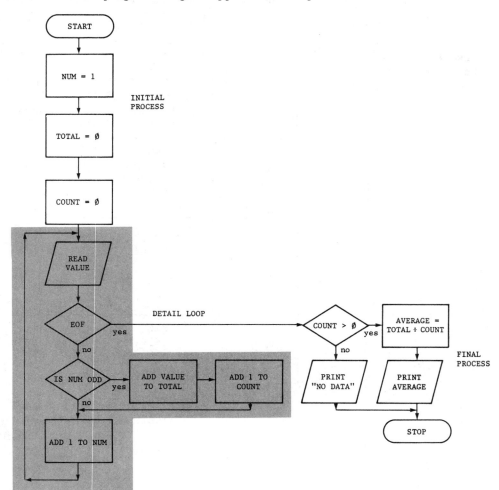

Example 1.1

Design a flowchart for a program that will

1. Read names and amounts.
2. Print each name and amount.
3. Print a total of the amounts and the number of records.

   The output requirements indicate the need for an accumulator, a counter, and detail printing (printing once per item). Because records will be read, a READ and EOF must be included. Listing the required items results in

1. ACCUMULATOR
2. COUNTER
3. DETAIL PRINT (NAME AMOUNT)
4. TOTAL PRINT

   Using Table 1.4 and this list produces the accompanying flowchart.

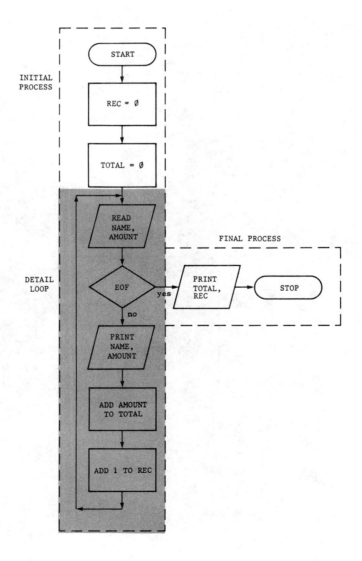

Example 1.2

Design a flowchart for a program that will

1. Read names and individual sale amounts from pre-alphabetized records. (Each record represents one sale.)
2. Print each agent's name and total sales. (A single name is to be printed only once.)
3. Print the number of sales and the total amount of the sales.

Program requirements:

1. TOTAL PRINT (number and amount)
2. ACCUMULATOR FOR TOTAL OF SALES
3. COUNTER FOR NUMBER OF SALES
4. DETAIL PRINT AGENT'S NAME
5. DETAIL PRINT AGENT'S SUBTOTAL
6. ACCUMULATOR FOR AGENT'S SUBTOTAL
7. NEW NAME CONTROL BREAK
8. FIRST RECORD CONTROL BREAK
9. READ AND EOF

The following flowchart results.

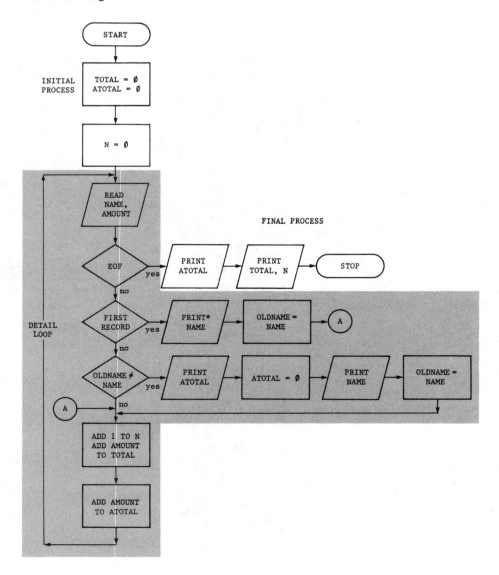

Exercises 1.9

Design flowcharts for programs that will carry out the following specifications. Assume that records have been alphabetized and that the last record is an end-of-file marker.

1. **a.** Read a name and an amount from each record.
   b. Print each name and amount (once per record).
   c. If none of the amounts is less than zero, print the total of the amounts; print "ERRONEOUS TOTAL" if any of the amounts is less than zero.

2. **a.** Read a name and an amount from each record.
   b. Print each name and amount that is not negative (once per record). Print the name and the words "NEGATIVE AMOUNT" if a negative amount is read.
   c. Print the number of records read.
   d. Print the number of different names.

3. **a.** Read a name and an amount from each record.
   b. Print each name and each amount (once per record).
   c. Print the number of records read.
   d. Print the number of different names.
   e. Print the total of the amounts.

4. **a.** Read a name and an amount from each record.
   b. Print each name once, along with the total of that individual's amount.
   c. Print the number of records.
   d. Print the number of different names.
   e. Print the total of all the amounts.

5. **a.** Read a name and an amount from 10 or fewer records. (Fewer will be read only if EOF is encountered.)
   b. Print each name and amount (once per record).
   c. Print an error message if fewer than 10 records were read.

6. **a.** Read a name and an amount from 10 or fewer records.
   b. Print each name once (no matter how many records are read).
   c. Print total of amounts if 10 records are processed.
   d. Print an error message (and not the total) if fewer than 10 records are read.

*7. **a.** Read a name and a sales amount from each record.
   b. Calculate and print the average of each individual's positive sales amounts.
   c. For each individual, if any sales amounts were less than zero, print the number of such amounts.
   d. Print the total of all amounts that are less than zero and the average of all positive sales amounts. (Assume that there will be at least one record with a positive amount for each individual.)

1.10 System Flowcharts

The flowcharts we have discussed so far are called **program flowcharts**. They represent program instructions to be executed by the computer. They do not represent the flow of data to or from the computer. **System flowcharts**, by comparison, represent the flow of data from original sources, through one or more programs, to its final output. System flowcharts represent programs as single processes and use special input/output symbols to represent data flow to and from those processes. Figure 1.35 is a system flowchart that might accompany the program described in Example 1.2.

Figure 1.35 A system flowchart for the program described in Example 1.2.

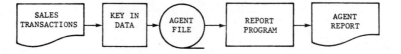

Figure 1.35 shows that original data in the form of documents (perhaps hand-written) is entered through a terminal or keyboard to produce an agent file on magnetic tape. The records from this file are read by the program, which in turn produces an agent report in the form of a printed document.

The specialized symbols that frequently occur in system flowcharts rarely occur in program flowcharts. These symbols can be divided into input/output symbols and specialized process symbols. The input/output symbols are used to represent either input or output, and they represent the medium specified.

Input/Output Symbols

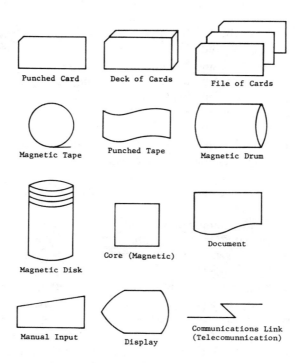

Specialized Process Symbols

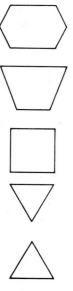

The **preparation symbol** represents some modification of instructions to change the operation of a program.

The **manual operation symbol** represents some operation done at human speed (rather than at computer speed).

The **auxiliary operation symbol** represents a process performed on equipment that is not directly controlled by the computer's central processing unit.

The **merge symbol** represents the merging of two or more sets of items.

The **extract symbol** represents selection of one particular set of items from another single set of items.

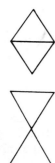

The **sort symbol** represents the sorting of a set of items into a specific order.

The **collate symbol** represents the formation of two or more sets from two or more other sets.

Figure 1.36 is a system flowchart that represents a fairly standard business operation. This flowchart shows sales receipts as documents being keyed in to create an unsorted file. The unsorted file is sorted, creating a sorted file that enters an edit program. The edit program checks for obvious errors in the sorted file and creates

Figure 1.36 System flowchart for a file maintenance program.

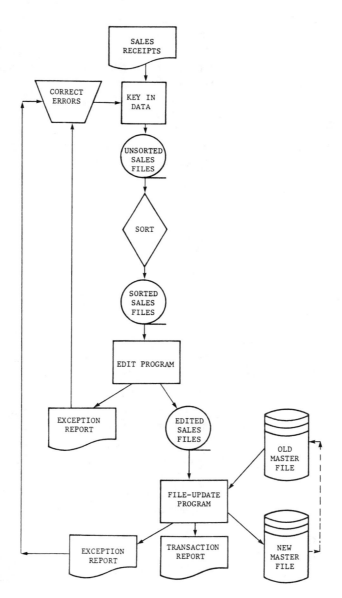

an edited sales file of correct records and an exception report that lists obvious errors. The edited sales file (on magnetic tape) is entered into the file-update program. This program uses the edited sales file and the old master file (on disk) to create a new master file. A report of each transaction and a second exception report are also printed. Data from each exception report is returned for correction and re-entry. The dotted line indicates that the new master for the current run will become the old master for the next run.

System flowcharts are concerned with origins and destinations of data and information. Because data may enter a system at various points and because output may be generated at various points, terminals are omitted and branches may begin or end with any input/output symbol.

Figure 1.36 is typical of a master file-update system. It involves programs (the edit program and the file-update program) that are considerably more complex than we will consider until the later chapters. The system flowcharts for programs in the earlier chapters will be similar to Figure 1.35 in that they will generally employ a single input and a single output.

Exercises 1.10

1. Design a system flowchart that describes a system to process records entered through a terminal from insurance policy records. The entered records will become a disk file to be used as input for a program to produce a printed report.

2. Design a system flowchart to describe a system to key in records from printed receipts to form a magnetic tape file. The file will be used as input to a program that produces punched cards and an exception report.

3. Design a system flowchart to describe a system to key in records from sales slips to create a disk file. The disk file is to be sorted, and the result will be used to update a master tape file. The update program is to produce an exception report to be used to correct and re-key individual records.

Review Questions

Completion

1. _____ is the flowchart symbol used to mark the point at which processing begins and ends.

2. _____ represents a branch in the flowchart.

3. To instruct the computer to print a particular word or other string of symbols, we enclose the word or string of symbols in _____.

4. A _____ is used to continuously repeat one or more operations.

5. A decision that transfers control after all data has been entered is called the

_____.

6. _____ is a structure that maintains a current total without affecting ongoing calculations or processing.

Definition

1. Algorithm
2. Computer program
3. Nested loops
4. Compare field

Discussion

1. What is the difference between a counter and an accumulator?
2. Explain the two operations of the READ command.
3. Explain the function of the loop exit decision.
4. Describe the processes that constitute a counter.
5. Describe the processes that constitute an indicator or switch.
6. Why, in a control-break program, must individual totals be printed after EOF is reached?
7. How are error messages used?
8. What happens when two instructions indicate that different values are to be stored at the same location?

True or False

1. _____ Individual instructions to a computer must be relatively simple.
2. _____ The use of connectors is always preferable to the use of upward flow direction lines.
3. _____ The end-of-file decision is generally placed before a READ instruction.
4. _____ The end-of-file marker (when present) is not normally included in a count of the records read.
5. _____ Counters are generally initialized within the loop that they count.
6. _____ Counters are generally incremented before the loop that they count.
7. _____ Accumulators are initialized before control enters the loop.
8. _____ The records to be processed by a control-break program are usually sorted.
9. _____ Each loop must contain its own exit decision.
10. _____ The reading of individual records usually occurs during the initial process.
11. _____ In programming, the equations $X = 3$ and $X = 5$ contradict each other.
12. _____ In storage commands, the expression to the left of the equals sign indicates the storage location.
13. _____ When a storage instruction is executed, the values stored at locations mentioned on the right of the equals sign are not changed.
14. _____ Decisions that contain equations should be understood as questions about the values stored at the locations mentioned.
15. _____ In programming, equations should be considered statements of fact.
16. _____ In programming, the expression $X = X + 1$ is a contradiction.

2. *The Logic Of Sets, I*

The logic of sets or **set theory**, as it is usually called, is a traditional branch of mathematical and philosophical logic. Set theory is especially applicable to programming. One function of computers is sifting through masses of information and extracting relevant pieces of that information for presentation in a usable format. Another function is determining relationships among various pieces of information. An understanding of the tools of set theory will facilitate the task of designing programs to sift data and determine relationships.

2.1 Definition of Set

The word *set* refers to any kind of collection of any sort of objects. The chairs in a room, for example, form a set; the cars in the parking lot form a set. We often use other expressions to refer to sets. For example, a set of cows, if it were large enough, would be called a herd of cows. Other more general substitutes for the word *set* include *bunch, group, collection,* and *class*.[1] The **members** of a set are simply the individuals that compose a set. George Washington, for example, is a member of the set of Presidents of the United States.

There are two ways of defining particular sets. They are

1. Listing the *name* of each member of the set.
2. Indicating the *kinds* of things that are members of the set.

The first method of defining sets is generally used only for sets with a small number of members. We could, for example, define set A as the set of even integers between 1 and 7 by listing the names of the members of set A. This is normally done using standard brace notation as follows:

A = {2,4,6}

This expression would be read: "Set A is identical with the set consisting of 2, 4, and 6." Similarly, B = {a,b,c,d} would be read: "Set B is identical with the set consisting of a, b, c, and d." And, B = {a,b,c,d} defines set B as the set consisting of the first four letters of the alphabet.

One could not, of course, list the names of the members of the set of even integers, because there are infinitely many such numbers. Nor is one likely to list the names of all human beings. These sets are more likely to be defined by indicating the *kinds* of things that are their members. For this purpose we would use the following notation:

C = {x | x is a human being}

This expression is read: "Set C is identical with the set of x's such that x is a human being." So, given this definition, C is the set of all human beings. D = {x | x is an

---

[1] We are not referring to these terms as they are used in formal mathematics.

42

even integer} is read: "Set D is identical with the set of x's such that x is an even integer" or, less formally, "Set D is the set of even integers."

The objects that make up a set may be objects of any sort. They need not be physical objects. They need not be real objects. A collection of dreams or a group of characters in a play would make a perfectly respectable set. The members of a set need not have any notable similarity to one another. Thus a set may consist of Richard Nixon's big toe, the bell tower at Washburn University, and Pegasus. We may find no use for such a set; nonetheless, it is a set. Things that are members of a set need not be located in the same place. All houses form the set of houses, even though the houses are widely distributed geographically. In short, a **set** is any collection of any sort of objects that one wants to consider a set.

2.2 The Universal Set and the Empty Set

Two special sets that are of interest to us are the universal set and the empty set. The **universal set** is the set of everything under discussion at a particular time. When using set theory, we generally assume that either the *number* of things or the *type* of things is limited in some way. Suppose, for example, that we were going to study the test-taking behavior of students at Lansing Community College and that no one else would be considered in that study. Whenever we mentioned students, it would be understood that we meant L.C.C. students, because we had intended to speak of no others. So, for that discussion, our universal set would be the set of students at L.C.C. The notation for the universal set is U.

The empty set may be thought of as the opposite of the universal set. The **empty set**, sometimes called the null set, is the set that has no members. This may seem peculiar in that a set is said to be a collection of objects. But defining sets by indicating types of members can easily result in the empty set. The set that contains all ten-legged horses is the empty set; so is the set that contains all even prime numbers greater than 3. The notation for the empty set is ∅ or { }.

2.3 Operations on Sets

Various **logical operations** combine or divide the members of various sets to form new sets. Of these various operations, we will be concerned with only three. They are union, intersection, and complement. The use of these operations always results in the creation of sets from other sets.

The **union** of two sets is the set composed of all the members of each set. That is, the union of two sets is the set that results when all the members of the two sets are combined to form a single set. For example, the union of the set of odd integers with the set of even integers results in the set containing all integers. The notation for the union of two sets is ∪. To say that A is the union of the sets B and C, we use the expression A = (B ∪ C). If B were the set of football players and C were the set of seniors, then (B ∪ C) would be the set of individuals who were *either* seniors *or* football players *or* both.

The **intersection** of two sets is the set composed of individuals that are members of both sets. The notation for the intersection of two sets is ∩. To say that D is the intersection of B and C, we use the expression D = (B ∩ C). If B were the set of football players and C were the set of seniors, (B ∩ C) would be the set of senior football players. In this situation, (B ∩ C) would be the set of individuals who are *both* seniors and football players.

The **complement** of a set is the set composed of all members of the universal set that were not in the original set. The notation for the complement of a set is ′, the symbol we read as "prime." To say that A is the complement of C, we would use the expression A = C′. If our universal set were the set of students at Washburn University and C were the set of seniors, then C′ would be the set of students at

Washburn who were not seniors. The following examples exhibit these three operations:

U = {1,2,3,4,5,6,7,8,9}

A = {1,2,3,4}   B = {2,3,4,5}   C = {5,6,7,8}

(A ∪ B) = {1,2,3,4,5}   (A ∩ C) = {   }

(A ∪ C) = {1,2,3,4,5,6,7,8}   A' = {5,6,7,8,9}

Because the effect of using operations is to produce another set, the results of operations can be combined to form more sets. The examples that follow use the definitions of U, A, B, and C that we have just established.
The complement of the union of A and B:

(A ∪ B)' = {6,7,8,9}

The union of the complements of A and B:

(A' ∪ B') = {1,5,6,7,8,9}

The complement of the intersection of A and B:

(A ∩ B)' = {1,5,6,7,8,9}

The intersection of the complements of A and B:

(A' ∩ B') = {6,7,8,9}

The union of A with the intersection of B and C:

(A ∪ (B ∩ C)) = {1,2,3,4,5}

The intersection of A with the union of B and C:

(A ∩ (B ∪ C)) = {2,3,4}

2.4 Venn Diagrams

Venn diagrams are used for various purposes in mathematics and logic. They are used to represent sets, to determine the equivalence of statements, and to assess the validity of arguments. In this section we will use Venn diagrams to provide graphic representations of operations in set theory.

A simple Venn diagram is drawn using a rectangle containing a single circle. The rectangle represents the universal set. The circle represents a set within that universe. In such a diagram there are two significant areas: the area inside the circle, representing the set, and the area outside it, representing the set's complement. The numbers in the following Venn diagram indicate those areas.

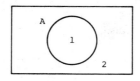

Area 1 contains all members of set A. Area 2 contains all things that are not members of set A. If the universal set were insurance company policy holders and set A represented those who smoke, then area 1 would contain all the smokers and area 2 would contain all the non-smokers.

Different sets are represented by shading different areas of Venn diagrams. The following diagrams represent set A and set A′, respectively.

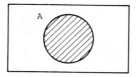

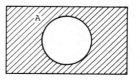

A (Smokers)   A′ (Non-Smokers)

A Venn diagram that is used to represent more than one set consists of a rectangle that represents the universal set and two or more overlapping circles that represent sets within the universal set. There are four significant areas in a Venn diagram for two sets. The following Venn diagram indicates those areas and describes the items that would occur in each. (Here, let set A represent policy holders who smoke and set B those who drink.)

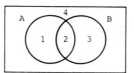

Area 1 contains all members of set A that are not members of set B (smokers who don't drink).

Area 2 contains all members of set A that are also members of set B (smokers who drink).

Area 3 contains all members of set B that are not members of set A (drinkers who don't smoke).

Area 4 contains all things that are members of neither set A nor set B (those who neither smoke nor drink).

By shading various areas of Venn diagrams, we can indicate various set-theoretical operations. To represent the set described by various operations, we simply shade the corresponding area.

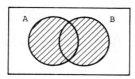

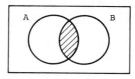

A ∪ B
(Both drinkers and smokers)

A ∩ B
(Smokers who drink or drinkers who smoke)

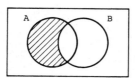

A ∩ B′
(Smokers who don't drink)

A′ ∩ B
(Drinkers who don't smoke)

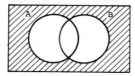

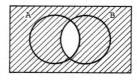

A′ ∩ B′
(Non-drinkers who don't smoke or non-smokers who don't drink)

A′ ∪ B′
(Both the non-smokers and the non-drinkers)

To ensure that Venn diagrams are correctly drawn from their descriptions, we can use the following, somewhat mechanical, procedure to construct them.

1. Start with the innermost component and work outward.
2. For unions and intersections:
   a. Shade entirely one of the components of the union or intersection with diagonal shading.
   b. Shade entirely the other component, using diagonals slanting in the other direction.
   c. The area where the diagonals cross is the intersection; the entire shaded area is the union.
   d. Copy the union or intersection, as appropriate, with diagonals in a single direction.
3. For complements:
   a. Shade the component.
   b. Copy the diagram, shading the opposite area.

Here is an example of the use of this method to draw a Venn diagram for (A ∩ B)′.

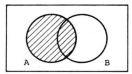

Shade area A with diagonals in one direction.

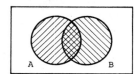

Shade area B with diagonals in the other direction.

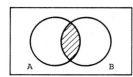

Copy the intersection.

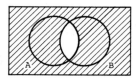

Shade the opposite area to represent the complement.

This method of drawing Venn diagrams is probably too mechanical for a set as simple as this, and perhaps we ought to rely on insight here. But this method is indispensable when sets become more complex – and particularly when we add a third component to the set. The following example approaches those that require the use of a step-by-step method.

$$((A \cup B) \cap (A \cap B)')$$

For $(A \cup B)$

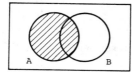

Shade A.

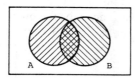

Shade B.

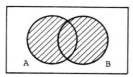

Copy the union.

For $(A \cap B)'$

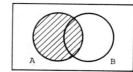

Shade A.

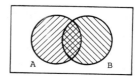

Shade B.

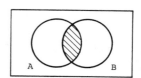

Copy the intersection.

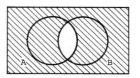

Draw the complement.

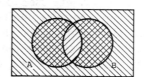

Combine components,
shading in different
directions.

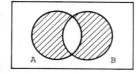

Copy the intersection.

After you become accustomed to working with Venn diagrams, you will be able to skip the initial steps and perhaps begin by drawing unions and intersections. However, when you must be certain that you are correct, completing each step is recommended even if this method is a bit tedious.

Exercises
2.1–2.4

1. Where U = the set of letters a through g, A = {a,b,c,d}, B = {d,e,f,g},
   C = {a,c,e,g}, and D = {b,d,f}, determine the membership of:
   a. A ∩ C   b. A ∪ C
   c. B ∩ D   d. A ∩ B
   e. (A ∩ B)′   f. ((A ∪ B)′ ∩ A)
   g. ((A ∩ C) ∪ D)   h. ((A ∩ B) ∩ D)
   i. ((A′ ∪ B) ∩ (C′ ∪ D))

2. Draw Venn diagrams to represent each of the following sets.
   a. D ∪ E′   b. D ∩ E′
   c. D′ ∩ E   d. D′ ∪ E′
   e. (D ∪ E)′   f. (D′ ∩ E)′

3. Using set-theory notation, name the set represented by the shaded areas in each
   of the following diagrams. Also describe the members of the set, assuming that A
   = {x | x smokes} and B = {x | x drinks}.

   a.
   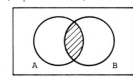

   b.

   c.
   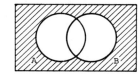

   d.
   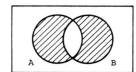

   e.
   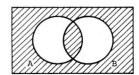

   f.
   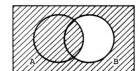

2.5 Venn
Diagrams for
Three Sets

Venn diagrams can be used to represent operations on more than two sets. In prin-
ciple, a Venn diagram could be drawn for any number of sets. But our ability to
visualize relationships is soon lost when more than four sets are represented. We will
confine ourselves to operations and statements using only three sets. To create a
Venn diagram for three sets, draw a rectangle with three overlapping circles enclosed.

There are eight significant areas in a Venn Diagram with three circles. The
following Venn diagram indicates those areas and describes the items that occur
there.

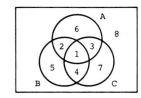

Area 1 contains all items that are members of sets A, B, and C.
Area 2 contains all members of set A that are members of set B but are not
members of set C.
Area 3 contains all members of set A that are members of set C but are not
members of set B.

Area 4 contains all members of set B that are members of set C but are not members of set A.

Area 5 contains all members of set B that are not members of either set A or set C.

Area 6 contains all members of set A that are not members of either set B or set C.

Area 7 contains all members of set C that are not members of either set A or set B.

Area 8 contains all items that are not members of set A, set B, or set C.

For any given set description, there is only one Venn diagram. However, there are many different ways of describing a single diagram. The following Venn diagrams are accompanied by various descriptions, each of which is correct.

Example 2.1

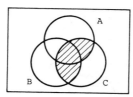

$(C \cap (A \cup B))$
$((A \cup B) \cap C)$
$((A \cap C) \cup (B \cap C))$
$((C \cap B) \cup (C \cap A))$

Example 2.2

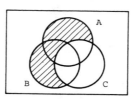

$((A \cup B) \cap C')$
$(C' \cap (A \cup B))$
$(A \cap C') \cup (B \cap C')$
$(C' \cap B) \cup (C' \cap A))$

The way one chooses to describe a particular diagram depends on how one sees the diagram. If we saw Example 2.1 as the overlap of two intersections, then we would describe it in either of the last two ways. If, on the other hand, we perceived it as that part of C where the union of A and B overlapped, we would describe it in either of the first two ways.

The key to describing a Venn diagram is recognizing the component parts of the diagram. This recognition is facilitated by the fact that a particular area of a diagram has the same name no matter how many circles are used in that diagram. As long as the same part of a diagram remains shaded, the addition of circles does not change the name of the shaded area. For example, the three diagrams in Example 2.3 all represent set A, even though two of them contain additional circles.

Example 2.3

A completely shaded circle always represents a single set, no matter what other features the diagram may have.

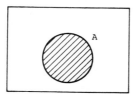 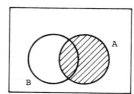 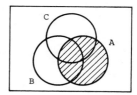

Examples 2.4 and 2.5 are pairs of diagrams; each pair exhibits the same set.

Example 2.4   (A ∩ B)

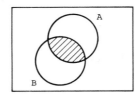 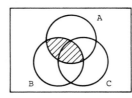

will always represent the intersection of two sets

Example 2.5   (C ∩ B′)

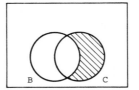 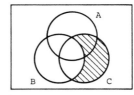 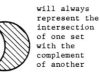

will always represent the intersection of one set with the complement of another

Many Venn diagrams are specified as the union of the components in the foregoing diagrams.

Example 2.6   ((B ∩ C′) ∪ (C ∩ B′))

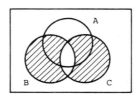

Example 2.6 is a combination of two figures from Example 2.5.

Example 2.7   (A ∪ (C ∩ B′))

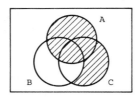

Example 2.7 is a combination of Examples 2.3 and 2.5.

Example 2.8   ((A ∩ B) ∪ (C ∩ B′))

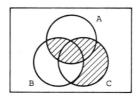

Example 2.8 is a combination of Examples 2.4 and 2.5.

Note that, in specifying the name for Example 2.7 one of the areas received "double coverage." The area ((A ∩ C) ∩ B′) occurs both in A and in (C ∩ B′). Frequently, the simplest name for a given set does, in fact, name an area twice. This "double coverage" should not be regarded as a defect, because avoiding it would result in a very long and, in some respects, redundant expression.

The following are examples of additional components that you should recognize readily.

Example 2.9

Example 2.9 represents the intersection of one set with the complements of two others.

Example 2.10

Example 2.10 represents the intersection of two sets with the complement of a third.

Example 2.11

Example 2.11 represents the intersection of three sets.

When we see Venn diagrams in terms of their various components, it is much easier to identify them. Look for these components in Examples 2.12 through 2.17.

Example 2.12

$(A \cap B) \cap C$

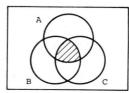

Example 2.13

$(A \cup B) \cap C$ or
$(A \cap C) \cup (B \cap C)$

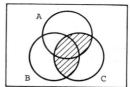

Example 2.14

$(A \cap B) \cup C$

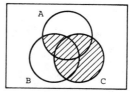

Example 2.15

$(A \cap B') \cap C'$

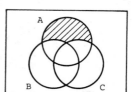

Example 2.16

$(A \cup B) \cap (A \cup C)$ or
$A \cup (B \cap C)$

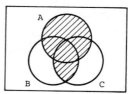

Example 2.17 $((A \cap B') \cap C') \cup (B \cap C)$

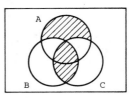

2.6 Translation from Natural Language to Set Theory

The usefulness of set theory in simplifying programming problems is limited to problems expressed in set notation. Because programming problems are generally expressed in natural language (English, Spanish, and so on), solving them is facilitated by set theory only to the extent that these problems can be expressed in set notation. In this section we will look at various English expressions that describe various combinations of unions, intersections, and complements.

A variety of English expressions describe sets, but there are some notable regularities.

1. Expressions that contain the word *not* or other symbols for negation indicate complements.
2. Expressions that enlarge sets indicate unions.
3. Expressions that restrict sets indicate intersections.

Note these regularities in the following examples.

$U = \{x \mid x \text{ is a customer}\}$ $C = \{x \mid x \text{ has a checking account}\}$
$S = \{x \mid x \text{ has a savings account}\}$ $M = \{x \mid x \text{ is a minor}\}$

Customers who don't have checking accounts
$$C'$$

Customers who have either a savings or a checking account
$$(S \cup C)$$

Customers who have both savings and checking accounts
$$(S \cap C)$$

Customers who have neither a savings nor a checking account
$$(S \cup C)' \quad \text{or} \quad (S' \cap C')$$

Customers with a savings account but no checking account
$$(S \cap C')$$

Customers other than those who have a savings account but no checking account
$$(S \cap C')'$$

Minor customers having both savings and checking accounts
$$(M \cap (S \cap C))$$

Minor customers having either a savings or a checking account
$$(M \cap (S \cup C))$$

Minor customers with savings accounts and adults with checking accounts
$$((M \cap S) \cup (M' \cap C))$$

Minor customers who have neither a savings nor a checking account
(M ∩ (S′ ∩ C′)) or (M ∩ (S ∪ C)′)

Savings account holders who are minors without checking accounts
(S ∩ (M ∩ C′))

Those without savings accounts, together with minors with checking accounts
(S′ ∪ (M ∩ C))

Savers and checkers who are not minors
((S ∪ C) ∩ M′)

Adult savers, together with minor checkers and also those with both a savings and a checking account
((M′ ∩ S) ∪ (M ∩ C) ∪ (C ∩ S))

Adult non-savers as well as minor checkers
((M′ ∩ S′) ∪ (M ∩ C))

Exercises 2.5–2.6

1. Translate each of these set descriptions into set-theory notation, using the following definitions.

U = {x | x is a library book}   O = {x | x is oversized}
R = {x | x is a reference book}   T = {x | x is a textbook}
L = {x | x is a book about logic}   F = {x | x is fiction}

a. the non-fiction books
b. the oversized non-fiction books
c. the reference and non-fiction books
d. the books that are neither reference nor fiction
e. the oversized reference books and textbooks
f. the standard-sized logic textbooks
g. the logic textbooks and oversized fiction books
h. logic books that are neither fiction nor texts
i. reference books, texts, and oversized non-fiction books
j. logic reference books that are oversized and non-fiction

2. Draw a Venn diagram to represent each of the following sets.
   a. ((D ∩ E) ∩ F)   b. ((D ∪ E) ∪ F)
   c. ((D ∪ E)′ ∪ F)   d. ((D ∪ E)′ ∩ (D ∪ F))
   e. ((D′ ∪ E′) ∪ (D ∪ F)′)   f. ((D′ ∩ E′) ∩ F′)

3. Name the set represented by the shaded areas in each of the following Venn diagrams.

a.
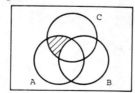

b.
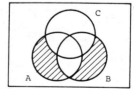

c.
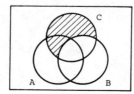

d.
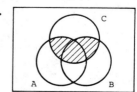

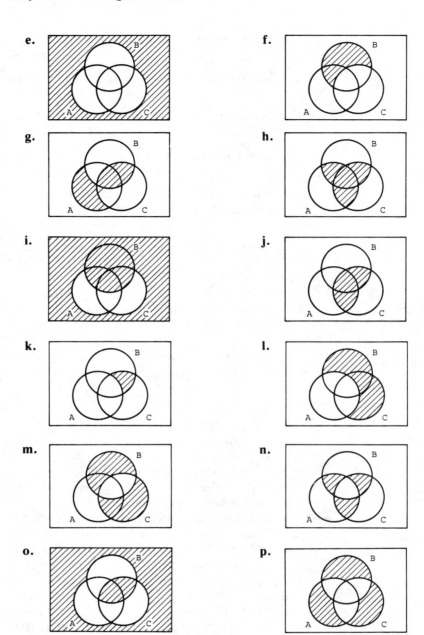

4. Translate the following set descriptions into colloquial English. Use the definitions given. (The first item is followed by the correct answer in brackets.)

$U = \{x \mid x \text{ is a component}\}$
$W = \{x \mid x \text{ is under warranty}\}$
$N = \{x \mid x \text{ is new}\}$
$S = \{x \mid x \text{ is in service}\}$

a. $N \cap W$ [The new components under warranty]
b. $N \cap S$
c. $((N \cap W) \cap S')$
d. $(N \cup W)$
e. $((N \cap S) \cup (N \cap W))$
f. $(N' \cap (S \cap W))$
g. $S' \cap W'$
h. $(S \cup (N \cap W))$
i. $((N' \cap W) \cup (N \cap S))$
j. $(W \cup S)'$

2.7 Extract Programs and Set Theory

The most natural application of set theory to program design is the extract program. **Extract programs** read files, select particular records, and create new files or reports from the selected records. The extract program is most often used to copy a relatively small number of records from a large master file onto another file. The smaller file can then be processed without processing the entire master file.

For example, an insurance company might consider a direct-mail advertising campaign in which each of its policy holders over 51 years of age was to be contacted. Suppose that the master file was arranged by policy number but the letters had to be sorted in order of zip code. An efficient programming solution would be first to create a file of the relevant records (policy holders over 51) and then to sort this smaller file by zip code. This procedure would avoid having to sort the entire master file. The extract program itself would read each record in the master file, determine whether each record met the appropriate conditions, and, if so, add that record to the new file.

Venn diagrams are useful in designing extract programs because they provide visual representations of the records to be selected and because they help simplify the logic required for the selection process. To use Venn diagrams, one assumes that the universal set (the rectangle) is the entire master file and that the component sets (circles) represent the conditions for selection (age, smoking habits, and so on). The flowcharts shown in Figure 2.1(a and b) represent extract programs that will examine an insurance company's file and create a file of the names of individuals who are over 51 years of age. Here, for the purposes of creating the accompanying Venn diagram (Figure 2.1c), we let $A = \{x \mid x \text{ is over } 51\}$.

Figure 2.1 (a and b) Extract programs that will examine an insurance company's file and create a file of the names of individuals who are over 51 years of age.
(c) Venn diagram.

(a)

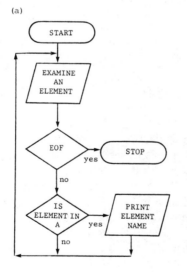

(b)

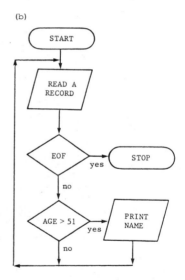

(c)

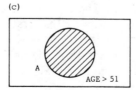

Note that the PRINT instruction in the input/output symbol is used both for printing reports and for adding records to a file. In the event that a program creates a file *and* prints a report, the input/output symbols also indicate which action is intended. In this chapter, we are most concerned with the logic of selection and will simply use the PRINT instruction, whether a report or a file is to be produced.

The flowchart shown in Figure 2.2 will print a single list or create a new file of all the policy holders who are over 51 or who have failed to renew their policies. We let A = {x | x is over 51} and B = {x | x has renewed his or her policy}.

Figure 2.2 (a) This program will print a single list or create a file of all the policy holders who are over 51 or who have failed to renew their policies. (b) Venn diagram.

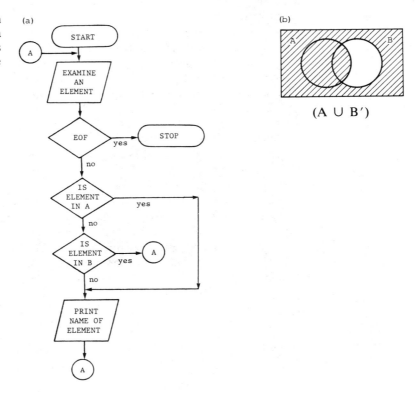

(A ∪ B′)

Note that the first decision causes the name of each element in set A to be printed, whether or not it is in set B. So, when control reaches the B decision, the only elements in (A ∪ B′) that are left to be printed are those that are not in A. The second decision causes all of the remaining elements of (A ∪ B′) to be printed.

The flowchart shown in Figure 2.3 will print a single list of policy holders who are 51 or younger and who have renewed their policies. We recognize that the set to be printed is the intersection of the complement of set A with set B. Here we let A = {x | x is over 51} and B = {x | x has renewed his or her policy}.

Because (A′ ∩ B) is the intersection of two sets, an element must be a member of both sets to be printed. The first decision ensures that members of A will not be printed, because members of A are not members of A′. Only members of A′ reach the second decision. The second decision diverts all those members of A′ that are not in B away from the PRINT statement. So control will reach the PRINT statement only for members of (A′ ∩ B).

The flowchart shown in Figure 2.4 will print a single list of policy holders who are neither smokers nor over 51 but who have renewed their policies, together with those smokers who didn't renew their policies.

Trying to comprehend this confusing assortment of conditions is a real challenge. However, the use of set theory makes the problem much easier to understand. If we first translate the description into set-theory notation, we can avoid keeping track of who smokes, who renews policies, and so on. If we go on to produce a Venn diagram for this set, the flowchart requirements become quite clear.

Figure 2.3 (a) This program will print a single list of policy holders who are 51 or younger and who have renewed their policies.
(b) Venn diagram.

(a)

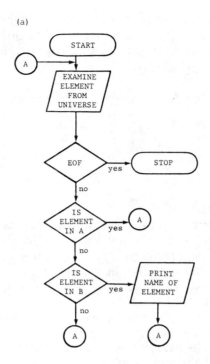

(b)

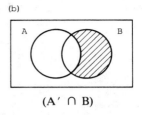

(A′ ∩ B)

Figure 2.4 (a) This program will print a single list of policy holders who are neither smokers nor over 51 but who have renewed their policies, together with those smokers who didn't renew their policies.
(b) Venn diagram.

(a)

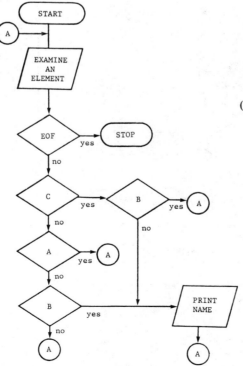

(b)

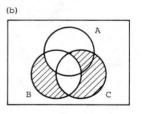

(B ∩ (A′ ∩ C′)) ∪ (C ∩ B′)

A = {x | x is over 51}

B = {x | x renewed his or her policy}

C = {x | x smokes}

With the Venn diagram drawn, there is a handy way to "desk check" this flowchart to ensure that the correct items will be printed. We do this by using the Venn diagram for the set (Figure 2.4b), along with the following diagram:

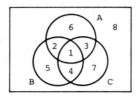

To "desk check" the diagram, we pick an imaginary element from each of the numbered areas and trace its path through the flowchart. When we reach the end of a path on the flowchart (here, a connector), we will see whether or not that item was printed. Next we refer to the original Venn diagram to determine whether or not it should have been printed. In checking Figure 2.4(a), we would start with an item from area 1 at the EXAMINE AN ELEMENT input. We would see that such an element would not be the EOF and would take the affirmative path at both decision B and decision C. The flow would now be at connector A and ready to return for another element. The name of the element from area 1 did not get printed; consulting the original Venn diagram, we see that indeed it *should not* get printed. So far, so good. Then we check areas 2 through 8. If *all* the correct names are printed and *only* the correct names are printed, the flowchart is correct.

Use this "desk checking" procedure to verify that the flowchart shown in Figure 2.5 prints the names of all non-students who have either health coverage or liability coverage.

Figure 2.5   (a) This program prints the names of all non-students who have either health coverage or liability coverage. (b) Venn diagram.

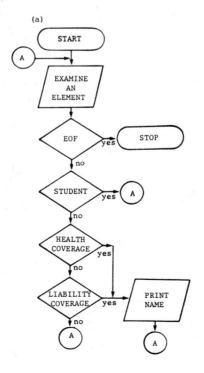

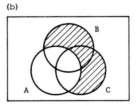

A = {x | x is a student}

B = {x | x has health coverage}

C = {x | x has liability coverage}

More complicated extract programs may require that different types of records be entered into different files or printed on different lists. The insurance company of our previous example might treat the non-smokers differently from the smokers and so require different processing for each. Rather than introduce multiple-file problems at this point, we shall simply specify that selected records be printed in different columns. (Again, this is because our interest is in the logic of selecting, not in the details of file creation.)

The flowchart shown in Figure 2.6 will print the names of individuals with both health coverage and liability coverage in column 1 and the names of those with health coverage but no liability coverage in column 2.

A = {x | x has health coverage}

B = {x | x has liability coverage}

Figure 2.6 (a) This program will print the names of individuals with both health coverage and liability coverage in column 1 and the names of those with health coverage but no liability coverage in column 2.
(b) Venn diagram.
(c) Sample input data.
(d) Sample report.

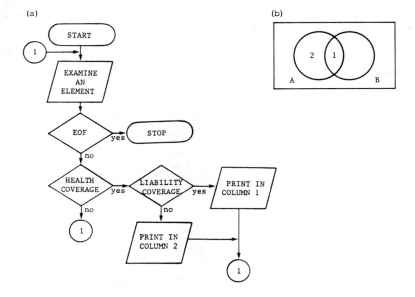

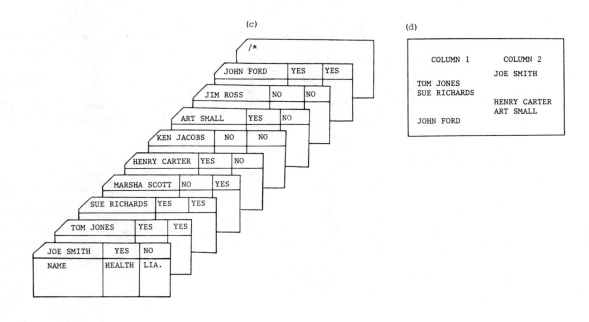

The flowchart shown in Figure 2.7 will print the names of all those over 51 who are non-smokers and who have not renewed their policies in column 1; the names of those smokers over 51 who have renewed their policies in column 3; and the names of smokers who have renewed their policies but are not over 51 in column 2.

A = {x | x is over 51}

B = {x | x has renewed his or her policy}

C = {x | x smokes}

Figure 2.7 (a) This program will print the names of all those over 51 who are non-smokers and who have not renewed their policies in column 1; the names of those smokers over 51 who have renewed their policies in column 3; and the names of smokers who have renewed their policies but are not over 51 in column 2.
(b) Venn diagram.
(c) Sample input data.
(d) Sample report.

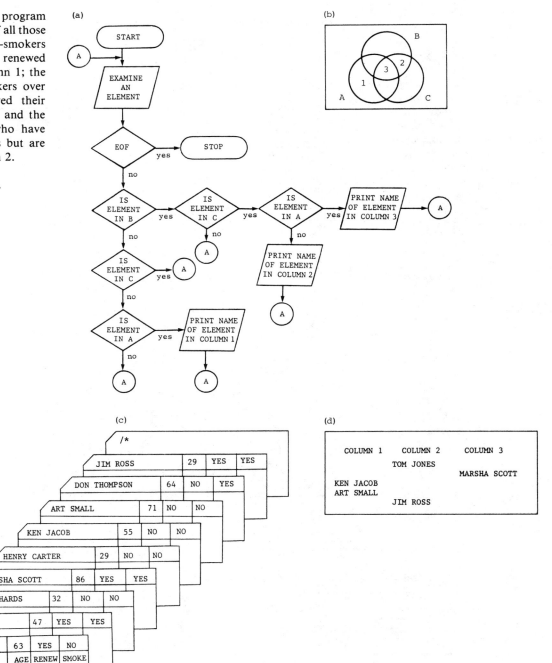

The flowchart shown in Figure 2.8 will print the names of those over 51 who don't smoke and haven't renewed their policies and the names of those who haven't renewed their policies and who aren't over 51 but who smoke in column 1, and the names of those who smoke and have renewed their policies but who aren't over 51 in column 2.

A = {x | x is over 51}

B = {x | x has renewed his or her policy}

C = {x | x smokes}

Figure 2.8 (a) This program will print the names of those over 51 who don't smoke and haven't renewed their policies and the names of those who haven't renewed their policies and who aren't over 51 but who smoke in column 1, and the names of those who smoke and have renewed their policies but who aren't over 51 in column 2.
(b) Venn diagram.

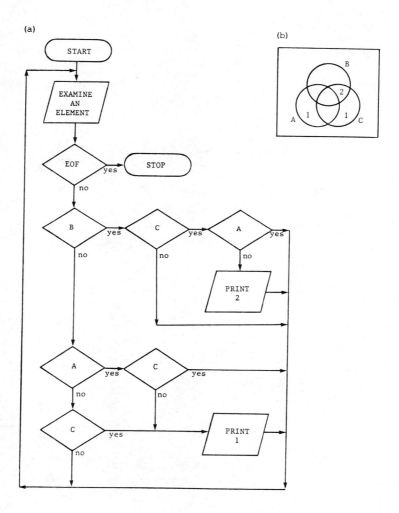

Simplification with Venn Diagrams

Venn diagrams not only help clarify the way data is to be selected. They also show how that selecting can be done more efficiently. Figure 2.9(a) represents the solution to a problem that can be simplified by using Venn diagrams. This problem is to print the names of everyone over 51 who has renewed the policy but does not smoke in column 1; the names of all smokers who have renewed their policies but are not over 51 in column 2; the names of all those who have renewed their policies, who are over 51, and who smoke in column 1; and the names of all those who are neither over 51 nor have renewed their policies but who do smoke in column 2. Just describing this problem with a Venn diagram simplifies things (see Figure 2.9(b)).

The Venn diagram makes it obvious that there are actually only two areas to be printed: (A ∩ B) in column 1 and (A′ ∩ C) in column 2.

When segments that are to undergo the same processing have a common border, as do ((A ∩ B) ∩ C′) and ((B ∩ A) ∩ C), the decision that is represented by the circle that creates that border (C) may be omitted.

Figure 2.9 (a) This program prints the names of everyone over 51 who has renewed the policy but does not smoke in column 1; the names of all smokers who have renewed their policies but are not over 51 in column 2; the names of all those who have renewed their policies, who are over 51, and who smoke in column 1; and the names of all those who are neither over 51 nor have renewed their policies but who do smoke in column 2.
(b) Venn diagram.

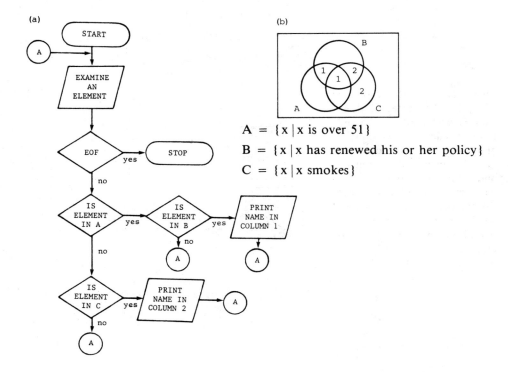

A = {x | x is over 51}

B = {x | x has renewed his or her policy}

C = {x | x smokes}

Figure 2.10 (a) This flow-chart shows how unnecessary decisions can be eliminated.
(b) Venn diagram.

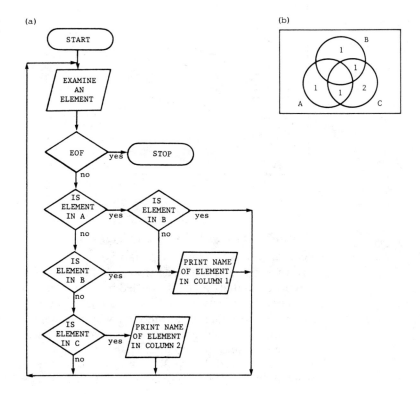

Figure 2.10(a) exhibits the elimination of unnecessary decisions. It was designed to print the lists described in the accompanying Venn diagram, Figure 2.10(b). Here the decision that would be represented by circle C in the Venn diagram would not affect the printing of column 1. Although circle C cuts across areas to be printed, the areas on each side of it are printed. A decision concerning circle C *is* relevant to Column 2 printing and is included at the proper place.

Exercises 2.7

1. Design flowcharts for programs that will examine a universe and print the names of the members of the sets indicated by the areas shaded in the following Venn diagrams.

   a.
   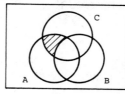

   b.
   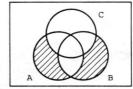

   c.
   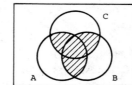

2. Design flowcharts for programs to print, in the corresponding columns, the names of members of the sets indicated by numerals in the following Venn diagrams.

   a.
   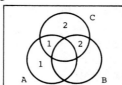

   b.
   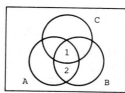

   c.
   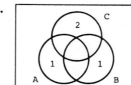

   d.
   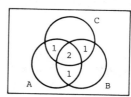

   e.
   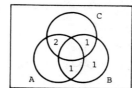

   f.
   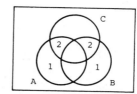

3. Design flowcharts that will print the members of each of the following sets. Use

   $A = \{x \mid x \text{ is an adult}\}$

   $B = \{x \mid x \text{ has a checking account}\}$

   $C = \{x \mid x \text{ has a savings account}\}$

   a. Minors who have either checking or savings accounts.
   b. Adults and those with checking accounts who also have savings accounts.
   c. Adults who have checking accounts and adults who have savings accounts.
   d. Those who are neither adults nor have checking accounts or savings accounts.

4. Design a flowchart for a program that will read names, ages, smoking habits, and policy renewals from cards and print the names of non-smokers over the age of 51 who have renewed their policies in column 1; the names of those over 51 who have not renewed their policies and who don't smoke in column 2; and the names of smokers who have renewed their policies in column 3.

2.8 Flowcharts Combining Sets, Counters, and Accumulators

Extract programs require only the selection and recording of records. More extensive programs require that information about records in a file be computed and recorded. A large retailer may want to know the number of employees in a particular division, the total sales of employees who are members of the stock plan, or perhaps whether average sales in one division exceeded those in another. To provide that information, a program must select the appropriate records and then use counters and accumulators to execute the proper calculations. Again, the Venn diagram is useful in visualizing the set or sets to be isolated.

Figures 2.11 to 2.16 represent programs that are designed to read sales records (each of which contains a name, a division, number of years employed, a stock incentive plan, and a sales amount) and to provide the information indicated.

Figure 2.11 determines and prints the number of agents in division 12 who have been employed more than 10 years and who are in the stock plan. This program differs from the extract programs only to the extent that it counts the members of the relevant set rather than printing their names or adding them to a file.

Figure 2.11 (a) This program determines and prints the number of agents in division 12 who have been employed more than 10 years and who are in the stock plan.
(b) Venn diagram.

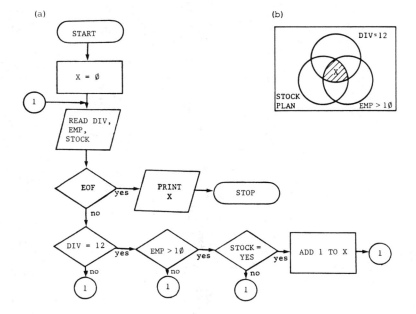

Figure 2.12 (a) This program counts those who have worked for fewer than 10 years and who are either in the stock plan or are in Division 2; it also counts those who have worked for at least 10 years and are not in Division 2.
(b) Venn diagram.

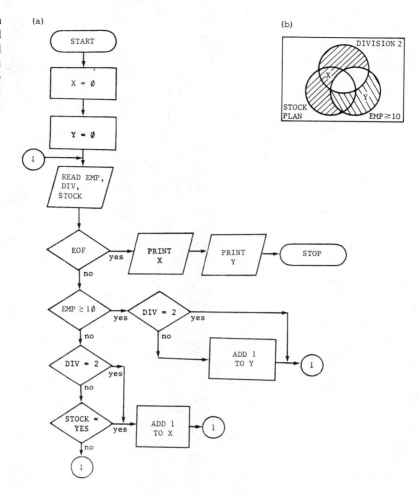

Figure 2.12 represents a program that counts two groups rather than one. It counts those who have worked for fewer than 10 years and who are either in the stock plan or are in Division 2; it also counts those who have worked for at least 10 years and are not in Division 2.

Figure 2.13 uses accumulators rather than counters and determines whether, among agents with more than 15 years of service, total sales of those in the stock plan exceeded total sales of those not in the stock plan.

A more enlightening sales comparison might be made between the average sales of those in the stock plan and the average sale of those who were not, again among those who have worked more than 15 years. Figure 2.14 uses both counters and accumulators to compute these averages.[2]

---

[2] We will assume that data will be sufficient to avoid division by zero.

Figure 2.13 (a) This program determines whether, among agents with more than 15 years of service, total sales of those in the stock plan exceeded total sales of those not in the stock plan.

(b) Venn diagram.

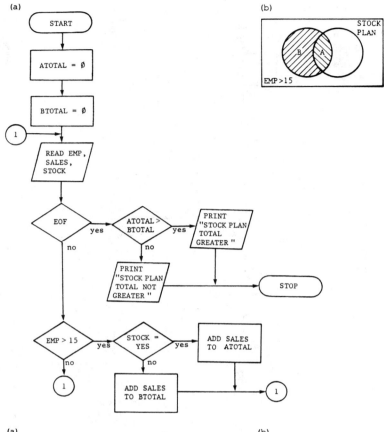

Figure 2.14 (a) This program compares the average sales of those in the stock plan with the average sales of those who were not, again among those who have worked more than 15 years.

(b) Venn diagram.

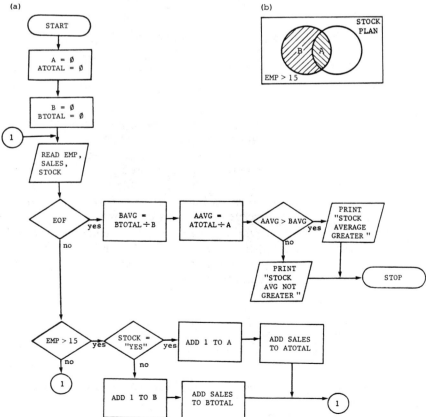

In the foregoing examples, the individuals for whom averages were calculated were in mutually exclusive groups. That is, no individual who was counted in one average was counted in another. Those in the stock plan were always different individuals from those not in the stock plan. It would be just as reasonable to calculate averages of groups that are not mutually exclusive (groups that overlap). For example, we could compare the average total sales of those who are in the stock plan with the average total sales of those who have been employed for more than 10 years. In calculating the averages, we would recognize that an individual could be in both of these groups and would direct control for every individual to both decisions. So, if our decision concerning the stock plan occurred first (as in Figure 2.15), we would have to direct control from both the affirmative and the negative branches of the stock decision back to the longevity decision.

Figure 2.15 (a) In this program, the groups that are compared are not mutually exclusive; they overlap. (b) Venn diagram.

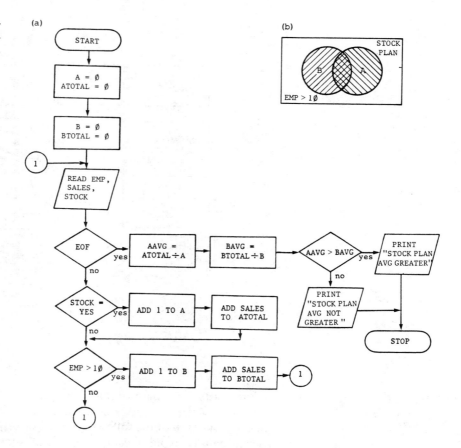

Note that the affirmative branch from the stock decision goes to the longevity decision rather than returning to the READ instruction. This ensures that anyone who both is in the stock plan and has more than 10 years of service will be counted and averaged with both groups. The Venn diagram (Figure 2.15(b)) highlights this overlap in decisions; the shaded areas cross each other.

Figure 2.16 calculates and prints the average sales of employees in the stock plan, of those employed more than 20 years, and of those in Division 5 but not in the stock plan. Note that control from the affirmative side of the stock decision bypasses the Division 5 decision and returns above the longevity decision. Division 5 was by-passed because we were to calculate an average for only those in Division 5 who were not in the stock plan. Control returned above the longevity decision because we were to calculate an average for all who were employed for more than 20 years.

Figure 2.16 (a) This program calculates and prints the average sales of employees in the stock plan, of those employed more than 20 years, and of those in Division 5 but not in the stock plan. (b) Venn diagram.

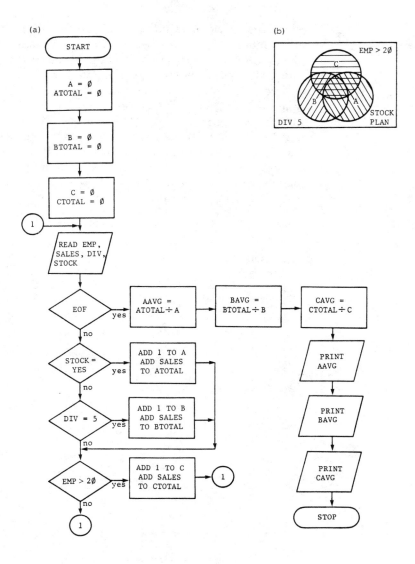

Exercises 2.8

1. Design flowcharts for programs that will read records that contain names, division numbers, years employed, stock plan membership, and sales amounts, and that will carry out each of the following sets of directions. Assume that there will be sufficient data to avoid division by zero and that the records are *not* sorted.
   a. Print the total sales of those in the stock plan who are also in Division 5.
   b. Print the average sales of those who are in the stock plan and are also in Division 5.
   c. Print the number of members of the stock plan, and print the average sales of those who have been employed more than 10 years.
   d. Determine and print whether the average sales in Division 5 exceeded the average of all employees of more than 10 years.
   e. Determine and print whether the average sales in Division 5 exceeded the average sales of those in the stock plan who have been employed more than 10 years.
   f. Determine and print whether everyone in Division 1 is in the stock plan. (The program is to read no more records than necessary to make the determination.)

g. Determine and print whether everyone in Division 1 whose sales exceeded $2000 is in the stock plan.

h. Print the total sales of Division 5 members who are in the stock plan. If any of those individuals' sales is negative, print "ERRONEOUS DATA" along with the total.

i. Print the total sales of individuals in Division 5 and the average sales of those in the stock plan. Print the name and "ZERO SALES" for each individual whose sales figure is zero. In the event that any individual's sales figure is less than zero, print "INVALID DATA" and terminate the program.

Review Questions

Completion

1. The _____ of two sets contains all of the members of the two sets.
2. The _____ of a Venn diagram represents the universal set.
3. The _____ of set A represents all members of the universal set that are not in set A.
4. There are _____ significant areas in a Venn diagram with three circles.
5. An expression that contains the word *not* indicates a _____.
6. An expression that restricts sets indicates a _____.

Definitions

1. Set
2. Empty set
3. Universal set
4. Union
5. Intersection
6. Complement

Discussion

1. What are the two methods of defining particular sets?
2. What is the function of extract programs?

True or False

1. _____ Set theory was specifically developed for use in designing computer programs.

2. _____ The members of a single set must be similar to one another.

3. _____ The intersection of two sets generally contains more members than either of the component sets.

4. _____ The membership of the complement of a set is related to the universal set.

5. _____ The membership of the complement of a set is related to the empty set.

6. _____ The rectangle of a Venn diagram is simply a "frame" for the diagram and has no logical significance.

7. _____ A Venn diagram that represents two sets includes two circles.

8. _____ For any given set description, there is only one correct Venn diagram.

9. _____ For any given Venn diagram, there is only one correct set description.

10. _____ A particular area of a Venn diagram has the same name no matter how many circles are used in that diagram.

3. The Logic of Sets, II

3.1 Boolean (Set Theory) Properties

Boolean properties are relationships among various sets. The properties that we will consider here are properties of identity. These properties arise because the same set can be described in a variety of ways. For example, the expression (A ∩ B) and (B ∩ A) both describe the set composed of the common elements of the sets A and B. We express this relationship by saying that (A ∩ B) is identical to (B ∩ A). By using this property, called commutation (COMM), and other Boolean properties, we are often able to reduce rather complicated set descriptions to rather simple ones. Ultimately, these Boolean properties can be used to simplify programming problems and facilitate program design.

Before applying Boolean properties, we will use Venn diagrams to verify those properties. This is done by diagramming, one at a time, the sets described on either side of the identity sign. If the diagrams match, the sets described are identical and the property described holds. If the diagrams don't match, the sets are not identical and the property described does not hold. As an example of this use of Venn diagrams, consider the statement (A ∩ B) = (B ∩ A).

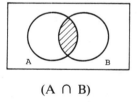

(A ∩ B)

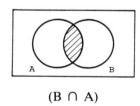

(B ∩ A)

The diagrams are identical, so we know that both expressions name the same set. The property holds, and the statement (A ∩ B) = (B ∩ A) is true. In addition to verifying the Boolean properties, Venn diagrams also help us understand them. Accordingly, you are encouraged to construct your own diagram for each of the properties described here.

Commutation

The commutative (COMM) property, like all other Boolean identity properties, applies to all sets. Hence, it applies to sets that are components of other sets. The following identity statements are examples of commutation with more complicated sets:

$$((A \cap B) \cap C) = ((B \cap A) \cap C)$$
$$((A \cap B) \cap C) = (C \cap (A \cap B))$$
$$((A \cap B)' \cap C) = (C \cap (A \cap B)')$$
$$(A \cap B)' = (B \cap A)'$$

In using the **commutative property**, one simply changes the order of two sets that occur on either side of a union or an intersection. But it is important to interchange the *complete sets* on either side of the union or intersection. When complete sets are not interchanged, the resulting sets are not equivalent. The following examples are incorrect uses of commutation, as indicated by their Venn diagrams.

$$((A \cup B) \cap C) \neq ((A \cup C) \cap B)$$
$$((A \cup B) \cap C) \neq ((C \cup B) \cap A)$$

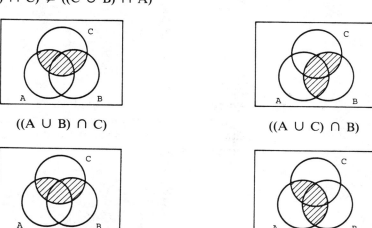

$((A \cup B) \cap C)$	$((A \cup C) \cap B)$
$((A \cup B) \cap C)$	$((C \cup B) \cap A)$

Association

The associative property of sets may be expressed as follows:

$$((A \cap B) \cap C) = (A \cap (B \cap C)) \quad \text{and}$$
$$((A \cup B) \cup C) = (A \cup (B \cup C))$$

Venn diagrams show that these statements are true identity statements.

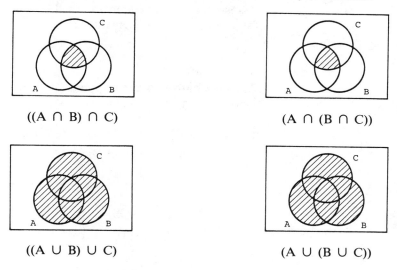

$((A \cap B) \cap C)$	$(A \cap (B \cap C))$
$((A \cup B) \cup C)$	$(A \cup (B \cup C))$

In plain language, the **associative property** states that, whenever three sets are joined by unions or are joined by intersections, the inner set of parentheses may be rearranged. But this property holds only when all three sets are joined by the same operation. If the sets are joined by both a union and an intersection, association does not hold. This is shown by the following set of Venn diagrams.

((A ∩ B) ∪ C)   (A ∩ (B ∪ C))

Association is also prohibited where the inner set of parentheses is followed by the complement sign. In fact, it is not clear what might be called "association" in such a situation. The following are Venn diagrams of several attempts to use association on such expressions.

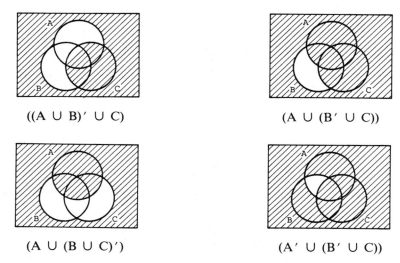

((A ∪ B)′ ∪ C)   (A ∪ (B′ ∪ C))

(A ∪ (B ∪ C)′)   (A′ ∪ (B′ ∪ C))

Note that none of the listed "possibilities" is equivalent to the original expression. Association simply cannot be used on an expression whose inner parentheses are followed by the complement sign.

Distribution

The **distributive property** applies to sets wherein unions and intersections are mixed. This rule may be stated

(A ∩ (B ∪ C)) = ((A ∩ B) ∪ (A ∩ C))   and

(A ∪ (B ∩ C)) = ((A ∪ B) ∩ (A ∪ C))

Distribution is verified by the following Venn diagrams.

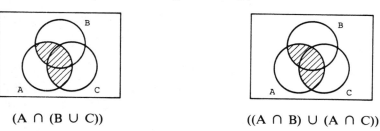

(A ∩ (B ∪ C))   ((A ∩ B) ∪ (A ∩ C))

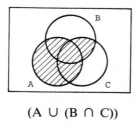

$$(A \cup (B \cap C))$$

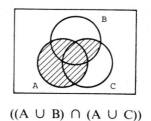

$$((A \cup B) \cap (A \cup C))$$

DeMorgan's Law

Perhaps the most useful of all the Boolean properties is **DeMorgan's law**. This property allows one to move the complement sign from outside of parentheses to inside them and to change unions to intersections, or vice versa. DeMorgan's law can be stated

$$(A \cup B)' = (A' \cap B') \qquad \text{and}$$
$$(A \cap B)' = (A' \cup B')$$

DeMorgan's law is verified by the following Venn diagrams.

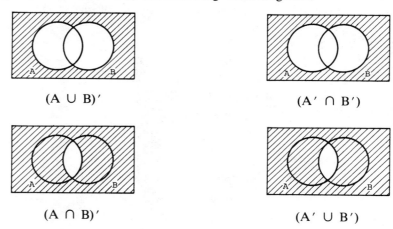

$(A \cup B)'$	$(A' \cap B')$
$(A \cap B)'$	$(A' \cup B')$

Note that DeMorgan's law always changes a union to an intersection, or vice versa. One cannot simply move the complements.

Absorption

Absorption is a property that could be proved from the other properties in this section, so including it is somewhat redundant. But that proof is quite involved (and not worth going through each time), so we shall use absorption just as we would any of the other properties. Absorption has two forms. They and their corresponding Venn diagrams follow.

$$(A \cup (A \cap B)) = A$$

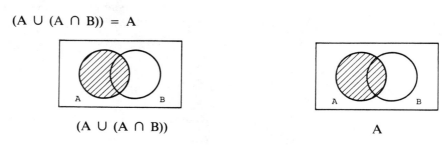

$$(A \cup (A \cap B)) \qquad\qquad\qquad\qquad A$$

$(A \cap (A \cup B)) = A$

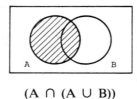

$(A \cap (A \cup B))$

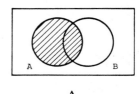

A

Other Properties

We shall also use several other Boolean properties that will not be verified by Venn diagrams. Each of these properties can be proved formally. But each of them involves only a single set, or a single set and the universal set or the empty set. Such properties cannot be diagrammed without expanding our procedures for the use of Venn diagrams. So we shall simply adopt them without verification. The properties are

tautology	$(A \cup A) = A$	(TAUT)
	$(A \cap A) = A$	(TAUT)
excluded middle	$(A \cup A') = U$	(ExM)
contradiction	$(A \cap A') = \emptyset$	(CON)
null union identity	$(A \cup \emptyset) = A$	(NU)
null intersection identity	$(A \cap \emptyset) = \emptyset$	(NI)
universal union identity	$(A \cup U) = U$	(UU)
universal intersection identity	$(A \cap U) = A$	(UI)
double negation	$(A')' = A$	(DN)
universal complement	$U' = \emptyset$	(UC)
null complement	$\emptyset' = U$	(NC)

The Boolean properties are more helpful when applied in combinations than when applied alone, because in combination they can be used to simplify rather complex expressions. Consider, for example, the set $((A \cup (B \cap C)) \cap (A \cup B))$. According to the distributive property, this set is identical to $(A \cup ((B \cap C) \cap B))$. This set is identical to $(A \cup ((C \cap B) \cap B))$ by the commutative property and identical in turn to $(A \cup (C \cap (B \cap B)))$ by the associative property. Finally, tautology shows this set to be equivalent to $((A \cup (C \cap B)))$. This last expression is preferable, because it is easier to read and understand. Nevertheless, it names the same set as $((A \cup (B \cap C)) \cap (A \cup B))$. The simplification of sets by this method is usually expressed on numbered lines, rather than in paragraphs. Rewriting our example in this more standard form results in

1. $((A \cup (B \cap C)) \cap (A \cup B))$	
2. $(A \cup ((B \cap C) \cap B))$	DIST
3. $(A \cup ((C \cap B) \cap B))$	COMM
4. $(A \cup (C \cap (B \cap B)))$	ASSOC
5. $(A \cup (C \cap B))$	TAUT

The following examples of simplification suggest ways to use other Boolean properties.

1. $((B \cap A') \cup (A \cup C)')$	
2. $((A' \cap B) \cup (A \cup C)')$	COMM
3. $((A' \cap B) \cup (A' \cap C'))$	DM
4. $(A' \cap (B \cup C'))$	DIST

1. $[((A \cap B)' \cup C')' \cup (C \cap (A' \cap B))]$	
2. $[((A \cap B) \cap C) \cup (C \cap (A' \cap B))]$	DM, DN
3. $[(A \cap (B \cap C)) \cup (C \cap (A' \cap B))]$	ASSOC
4. $[(A \cap (B \cap C)) \cup (C \cap (B \cap A'))]$	COMM
5. $[(A \cap (B \cap C)) \cup ((C \cap B) \cap A')]$	ASSOC
6. $[((B \cap C) \cap A) \cup ((C \cap B) \cap A')]$	COMM
7. $[((B \cap C) \cap A) \cup ((B \cap C) \cap A')]$	COMM
8. $((B \cap C) \cap (A \cup A'))$	DIST
9. $((B \cap C) \cap U)$	ExM
10. $(B \cap C)$	UI

1. $((B \cup A) \cap (B \cup A'))$	
2. $(B \cup (A \cap A'))$	DIST
3. $(B \cup \emptyset)$	CON
4. B	NU

Some programming books present truth tables along with their treatment of Boolean properties. This text does not do so because of the important theoretical differences between sets and statements. Truth functional logic, including truth tables, is presented in Chapter 5.

Exercises 3.1

1. Use Boolean properties to simplify the following expressions.
   a. $(A \cup (B \cup A'))$
   b. $((A \cup B) \cap (B' \cup A))$
   c. $((A \cup B')' \cup (A \cup C')')$
   d. $((B \cup A)' \cup A)$
   e. $[((A \cup C) \cap (A \cup B)) \cap (A \cup C')]$
   f. $[(((B \cup A) \cup A') \cap B') \cup A]$
   g. $[((A \cup C) \cap (A \cup C')) \cap ((A' \cap B) \cup (A \cup B)')]$
   h. $[(A' \cup B') \cap (A' \cup B')]'$
   i. $[(A \cap (C \cup B)') \cup (A \cap (C \cup B')')]$
   j. $(B \cap (A \cup B'))$

2. Use Venn diagrams to check your work in Exercise 1 by comparing a diagram of your results with a diagram of the original expression.

3.2 Simplified Flowcharts

One reason for simplifying the name of a set is to better understand the set. A second reason is to simplify programs involving that set. In Section 2.7, flowcharts were simplified via Venn diagrams. That method works well when only two or three component sets are involved. When more than four sets are involved, however, Venn diagrams become confusing, and simplification should be accomplished through the use of Boolean properties. Figure 3.1 and Figure 3.2 both exhibit a pair of solutions. In each case, part (a) is the version that might be attempted if flowcharting were done without first simplifying the expression.

Figure 3.1 (a) Flowchart for the unsimplified expression ((B ∪ A) ∩ (B ∪ A′)).
(b) Flowchart for the same expression after it is simplified to B via Boolean properties, as follows:

(B ∪ A) ∩ (B ∪ A′)	
(B ∪ (A ∩ A′))	DIST
(B ∪ ∅)	CON
B	NU

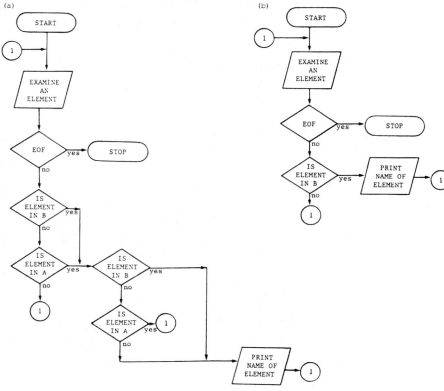

Figure 3.2 (a) Flowchart for the unsimplified expression (A ∪ B) ∪ (A ∪ B′). (b) Flowchart for the same expression after it is simplified to U via Boolean properties, as follows:

((A ∪ B) ∪ (A ∪ B′))	
((A ∪ B) ∪ (B′ ∪ A))	COMM
(A ∪ (B ∪ (B′ ∪ A)))	ASSOC
(A ∪ ((B ∪ B′) ∪ A))	ASSOC
(A ∪ (U ∪ A))	ExM
(A ∪ U)	UU
U	UU

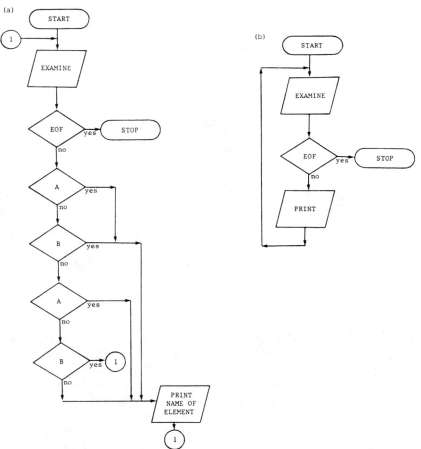

Not every complex set description can be simplified as those we used in Figures 3.1 and 3.2 can. But when expressions *can* be simplified, the corresponding programs can be simplified also.

Exercises 3.2

Design a flowchart for a program to carry out each of the following sets of instructions. Before starting the flowchart, translate the directions into set-theory notation and simplify.

1. Print a list of the smokers who also drink and who are overweight, together with drinkers who smoke but who are not overweight.

2. Print a list of those who are overweight but neither drink nor smoke, and add to that list those overweight drinkers who are non-smokers.

3. Print a single list of smokers who don't drink, drinkers who don't smoke, overweight smokers who drink, and drinkers who are not overweight but who smoke.

4. Print a two-column report. In column 1 list the overweight non-smokers who don't drink and the overweight non-drinking smokers. In column 2, list those who are overweight and who drink but don't smoke.

3.3 Statements in Set Theory

Up to this point, we have considered only descriptions of sets and ways of representing and simplifying those descriptions. An equally important aspect of set theory involves the use of set-theory notation to make statements. Statements in set theory differ from descriptions in an important respect. Statements assert something that is either true or false, whereas descriptions merely define sets in terms of operations and component sets. Statements, when they are true, tell how various sets are related; descriptions just name sets.

Statements in set theory are constructed by placing, between the names of two sets, "verbs" that designate relations. Here we will consider only three such verbs. They are "____ *is identical to* ____," "____ *is a subset of* ____," and "____ *is a proper subset of* ____." The statement "A is identical to B" (A = B) says that sets A and B have exactly the same members. A is identical to B if and only if every member of A is a member of B, and every member of B is a member of A. The order in which the members of the sets are written is not relevant to their identity. So, for example, {1,2,3} is identical to {1,3,2}.

The statement "A is a subset of B" says that every member of set A is a member of set B. "A is a subset of B" is expressed as A $\subseteq$ B. {1,2,3}, {3,2}, and {1,2,3,4} are all **subsets** of {1,2,3,4}. From the definitions of identity and subset, it follows that identical sets are also subsets of each other. However, as our examples show, not all subsets are identical. It also follows, though it may run counter to our intuition, that the empty set is a subset of every set.

The statement "A is a proper subset of B" says that every member of set A is a member of set B, but not vice versa. That is, every member of A is a member of B, but at least one member of B is not a member of A. "A is a proper subset of B" is expressed as A ⊂ B. {1,2,3}, {3,1}, and {4} are all **proper subsets** of {1,2,3,4}. Every proper subset is a subset, but identical sets are *not* proper subsets of each other.

To express the denial of a set-theory statement, one simply places a slash (/) through its verb. The expression A ⊄ B states that A is not a proper subset of B. If a statement is true, then its denial is false, and vice versa. So, if A = B is true, then A ≠ B is false.

Assume that the component sets are defined as

U = the first 10 letters of the English alphabet

A = {a,b,c,d,e}   C = {a,c,e}

B = {a,c,e,g,i}   D = {a,b,c,e}

Then the following statements are true.

1. A ⊆ (B ∪ C′)	6. (A ∪ B) ⊄ C′
2. B ≠ C′	7. (A ∪ B) ≠ U
3. D ⊂ A	8. { } ⊆ D
4. A ⊄ (C ∪ D)	9. U′ = ∅
5. (A ∩ C) ⊆ D	

And the following statements are false.

1. B ⊂ C′	5. (A ∩ B) ⊄ D
2. D ⊆ (C ∩ B)	6. (A ∪ C) ⊆ B
3. A ⊆ C	7. D ⊆ C′
4. (D ∩ B) ⊄ C	

The truth of any statement depends in part on the definitions of its terms. The truth of many set-theory statements also depends on the definition of the universal set. Even when all other definitions are held constant, the truth (or falsehood) of a set-theory statement may change if the universal set is altered. Consider how the truth value of the statement A ⊂ B varies with changes in the universal set when A and B are defined as follows:

A = {x | x is an odd number}

B = {x | x is a prime number}

U = {1,2,3,4,5,6,7,8}	A ⊂ B is true.
U = {1,2,3,4,5,6,7,8,9}	A ⊂ B is false.
U = {1,3,5,7}	A ⊂ B is false.
U = {11,12,13,14,15}	A ⊂ B is false.

So a statement that is true given one universal set may be false given a different universal set.

Some other statements of set theory depend on neither the definition of the universal set nor the definition of their component sets. These statements are called **logical truths**. Their truth or falsehood depends on the definitions of operations and verbs. We will not consider general methods for determining logical truth. The following list of logical truths contains those that one is apt to encounter in simplifying statements in set theory. We omit a list of logical falsehoods; they are merely the denial of the logical truths. The logical truths you can expect to use in set theory are

$$A = A \qquad \emptyset \subseteq A$$
$$A \subseteq A \qquad A \not\subseteq \emptyset$$
$$A \not\subseteq A \qquad U \not\subseteq A$$
$$A \subseteq U$$

Recognizing these logical truths and the corresponding logical falsehoods is important in programming, because there is no point in designing a program to determine the obvious.

3.4 Set-Theory Statements and Flowcharts

Figure 3.3 This flowchart determines the truth or falsehood of the statement A ⊆ B.

Using some of the techniques developed in Section 3.2, we can design flowcharts for programs that will test a particular statement on various universal sets and determine the truth or falsehood of that statement for each universe. Figure 3.3 is an example for a rather simple statement.

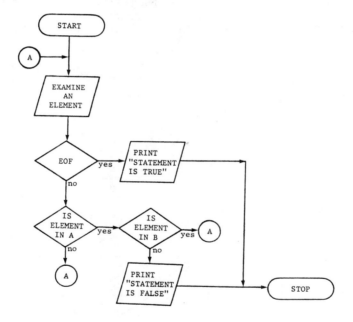

This program will examine an element. If the element is not in A, the next element is examined. If the element is in A, then, if it is not in B, the "false" message is printed and the program stops. When an element is in both A and B, a new element is examined. If every element is examined without encountering an element that is in A but not in B, the "true" message is printed and the program stops.

Note that determining whether A ⊆ B is true requires examination of the entire universal set. It can be shown false, on the other hand, by a single element. This is so because every member of A must be a member of B for the statement to be true. To confirm this, each and every member of the universe has to be examined, at least to determine whether it is a member of A. But a single member of A that is not a member of B is sufficient to prove the statement false. This element could even be the first element examined. Once *any* such element is found, there is no point in examining those that remain.

Figures 3.4 through 3.11 show how other set-theory statements can be tested.

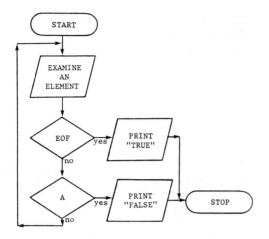

Figure 3.4 This flowchart determines the truth or falsehood of the statement A = ∅.

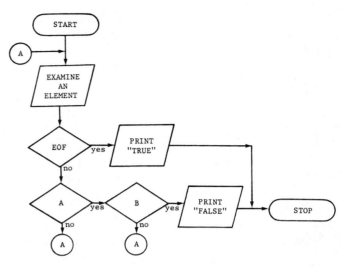

Figure 3.5 This flowchart determines the truth or falsehood of the statement (A ∩ B) = ∅, which says that nothing is in both set A and set B.

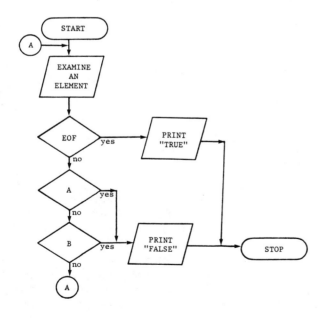

Figure 3.6 This flowchart determines the truth or falsehood of the statement (A ∪ B) = ∅, which says that nothing is in either set A or set B.

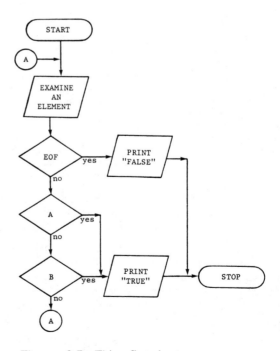

Figure 3.7 This flowchart determines the truth or falsehood of the statement (A ∪ B) ≠ ∅, which says that something is in set A or in set B.

Figure 3.8 This flowchart determines the truth or falsehood of the statement (A ∩ B) ≠ ∅, which says that something is in set A and also in set B.

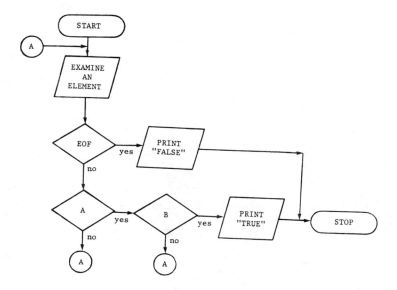

Figure 3.9 This flowchart determines the truth or falsehood of the statement (A ∪ B) ⊆ (C ∩ D), which says that whatever is in either set A or set B is also in set C and set D.

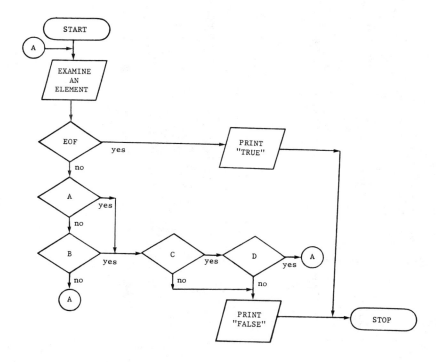

Note that, in Figure 3.10, X is used as an indicator. X will have the value 1 if any members of set B are not members of set A.

To determine that A is a *proper* subset of B, it is necessary to determine both that A is a subset of B and also that there is at least one member of B that is not a member of A. The program determines that A is a subset of B, just as it did in Figure 3.3. To determine that at least one member of B is not a member of A, it checks each element that is not a member of A to see whether it is a member of B. If even one such member is found, X is given the value 1 and keeps that value throughout the program. As in Figure 3.3, the EOF decision is reached only if A is a subset of B. In Figure 3.10, a decision placed after EOF checks the value of X to determine whether the subset is a proper subset. If X is still 0, then no members of B were found that

Figure 3.10 This flowchart determines the truth or falsehood of the statement A ⊂ B.

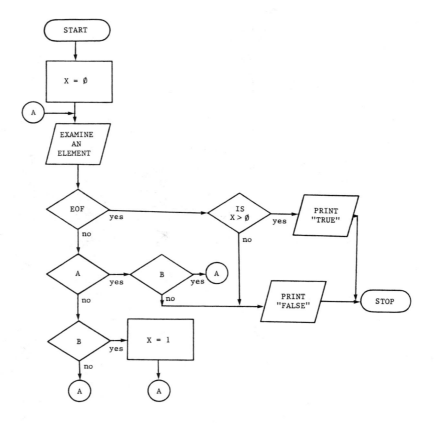

Figure 3.11 This flowchart determines the truth or falsehood of the statement (A ∩ B) ⊂ C.

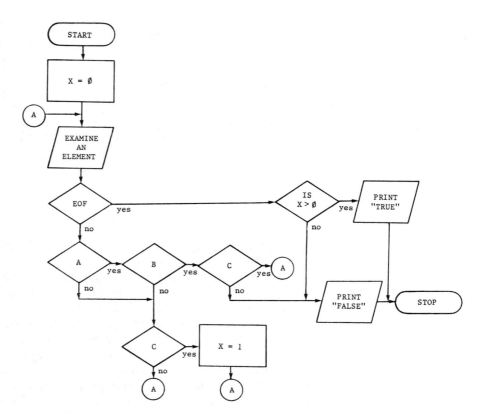

were not also members of A, and therefore the subset is not proper. If X is 1, then at least one member of B was found that was not a member of A, and the subset is proper.

Each of the flowcharts shown in Figures 3.3 through 3.11 will test its statement for truth on various universes. Each will also test equivalent statements for truth. For example, A ⊂ C is equivalent to ((A ∪ B) ∩ (A ∪ B′)) ⊂ C, because A is equivalent to ((A ∪ B) ∩ (A ∪ B′)). But the flowchart drawn for A ⊂ C is much less complex than one that might be drawn for ((A ∩ B) ∩ (A ∪ B′)) ⊂ C. Again, it is worthwhile to use the Boolean properties to simplify expressions before drawing flowcharts for them.

Exercises 3.3–3.4

1. Determine whether the statements below are true or false, given the following definitions.

    Universal set = {x | x is an integer and 0 < x < 10}
    A = {x | x is even}   B = {x | x is odd}   C = {2,4}   D = {3,5}

    a. A ⊆ B′   **b.** A ⊂ B′
    c. A = B′   **d.** C ⊄ A
    e. D ⊂ A   **f.** D ⊂ B
    g. D ⊄ A   **h.** D ∩ C = ∅
    i. A ∩ B = U   **j.** (A ∪ D)′ ⊄ B
    k. (B ∪ C)′ ⊆ (D ∪ C)′   **l.** (B ∪ C)′ ⊈ (A ∩ D)′

2. Determine the truth or falsehood of each of the statements in Exercise 1, if the universe is defined as follows:

    U = {x | x is an integer and 0 < x < 6}

3. For each of the following statements, design a flowchart that will examine the elements of a universe and determine whether the statement is true. When possible, use Boolean properties to simplify the statements before designing the flowchart.

    a. C ⊆ D   **b.** C ∪ D = ∅
    c. (C ∩ D) ⊂ E   **d.** (C ∩ D) ≠ (E ∩ E′)
    e. A′ ∩ (B ∪ A)′)′ ⊆ C   **f.** (A ∪ B) = U
    g. (A′ ∩ B′) ⊂ C   **h.** (C ∪ (B ∩ D)) ≠ ∅
    i. ((B ∪ C′) ∩ D) ⊆ E   **j.** (A ∪ B) ⊂ C

3.5 Symbolizing Natural-Language Statements

Many natural-language statements are equivalent to set-theory statements, provided that component sets are properly defined. Writing programs that make use of such natural-language statements can be facilitated by translating those statements into set theory. The translations done in Section 3.2 will be applicable here in describing the sets on either side of the verb. What remains is to learn how to use the verbs of set theory. Most of the statements that can be translated using the set theory we have developed so far represent one of the following types of sentences. Each of these sentence types can be translated using either the subset notation or the identity notation.

Models Using Subset Notation

All S is P	S $\subseteq$ P	Every member of S is a member of P.
No S is P	S $\subseteq$ P $'$	Every member of S is a member of the complement of P.
Some S is P	S $\not\subseteq$ P $'$	Not every member of S is a member of the complement of P.
Some S is not P	S $\not\subseteq$ P	Not every member of S is a member of P.

Models Using Identity Notation

All S is P	(S $\cap$ P$'$) = $\emptyset$	Nothing is in the intersection of S and the complement of P.
No S is P	(S $\cap$ P) = $\emptyset$	Nothing is in the intersection of S and P.
Some S is P	(S $\cap$ P) $\neq$ $\emptyset$	Something is in the intersection of S and P.
Some S is not P	(S $\cap$ P$'$) $\neq$ $\emptyset$	Something is in the intersection of S and the complement of P.

As expressions become more complicated, the sets that replace S and P in the foregoing models also become more complicated. Nevertheless, most statements that can by symbolized follow one of these four basic patterns.

For our examples, we will use a series of statements concerning billing procedures and define our sets in the following way:

U = {x | x is a customer}

C = {x | x is a preferred customer}

P = {x | x made a payment}

S = {x | x was sent a bill}

Every preferred customer made a payment.
(C $\subseteq$ P)   (C $\cap$ P$'$) = $\emptyset$

Every preferred customer who was sent a bill made a payment.
(C $\cap$ S) $\subseteq$ P   ((C $\cap$ S) $\cap$ P$'$) = $\emptyset$

Every preferred customer who made a payment was sent a bill.
(C $\cap$ P) $\subseteq$ S   ((C $\cap$ P) $\cap$ S$'$) = $\emptyset$

No preferred customer made a payment.
(C $\cap$ P) = $\emptyset$ C $\subseteq$ P$'$

No one who made a payment is a preferred customer.
(P $\cap$ C) = $\emptyset$ P $\subseteq$ C$'$

No preferred customer who made a payment was sent a bill.
((C $\cap$ P) $\cap$ S) = $\emptyset$ (C $\cap$ P) $\subseteq$ S$'$

Some preferred customer made a payment.
(C $\cap$ P) $\neq$ $\emptyset$ C $\not\subseteq$ P$'$

Some preferred customer who made a payment was sent a bill.
((C $\cap$ P) $\cap$ S) $\neq$ $\emptyset$ (C $\cap$ P) $\not\subseteq$ S$'$

Someone who was sent a bill is not a preferred customer.
(S $\cap$ C$'$) $\neq$ $\emptyset$ S $\not\subseteq$ C

Someone who was sent a bill is not a preferred customer who made a payment.
(S $\cap$ (P $\cap$ C)$'$) $\neq$ $\emptyset$ S $\not\subseteq$ (P $\cap$ C)

Preferred customers and those who made a payment were not sent bills.

$(C \cup P) \subseteq S'$ $((C \cup P) \cap S) = \emptyset$

Those who made payments are preferred customers or were sent bills.

$P \subseteq (C \cup S)$ $(P \cap (C \cup S)') = \emptyset$

Some who made payments are preferred customers or were sent bills.

$(P \cap (C \cup S)) \neq \emptyset$ $P \nsubseteq (C \cup S)'$

Some preferred customers who made payments were sent bills.

$((C \cap P) \cap S) \neq \emptyset$ $(C \cap P) \nsubseteq S'$

Every customer made a payment.

$U \subseteq P$ $P' = \emptyset$

No customer made a payment.

$P = \emptyset$ $U \subseteq P'$

3.6 Flowcharts and Natural-Language Statements

The ability to reduce natural-language statements to set-theory statements and the ability to design flowcharts to determine the truth or falsehood of set-theory statements allows one to design programs to discover various facts about data. A particular program might require that different processing take place, depending on the relationships of previously read data. For example, a program might require one process to be completed (say, execute a particular report routine) if *any* preferred customer made a payment and another process (say, print a message to advertising) if *no* preferred customer made a payment. Referring to the example "Some preferred customer made a payment" in the foregoing list, we see how to reduce the condition to set-theory notation. Figure 3.8 is a model for Figure 3.12, which represents a program to accomplish the required processing.

Figure 3.12 This flowchart executes a report routine if at least one preferred customer made a payment.

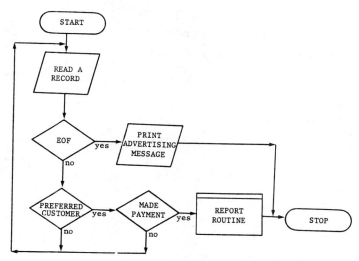

Figure 3.13 represents a program that determines whether every preferred customer and every customer who made a payment was sent a bill. If so, it executes a report routine; if not, it prints an error message. The execution of the report routine requires a bill for each preferred customer and for each customer who made a payment. Consequently, if a single one of these individuals did not get a bill, the error message is printed and the program stops.

Figure 3.13 This flowchart executes a report routine if every preferred customer and every customer who made a payment was sent a bill.

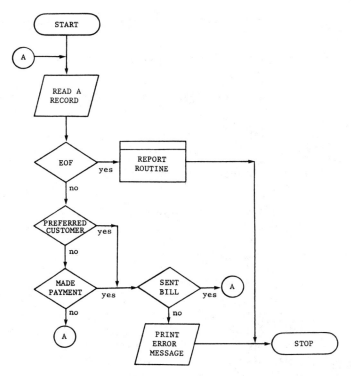

Figure 3.14 represents a program that prints a message if the preferred customers who didn't make payments and weren't registered *and* the registered preferred customers who didn't make payments were all sent bills. Otherwise the program carries out a report routine. These rather complicated instructions were reduced to set theory and simplified before the flowchart was drawn. Here,

A = {x | x is a preferred customer}

B = {x | x made a payment}

C = {x | x was registered}

D = {x | x was sent a bill}

Figure 3.14 This flowchart prints a message if every preferred customer who didn't make a payment was sent a bill. This simplified statement of the problem results from the following application of Boolean properties:

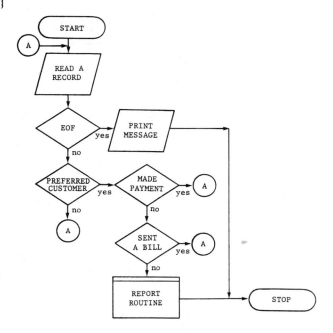

[(A ∩ (B′ ∩ C′)) ∪ ((C ∩ A) ∩ B′)] ⊆ D	
[(A ∩ (B′ ∩ C′)) ∪ ((A ∩ C) ∩ B′)] ⊆ D	COMM
[(A ∩ (B′ ∩ C′)) ∪ (A ∩ (C ∩ B′)] ⊆ D	ASSOC
[A ∩ ((B′ ∩ C′) ∪ (C ∩ B′))] ⊆ D	DIST
[A ∩ ((B′ ∩ C′) ∪ (B′ ∩ C))] ⊆ D	COMM
[A ∩ (B′ ∩ (C′ ∪ C))] ⊆ D	DIST
[A ∩ (B′ ∩ U)] ⊆ D	ExM
[A ∩ B′] ⊆ D	UU

Exercises 3.5–3.6

1. Using set-theory notation, symbolize each of the following natural-language statements, where

   F = {x | x is a football player}
   S = {x | x is a senior}
   J = {x | x is a junior}
   E = {x | x was excused}

   a. Every football player was excused.
   b. No football player was excused.
   c. Some football player was excused.
   d. Some football player was not excused.
   e. Some senior football player was excused.
   f. Some junior is not a football player.
   g. No junior is a senior football player.
   h. No junior football player was excused.
   i. No senior football player is a junior who is excused.
   j. Juniors and seniors were excused.
   k. Only football players were excused.
   l. All senior football players were excused.
   m. Some senior who was excused is not a football player.
   n. Some junior football player was not excused.
   o. No junior is a senior who was excused.

2. Using set-theory notation, symbolize each of the following natural-language statements. Where appropriate, use Boolean properties to simplify each. Design a flowchart for a program to execute a report routine if the statement is true of a given set of records and to print an error message if the statement is false.

   S = {x | x is a salesperson}   M = {x | x met his or her quota}
   F = {x | x is in district 1}   B = {x | x received a bonus}
   T = {x | x is in district 2}

   a. Every salesperson in the first district met his or her quota.
   b. Some salesperson in the second district failed to meet his or her quota.
   c. No salesperson in district 1 who met his or her quota received a bonus.
   d. The salespersons in district 1 who met their quotas, together with those in district 2 who met their quotas, all received bonuses.
   e. Salespersons in district 1, as well as those who are not in district 1, received bonuses.

Review Questions

Completion

1. The _____ simply changes the order of the two sets that occur on either side of a union or an intersection.
2. The statement _____ asserts that every member of A is a member of B, but not vice versa.
3. To express the denial of a set-theory statement, one places a _____ through the statement's _____.

4. The truth of a set-theory statement (except for logical truths and falsehoods) depends on the definitions of its _____ and on the definition of the _____ .

5. To determine that A is a proper subset of B, it is necessary to determine both that _____ and that _____ .

Definitions

1. Subset   2. Proper subset

Discussion

1. State the following Boolean properties:
   a. Commutation
   b. Association
   c. DeMorgan's law

2. Why is the flowchart for a program to determine the truth of a subset statement simpler than one to determine the truth of a proper subset statement?

3. Why is it possible to determine the truth of a set-theory statement without examining all elements in the universe?

4. Explain the difference between subsets and proper subsets.

True or False

1. _____ DeMorgan's law always changes a union to an intersection, or vice versa.

2. _____ Association permits the rearrangement of interior sets of parentheses of appropriate set descriptions.

3. _____ $A \subseteq B$ and $B \subseteq A$ may both be true.

4. _____ $A \subset B$ and $B \subset A$ may both be true.

5. _____ The truth of set-theory statements is independent of the definition of the universal set.

6. _____ $A \subset A$ is true when A is defined as the empty set.

7. _____ DeMorgan's law establishes that $(A \cap B)'$ is equivalent to $(A' \cap B')$.

8. _____ The empty set is not a proper subset of any set.

9. _____ $A = B$ and $A \subseteq B$ may both be true.

10. _____ $A = B$ and $A \subset B$ may both be true.

4. Structured Flowcharts

In its simplest form, designing **structured programs** is a matter of dividing tasks into logically independent units (or modules) and then joining these units in a limited number of predefined ways. Structured programs have several advantages. They are easier to understand because (1) the modules can be considered individually, and one need not comprehend an entire program before understanding its individual parts; and (2) the limitation on the ways the modules can be arranged makes it easier to identify the structure of a particular program. These factors are particularly important when we are trying to understand programs that were designed and coded by someone else. Structured programs are easier to maintain or change, because the individual modules can be changed or corrected without changing the entire program. Finally, structured programs are ultimately (though not initially) easier to design because the modules can be designed independently.[1] This means that the designer need not keep the whole project in mind at once and that parts of a complex project can be assigned to several different individuals.

Structured flowcharts contain precisely the same symbols as unstructured flowcharts. They differ in that structured flowcharts must meet the following conditions:

1. Each part of the chart must be one of three or four specified structures.
2. Control must enter each part at exactly one place and must leave each part at exactly one place.

These two conditions have the general effect of producing structured programs. The second condition tends to result in logically independent units; the first condition tends to limit the different organizational patterns of those units.

4.1 Requirements for Structured Flowcharts

The logical structures that are typically permitted in structured flowcharts include

1. Sequence
2. If-then (or if-then-else)
3. Do-while
4. Do-until
5. Case

We will adopt all five of these, even though doing so involves some redundancy. One could easily get along without do-while or without do-until. Here they will both be included so that you will understand both. Case is entirely dispensable, but it is useful in avoiding needlessly complicated flowcharts.

The decision in each of the logical structures represents a single condition. The process(es) in each logical structure represent(s) either a single operation or one or more of the permissible logical structures.

---

[1] Textbook problems in beginning language courses are not usually complex enough to make this advantage obvious.

Sequence represents any series of operations of permissible logical structures.

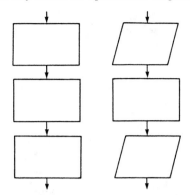

If-then (or **if-then-else**) represents a decision that controls further processing. The important feature of if-then that distinguishes it from unstructured decisions is that flowlines from both sides of the decision meet before control passes from this structure. However, process symbols need not be included on both flowlines from the decision.

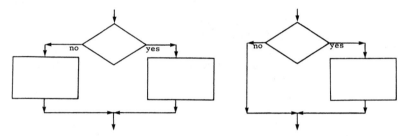

Do-while is a loop with an exit decision that occurs before processing within the loop. The important feature of this loop is that, after processing, control returns to a point immediately before the decision. Because the exit decision occurs first in the do-while loop, it is possible for the processing within that loop to be avoided entirely.

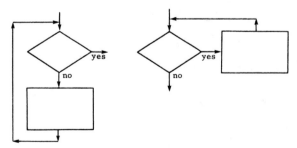

Do-until is a loop with an exit decision that occurs after processing. The do-until loop returns control to a point immediately before the first symbol in the loop. Because the exit decision occurs last in the loop, the processing within that loop is always completed at least once.

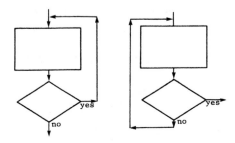

Case represents a decision with more than two possible outcomes; each outcome has its own process. The decision symbol indicates what condition is being checked, and each branch indicates a possible alternative. For example, the decision could contain AGE and the branches could be labeled UNDER 10, 10-21, and OVER 21 to indicate the flow for individuals in those age groups.

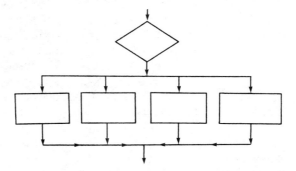

Note that all of these structures have an important feature in common: Control enters at exactly one point and exits at exactly one point.

Figures 4.1 and 4.2 show structured flowcharts that read SALES and print a total sales figure. Figure 4.1 contains a do-while loop; Figure 4.2 contains a do-until loop.

Comparing these flowcharts, we find an ''extra'' READ in Figure 4.1 and an ''extra'' EOF in Figure 4.2. Each of these ''extra'' symbols is necessitated by the fact that loop exit decisions must be either the first symbol or the last symbol in their loops. In Figure 4.1, control can't be returned above the READ, because the exit decision would then be the second item in the loop. So an additional READ is placed

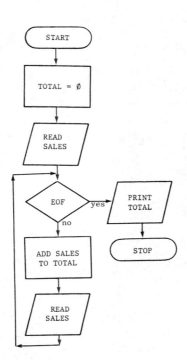

Figure 4.1 This flowchart reads SALES and prints a total sales figure. It contains a do-while loop.

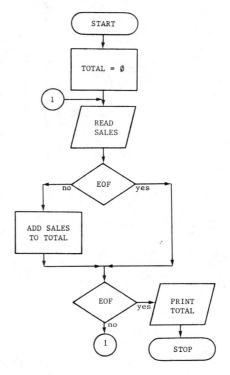

Figure 4.2 This flowchart uses a do-until loop to accomplish the same task as Figure 4.1.

at the bottom of the loop to read a record within the loop, just before the EOF decision. In Figure 4.2, EOF is to be the exit decision of a do-until loop. It must be placed at the end of the loop. Without the "extra" EOF just after the READ, the program would attempt to process an end-of-file marker.

Structured flowcharts contain only two kinds of decisions: loop exit decisions and if-then-else decisions. In reviewing the examples in this section, note that loop exit decisions are drawn with their negative branch at the bottom corner and that if-then-else decisions are drawn with their negative branch to the left. Adhering to this informal convention results in flowcharts that are easier to read and understand.

Figure 4.3 shows a structured flowchart that combines sequence, do-while and if-then. It represents a program that will read amounts, keep track of the number of amounts greater than 50, print the number of amounts over 50, and print the total of all amounts.

Figure 4.3 This flowchart contains a sequence, a do-while, and an if-then.

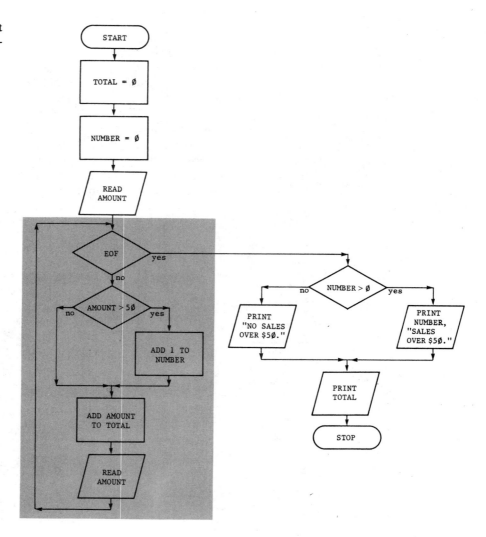

The overall structure of this program is a sequence. That sequence consists of an initial sequence, a do-while loop, an if-then, and a final sequence. The do-while loop contains a sequence with an if-then. The flowchart is structured because it is composed of only the permissible logical structures.

Note that this flowchart contains an "extra" READ statement. This is required because do-while loops must return control to a point immediately before their exit decision. So an initial READ is required before the loop, and a second READ is required within the loop.

Now compare Figure 4.3 to Figure 4.4. The latter describes a comparable program, but it uses a do-until loop rather than a do-while loop.

Unlike Figure 4.3, this flowchart requires only one READ instruction. But it requires an "extra" decision. This program is intended to read until EOF. But the EOF that immediately follows the READ cannot be the loop exit decision, because

Figure 4.4 This flowchart is much like Figure 4.3, but it uses a do-until loop rather than a do-while.

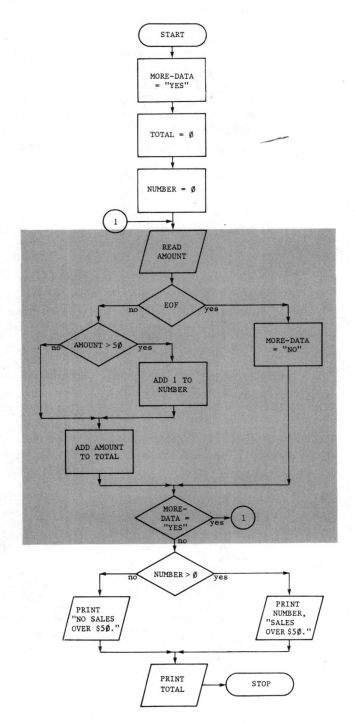

the loop exit decision must be the last symbol of the do-until loop. Placing a single EOF at the end of the loop would result in processing the end-of-file marker. To avoid processing the EOF marker and still meet the do-until requirements, Figure 4.4 includes an indicator called MORE-DATA. Initially this indicator is given the value YES, which it retains until the EOF marker is read. When the EOF marker is encountered, the value of MORE-DATA is set to NO, and control passes from the loop at the MORE-DATA decision. So, in this flowchart, MORE-DATA becomes the loop exit decision. The remainder of Figure 4.4 is essentially the same as Figure 4.3. (The MORE-DATA indicator could be eliminated by using a second EOF decision, as is done in Figure 4.2.)

From a purely logical point of view, it makes no difference whether a flowchart contains the do-while loop or the do-until loop. But from the point of view of the intended programming language, there may be important differences. In COBOL, for example, the standard "Perform-until" loop is essentially a do-while loop; in FORTRAN IV the standard "Do" loop is a do-until loop. Coding a program from a flowchart is facilitated by using the most appropriate loop.

The construction of structured flowcharts will not at first seem natural; their restrictions will seem artificial. But structured flowcharts can be an important step in structured programming, and structured techniques are well worth learning.

4.2 Examples of Structured Flowcharts

The next several flowcharts are structured representations of programs that correspond to unstructured flowcharts that we examined in earlier chapters. The flowcharts below are structured versions of Figure 2.1.

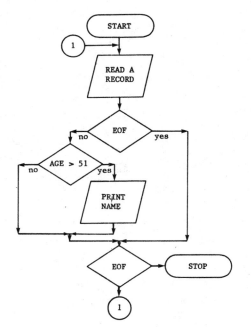
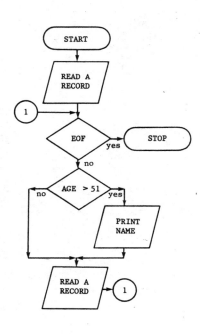

Figures 4.5 and 4.6 are structured models of the program described by Figure 1.21. The difference is, of course, that Figure 4.5 contains a do-while loop and Figure 4.6 contains a do-until loop. The difference between these flowcharts is comparable to the differences between Figure 4.1 and Figure 4.2. Compare these four flowcharts. Observe the difference in the way the two types of loops handle the READ instruction and the EOF decision. Note that the structured flowcharts are more complicated than the unstructured flowcharts.

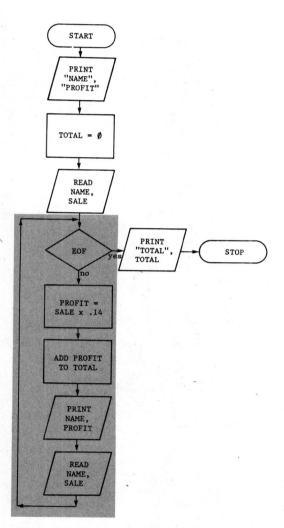

Figure 4.5 This flowchart is a structured model of the program described by Figure 1.21. It contains a do-while loop.

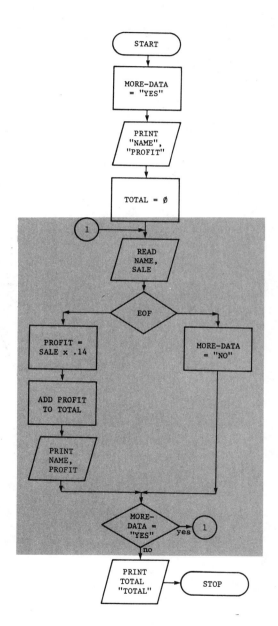

Figure 4.6 This flowchart is like Figure 4.5, except that it contains a do-until loop instead of a do-while.

Figures 4.7 and 4.8 are structured models of the program described by Figure 2.4. Figure 4.7 contains a do-while loop; Figure 4.8 contains a do-until loop.

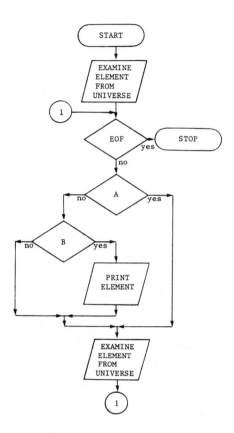

Figure 4.7 This flowchart, a structured model of the program described by Figure 2.3, contains a do-while loop.

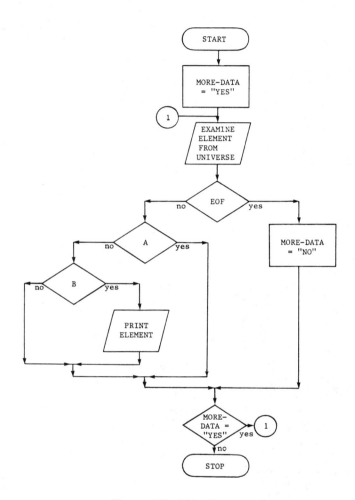

Figure 4.8 This flowchart is like Figure 4.7, except that it contains a do-until loop instead of a do-while.

Figures 4.9 and 4.10 are structured models of the program described by Figure 1.20. Both of these structured flowcharts required indicators, whereas the unstructured flowchart shown in Figure 1.20 did not. Note that, in Figure 1.20, there are two ways to exit the loop (when NUMBER is greater than 25 and at EOF). But having two exits from a loop is forbidden in structured programming. To accommodate the "one exit" requirement, we insert an indicator (DONE) to control the loop exit. This indicator is changed if either of the events occurs that would result in stopping the flowchart shown in Figure 1.20. So both of these structured flowcharts would stop under the same conditions as the flowchart shown in Figure 1.20.

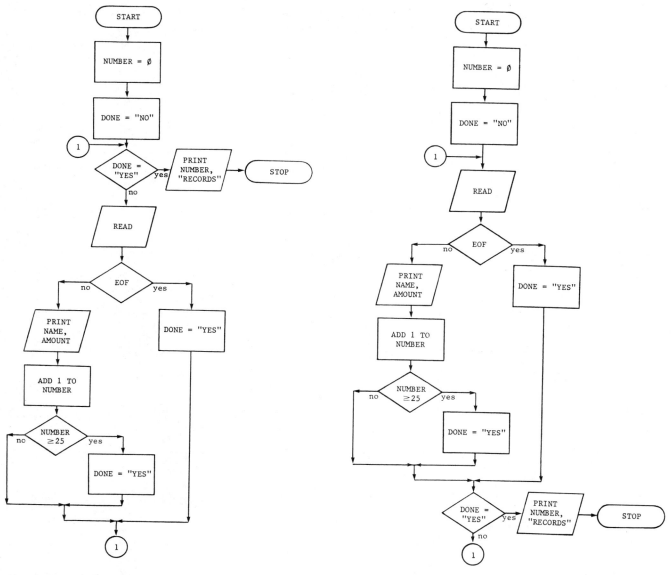

Figure 4.9 A structured model of the program described by Figure 1.20.

Figure 4.10 Another structured model of the program described by Figure 1.20.

Note that, when EOF is not the loop exit decision (as in Figures 4.9 and 4.10), the "extra" READ and the "extra" EOF are eliminated. The "extra" READ and the "extra" EOF can always be eliminated when EOF is not used as the loop exit decision. The only difference between these flowcharts is the placement of the loop exit decision.

Figure 4.11 is a structured model of the control-break program represented by the flowchart that appears in Example 1.2 on page 36.

Figure 4.11 This flowchart is a structured model of the control-break program illustrated on page 36.

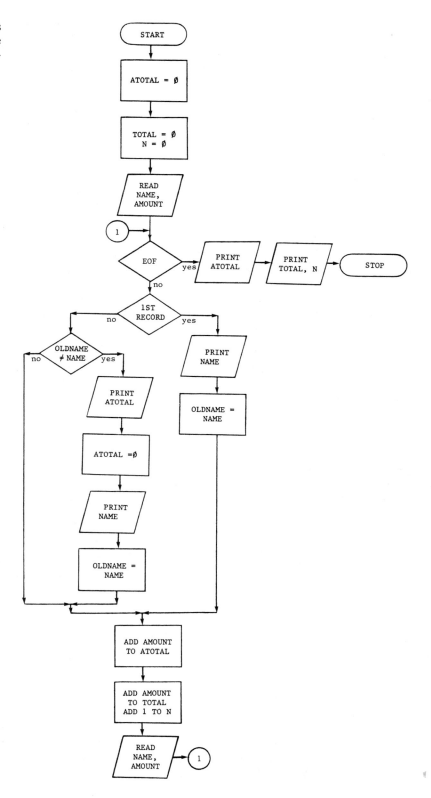

4.3 Modular Flowcharts

Structuring alone does much to enhance our understanding of programs. But even with structured flowcharts, the number of details in a typical program can obscure our understanding of the overall program. In reading flowcharts we become immersed in the details and are unable to recognize either the program's major components or the organization of its components. The addition of modular flowcharting to structured flowcharting greatly enhances readability by using a control module that eliminates most details in favor of predefined processes. The **control module** is an abbreviated flowchart that represents each major program component with a single striped process symbol. The control module describes program flow between program components and gives an overall picture of the program. The detail processing within each major component is described by a subordinate flowchart called a **submodule**. Each striped process symbol is "defined" by a submodule. Figure 4.12 is a modular version of Figure 4.5.

Figure 4.12 A modular flowchart. (a) The control module. (b, c, d, and e) Submodules.

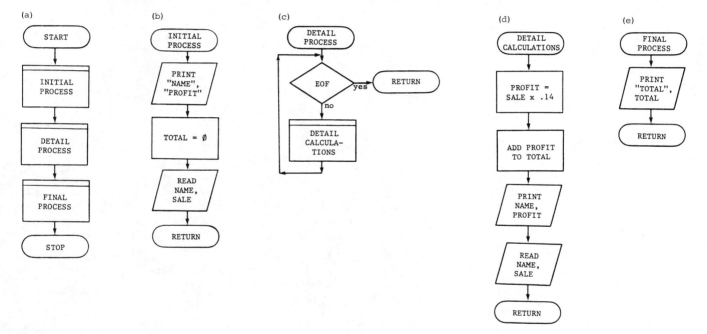

A **modular flowchart** is, in effect, a series of flowcharts. The first flowchart in the series is the control module, which represents the program's overall structure and contains the program's START and STOP terminals. The remaining flowcharts are submodules, each of which describes in greater detail the process named by a striped process symbol. Each submodule begins with a terminal containing the name of the process to be represented; each ends with a terminal containing RETURN. Each striped process symbol, whether in the control module or in a submodule, indicates that control is to be transferred to the named submodule. The RETURN terminal of the submodule indicates that control is to be returned to the previous flowchart at the point where control departed.

Each of the submodules in Figure 4.12 represents a single structure from our list of permissible logical structures. It is always possible to modularize a program in this much detail, but often it is confusing and not helpful to do so. Figure 4.13 is a modular version of Figure 4.11 that does not divide components to the single-structure level.

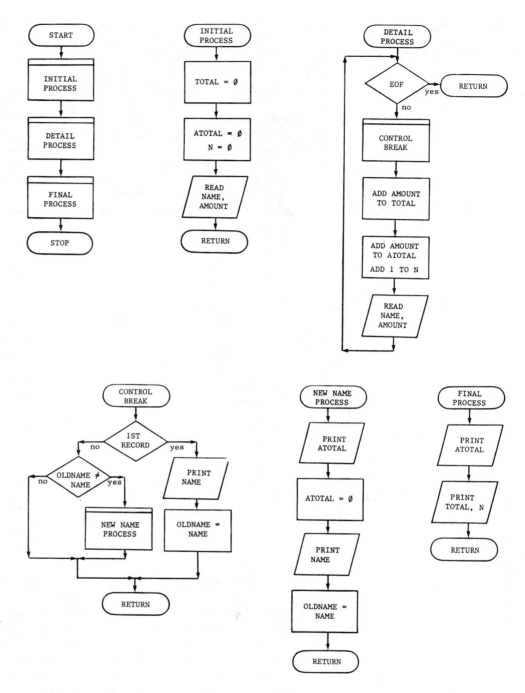

Figure 4.13 This version of Figure 4.11 does not modularize the program in so much detail.

Each submodule in both Figure 4.12 and Figure 4.13 has a single entry and a single exit. This is a requirement of all modular flowcharts. And it is this requirement that makes modular flowcharts compatible with structured flowcharts and makes possible the modular structured flowchart.

An Example of a Modular Structured Flowchart

Figure 4.14 describes a program that will produce a payroll summary. The modular aspect of this program is particularly effective in describing the three different compensation schedules based on total dollar sales.

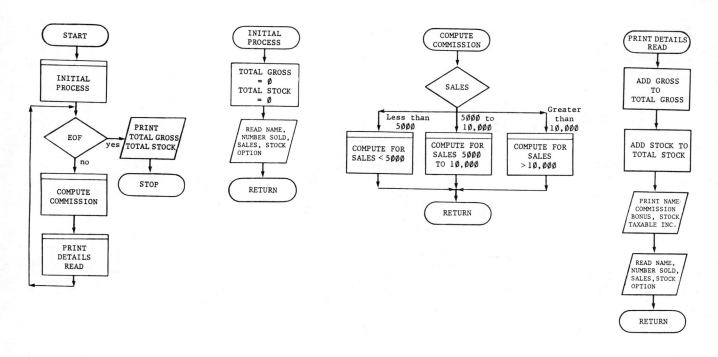

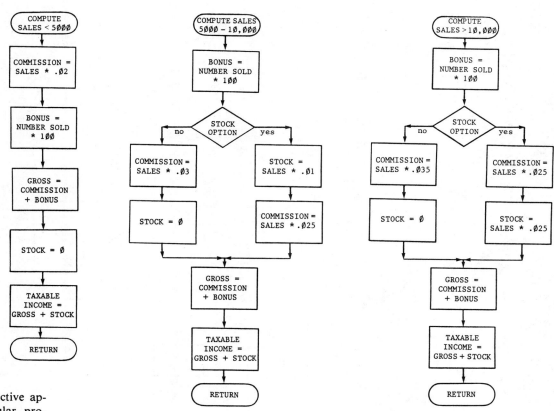

Figure 4.14 An effective application of a modular program.

Exercises
4.1–4.3

1. Identify the structures in each of the following flowcharts.

a.   b.

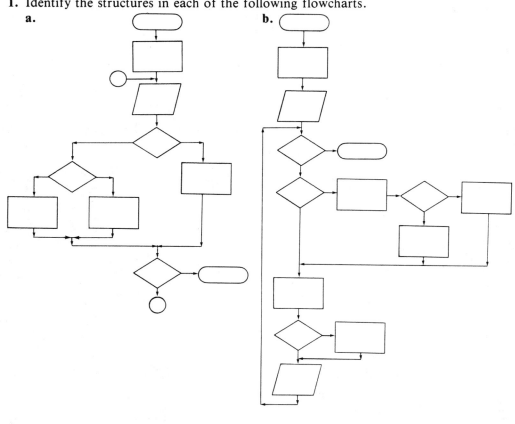

c.

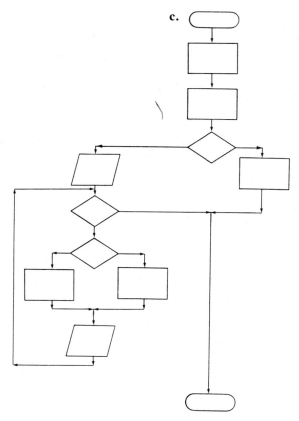

2. Design a structured flowchart using do-while loops for each of the following programs (Exercises 2 and 3 on page 22).
   a. Read SALES from each record, print each sales amount, and print the total of the sales amounts.
   b. Read SALES from each record and print the average of the sales amounts.

3. Design a structured flowchart using do-until loops for each of the programs described in Exercise 2 above.

4. Design structured flowcharts using do-while loops for the following program (Exercise 4 on page 33).

   Read names and grades. The program is to print each name and grade and to calculate and print the average of all grades. The program is to print one error message for every grade that is less than 0 and another for every grade over 100.

5. Design a structured flowchart using do-until loops for the program described in Exercise 4 above.

6. Design a structured flowchart using do-until loops for the following program (part 5 of Exercise 1 on page 37).

   Read a name and an amount from 10 or fewer records. Print each name and amount. Print an error message if fewer than 10 records were read.

7. Using the loop indicated, design structured flowcharts for programs to print, in the corresponding columns, the names of the members of the sets indicated by numerals in the following Venn diagrams. (These diagrams are taken from parts a and e of Exercise 2 on page 63.)

   a. 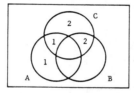   b.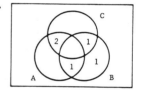

         DO-WHILE   DO-UNTIL

8. Using the loop indicated, design structured flowcharts for programs that will read records that contain names, division numbers, years employed, stock plan membership, and sales amounts, and that will carry out one of the following sets of directions (from parts c, f, g, and h of Exercise 1 on pages 68-69).
   a. Print the number of members in the stock plan and print the average sales of those who have been employed more than 10 years. Assume sufficient data to avoid division by 0. (DO-WHILE)
   b. Determine and print whether or not everyone in Division 1 is in the stock plan. (The program is to read no more records than necessary to make the determination.) (DO-UNTIL)
   c. Determine and print whether or not everyone in Division 1 whose sales exceed 2000 is in the stock plan. (DO-WHILE)
   d. Print the total sales of Division 5 members who are in the stock plan. If any of those individuals' sales is negative, print "ERRONEOUS DATA" along with the total. (DO-UNTIL)

4.4 Control Breaks Re-examined (with the Do-While Loop)

The FIRST RECORD decision employed by the flowcharts shown in Figures 1.26 through 1.29 provided a straightforward way of handling the special processing required for the first record of a control-break program.[2] In particular, the FIRST RECORD decision was used to avoid control-break processing for the first record. But none of these programs is structured. When the do-while structure is placed on the control-break program, the FIRST RECORD decision can be conveniently eliminated. Because the do-while loop usually requires two READS, control-break indicators can be placed after the second READ symbol only so that the FIRST RECORD will not result in a control break. Figure 4.15 represents a simplified version of this logic.

Figure 4.15 A standard control-break program using a do-while loop.

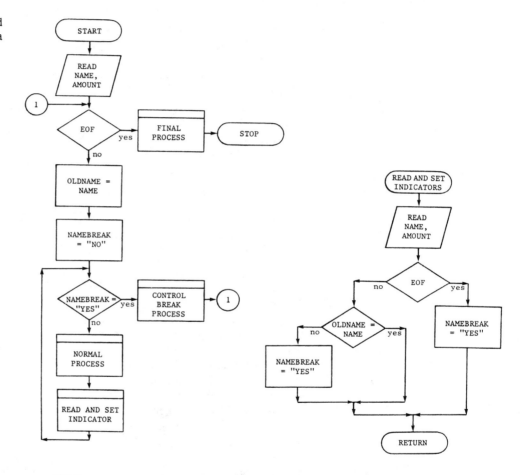

While the initial READ remains at the top of the flowchart, subsequent READS occur within the innermost loop. Control must leave this innermost loop for either a control break or EOF, so a control-break indicator (NAMEBREAK) is used in the loop exit decision. As processing for each new name begins, NAMEBREAK is set to "NO." Processing continues within the inner loop until either a new name or EOF is read. Then NAMEBREAK is set to "YES" and control escapes from the inner loop, control-break processing is accomplished, and control is transferred to the EOF decision.

Figure 4.16 represents a program comparable to that of Figure 1.27. But this structured flowchart uses the indicator NAMEBREAK to cause control to break if either a new name or EOF is reached. Note that, if EOF did *not* cause a control break by changing NAMEBREAK to "YES" the program would not stop when it

[2] This method also reflects the fixed logic cycle of RPG.

Figure 4.16 A structured flowchart that uses a do-while loop and a NAMEBREAK indicator to eliminate the FIRST RECORD decision.

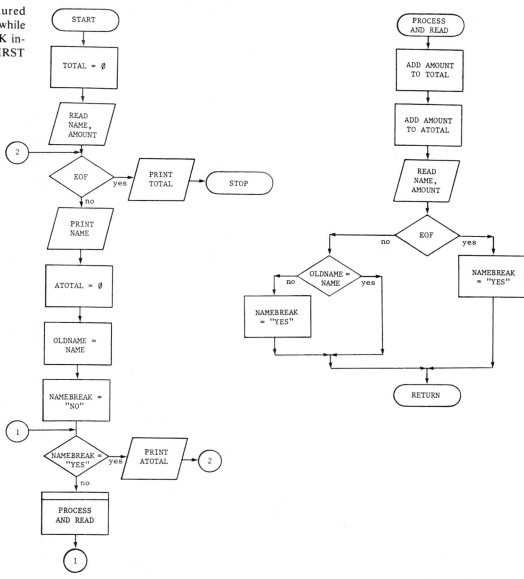

reached the end of the file. Instead it would continue to loop and try to read again. By changing **NAMEBREAK** to "YES" at EOF, the program escapes the loop and prints the last **ATOTAL**. Control is then directed to the EOF decision and the program stops.

Two-Level Control Break

A two-level control-break program interrupts normal processing if the data of either of two fields is changed. A program might process records that list both an agency and an agent, as well as a sales figure, and compute agent totals, agency totals, and a grand total. Such a program would contain an **AGENTBREAK** and an **AGENCY-BREAK**. Figure 4.17 shows this program. Note that both EOF and an agency change execute both control breaks and that an agent change executes only one. Generally, in multiple-level control-break programs, each control break causes each of its subordinate breaks to be executed. So if there were also districts to be considered, in addition to an agency and agents, the district control break would cause an agency control break and an agent control break, and EOF would cause all three breaks.

Figure 4.17 A two-level control-break program.

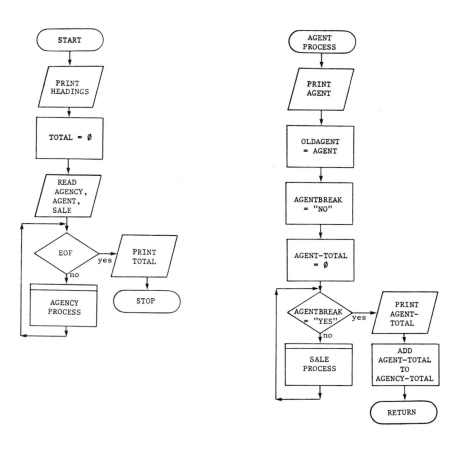

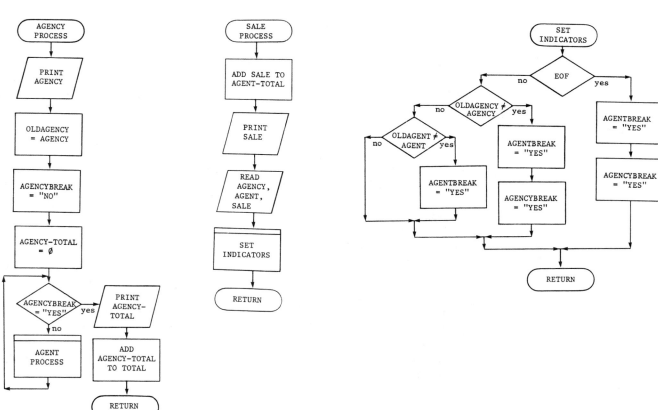

Exercises 4.4

1. Design a structured flowchart using do-while loops for a program that will read names and amounts from records sorted by name. Each name is to be printed once (even though it may occur on several records) and the total of all amounts is to be printed. (Exercise 3 on page 27.)

2. Design a structured flowchart using do-while loops for a program that will read names and amounts from records sorted by name. Each name is to be printed once, along with the total of that individual's amounts. The total of all amounts is to be printed. (Exercise 5 on page 27.)

*3. Design a structured flowchart with do-while loops for a program that will read a department number, a name, and a sales amount from records that have been sorted by department and then by name. Each department number and each name are to be printed once (even though they may occur on several records). The sale from each record, departmental totals, and a grand total are to be printed.

*4. Design a structured flowchart with do-while loops for a program to read a department number, a name, a sales amount, and an item cost. The records are sorted by department and by name. Print each department number once. For each record, print the name, the item cost, the sales amount, the profit, and percent profit (profit = sale amount − item cost). Print the total sales and item cost for each individual and the average percent profit for each individual. Print total sales, item cost, and average percent profit for each department.

4.5 Structured Flowcharts for Printing Tables

The programs that we have considered so far have depended on input (reading records) to supply the information necessary to produce output. Some programs do not rely on input. They combine fixed starting points (initial values) with calculations to produce output. Among the most straightforward of such programs are those that print tables of values based on mathematical equations. Such tables have limited application. But the logic used in their construction is important because it paves the way for understanding the logic of array processing to be treated in Chapter 8.

The programs to be designed create tables by calculating and printing the value of one variable of an equation, given the values of other variables. The flowchart shown in Figure 4.18 creates a table for the two-variable equation X = 3Y by

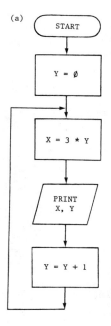

(a)

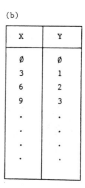

(b)

X	Y
$\emptyset$	$\emptyset$
3	1
6	2
9	3
.	.
.	.
.	.
.	.

Figure 4.18 (a) Flowchart for the two-variable equation X = 3Y. (b) The resulting table.

calculating and printing the value of X for each positive integer value of Y. Of course, the resulting table (Figure 4.18(b)) could never be completed because there are an infinite number of positive-integer values to assign to Y. This fact is reflected by the endless loop of Figure 4.18(a). A more practical program would place limits on the possible values of Y and thereby make the table "completable."

The flowchart shown in Figure 4.19 adds this limitation by using a decision to transfer control when the value of Y reaches 7. This limits the printed values of Y to positive integers less than 7.

Figure 4.19 (a) Flowchart for the equation X = 3Y, with limits on the possible values of Y. (b) The resulting table.

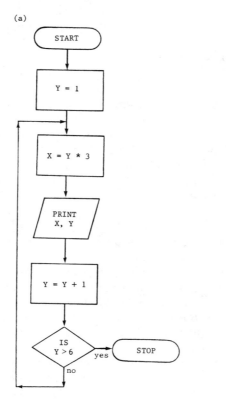

(a)

(b)

Y	X
1	3
2	6
3	9
4	12
5	15
6	18

Two-dimensional tables for equations with three variables can also be generated. Such tables are similar in appearance to Table 4.1. The values across the top and along the left side of the table represent the given values. The values in the table itself are the calculated values (in this case, the values of X).

Table 4.1 Table for the three-variable equation X = Y + Z.

Y \ Z	1	2	3	4	5
1	2	3	4	5	6
2	3	4	5	6	7
3	4	5	6	7	8
4	5	6	7	8	9
5	6	7	8	9	10

A flowchart designed to generate Table 4.1 would use a process symbol to calculate values for X and would then use a print symbol to print that value, just as

Figure 4.20 This flowchart generates Table 4.1.

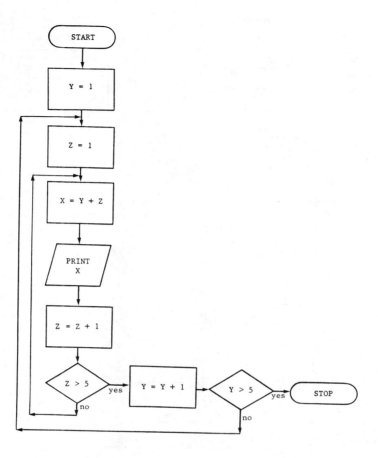

Figure 4.19 did. The chief difference would be that a flowchart for Table 4.1 would use nested loops to initialize, increment, and check two variables rather than one.

The order in which the two variables are initialized, incremented, and checked is vital. In Figure 4.20,

1. Y is initialized first and held constant while Z is initialized and incremented through its full range of values. With each change in Z's value, a new value for X is calculated and printed.
2. Y is incremented and then again held constant while Z is reinitialized and incremented, and while values for X are printed.
3. The process is repeated until a different value for X is calculated for each value of Y and Z.

The regularity to be observed is that the first variable initialized is the last variable incremented, and the last variable initialized is the first variable incremented. This pattern holds true in both table-building flowcharts and array-processing flowcharts.

There is no need for the values of the variables in tables to be positive integers and no need for them to be incremented by 1. The flowchart shown in Figure 4.21 describes a program that generates values for a table where the given values are negative and the intervals are 2 and 3. The only changes required from Figure 4.20 are the initial values, the amount of each increment, and the values in the decisions.

Both Figure 4.20 and Figure 4.21 represent programs that calculate values by horizontal rows rather than by vertical columns. That is, all the values for the top row are calculated and printed before any values for the second row are calculated. The flowcharts do this by holding the value of Y constant while Z is incremented

Figure 4.21 (a) Flowchart to generate a table containing negative values. (b) The resulting table. Here the given values are negative, and the intervals are 2 and 3.

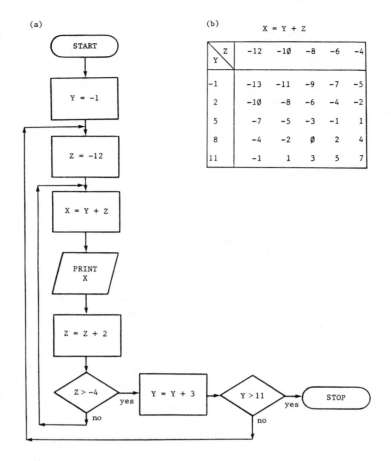

(a)

(b)

X = Y + Z

Y \ Z	−12	−1Ø	−8	−6	−4
−1	−13	−11	−9	−7	−5
2	−1Ø	−8	−6	−4	−2
5	−7	−5	−3	−1	1
8	−4	−2	Ø	2	4
11	−1	1	3	5	7

through its range of values. As long as the value of Y remains constant, successive calculations based on a changing Z determine the values of a single row. When Y is incremented and Z is reinitialized, calculations for the next row begin. Had Z been initialized first and held constant while Y was incremented, values would have been calculated by column rather than by row. (They could not be printed in this order, because printers print a row at a time.)

Calculations in Figure 4.21 were done by rows, so it is easy to augment that flowchart in order that its program will also calculate and print a total for each row. The flowchart shown in Figure 4.22 accomplishes this by adding an accumulator called TOTAL. This flowchart initializes an accumulator and then increments it each time a value for X is calculated. The total is printed and the accumulator reset each time Z reaches its final value. As a result, the total for each row is printed.

Figure 4.22 (a) Flowchart that calculates and prints row totals in addition to other values. (b) The resulting table.

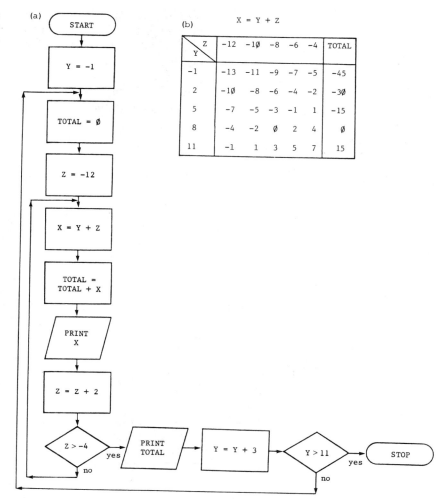

(a)

(b)

X = Y + Z

Z / Y	−12	−1Ø	−8	−6	−4	TOTAL
−1	−13	−11	−9	−7	−5	−45
2	−1Ø	−8	−6	−4	−2	−3Ø
5	−7	−5	−3	−1	1	−15
8	−4	−2	Ø	2	4	Ø
11	−1	1	3	5	7	15

Calculation by row makes sense if one's aim is to print the table, because printers print a row at a time. It is also an appropriate way of accumulating row totals. But suppose that, instead of printing the table and row totals, we wanted only to print the total for each column. In that case, we would design a program that would calculate values by columns. It would do this by holding the "top" variable constant while the "side" variable was incremented. The flowcharts shown in Figures 4.23 and 4.24 follow this strategy.

Figure 4.23 (a) A structured flowchart that uses do-while loops to calculate column totals. (b) The resulting table.

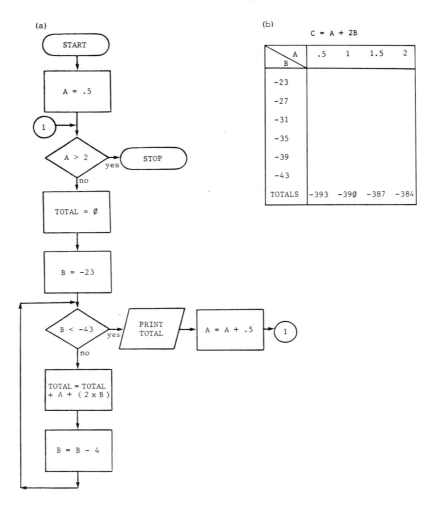

(b)

C = A + 2B

A / B	.5	1	1.5	2
-23				
-27				
-31				
-35				
-39				
-43				
TOTALS	-393	-390	-387	-384

Figure 4.24 calculates and prints both column totals and a grand total. By initializing the column variable (the variable at the top) first and holding it constant while the row variable changes, the program calculates values and totals for one column at a time. After each column total (TOTAL) is calculated and printed, its value is added to the value of the grand total, which is printed after the final column has been completed.

Figure 4.24 (a) A structured flowchart that uses do-until loops to calculate column totals and a grand total. (b) The resulting table.

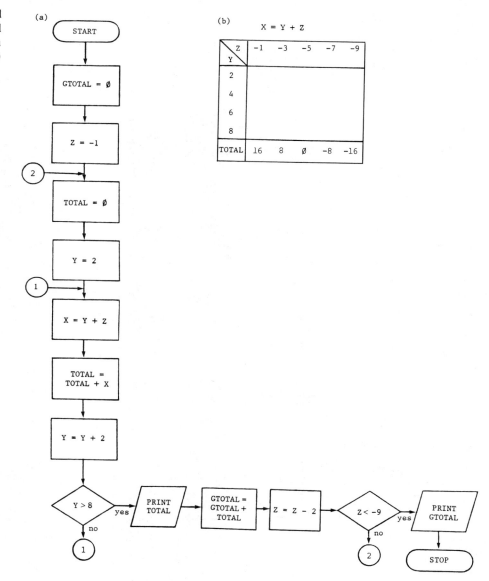

One last "natural" expansion of the logic of tables remains. Up to this point, our flowcharts have calculated and printed the content of the tables, including totals, but they have not printed the values of the variables along the top and side. The flowchart shown in Figure 4.25 includes an initial loop to calculate and print the values along the top of a table. It also appropriately augments the main program so the values along the left side will be printed.

Figure 4.25 A structured flowchart that prints the initial values along the top and left side of the table as well as the computed values within the table.

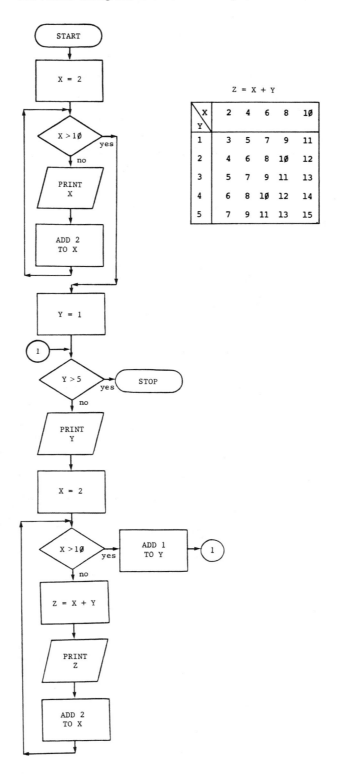

Both of the flowcharts shown in Figure 4.26 represent programs to calculate and print the values required for Table 4.1. Both are structured, and both represent programs that would calculate correctly. The important difference between them is that Figure 4.26(a) exhibits a nested-loop structure, whereas Figure 4.26(b) exhibits an if-then-else structure within its single loop. Flowcharts with the nested-loop structure are preferable because they are more efficient.

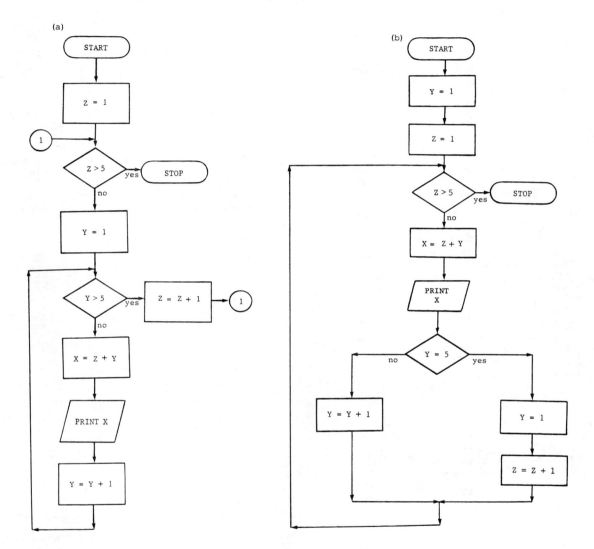

Figure 4.26 These flowcharts both represent programs to calculate and print the values required for Table 4.1. (a) This flowchart contains a nested-loop structure. (b) This one contains an if-then-else structure.

Note that, in Figure 4.26(b), both the decision involving Z and the decision involving Y are encountered for every change in Y. In Figure 4.26(a), the Y decision is encountered for every change in Y, but the Z decision is encountered only when Z changes. Both flowcharts represent structured methods, so the more efficient nested-loop method is recommended.

Exercises 4.5

1. Design *structured flowcharts* using do-until loops that will generate the values required to complete the following tables.

   a. $3X = Y$

Y	X
1	
3	
5	
7	
9	

   b. $X = Y^2 + Z$

Y \ Z	-2	-5	-8	-11	-14
3					
7					
11					
15					
19					
23					
27					

2. Design *structured flowcharts* using do-while loops to complete the tables in Exercise 1.

3. Design a *structured flowchart* using nested do-while loops to calculate and print the totals of the columns of the table in part b of Exercise 1.

4. Design a *structured flowchart* using nested do-until loops to calculate and print the total for each row, starting with the bottom row of the table in part b of Exercise 1.

5. Design a *structured flowchart* to calculate and print the total of the values on the diagonal from top left to bottom right of the following table.

   $X = Z + Y^2$

Y \ Z	4	9	14	19	24
7					
14					
21					
28					
35					

*6. Design a structured flowchart using do-until loops for a program to print the table in Exercise 5. The program is to print the values for Y and Z, as well as the computed values for X. The program is also to print a total for each row.

Review Questions

Completion

1. _____ represents a decision that controls further processing.
2. _____ represents any series of operations or permissible logical structures.
3. In a do-while loop, the exit decision occurs _____ processing within the loop; after processing, control returns to a point _____.
4. _____ represents a decision with more than two possible outcomes.
5. A structured flowchart with a loop that must be exited if either of two conditions occurs uses _____.
6. In programs designed to print two-dimensional tables, the first variable initialized is the _____ variable incremented.
7. In calculating values for tables, the _____ structure is preferred to an _____ within a single loop.

Discussion

1. List and draw each of the permitted logical structures for structured flowcharts.
2. What are the two conditions that structured flowcharts must meet?

3. What important feature of the if-then structure distinguishes it from unstructured decisions?

4. Describe the informal convention recommended for placing the negative branches for decisions.

5. Describe the conditions under which the "extra" READ and "extra" EOF can be eliminated from structured flowcharts.

True or False

1. _____ Structured programs are easier to update than unstructured programs.

2. _____ Structured programs run more efficiently than unstructured programs.

3. _____ Structured programs use a greater variety of symbols than unstructured programs.

4. _____ A structured flowchart that includes no do-until loops can be constructed.

5. _____ From a logical point of view, the do-while loop is generally preferred to the do-until loop.

6. _____ A do-while loop frequently uses two loop exit decisions.

7. _____ Every structured flowchart that uses do-while loops includes two READ instructions.

8. _____ The "perform-until" loop of COBOL is a do-until loop.

9. _____ The "do" loop of FORTRAN is a do-until loop.

10. _____ In modular flowcharts, the RETURN terminal indicates that control is to return to the previous flowchart at the point where control departed.

11. _____ In programs for tables with three variables, the first variable initialized is usually the first variable incremented.

12. _____ Printers generally print by rows rather than by columns.

5. Truth Functional Logic and Decision Tables

In Chapters 2 and 3 we saw how the logic of sets can be useful in understanding and simplifying problems in preparation for designing programs. **Truth functional logic** is another branch of logic that can be similarly useful. Like set theory, truth functional logic is much older than computer programming and was not intended as a programming tool. It was originally used to construct and evaluate arguments and proofs. But the analysis of language that is required to deal with arguments and proofs is also directly applicable to many programming problems. Truth functional logic can be a powerful tool in understanding program requirements and in designing the most efficient solutions. We will first consider the relevant aspects of truth functional logic without reference to programming applications. Then, armed with some understanding of truth functional logic, we will investigate the application of its results to programming situations.

5.1 Truth Functional Sentence Connectives

Truth functional logic deals with compound sentences that are constructed from component sentences via connectives such as *and*, *or*, and *only if*. Examples of these compound sentences include

1. The EOF indicator is on *only if* there are no more records.
2. The AGENT-INPUT FILE was read *or* the CUSTOMER-INPUT FILE was read *and* the CUSTOMER-OUTPUT RECORD was written.
3. The 01 indicator is on *and* the LR indicator is on.

Each of these examples is composed of two or more sentences (called **atomic sentences**) joined by one or more connectives. Each also exhibits a characteristic that allows truth functional analysis. The truth value of the entire sentence can be determined from the truth value of its atomic sentences. Consider Sentence 3 above. It is true when both its atomic sentences are true, and it is false otherwise. That is:

when ''The 01 indicator is on'' is true

and ''The LR indicator is on'' is true,

then ''The 01 indicator is on and the LR indicator is on'' is true;

otherwise ''The 01 indicator is on and the LR indicator is on'' is false.

This analysis of truth values has, of course, nothing to do with the meanings of the component sentences themselves. What makes the analysis possible is the meaning of the word *and*. A comparable discussion would be appropriate for most other sentences composed of two atomic sentences joined by *and*.

118

The analysis of *and* can be summarized in the following table, which is called a **truth table**.

A	B	(A and B)
T	T	T
T	F	F
F	T	F
F	F	F

Truth tables specify the truth value of compound sentences on the basis of each of the possible combinations of truth values of their atomic sentences. Correctly understood, the table says that, no matter what sentences are represented by A and by B, the sentence (A and B) will be true only if both A and B are true. A sentence connective whose logical meaning can be summarized in a truth table is called a **truth functional sentence connective**. These truth functional sentence connectives provide the foundation for truth functional logic.

Many English-language connectives are not truth functional and cannot be summarized by a truth table. *Because* is a typical example of a non-truth-functional connective. Consider the following example:

The Mets lost because Ryan pitched.

Obviously, this sentence is false if either of its components is false. But if both components are true, one cannot determine the truth value of the sentence as a whole from that of its components. Even if we knew that the Mets lost and that Ryan pitched, we still might not know that the loss was caused by Ryan's pitching. If we were to attempt to construct a truth table for *because*, we would be unable to complete its top row. Thus the complete meaning of *because* can't be summarized in a truth table. And therefore, *because* is not truth functional. *Because* and other non-truth-functional connectives are not subject to truth functional analysis, and we shall not consider them further.

Negation

The word *not* is a somewhat unusual connective in that it does not connect two sentences; instead it is attached to a single sentence to form a compound sentence. It is truth functional, however, and deserves treatment on a par with other connectives. Negation is represented by a wide variety of expressions in addition to *not*:

The program *failed* to run.

The 01 indicator *isn't* on.

It is not the case that the bill was sent.

In each of its uses, negation simply denies the statement to which it is attached. The meaning of *not* is summarized in the following truth table.

A	Not A
T	F
F	T

When A is true, "not A" is false; when A is false, "not A" is true.

The examples we have considered so far have been quite simple. They can be understood without the use of truth tables, and their truth values can be determined without the use of truth functional analysis. But, when sentences are not so simple as our previous examples, truth functional analysis can be very helpful – perhaps even necessary.

The truth functional anlaysis of more complex sentences uses both the truth tables for their connectives and the truth value of their atomic sentences. Truth functional analysis uses truth tables as directions for computing the values of larger and larger sections of a sentence until a final value (true or false) is reached. The following example shows the step-by-step analysis of "not (A and not B)," assuming that A is a true sentence and that B is false.

not (A and not B) T F	(Values are placed under the respective sentences.)
not (A and not B) T T F	(The value of "not B" is calculated and written under the *not*.)
not (A and not B) T̄ T T̄ F	(The value of "A and not B" is calculated and written under the *and*.)
not (A and not B) F T̄ T̄ T̄ F	(The sentence is false when its components have the values assigned.)

Truth functional analysis is accomplished in a stepwise manner, starting with the smallest component and working toward larger ones until a final value is reached. Normally we carry out all of the steps on a single line, writing the expression only once, so that only the final line is recorded. This same step-by-step procedure can be used on even the most complicated examples. So long as a sentence's connectives are truth functional, its truth value can be determined from the truth values of its components.

Exercises 5.1

Use truth functional analysis to determine the truth value of each of the following expressions. Assume that A is true, B is false, and C is true.

1. (not A and B)
2. (not (A and B) and C)
3. not (not A and B)
4. (not (not A and not B) and C)
5. (not C and (B and not A))

5.2 Symbolization

We started symbolizing when we replaced sentences with A's and B's in the foregoing examples. There we used symbols because the particular sentence made no difference to the logical analysis, and the logic itself became clearer. For similar reasons we shall adopt symbols for connectives. Often several different English-language connectives have the same logical force, and it makes no logical difference which is used. So, to simplify our logic, we shall use a single symbol for each set of logically equivalent connectives. Starting with *and* and *not* because they have already been introduced, we assign the inverted wedge (∧) to *and* and the tilde (~) to *not*. Given this assignment, the expression 'not both A and not B' becomes ~(A ∧ ~B).

Examples of Symbolization and Truth-Value Analysis

A represents 'The water is cold'; B represents 'Mary went swimming'; and C represents 'John went swimming.' The truth-value analysis assumes that A is true, B is false, and C is true.

1. Mary went swimming and John did not.
   (B ∧ ~C)
   F F F T

2. Mary and John did not both go swimming.
   ~(B ∧ C)[1]
   T F F T

3. Mary and John both did not go swimming.
   (~B ∧ ~C)[1]
   T F F F T

4. The water was cold and Mary, but not John, went swimming.
   (A ∧ (B ∧ ~C))
   T F F F F T

5. John went swimming and John and Mary did not both go swimming.
   (C ∧ ~ (C ∧ B))[1]
   T T T T F F

Inclusive and Exclusive Disjunction

The English word *or* is genuinely ambiguous. It has at least two clearly distinct meanings. In some of its uses, *or* means *and/or*. For example, "Please bring a pencil or a pen" invites one to bring a pencil, a pen, or both. The truth table for this, the **inclusive** use of *or*, is

p	q	p or q
T	T	T
T	F	T
F	T	T
F	F	F

The other use of *or* means that exactly one of the alternatives is to be selected. It might be expressed as ". . . or . . . and not both." When a child asks for both pie and cake but is told by a parent that he or she may have pie or cake, it should be clear that the child may have only one of the desserts. The truth table for this, the **exclusive** use of *or*, is

p	q	p or q
T	T	F
T	F	T
F	T	T
F	F	F

The difference between these two uses of *or* is shown on the top line of their truth tables. The inclusive *or* includes p and q both true among the ways to make "p or q" true. The exclusive *or* excludes p and q both true as a way of making "p or q" true. Unfortunately, the English language often doesn't distinguish between these uses of *or*. Sometimes the content of a sentence will make the meaning of the *or* clear, as in the foregoing examples. But when the precise meaning of *or* is unclear, it is important to determine (perhaps by asking) what is intended.

   We shall use the wedge (∨) as the symbol for the inclusive *or*. No symbol is adopted for the exclusive *or*, because it can be symbolized by using the wedge, the

---

[1] Note that the word *both* becomes a left parenthesis in these examples. The word *either* will also become a left parenthesis when the word *or* is used.

inverted wedge, and the tilde. When the *or* in "A or B" is understood in its exclusive sense, it is symbolized as (A ∨ B) ∧ ~ (A ∧ B). In our examples, when the sense of *or* cannot be determined, it will be assumed to be inclusive. (In "real-world" programming, however, making any such assumption could be disasterous.)

In symbolizing sentences containing *or*, we use the left parenthesis to represent the word *either*. So the expression "not either Alice or Betty attended the lecture" would be translated ~ (A ∨ B). And, because *neither* means *not either*, "Neither Alice nor Betty attended the lecture" would also be translated ~ (A ∨ B).

Examples of Symbolization with Truth-Value Analysis

In each of the following examples, A represents "The Tigers won," B represents "The Royals won," and C represents "The Yankees won." The truth-value analysis of these examples assumes that the Tigers won, that the Royals did not win, and that the Yankees did win. (Assume that there could be no ties.)

1. Both the Tigers and the Royals won.
   (A ∧ B)
    T F F

2. Neither the Tigers nor the Royals won.
   ~ (A ∨ B)
   F T T F

3. Either the Tigers and the Yankees both won or the Royals won.
   ((A ∧ C) ∨ B)
    T T T T F

4. Both the Tigers and either the Yankees or the Royals won.
   (A ∧ (C ∨ B))
    T T T T F

5. The Yankees and the Tigers didn't both win.
   ~ (C ∧ A)
   F T T T

6. The Yankees didn't win; neither did the Tigers or the Royals.
   (~ C ∧ ~ (A ∨ B))
    F T F F T T F

7. The Tigers and the Royals didn't both lose.
   ~ (~ A ∧ ~ B)
   T F T F T F

8. Either the Tigers won or both the Tigers and the Yankees lost.
   (A ∨ (~ A ∧ ~ C))
    T T F T F F T

5.3 Alternative Notation for Disjunction and Conjunction

In English there are many ways of expressing conjunction, disjunction, and negation. As soon as one moves beyond the textbook to solve programming problems, one finds truth functional connectives expressed in a wide variety of ways. The following rules of thumb will help in translating those expressions.

A and B A but B A yet B A although B (A ∧ B) A albeit B A while B A even though B	A or B A unless B (A ∨ B) A without B

Exercises
5.2–5.3

1. Using the rules of thumb that we have cited, symbolize each of the following sentences, letting A stand for "Mary went to the movies," B for "Mary's sister went to the movies," and C for "It rained."
   a. It rained and Mary went to the movies.
   b. Mary went to the movies or it rained.
   c. Mary and her sister went to the movies.
   d. Mary or her sister went to the movies.
   e. Although it rained, both Mary and her sister went to the movies.
   f. Unless it rained, Mary went to the movies.
   g. Mary didn't go to the movies without her sister.
   h. It didn't rain, yet neither Mary nor her sister went to the movies.
   i. While her sister didn't go to the movies, Mary went even though it rained.
   j. Mary didn't go to the movies unless it rained.
   k. It rained, but Mary went to the movies.
   l. Mary didn't go to the movies without her sister, unless it rained.
   m. Although Mary and her sister didn't both go to the movies, Mary went to the movies unless her sister did.
   n. Neither Mary nor her sister went to the movies, unless it failed to rain.

2. Determine the truth value for each sentence in Exercise 1, assuming that Mary went to the movies, that Mary's sister did not go to the movies, and that it didn't rain.

5.4 Equivalence

Truth functional analysis is an effective method of determining whether two expressions are **equivalent** and, therefore, say essentially the same thing. To determine equivalence between a pair of truth functional expressions, we calculate the truth value of the expressions for each possible combination of truth values of their atomic sentences. If the truth values of the expressions match given every possible combination of values, the expressions are equivalent. But if there is even one assignment of truth values that makes one expression true and the other false, those expressions are not equivalent.

Truth tables provide the most effective means of determining equivalence, because they incorporate all possible assignments of values to the atomic sentences of an expression. To use truth tables to determine equivalence, place both expressions at the top of the same truth table and evaluate the expressions for each of the possible combinations of value assignments. If the two expressions have identical values for each value assignment, they are equivalent. If the final values for the expressions differ on any row, the expressions are not equivalent.

The following step-by-step procedure shows that $\sim(A \wedge B)$ is equivalent to $(\sim A \vee \sim B)$.

A	B	$\sim(A \wedge B)$		$(\sim A \vee \sim B)$	
T	T	T	T	T	T
T	F	T	F	T	F
F	T	F	T	F	T
F	F	F	F	F	F

(Place the appropriate values under the variables.)

A	B	$\sim(A \wedge B)$		$(\sim A \vee \sim B)$	
T	T	T T T		F T F T	
T	F	T F F		F T T F	
F	T	F F T		T F F T	
F	F	F F F		T F T F	

(Referring to the truth tables for $\sim$ and $\vee$, determine intermediate values.)

A	B	~(A ∧ B)	(~A ∨ ~B)
T	T	F T T T	F T F F T
T	F	T T F F	F T T T F
F	T	T F F T	T F T F T
F	F	T F F F	T F T T F

(The statements are equivalent because, given every possible combination of values, they have the same final value.)

There are four rows in this table, because there are four possible combinations of T's and F's when two atomic sentences are used in the expressions.

Surprisingly, compound sentences may be equivalent even though they don't have the same atomic sentences. Consider the following completed truth table, which shows A to be equivalent to ((A ∧ B) ∨ (A ∧ ~B)).

A	B	A	((A ∧ B) ∨ (A ∧ ~B))
T	T	T	T T F
T	F	T	F T T
F	T	F	F F F
F	F	F	F F F

Truth tables that are used to test the equivalence of two expressions must contain (on the left side) every component that occurs in *either* of the statements. So, for example, to test (A ∧ ~B) and ~(~A ∧ C) for equivalence, we would need a basic table that looks like this:

A	B	C	(A ∧ ~B)	~(~A ∧ C)
T	T	T	F	T
T	T	F	F	T
T	F	T	T	T
T	F	F	T	T
F	T	T	F	F
F	T	F	F	T
F	F	T	F	F
F	F	F	F	T

Note that, when there are 3 variables, there are 8 different combinations of T's and F's. So a table with 3 variables contains 8 rows. The general formula for determining the number of rows in a truth table is $r = 2^n$, where r = the number of rows and n = the number of variables.

The following truth tables show that their respective pairs of sentences are not equivalent. We know that the sentences are not equivalent because they have different values on at least one row of their truth tables.

A	B	~(A ∧ B)	(~A ∧ ~B)
T	T	F T T T	F T F F T
T	F	T T F F	F T F T F
F	T	T F F T	T F F F T
F	F	T F F F	T F T T F

A	B	C	D	~(A ∧ (B ∨ C))	((B ∨ D) ∧ C)
T	T	T	T	F T T T T T	T T T T T
T	T	T	F	F T T T T T	T T F T T
T	T	F	T	F T T T T F	T T T F F
T	T	F	F	F T T T T F	T T F F F
T	F	T	T	F T T F T T	F T T T T
T	F	T	F	F T T F T T	F F F F T
T	F	F	T	T T F F F F	F T T F F
T	F	F	F	T T F F F F	F F F F F
F	T	T	T	T F F T T T	T T T T T
F	T	T	F	T F F T T T	T T F T T
F	T	F	T	T F F T T F	T T T F F
F	T	F	F	T F F T T F	T T F F F
F	F	T	T	T F F F T T	F T T T T
F	F	T	F	T F F F T T	F F F F T
F	F	F	T	T F F F F F	F T T F F
F	F	F	F	T F F F F F	F F F F F

5.5 Tautologies and Contradictions

Tautologies and contradictions are special cases of compound sentences. **Tautologies** come out true no matter what values are assigned to their atomic variables, or (and this amounts to the same thing) they are true no matter what happens. **Contradictions** are false no matter what values are assigned to their variables. Recognizing that an expression is a tautology is important because tautologies don't say anything. Suppose you pay for a prediction concerning the stock market and the prediction you receive is "XYZ, Inc. stock will go up in price or it won't go up in price." You may be surprised that someone would charge for such a prediction, but you won't be able to argue that it turned out false. It will be true no matter what happens to the stock price. On the other hand, this advice won't help you to invest your capital because it doesn't predict anything. You know nothing more than you did before. The sentence says nothing. Your prediction is a tautology. Contradictions are equally unhelpful. Suppose you are told that XYZ, Inc. stock both will and will not go up in price. You will disregard this advice; it will be false no matter what happens.

Tautologies and contradictions would pose no problem if they were all as easy to recognize as these. We would simply avoid them. But many are not so easily recognized. Truth tables provide a convenient method of determining whether an expression is a tautology or a contradiction. To use this method, construct a table to represent the appropriate number of atomic sentences. Compute the value of the sentence for each row. If the sentence comes out false under every assignment to its atomic sentences, it is a contradiction:

A	B	(~A ∧ B) ∧ A
T	T	F T F T F T
T	F	F T F F F T
F	T	T F T T F F
F	F	T F F F F F

If it comes out true under every assignment to its atomic sentences, it is a tautology:

A	B	A ∨ (B ∨ ~A)
T	T	T T T T F T
T	F	T T F F F T
F	T	F T T T T F
F	F	F T F T T F

Sentences that are neither tautologies nor contradictions are called **contingent sentences**:

A	B	C	(~(A ∧ B) ∨ C)
T	T	T	F T T T T T
T	T	F	F T T T F F
T	F	T	T T F F T T
T	F	F	T T F F T F
F	T	T	T F F T T T
F	T	F	T F F T T F
F	F	T	T F F F T T
F	F	F	T F F F T F

Exercises 5.4–5.5

1. Determine which of the following pairs of statements are equivalent.
   a. ~(A ∧ B),   (~A ∨ ~B)
   b. ~(A ∨ B),   ~(~A ∨ ~B)
   c. [(A ∨ B) ∧ (A ∨ ~B)],   A
   d. (A ∨ (B ∨ C)),   ((A ∨ B) ∨ (A ∨ C))
   e. (A ∧ (B ∨ C)),   ((A ∨ B) ∨ C)

2. Use truth tables to determine whether each of the following statements is a tautology, a contradiction, or a contingent sentence.
   a. ((A ∨ B) ∧ ~A)
   b. ((A ∧ B) ∨ (~A ∧ ~B))
   c. ((A ∧ B) ∨ (~A ∨ ~B))
   d. ((A ∨ B) ∧ ~B)
   e. (~(A ∧ B) ∨ (~A ∨ ~B))
   f. (~C ∧ ((A ∨ B) ∧ C))

3. Symbolize each of the following sentences and determine whether it is a tautology, a contradiction, or a contingent sentence.
   a. The interest was either credited or paid, even though it was credited but not paid.
   b. Interest was either credited or paid unless it wasn't credited.
   c. Interest was credited but not paid, although it was paid but not credited.
   d. Interest was either credited or paid, but not both.
   e. Interest was neither credited or paid, but it was not unpaid unless credited.

5.6 Conditional Statements

Conditional statements are among the most misunderstood statements in English. They are also among the most important for writing programs. The basic conditional statement has the form "if. . . then. . . ." The symbol that we shall adopt for the conditional statement is the arrow ($\rightarrow$). The truth table for the conditional statement is:

A	B	$(A \rightarrow B)$
T	T	T
T	F	F
F	T	T
F	F	T

The first component of a conditional statement (A in this truth table) is called the **antecedent**; the second is called the **consequent**.

Examples of Conditional Statements and Symbolizations

The truth functional analysis of these examples assumes that indicator A is on, that indicator B is off, and that C is printed.

1. If both indicators A and B are on, then C will be printed.
   $((A \wedge B) \rightarrow C)$
   T F F T T

2. If indicator A is on, then if B is on, C will be printed.
   $(A \rightarrow (B \rightarrow C))$
   T T F T T

3. If either A or B is on, then C will not be printed.
   $((A \vee B) \rightarrow \sim C)$
   T T F F F T

4. If A is on, then B is not on and C will be printed.
   $(A \rightarrow (\sim B \wedge C))$
   T T T F T T

5. If C is printed, then A and B are on.
   $(C \rightarrow (A \wedge B))$
   T F T F F

Most difficulties with conditional statements involve the translation from English to logical notation. This difficulty is particularly common when the English statements consist, in part, of alternative notation for "if. . . then. . . ." The following is a partial list of commonly used alternative expressions. In reviewing this list, be sure to note that the order of the components is reversed in several of the expressions.

If A then B
B, if A
A only if B
B on the condition that A
A only on the condition that B $\Big\}$ $(A \rightarrow B)$
B, assuming A
A is a sufficient condition for B
B is a necessary condition for A

Even armed with a list of alternative expressions like this one, students of logic (and others) often make mistakes in symbolization. The most frequent mistakes involve reversing the order of antecedents and consequents. Reversing the order of the components of conjunction or disjunction (*and* or *or*) causes no problem, because reversing those expressions produces equivalent expressions. But the same is not true of conditional statements. The truth table below shows that reversing the antecendent and the consequent in a conditional statement does not result in an equivalent statement.

A	B	A → B	B → A
T	T	T T T	T T T
T	F	T F F	F T T
F	T	F T T	T F F
F	F	F T F	F T F

The following examples in English support this result. Note that, in each, the first sentence is true and the second false.

> If a pail will hold a gallon, then it will hold a quart.
> If a pail will hold a quart, then it will hold a gallon.

> If a number is evenly divisible by 9, then it is evenly divisible by 3.
> If a number is evenly divisible by 3, then it is evenly divisible by 9.

> If John has the mumps, then he has a contagious illness.
> If John has a contagious illness, then he has the mumps.

The expressions A → B and B → A are simply *not* interchangeable. On some occasions they might both be true. But such occasions are matters of coincidence and not of logic. When we infer B → A from A → B or translate one for the other, we commit the fallacy of **illicit conversion**.

A second difficulty that arises in symbolizing conditional statements results from a rather loose use of the phrase "only if." On some occasions, ". . .only if . . ." is used in place of ". . . if and only if . . . ." And "A only if B" is intended to be understood as "A if and only if B." For example, when a mother tells her child that he may go swimming only if he does the dishes, she means that if he does the dishes, then he may go swimming and if he doesn't do the dishes, then he may not go swimming. The truth table for this meaning of ". . . only if . . ." is

A	B	((A → B) ∧ (~A → ~B))
T	T	T T T
T	F	F F T
F	T	T F F
F	F	T T T

This is equivalent to the table for "if . . . and only if . . ." ((B → A) ∧ (A → B)).

Sometimes one means merely "if . . . then . . ." by ". . . only if . . . ." For example,

A number is evenly divisible by 9 only if it is evenly divisible by 3.

In this case, interpreting ". . . only if . . ." as ". . . if and only if . . ." would change the otherwise true sentence into a false sentence.[2] Here it is clear that ". . . only if . . ." was intended. But it is not always clear what someone means by

---

[2] While it is true that a number is evenly divisible by 9 *only if* it is evenly divisible by 3, it is not true that a number is evenly divisible by 9 *if* it is divisible by 3. The number 6 is an example.

". . . only if . . . ." The only way to be sure what is meant by "only if" is to ask.[3] When writing a program, it is vital to determine what the boss or customer means. Unfortunately, the boss or customer may not have considered distinctions such as this. Further, he or she may not appreciate your mentioning it! Even so, you *must* get a clear statement of the problem before you attempt to program a solution.

A third difficulty with the "if . . . then . . ." statement is a tendency to think that the *then* indicates *when* events occurred. This is not the case. The statement "if A then B" could be true if B occurred before A or if B occurred after A. The order in time of A and B does not affect their truth functional relationships. In each of the following examples, the *then* occurred first.

If my car is now in the parking lot, then I did not walk to the office earlier this morning.

If the Lions are in the playoffs today, then they won last week.

Exercises 5.6

Translate each of the following into the notation of symbolic logic. Use the first letter of each word printed in all capital letters to stand for an atomic sentence.

1. A TOTAL is printed only if FIFTY records were read.
2. COST was negative, as was SALES.
3. Although the FILE was read, no NAMES were printed.
4. The FILE was read if the program RAN.
5. If there were no TOTALS, then the RECORDS were not processed.
6. Either the SALE was 0 or there were no RECORDS processed.
7. Neither the 01 nor the LR indicator is on.
8. If a CONTROL break occurs while the TOTAL is zero, an error MESSAGE will be printed.
9. This is a CONTROL break or the end of the FILE, not both.
10. The TRANSACTION file can't be processed without the MASTER file being processed.
11. Unless TWENTY records are processed, no totals will be PRINTED.
12. TOTAL and SALES can't both be zero.
13. A TOTAL was printed even though no RECORDS were read.
14. The END-OF-FILE indicator is on, provided that there are no more RECORDS.
15. COST was negative, but SALES was positive.
16. COST and SALES were both positive, provided that TOTAL was greater than 10,000.
17. Only if the PROGRAM is structured will it be ACCEPTABLE.
18. TOTAL and SALES both are not zero.
19. An END-OF-FILE record is necessary for proper TERMINATION.
20. The FILE is empty unless the PROGRAM ran.
21. The data will be PROCESSED if and only if it has been EDITED.
22. The data will not be PROCESSED unless it is EDITED.

---

[3] Sometimes the context of the statement makes the meaning clear.

5.7
Simplification
by Truth
Functional
Analysis

Truth functional analysis provides an effective method of simplifying complicated and perhaps redundant sets of instructions. And even when no simplification of directions is possible, truth tables provide clear guidelines for the construction of flowcharts for these directions.

Suppose we wanted to design a program that would update a tape file if either there was a sale and no commission or there was both a sale and a commission. We might start with Figure 5.1. But examination of Figure 5.1 reveals that it is unnecessarily complex. The COMMISSION decision makes no difference in this program, because the file is updated in either case. So the COMMISSION decision could be eliminated without changing the output of this program.

Figure 5.1 A needlessly complex flowchart.

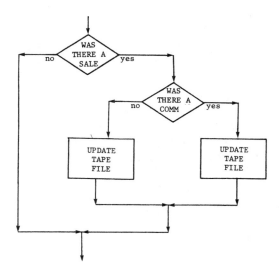

The following truth table for "either there was a sale and no commission or there was both a sale and a commission" also shows that the COMMISSION decision was unnecessary.

S	C	$((S \land \sim C) \lor (S \land C))$[4]		
T	T	F	T	T
T	F	T	T	F
F	T	F	F	F
F	F	F	F	F

Note that this table comes out true when S is true and false when S is false. The expression is equivalent to S. So the SALES decision is the only one that affects the outcome. There is no reason to include a COMMISSION decision in the flowchart; updating the tape file doesn't depend on that decision. Figure 5.2 would be just as effective as Figure 5.1 and would lead to a more efficient program.

The foregoing example is fairly obvious. Reasonable familiarity with flowcharts and programming would lead anyone to avoid Figure 5.1 and use Figure 5.2. Other cases are not so transparent. Consider the following set of directions:

> Update a tape file if either a sale and a payment were made but no commission was paid, or a payment was made but there was neither a sale nor a commission.

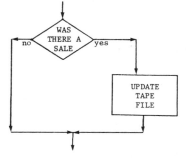

Figure 5.2 This flowchart describes a more efficient program that yields the same results as the program described by Figure 5.1.

---

[4] Columns representing detail calculations will often be omitted in future examples of truth tables so that the remaining work will be clearer.

From the viewpoint of truth functional logic, this example is only slightly more complicated than the previous one. But attempting to understand it and to design a program for it is quite difficult without logical analysis. Using truth functional analysis, however, makes program design much easier. To use this analysis, we (1) translate the directions into truth functional notation, (2) draw a complete truth table for the set of conditions (the antecedent of the "if. . . then. . ." statement), (3) identify the rows of the table that make the condition true, and (4) design a flowchart (or other program design tool).

To design a flowchart for the second set of directions, first translate the directions into truth functional notation.

$$[((S \wedge P) \wedge \sim C) \vee (P \wedge \sim (S \vee C))] \rightarrow U$$

Completing a truth table for the set of conditions yields Table 5.1.

Table 5.1

S	P	C	((S ∧ P) ∧ ~C) ∨ (P ∧ ~(S ∨ C))
T	T	T	T F F F T F F
T	T	F	T T T T T F F
T	F	T	F F F F F F F
T	F	F	F F T F F F F
F	T	T	F F F F T F F
F	T	F	F F T T T T T
F	F	T	F F F F F F F
F	F	F	F F T F F F T

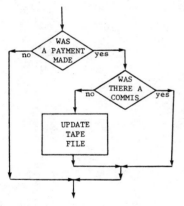

Figure 5.3 This program was simplified using truth functional analysis represented by Table 5.1.

Examination of the truth values in this truth table reveals that the condition is true on every row where both P is true and C is false and that it is false on every other row. This is the case no matter what value S has. So the file is to be updated when P is true and C is false and at no other time. S has no effect on the outcome of the table, so there is no need for a decision for S. Figure 5.3 appropriately characterizes the original directions. This flowchart is considerably simpler than one might have expected when reading the directions. The use of truth tables for complicated sets of directions makes the required programming clearer and, as in this case, may eliminate some decisions entirely.

Consider the following example, in which the effect of truth functional analysis is more dramatic.

Print a bill if the customer is residential and either has both gas and electric service or is residential.

Table 5.2 is the truth table for this.

Table 5.2

R	G	E	[R ∧ ((G ∧ E) ∨ R)]
T	T	T	T
T	T	F	T
T	F	T	T
T	F	F	T
F	T	T	F
F	T	F	F
F	F	T	F
F	F	F	F

This table shows that the truth of the condition depends entirely on R and that no decisions concerning G or E need be made. Figure 5.4 appropriately characterizes this example.

Figure 5.4 A simplified flow-chart based on Table 5.2.

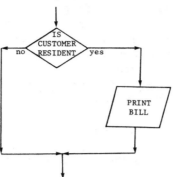

Table 5.3

A	B	C	
T	T	T	F
T	T	F	T
T	F	T	F
T	F	F	T
F	T	T	T
F	T	F	F
F	F	T	T
F	F	F	F

Figure 5.5 A simplified flow-chart based on Table 5.3.

Of course, not every set of instructions is so easily resolved. Consider the set of directions to print M when a condition is met whose truth table is as shown in Table 5.3. At first there seems to be no regularity in the value column. The expression's truth value isn't related to one single condition or even to pairs of conditions. But with enough study, we notice two patterns. There is one pattern when A is true and another when A is false. When A is true, the expression is true when C is false. When A is false, the expression is true when C is true. This insight reveals that B's truth value has no effect on the outcome of this program. Consequently there will be no decision for B. It also suggests a way to construct the flowchart. We begin with a decision for A and add decisions for C on each branch from A. Input/output symbols are added to complete the details. (See Figure 5.5.)

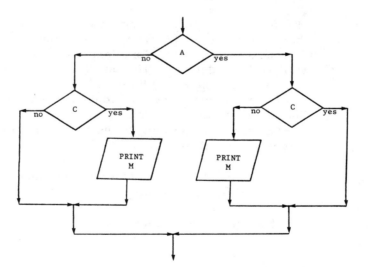

In using truth tables to simplify conditions, it is sometimes easier to examine the table with a view to determining when the table comes out false. This is the case, for instance, when there are many more F's than T's. Consider the truth table shown in Table 5.4.

The expression that generates such a table will be false when B is false and C is true, and it will be true in any other event. If a process N is to be carried out when the expression is true, then our flowchart will show the branch from B (F) and C (T) returning directly to the main program, whereas all other branches go to N (see Figure 5.6).

Table 5.4

A	B	C	
T	T	T	T
T	T	F	T
T	F	T	F
T	F	F	T
F	T	T	T
F	T	F	T
F	F	T	F
F	F	F	T

Figure 5.6 This flowchart was designed by isolating the false rows of Table 5.4 and placing process symbols on branches that represent other rows.

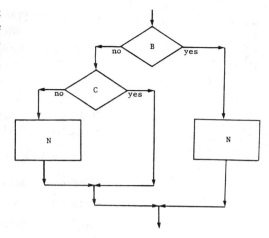

In each of the foregoing examples, the process to be carried out and the conditions of that process were specified in a single statement. This will not always (or even usually) be the case. Often a process will be based on conditions stated in more than one sentence. For example:

> Print D if A and B, and also print D if B or C.

The use of truth tables to simplify directions such as these is facilitated by combining the sets of conditions into a single antecedent by placing a wedge (∨) between them. Applying this technique to the foregoing example changes

$$((A \wedge B) \rightarrow D) \wedge ((B \vee C) \rightarrow D)$$
to
$$[((A \wedge B) \vee (B \vee C)) \rightarrow D].$$

The truth table for the combined condition is shown in Table 5.5.

Table 5.5

A	B	C	((A	∧	B)	∨	(B	∨	C))
T	T	T	T		T		T		
T	T	F	T		T		T		
T	F	T	F		T		T		
T	F	F	F		F		F		
F	T	T	F		T		T		
F	T	F	F		T		T		
F	F	T	F		T		T		
F	F	F	F		F		F		

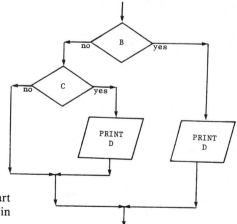

Figure 5.7 This flowchart reflects the truth values in Table 5.5.

Noting that the condition comes out false only when B and C are both false would lead to construction of Figure 5.7.

This method of combining conditions (or antecedents) may also be used when more than two sentences are involved, provided that the consequent or operation described is the same in each sentence. The following set of directions comprises such an example:

Design a program that will read cards with customer information and then do each of the following:

1. Send the SPECIAL DEAL brochure if a customer is more than 25 years old or has both a home insurance policy and a life insurance policy.

2. If a customer earns more than $45,000 and has a home insurance policy, or is over 25 and has a life insurance policy, send the SPECIAL DEAL brochure.

3. If a customer neither is over 25 nor has a home insurance policy, send the SPECIAL DEAL brochure.

Here we designate the conditions as follows:

A = is over 25 years old

B = earns more than 45,000

C = has home insurance

D = has a life insurance policy

S = send the SPECIAL DEAL brochure

Then the instructions called for can be symbolized as

1. $(A \lor (C \land D)) \rightarrow S$
2. $((B \land C) \lor (A \land D)) \rightarrow S$
3. $\sim(A \lor C) \rightarrow S$

Combining the antecedents and drawing a truth table produces Table 5.6.

Table 5.6

A	B	C	D	$(A \lor (C \land D)) \lor (((B \land C) \lor (A \land D)) \lor \sim(A \lor C))$			
T	T	T	T	T	T	T	T F
T	T	T	F	T	T	T	T F
T	T	F	T	T	T	T	T F
T	T	F	F	T	T	F	F F
T	F	T	T	T	T	T	T F
T	F	T	F	T	T	F	F F
T	F	F	T	T	T	T	T F
T	F	F	F	T	T	F	F F
F	T	T	T	T	T	T	T F
F	T	T	F	F	T	T	T F
F	T	F	T	F	T	F	T T
F	T	F	F	F	T	F	T T
F	F	T	T	T	T	F	F F
F	F	T	F	F	F	F	F F
F	F	F	T	F	T	F	T T
F	F	F	F	F	T	F	T T

Figure 5.8 This flowchart is based on Table 5.6.

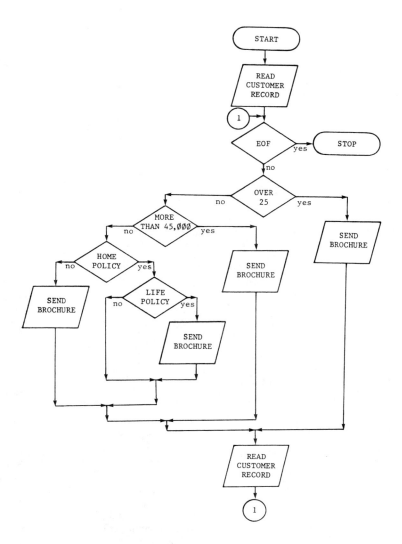

This truth table shows only a single case in which the set of conditions comes out false. Figure 5.8 incorporates these conditions. Note that, even though each decision was required, none had to be repeated. Even when decisions must be repeated several times, truth tables make program design easier. They clearly show what decisions must be made and what the outcome of decisions must be.

Examples of Simplification by Truth Functional Analysis

Example 5.1

If a preferred customer made a purchase but didn't return an item, or if a preferred customer neither made a purchase nor returned an item, then print a bill.

A = customer is preferred

B = customer made a purchase

C = customer returned an item

A	B	C	(A ∧ (B ∧ ~C)) ∨ (A ∧ ~(B ∨ C))
T	T	T	F
T	T	F	T
T	F	T	F
T	F	F	T
F	T	T	F
F	T	F	F
F	F	T	F
F	F	F	F

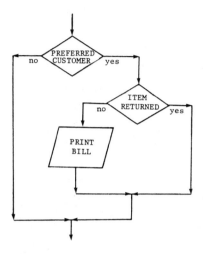

Example 5.2

Print a bill if any of the following circumstances occurs.

1. A preferred customer who returned an item didn't make a purchase.
2. An individual who is not a preferred customer both returned an item and bought an item.
3. An individual who neither is a preferred customer nor returned an item, bought an item.

A = customer is preferred

B = customer returned an item

C = customer made a purchase

A	B	C	((A ∧ B) ∧ ~C) ∨ ((~A ∧ (B ∧ C)) ∨ (~(A ∨ B) ∧ C))
T	T	T	T T T F F T F F T F T T T F F T T T F T
T	T	F	T T T T T T F T F T F T F F F F T T T F F
T	F	T	T F F F F T F F T F F F T F F T T F F T
T	F	F	T F F F T F F F T F F F F F F T T F F F
F	T	T	F F T F F T T T T F T T T T T F F T T F T
F	T	F	F F T F T F F T F F T F F F F F T T F F
F	F	T	F F F F F T T T T F F F F T T T F F F T T
F	F	F	F F F F T F F T F F F F F F T F F F F F

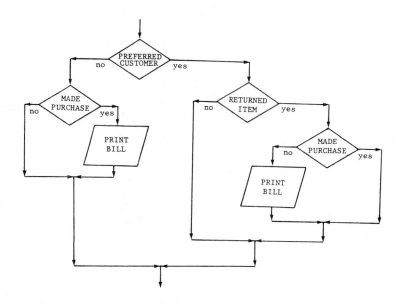

A Word of Caution

Truth functional analysis is a powerful tool in simplifying sets of complex conditions. Programs that result from this simplification are both shorter and more efficient. However, they may bear little resemblance to the original programming specifications. In such cases, adequate documentation must be included to facilitate program maintenance. Because the techniques discussed in this section and in Sections 5.9 through 5.12 may inhibit program maintenance, they must be used with discretion as well as documentation.

Exercises 5.7

1. Design structured flowcharts that will print M when the expressions represented by the truth tables a through j are true.

A	B	a.	b.	c.	d.	e.
T	T	T	F	F	F	F
T	F	T	F	T	T	F
F	T	T	F	T	F	T
F	F	F	T	F	T	T

A	B	C	f.	g.	h.	i.	j.
T	T	T	T	F	F	F	T
T	T	F	F	F	F	F	F
T	F	T	T	T	F	T	F
T	F	F	T	F	F	T	T
F	T	T	T	F	T	F	T
F	T	F	F	F	F	F	F
F	F	T	T	T	T	F	F
F	F	F	T	F	F	F	T

2. Design structured flowcharts that will carry out the following sets of instructions for each account after reading a record with input for that account.

    a. Print a bill if and only if the account:
        — is non-commercial and has either a current or past-due balance, or
        — is commercial with a past-due balance.

    b. Print a bill if and only if the account:
- is commercial and has a current balance due, or
- has both current and past-due balances.

    c. Print a bill if and only if an account either:
- is commercial and either has a current balance or doesn't have a past-due balance, or
- has a current balance or is a commercial account with a past-due balance.

    d. Print bills for commercial accounts that have neither current nor past-due balances and also for non-commercial accounts that don't have both current and past-due balances.

    e. Print bills for all accounts that:
- neither are commercial nor have current or past-due balances, and
- have both current and past-due balances.

3. Design structured flowcharts for programs that will carry out the following instructions. (Design a single flowchart for each of a, b, and c.)

    a. Send a bill on the condition that the account is residential or past due. If the account is past due or has a negative balance, then send a bill.

    b. Update the file if an account is residential but is not current. When an account is past due and non-residential, update the file.

    c. Update the file if an account is neither residential nor current. But if it is not past due and is residential, then update the file. On the other hand, update the file if the account is current and past due.

5.8 The Conditional And Flowcharts

When "if . . . then . . ." occurs in computer programs, the *if* clause contains a condition or set of conditions and the *then* clause contains one or more operations to be completed. The programming "if . . . then . . ." is represented by a decision that contains the condition and a process or input/output symbol that contains the operation. So the programming statement "If 01 is on then read a record" would be represented by the flowchart shown in Figure 5.9.

Figure 5.9 This flowchart represents the programming statement "If 01 is on then read a record."

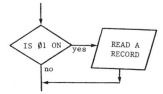

More extensive conditionals are represented by flowcharts with a greater number of decisions, as indicated by Figures 5.10 and 5.11.

Figure 5.10 This flowchart represents the programming statement "If 01 is on and 02 is on then read a record."

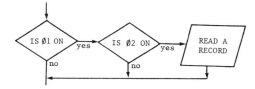

Figure 5.11 This flowchart represents the programming statement "If 01 is on or 02 is on then read a record and print a record."

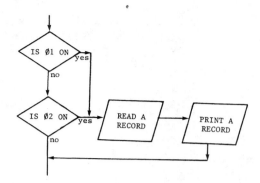

Drawing flowcharts to represent conditionals in well-written programs is a fairly easy task. It is a greater challenge to design flowcharts for conditionals from directions given in ordinary English. One reason is that directions in English don't always specify conditions in the antecedent and operations in the consequent. Consider the following directions:

Send a bill only if no payment has been made.

Truth functionally, this statement is represented by $S \rightarrow \sim P$. This expression could not be flowcharted as written, because the operation (send a bill) is in the antecedent and the condition (there is no payment) is in the consequent, whereas, in a flowchart, the antecedent is placed in the decision.

In Section 5.6 we saw that it would be a logical mistake merely to reverse the order of the antecedent and the consequent of a conditional. To do so would be to commit the fallacy of illicit conversion. But flowchart design requires that conditions be specified in the antecedent. To accomplish this, we use a rule of logic called contraposition. **Contraposition** may be stated in any of the following forms:

$$(p \rightarrow q) :: (\sim q \rightarrow \sim p)$$
$$(\sim p \rightarrow q) :: (\sim q \rightarrow p)$$
$$(p \rightarrow \sim q) :: (q \rightarrow \sim p)$$
$$(\sim p \rightarrow \sim q) :: (q \rightarrow p)$$

The expressions within each of these pairs are equivalent. This could be proved with truth tables.

Applying the rule of contraposition to the expression

$$S \rightarrow \sim P$$

reveals that it is equivalent to

$$P \rightarrow \sim S.$$

In other words, "send a bill only if no payment has been made" says "If a payment has been made, then don't send a bill." The expression tells when not to send a bill rather than when to send it. Example 5.3 shows how this direction would be included in a flowchart.

Example 5.3

Design a program that will read cards with billing information, calculate bills for each account, and print bills for residential accounts. But it is to print bills only if no payment has been made.

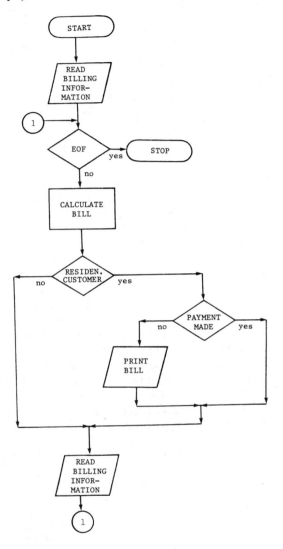

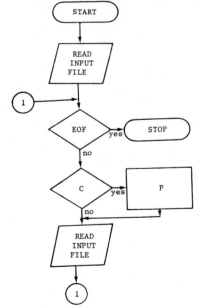

Figure 5.12 This flowchart represents "P only if C" when no other decisions are included.

Understanding the difference between programming C → P and programming P → C is difficult if we are considering a program that contains only one decision and one process. In a program this simple, there is no difference between C → P and P → C. Instructions that represented "P, if C" would also represent "P only if C" and "P if and only if C." Figure 5.12 represents the program that would carry out all of these instructions.

When C is the only decision that is relevant to P, the directions C → P and P → C specify the same program, and the distinction between them is insignificant. The distinction between C → P and P → C is significant when those statements are to be included within programs containing other decisions. Suppose, for example, we were to add one of these instructions to an existing program such as that represented by Figure 5.13. The distinction between C → P and P → C would then be very important.

Figures 5.14 and 5.15 incorporate the *additional* instructions. Compare them with each other and with Figure 5.13, and note the relationship of C to P.

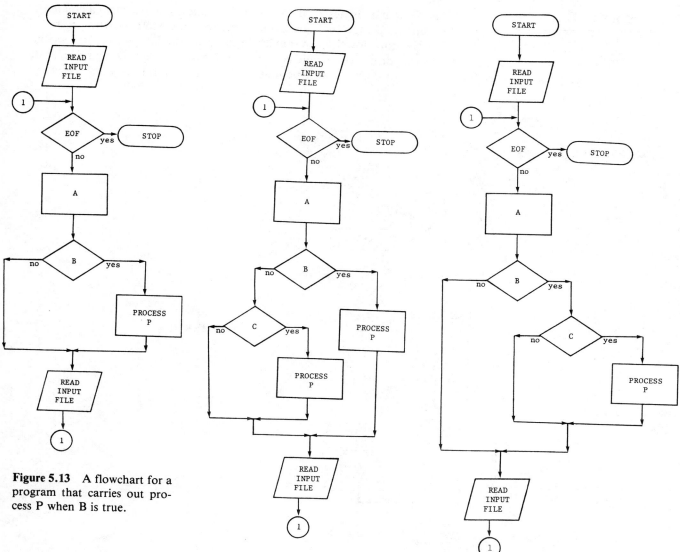

Figure 5.13 A flowchart for a program that carries out process P when B is true.

Figure 5.14 This flowchart adds the instruction "C → P, Do P if C" to the flowchart in Figure 5.13.

Figure 5.15 This flowchart adds the instruction "P → C, Do P only if C" to the flowchart in Figure 5.13.

Figure 5.14 will (potentially) increase the frequency with which PROCESS P is executed; it will execute P for each record that results in an affirmative decision at C. It will do P if C. Figure 5.15 will (potentially) decrease the frequency with which PROCESS P is executed. It ensures that P won't be executed if C is negative.

The addition of the instruction "Do P only if C" to preexisting instructions is not a matter of simple truth functional conjunction. This is due to the fact that the preexisting instructions are assumed to have priority, and this fact cannot be represented by the inverted wedge, ∧. The additional instruction is intended to augment the original – but not to have an equal status. To conjoin all these instructions and then simplify them with truth tables yields misleading results and may lead to erroneous program design. To avoid such misleading results, complete all simplification *before* adding the only-if statements.

Exercises 5.8

The following flowchart is designed to read information from cards, calculate the balance due, update a tape file, and print a bill for all customers who are billed monthly. Redesign this flowchart so that it will carry out the following *additional* instructions (whether or not you would run your business that way). Design a separate flowchart for each of these five instructions, and use contraposition when necessary.

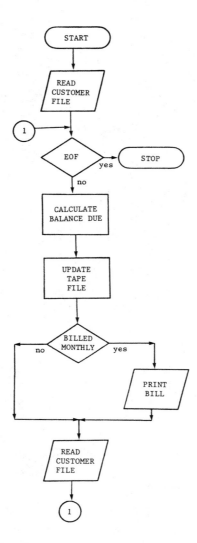

1. Print a bill only if there is a negative balance.
2. Print a bill on the condition that there is a negative balance and no payment has been made.
3. Having a negative balance is a sufficient condition for printing a bill.
4. Print a bill only on the condition that there has been no payment.
5. Print a bill if either no payment has been made or there is a negative balance.

5.9 Equivalence Rules

Truth tables provide an infallible method for determining equivalence, and they are an effective means of simplifying statements. But constructing truth tables can be both time-consuming and tedious. Some pairs of equivalent statements occur frequently enough to warrant memorizing them. Because these pairs occur in many deductive systems of logic, they have acquired the status of named rules. The most useful of these rules are shown at the top of page 143.

Equivalence Rules

$\sim(A \land B) :: (\sim A \lor \sim B)$

Not both A and B :: Either not A or not B

$\sim(A \lor B) :: (\sim A \land \sim B)$

Not either A or B :: Both not A and not B

DeMorgan's law (DM)

$(A \land B) :: (B \land A)$

A and B :: B and A

$(A \lor B) :: (B \lor A)$

A or B :: B or A

Commutation (COMM)

$(A \to B) :: (\sim B \to \sim A)$

If A then B :: If not B then not A

Contraposition (CONTR)

$(A \to B) :: (\sim A \lor B)$

If A then B :: Either not A or B

Implication (IMP)

$(A \land (B \lor C)) :: ((A \land B) \lor (A \land C))$

A and either B or C :: Either A and B or A and C

$(A \lor (B \land C)) :: ((A \lor B) \land (A \lor C))$

Either A or both B and C :: Both A or B and A or C

Distribution (DIST)

$(A \land A) :: A$

$(A \lor A) :: A$

Tautology (TAUT)

$\sim \sim A :: A$

$A :: \sim \sim A$

Double negation (DN)

$(A \lor)(B \lor C)) :: ((A \lor B) \lor C)$

$(A \land)(B \land C)) :: ((A \land B) \land C)$

Association (ASSOC)

You will notice a great deal of similarity between the equivalence rules for truth functional logic and those for set theory. In fact, interchanging symbols on the basis of the following table would convert several of the set-theory rules to truth functional rules.

$'$	$\sim$
$\cap$	$\land$
$\cup$	$\lor$

Even though many of the equivalence rules for truth functional logic bear a striking similarity to those of set theory, there are important differences between these logics. The most significant and (we hope) the most obvious difference is that truth functional logic deals with sentences, whereas set theory deals with sets. Furthermore, truth functional logic contains no symbols corresponding to the verbs of set theory ($\subset$, $\subseteq$, and $=$), and set theory has no symbols corresponding to the arrow of truth functional logic. So, even though some resemblances exist, it would be a mistake to regard truth functional logic as a rehash of Boolean algebra.

Just as is the case with Boolean algebra, truth functional equivalences are valid when applied to complex expressions. Each of the following is an example of DeMorgan's law applied to a complex expression.

$$\sim((p \to r) \wedge r) :: (\sim(p \to r) \vee \sim r)$$
$$\sim(\sim p \wedge \sim r) :: (p \vee r)$$
$$(\sim(p \wedge q) \vee \sim r) :: \sim((p \wedge q) \wedge r)$$
$$(p \to \sim(q \vee r)) :: (p \to (\sim q \wedge \sim r))$$

Several other pairs of statements are worth memorizing because they are *not* equivalent but are often mistaken for equivalent sentences. One could always use truth tables to be sure that a pair of sentences was in fact equivalent. But often the following pairs seem so obviously equivalent that one never thinks of testing them with truth tables. They are given special attention here and in the exercises that follow so that you will recognize them when you encounter them in actual programming situations.

Non-Equivalent Statements

$(p \to q)$	$(q \to p)$
If p then q	If q then p
$(p \to q)$	$(\sim p \to \sim q)$
If p then q	If not p then not q
$\sim(p \wedge q)$	$(\sim p \wedge \sim q)$
Not both p and q	Not p and not q
$\sim(p \vee q)$	$(\sim p \vee \sim q)$
Neither p nor q	Not p or not q

Exercises 5.9

Some of the following pairs are instances of the equivalence rules; some are not. Indicate the name of each instance of an equivalence rule, and write "not equivalent" for the rest. (It may be helpful to translate the sentences into logical notation first.)

1. A bill will be printed only if no payment is received.
    If no payment is received, a bill will be printed.
2. A receipt won't be given without a deposit being made.
    If a receipt is given, then a deposit is made.
3. X is not equal to both 6 and 3.
    X is not equal to 6 and not equal to 3.
4. A statement and a past-due notice won't both be printed.
    Either a statement won't be printed or a past-due notice won't be printed.
5. A bill and either a past-due notice or a preferred-customer letter will be printed.
    A bill and a past-due notice will be printed, or a bill and a preferred-customer letter will be printed.
6. If a bill is paid, a receipt is issued.
    If no receipt is issued, then the bill is not paid.
7. The L1 indicator is not on and the OF indicator is not on.
    The L1 indicator and the OF indicator are not both on.
8. If OF is on, headings will be printed.
    If OF is not on, headings will not be printed.

9. Neither 22 nor 23 is on.
   Either 22 is not on or 23 is not on.

10. Either 22 is not on or 23 is not on.
    22 and 23 are not both on.

11. A payroll deduction won't be made unless the customer has a preferred account.
    If a payroll deduction is made, the customer has a preferred account.

12. Unless X is even, the loop will be repeated.
    If X is not even, the loop will be repeated.

13. If X is even, the loop will be repeated.
    If X is not even, the loop won't be repeated.

14. The loop will be repeated if X is even.
    If the loop is repeated, then X is even.

15. If X is even, both L1 and L2 indicators are not on.
    If X is even, neither L1 nor L2 indicator is on.

16. If the loop is repeated, neither X nor Y will be 0.
    If the loop is repeated, either X will be 0 or Y will be 0.

17. Either $X \neq 0$ or $Y \neq 0$.
    X and Y are not both equal to zero.

18. A bill will be printed and sent to either a home address or an office address.
    Either a bill will be printed and sent to a home address or a bill will be printed and sent to an office address.

19. Either a detail line is printed or an error message is printed.
    Either an error message or a detail line is printed.

20. A detail line is printed on the condition that an error message is generated.
    Either no error message is generated or a detail line is printed.

21. An error message and a detail line are not both printed.
    An error message is not printed and a detail line is not printed.

22. If no error message is generated, then a detail line is printed.
    A detail line is printed if an error message is generated.

23. Neither the detail line nor the error message is printed.
    Both the detail line and the error message are not printed.

24. A detail line was not printed even though an error message was generated.
    It is not the case that a detail line was printed and an error message was not generated.

25. A detail line and either an error message or an exception report are printed.
    A detail line and an error message are printed, or a detail line and an exception report are printed.

26. Generating an error message is a necessary condition for printing a detail line.
    Failing to generate an error message is a sufficient condition for failing to print a detail line.

27. An error message isn't generated unless a detail line is printed.
    The generation of an error message is a sufficient condition for printing a detail line.

5.10
Simplification
by Equivalence
Rules

The equivalence rules for truth functional logic can be used in a series of steps to simplify expressions. The simplification of statements may allow one to reduce the number of occurrences of individual sentences, and it may eliminate the occurrence of a sentence completely.

<table>
<tr><td>

Example 5.4

</td><td>

If the quota is met, send the gold award and if a 50% increase is achieved, send the gold award.

</td></tr>
</table>

$((A \rightarrow B) \wedge (C \rightarrow B))$
$((\sim A \vee B) \wedge (\sim C \vee B))$ IMP   (twice)
$((B \vee \sim A) \wedge (B \vee \sim C))$ COMM   (twice)
$(B \vee (\sim A \wedge \sim C))$ DIST
$(B \vee \sim (A \vee C))$ DM
$(\sim (A \vee C) \vee B)$ COMM
$((A \vee C) \rightarrow B)$ IMP

Example 5.5

It is false that, if the train was on time and the bus was late, then the train and plane were not both on time.

$\sim [(A \wedge B) \rightarrow \sim (A \wedge C)]$
$\sim [\sim (A \wedge B) \vee \sim (A \wedge C)]$ IMP
$\sim \sim [(A \wedge B) \wedge (A \wedge C)]$ DM
$[(A \wedge B) \wedge (A \wedge C)]$ DN
$[((A \wedge B) \wedge A) \wedge C]$ ASSOC
$[(A \wedge (A \wedge B)) \wedge C]$ COMM
$[((A \wedge A) \wedge B) \wedge C]$ ASSOC
$[(A \wedge B) \wedge C]$ TAUT

The simplification in Examples 5.4 and 5.5 involved only the equivalence rules introduced in Section 5.9. But that set of rules is incomplete, because it fails to provide directions for tautologies and contradictions. Suppose, for example, that the simplification of an expression resulted in $(A \wedge (B \vee \sim B))$. A truth table would show that this expression is equivalent to A. But the rules presented so far do not allow further reduction of $(A \wedge (B \vee \sim B))$. These rules can be augmented by the rules in the following table to provide for the reduction of expressions that contain tautologies and/or contradictions. (In expressing these rules, we use T to indicate a tautology and $\perp$ to indicate a contradiction.)

Excluded middle	$(A \vee \sim A) = T$	(ExM)
Contradiction	$(A \wedge \sim A) = \perp$	(CON)
Contradictory disjunct	$(A \vee \perp) = A$	(CD)
Contradictory conjunct	$(A \wedge \perp) = \perp$	(CC)
Tautologous disjunct	$(A \vee T) = T$	(TD)
Tautologous conjunct	$(A \wedge T) = A$	(TC)
Negation of tautology	$\sim T = \perp$	(NT)
Negation of contradiction	$\sim \perp = T$	(NC)

Any expression that reduces to T or $\perp$ is a tautology or a contradiction, respectively. Examples 5.6 and 5.8 make use of the additional equivalence rules.

Example 5.6

$\{ \sim (B \vee \sim A) \vee \sim (A \rightarrow \sim B) \}$
$\{ (\sim B \wedge A) \vee \sim (A \rightarrow \sim B) \}$ DM
$\{ (\sim B \wedge A) \vee \sim (\sim A \vee \sim B) \}$ IMP
$\{ (\sim B \wedge A) \vee (A \wedge B) \}$ DM
$\{ (A \wedge \sim B) \vee (A \wedge B) \}$ COMM
$\{ A \wedge (\sim B \vee B) \}$ DIST
$\{ A \wedge T \}$ ExM
A TC

Example 5.7

$((A \wedge B) \vee (A \wedge \sim B)) \vee \sim (B \vee (C \vee \sim B))$

$(A \wedge (B \vee \sim B)) \vee \sim (B \vee (C \vee \sim B))$	DIST
$\{(A \wedge T) \vee \sim (B \vee (C \vee \sim B))\}$	ExM
$\{A \vee \sim (B \vee (C \vee \sim B))\}$	TC
$\{A \vee \sim (B \vee (\sim B \vee C))\}$	COMM
$\{A \vee \sim ((B \vee \sim B) \vee C)\}$	ASSOC
$\{A \vee \sim (T \vee C)\}$	ExM
$\{A \vee \sim (T)\}$	TD
$\{A \vee \perp\}$	NT
A	CD

Example 5.8

$\{(A \wedge (C \rightarrow C)) \wedge (\sim (D \vee B) \rightarrow (B \vee \sim D))\}$	
$\{(A \wedge (\sim C \vee C)) \wedge (\sim (D \vee B) \rightarrow (B \vee \sim D))\}$	IMP
$\{(A \wedge T) \wedge (\sim (D \vee B) \rightarrow (B \vee \sim D))\}$	ExM
$\{A \wedge (\sim (D \vee B) \rightarrow (B \vee \sim D))\}$	TC
$\{A \wedge (\sim \sim (D \vee B) \vee (B \vee \sim D))\}$	IMP
$\{A \wedge ((D \vee B) \vee (B \vee \sim D))\}$	DN
$\{A \wedge (D \vee (B \vee (B \vee \sim D)))\}$	ASSOC
$\{A \wedge (D \vee ((B \vee B) \vee \sim D))\}$	ASSOC
$\{A \wedge (D \vee (B \vee \sim D))\}$	TAUT
$\{A \wedge ((B \vee \sim D) \vee D)\}$	COMM
$\{A \wedge (B \vee (\sim D \vee D))\}$	ASSOC
$\{A \wedge (B \vee T)\}$	ExM
$\{A \wedge T\}$	TD
A	TC

Simplification by equivalence rules and simplification by truth tables are logically comparable. A statement that can be simplified by equivalence rules can also be simplified by truth tables, and vice versa. The use of equivalence rules usually takes less time for an experienced logician. But it requires greater insight than the use of truth tables. Truth tables are more mechanical and more tedious, but they are the final court of appeal in questions of truth functional equivalence. Both methods of simplification have been presented here because potential programmers should be able to avail themselves of either.

Exercises 5.10

1. Use equivalence rules to show that the following are equivalent.
   a. $(A \vee (\sim B \vee C))$ $((\sim A \rightarrow \sim B) \vee C)$
   b. $\sim (A \wedge B)$ $(A \rightarrow \sim B)$
   c. $\sim (B \wedge A)$ $(A \rightarrow \sim B)$
   d. $(\sim C \rightarrow (\sim A \vee \sim B))$ $((A \wedge B) \rightarrow C)$
   e. $A \vee (C \wedge A)$ $(A \wedge (A \vee C))$
   f. $A \wedge (B \vee C)$ $\sim ((A \rightarrow \sim B) \wedge (A \rightarrow \sim C))$
   g. $(C \rightarrow A)$ $\sim (\sim A \wedge C)$
   h. $((A \vee B) \wedge (A \vee C))$ $(\sim (B \wedge C) \rightarrow A)$
   i. $(\sim C \rightarrow (\sim A \vee \sim B))$ $((A \wedge B) \rightarrow C)$
   j. $\sim (A \vee (B \wedge \sim C))$ $(\sim A \wedge (\sim C \rightarrow \sim B))$

2. Use equivalence rules to simplify the following expressions. Construct flowcharts to print when each of the expressions is true.
   a. $\sim [(C \vee B) \vee (\sim B \vee \sim (A \wedge \sim A))]$
   b. $[((A \wedge B) \vee (A \wedge \sim B)) \vee ((B \vee A) \wedge (B \vee \sim A))]$
   c. $[((C \vee A) \wedge (\sim A \vee C)) \wedge \sim (B \wedge \sim B)]$
   d. $[(B \wedge (C \wedge A)) \vee ((C \wedge \sim B) \wedge A)]$
   e. $[\sim (C \vee \sim (B \rightarrow B)) \rightarrow (C \vee \sim (A \rightarrow A))]$

5.11 Decision Tables

The **decision table** is a major tool for problem definition and program design. It is most useful in designing programs that must relate several different processes to a variety of conditions. Consider the following example.

Example 5.9

Design a program that will:

1. Send a "preferred customer" notice if a given customer has made a purchase and a payment.
2. Send a marketing brochure and special flyer if the customer has made a purchase or a payment (but not both).
3. If a customer has made neither a purchase nor a payment, send only the special flyer.

Truth tables would not be used for this example, because several different processes are related to the same set of conditions. Instead, a decision table like Figure 5.16(a) would be used. In a table such as this, X indicates that a corresponding condition holds or that an action is specified. This decision table indicates, for example, that when a purchase was made and a payment was not made, the brochure and special flyer are to be sent. It appropriately reflects the other directions as well. This presentation of requirements is much clearer than the directions in English. The decision table makes flowcharting these directions easier. An additional advantage of using decision tables (as opposed to flowcharting from the directions) is that all of the possible outcomes of the conditions are considered, and the programmer is less likely to overlook one of them.

To design a flowchart from a decision table, start with the condition at the top of the table and represent it by one or more decisions. Then continue by representing each subsequent condition as one or more decisions below each branch of each previous decision. When all of the conditions have been represented, add appropriate process or input/output symbols to represent the indicated actions. Figure 5.16(b) represents the decision table given in Figure 5.16(a). Examine Figure 5.16(b) and review the directions given in English to see that those directions would be car-

(a)

Purchase	Made	X	X		
	Not Made			X	X
Payment	Made	X		X	
	Not Made		X		X
Send "P.C." Notice		X			
Send Brochure			X	X	
Send Special Flyer			X	X	X

(b)

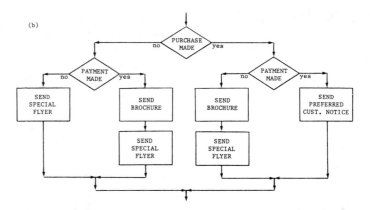

Figure 5.16 (a) Decision table. (b) The flowchart that represents it.

Decision tables consist of a top part that specifies conditions and a bottom part that specifies actions. The top part lists each condition and each possible combination of outcomes of those conditions. To determine the total number of possible outcomes, multiply the number of alternatives for each condition by the number (or numbers) of alternatives for each other condition. Two conditions consisting of three alternatives each would have nine possible outcomes; three conditions consisting of two alternatives each would have eight possible outcomes. Each possible outcome of the set of conditions is represented by a different column in the table. The number of possible outcomes of a given set of conditions is a matter of logic and is the same for any table with that number of conditions and alternatives.

The bottom portion of the decision table lists the actions to be carried out. An X indicates the conditions under which each action is to take place. The placement of X's in the bottom portion of a given decision table is determined by the requirements of the program for which it is constructed and varies from program to program.

Figure 5.17(a) combines decisions with two and three alternatives. Figure 5.17(b) represents that table.

(a)

Sex	Male	X	X	X			
	Female				X	X	X
Age	Under 18	X			X		
	18-23		X			X	
	Over 23			X			X
Brochure 1		X		X			X
Brochure 2						X	
Brochure 3		X				X	
Brochure 4		X	X	X			

(b)

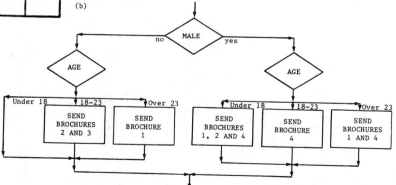

Figure 5.17 (a) Decision table for Example 5.10. (b) A corresponding flowchart.

Example 5.10   Design a program that will:

1. Send brochures 1 and 3 to males under 18 years of age.
2. Send brochures 2 and 3 to females between 18 and 23.
3. Send brochure 1 to everyone over 23.
4. Send brochure 4 to all males.

In creating a decision table of some complexity, it is advantageous first to isolate the conditions and the various alternatives for each (that is, make a note of each before starting to design the table). In this example there are two conditions: age and sex. Age has three alternatives; sex has two. The resulting table [Figure 5.17(a)] therefore has six columns.

Because the first or top condition of this decision table was a two-alternative condition (male and female), half of the top row (indicating males) contains X's, and half of the second row (indicating females) contains X's. If the first decision had been a three-alternative decision, one-third of the top row would have contained X's. Each successive condition divides the previous condition into a number of parts equal to the number of parts in the successive condition. So here, the age condition divides both the males and the females into three equal groups.

Figure 5.18   (a) Decision table for Example 5.11. (b) A corresponding flowchart.

(a)

Sex	Female	X	X	X	X	X	X						
	Male							X	X	X	X	X	X
Age	Under 39	X	X	X				X	X	X			
	Not under 39				X	X	X				X	X	X
Zip	Ø3, Ø5, Ø6	X			X			X			X		
	Ø2, Ø4, 1Ø		X			X			X			X	
	All Others			X			X			X			X
Brochure 1					X	X	X	X	X	X	X	X	X
Brochure 2		X	X	X	X	X	X	X	X	X	X		
Brochure 3		X	X	X		X		X	X	X	X	X	X
Brochure 4					X	X	X				X	X	X

(b)

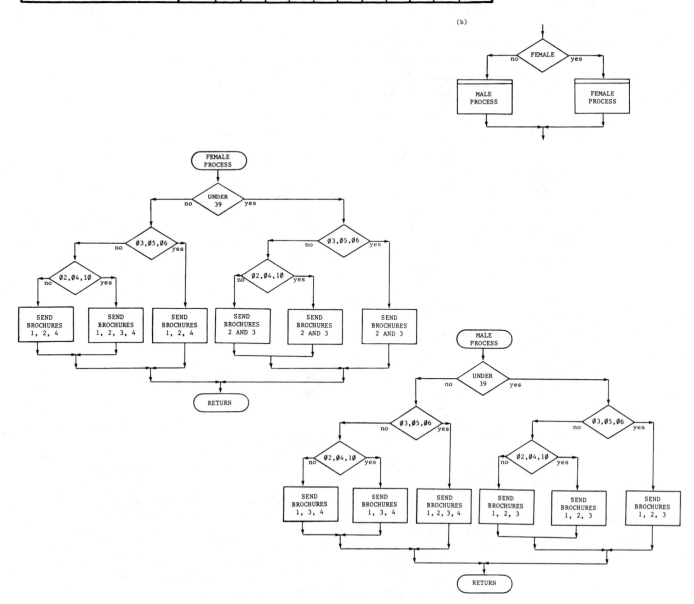

Example 5.11

For a more extensive example of a decision table, suppose that your company will conduct a direct-mail advertising campaign and will target various audiences by sex, by age, and by address. The company has four different brochures to be sent, on the basis of the following conditions:

1. Send brochures 1 and 3 to males.
2. Send brochure 2 to females.
3. Send brochures 2 and 3 to those under 39 years of age.
4. Send brochures 1 and 4 to those 39 and older.
5. Send brochure 2 to those with zip codes ending in 03, 05, or 06.
6. Send brochure 3 to those with zip codes ending in 02, 04, and 10.

As constructed, the decision table shown in Figure 5.18(a) records the appropriate actions to be carried out, ensures that each of the possible sets of conditions is considered, and ensures that contradictory actions are not specified for any single set of conditions. Figure 5.18(b) represents this decision table.

An examination of Figure 5.18(b) reveals that the zip code decision makes no difference for people under 39 years of age. That is, the same process will be carried out no matter how that decision turns out. This fact may tempt one to achieve greater efficiency by eliminating those zip code decisions. Indeed, the program *would* run faster if the unnecessary decisions were eliminated. But such programming could prove to be a false efficiency if a change in business operations later required a change in programming. Reinserting the zip code decision in the right place would be much more difficult than including it in the program to begin with. This is especially true if the maintenance programmer is not the original programmer. Even though there are algorithms for simplifying decision tables to avoid unnecessary decisions (such as zip code in this example), they are not presented here because programs that are produced through their use are generally less "maintainable."

5.12 Decision Table Examples

This section contains examples of decision tables and appropriate flowcharts. A review of these tables should prepare you to do the exercises at the end of this section.

Example 5.12

Design a program that will read customer data from a file and then:

1. Send a brochure to each customer over 31 years of age.
2. Send a special flyer to each customer who is between 18 and 31 or who has a credit balance.
3. Send a preferred-customer notice to all customers who have a credit balance and to all customers over 31.
4. Send the regular ad to customers under 18 who have no credit balances.

	Under 18	X	X				
Age	18 - 31			X	X		
	Over 31					X	X
Credit	Balance	X		X		X	
	No Balance		X		X		X
Brochure						X	X
Special Flyer		X		X	X	X	
Preferred Notice		X		X		X	X
Regular Ad			X				

Example 5.12 continued

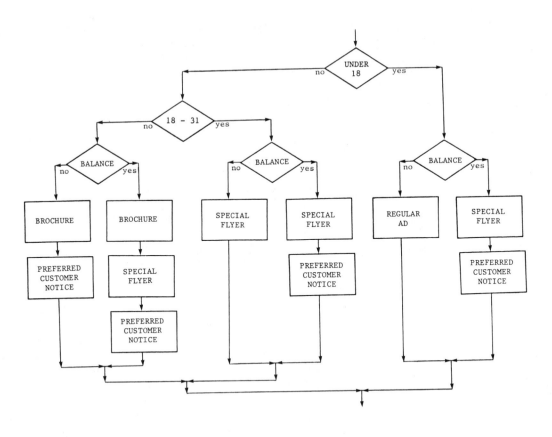

Example 5.13

Design a program that will read employee data for members of the sales, shipping, and assembly departments and then:

1. Add a 10% cash bonus to members of sales departments and to those earning less than $7,000.00.
2. Add stock bonuses to those earning over $12,000.00 and to those in assembly departments.
3. Deduct a retirement contribution from those earning $20,000.00 or less.

Salary Range	Under 7,ØØØ	X	X	X									
	7,ØØØ–12,ØØØ				X	X	X						
	12,ØØ1–2Ø,ØØØ							X	X	X			
	Over 2Ø,ØØØ										X	X	X
Dept.	Shipping	X			X			X			X		
	Sales		X			X			X			X	
	Assembly			X			X			X			X
10% Bonus (Cash)		X	X	X		X			X			X	
Stock Bonus				X			X	X	X	X	X	X	X
Deduct Retirement		X	X	X	X	X	X	X	X	X			

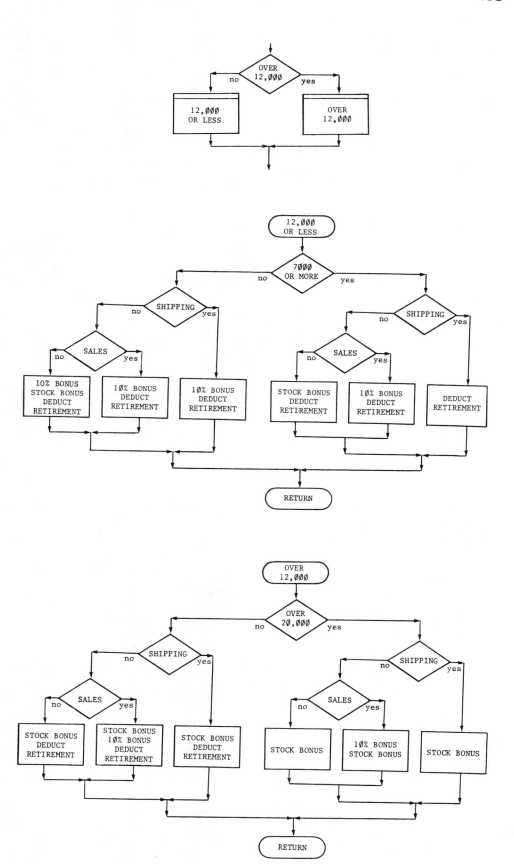

<table>
<tr><td>Example 5.14</td><td>Design a decision table and flowchart that will adjust the net pay of employees in the sales, assembly, and shipping departments of the Lansing, Logan, and Topeka offices as follows:</td></tr>
</table>

1. Add incentive pay to members of the sales and assembly departments of the Logan office.
2. Add cash bonuses to the Lansing and Topeka offices.
3. Add stock bonuses to the Logan shipping department employees.
4. Add stock bonuses to all sales departments.
5. Add incentive pay at all shipping departments.

Office	Lansing	X	X	X						
	Logan				X	X	X			
	Topeka							X	X	X
Dept	Sales	X			X			X		
	Shipping		X			X			X	
	Assembly			X			X			X
Add Incentive Pay			X		X	X	X		X	
Add Cash Bonus		X	X	X				X	X	X
Add Stock Bonus		X			X	X		X		

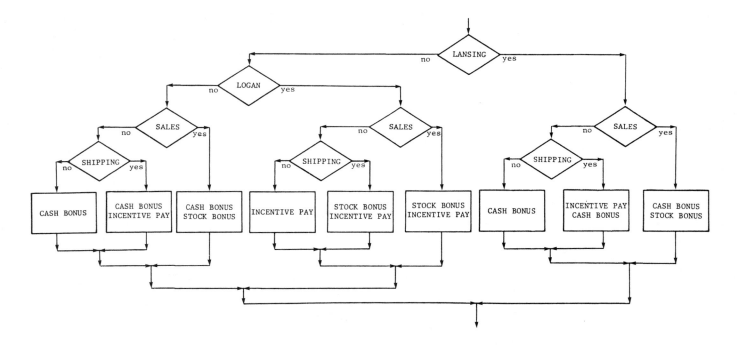

Exercises 5.11–5.12

1. Use a decision table to design a flowchart for a program to read a file and assign applicants for insurance to risk categories as follows:
   a. Applicants who have had moving violations and accidents during the last 12 months are assigned to risk category A.
   b. Applicants who have had either a moving violation or an accident (but not both) during the last 12 months are assigned to risk category B.
   c. Other applicants are assigned to the no-risk category.
   d. Applicants who have had accidents during the last 12 months are assigned a surcharge in addition to a risk category.

2. Using decision tables, design a structured flowchart that will obtain input from cards and:
   a. Assign a surcharge to all applicants under 21 years of age.
   b. Assign all males who either are under 25 and married or who are 25 or over and single to risk category B.
   c. Assign those under 25 to risk category A if they are single males or are females.
   d. Assign all others to the no-risk category.
3. Use a decision table to design a flowchart for a program that will read cards and assign risk categories as follows:
   a. If an applicant has a chargeable accident but no DWI during the past 3 years, assign him or her to risk category B.
   b. Reject all applicants with chargeable accidents and DWI convictions during the past 3 years.
   c. Assign to risk category A all those who have had moving violations (other than DWI) during the past 3 years but who have had neither accidents nor DWI convictions during that time.
   d. Those who have had no accidents, DWI convictions, or moving violations during the last 3 years are to be classified as good drivers.
   e. Reject all other applicants.

Review Questions

Completion

1. A sentence connective whose logical meaning can be summarized in a truth table is called a _____ .
2. Truth functional analysis starts with the _____ component and works toward the _____ components until a final value is reached.
3. So long as a sentence's connectives are _____ , its truth value can be determined from the truth values of its components.
4. In symbolizing sentences containing *or*, we let the left parenthesis represent the word _____ .
5. In symbolizing sentences, we represent the word *both* by _____ .
6. Decision tables consist of a top part that specifies _____ and a bottom part that specifies _____ .

Discussion

1. What is the difference between truth functional and non-truth-functional connectives?
2. List several English-language alternatives for the word *not*.
3. List several English-language alternatives for the words *if . . . then . . . .*
4. List several English-language alternatives for the word *and*.
5. How is the number of rows for a truth table determined?
6. How is the number of columns for a decision table determined?

True or False

1. _____ Truth functional logic was specifically designed for computer programming.
2. _____ So long as a sentence's connectives are truth functional, its truth value can be determined from the truth values of its components.

3. _____ *Because* is a truth functional connective.

4. _____ The expression *and/or* has the same meaning as the exclusive *or*.

5. _____ The word *either* may be represented by a left parenthesis.

6. _____ Expressions may be equivalent even though they contain different variables.

7. _____ Tautologies say nothing.

8. _____ The first component of a conditional statement is called the antecedent.

9. _____ Truth tables provide an infallible method for determining equivalence.

10. _____ Equivalence rules for set theory are essentially the same as those of truth functional logic.

11. _____ Decision tables are tools specifically designed for use in programming.

12. _____ The number of columns in a decision table is a matter of logic.

13. _____ The placement of X's in the bottom part of a decision table is a matter of logic.

6. Warnier/Orr Diagrams for Program Design[1]

Warnier diagrams[2] are structured design tools that combine braces and informal notation to describe computer programs. Warnier diagrams represent the traditional structures of structured programming, including sequence, loops, if-then-else, and case. They also include elements called universals that facilitate and emphasize program modularization.

Warnier diagrams may be preferred to flowcharts because Warnier diagrams more naturally reflect structured programming and do not require apparently arbitrary restrictions, as structured flowcharts do. The brace notation of Warnier diagrams emphasizes the modularization of a program and, more important, clearly describes its hierarchy. By comparison, flowcharts (even modular structured flowcharts) emphasize sequence rather than hierarchy. Because a clear understanding of a program's hierarchy is essential when "real-world" programs are considered, Warnier diagrams are superior for both program design and program documentation.

6.1 Warnier Structures and Terminology

Hierarchy

The capacity of Warnier diagrams to represent the modularization and structure of computer programs results from the fact that the Warnier diagram emphasizes hierarchy rather than sequence. Hierarchy is often formally represented in business organization charts similar to the one shown in Figure 6.1. A Warnier diagram is similar to a business organization chart. The chief differences between them are that Warnier diagrams are read from the left rather than from the top, that braces are used in place of lines and boxes and, of course, that Warnier diagrams deal with program structure rather than business organization.

---

[1] Warnier diagrams are often used in systems design and analysis also. Here they are presented as program-design tools.

[2] Jean Dominique Warnier, *Logical Construction of Programs,* trans. by B. M. Flanagan (New York: Van Nostrand Reinhold, 1976). Also reported in Kenneth T. Orr, *Structured Systems Development* (New York: Yourdon Press, 1977). Our presentation differs somewhat from those of Warnier and Orr, especially in the representation of loop exit decisions.

Figure 6.2 shows a Warnier diagram that represents the same hierarchy as the organization chart shown in Figure 6.1.

Figure 6.1   Business organization chart.

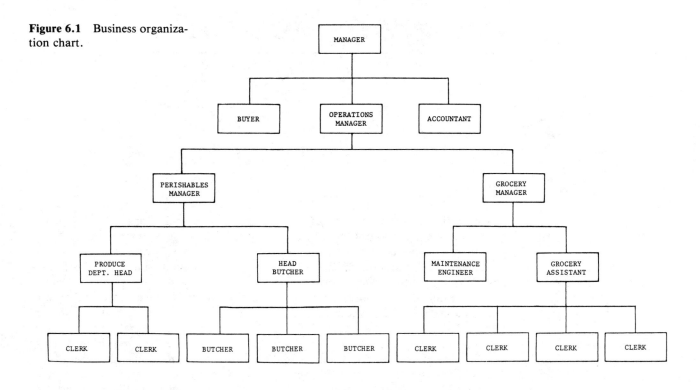

Figure 6.2   Business organization Warnier.

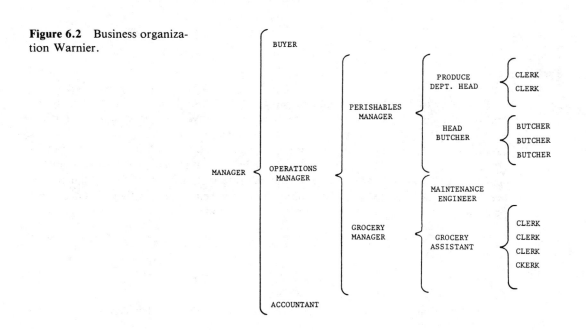

Univerals, Executables, and Decisions

In addition to their braces, Warnier diagrams consist of three types of elements: universals, executables, and decisions. **Universals** are the names of procedures, and they do not indicate executable instructions. They are comparable to the predefined processes of modular flowcharts. Because universals do not represent executable instructions, they occur in coded programs only as comments or procedure names. **Executables** represent executable statements. They are comparable to the instructions found in the input/output symbols and the process symbols of conventional flowcharts. Executables are easily distinguished by the fact that they are not followed by braces. Decisions will be represented by special notation to be introduced later.

In the following Warnier diagram, the universals are A, D, G, I, and N, and the executables are B, C, E, F, H, J, K, L, M, O, and P.

Universals are names of general operations rather than particular tasks to be performed. A universal might, for example, be CALCULATE NET PAY. The brace of such a universal could contain the instructions MULTIPLY HOURS BY RATE, CALCULATE DEDUCTIONS, SUBTRACT DEDUCTIONS FROM GROSS PAY. When the instructions within the brace following CALCULATE NET PAY have been completed, the net pay has been calculated. The universal CALCULATE NET PAY doesn't represent an additional operation.

In general, when the instructions within a brace have been completed, the operation described by the universal is completed. Universals do not represent tasks in addition to those within their braces. By contrast, executables do represent specific tasks, and they represent specific executable statements in a computer program. Both Warnier diagrams and flowcharts represent executables and decisions, but the universals of Warnier diagrams are not represented in flowcharts except as predefined processes.

Sequence

Sequence is represented as a series of entries, aligned vertically within a brace. To read the Warnier diagram in sequential order, read the universal in front of the brace, then read items within the brace from top to bottom. The following diagram indicates the sequential order represented by a single brace. A is read first, and then B, C, and D are read.

A Warnier diagram is always read from left to right and from top to bottom. Braces to the right of a universal are always completed before moving down from the universal. The order of occurrence of executables (and later decisions) determines the sequence of program execution. The following diagram shows the sequence of operations of a Warnier diagram that contains several universals.

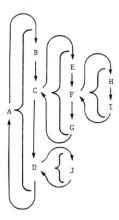

This Warnier diagram should be read in the following order: A, B, C, E, F, H, I, (check to see whether F is to be repeated), G (check to see whether C is to be repeated), D, J, (check to see whether D is to be repeated), (check to see whether A is to be repeated). Note that, in every case, a brace to the right of a universal is completed before control moves down from that universal.

Loops

Loops are indicated by parenthetical expressions placed beneath universals. These expressions may be either numerals or expressions that designate loop exit decisions. When numerals are used, they indicate the number of times that the content of the brace is to be executed. When no parenthetical expression accompanies a universal, a (1) is assumed, and that brace is completed once. The following Warnier diagram uses numerals to indicate loops.

$$
A \atop (1) \left\{ \begin{array}{l} B \atop (2) \left\{ \begin{array}{l} F \\ G \\ H \end{array} \right. \\[2em] C \atop (1) \left\{ \begin{array}{l} I \\ J \end{array} \right. \\[2em] D \atop (3) \left\{ \begin{array}{l} K \\ L \end{array} \right. \end{array} \right.
$$

The order in which this chart is to be read, taking account of repetition, is A, B, F, G, H, F, G, H, C, I, J, D, K, L, K, L, K, L. The order in which the executable statements will be executed is F, G, H, F, G, H, I, J, K, L, K, L, K, L. Figure 6.3 compares the representation of loops using a flowchart with that of loops using a Warnier diagram.

Figure 6.3 (a) A Warnier diagram representing loops with numerals. (b) A corresponding flowchart.

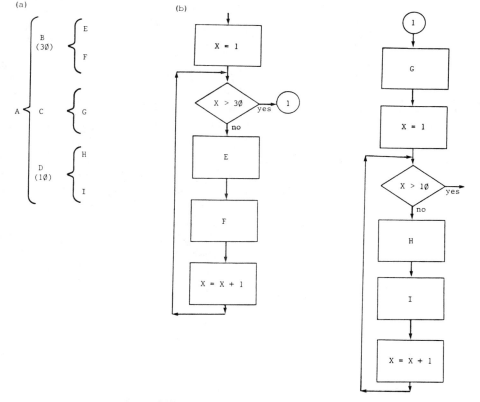

Loop-Until and Loop-While

The do-while loop and the do-until loop of structured design are indicated by placing either the word WHILE or the word UNTIL, along with a loop exit condition, in parentheses beneath the universal. WHILE indicates that the loop exit decision occurs before any processing within the loop. UNTIL indicates that the loop exit decision occurs after all processing within the loop. Figure 6.4 compares a Warnier do-until loop with a corresponding flowchart. Figure 6.5 compares a Warnier do-while loop with a corresponding flowchart. Both of these figures represent programs to read and print 50 names.

Figure 6.4 (a) Warnier diagram that includes a do-until loop. (b) A corresponding flowchart.

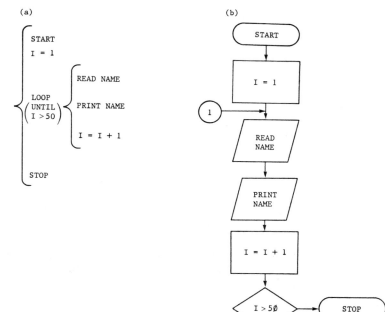

Figure 6.5 (a) Warnier diagram that includes a do-while loop. (b) A corresponding flowchart.

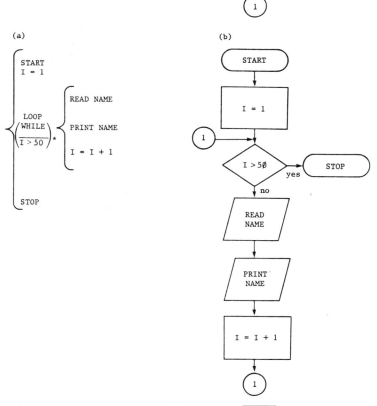

* The bar over I > 50 indicates negation. WHILE $\overline{I > 50}$ is read as "while I is not greater than 50."

Figure 6.6 The program that this Warnier diagram represents completes its loop once.

```
START
X = 1Ø

LOOP        READ NAME
(UNTIL)
(X > 5)     PRINT NAME

STOP
```

Loop-until, like all do-untils, completes the loop before checking the condition. In other words, loop-until completes the process within a loop at least once, no matter what condition is initialized. So, for example, the program represented by Figure 6.6 completes its loop once. Even though X is initialized at 10 and is greater than 5 to begin with, the loop is completed once and one name is read and printed.

Note that both the WHILE _____ of the loop-while and the UNTIL _____ of the loop-until represent decisions and are the counterparts of decision symbols of flowcharts.

Figure 6.7 compares a Warnier diagram (a) with a flowchart (b) for a program that contains a nested loop-while. This program calculates and prints the values needed to complete the multiplication table for Z = X × Y given in Figure 6.7(c). Note that both X and Y are initialized outside the braces and are incremented inside at the bottom of the brace.

(a)

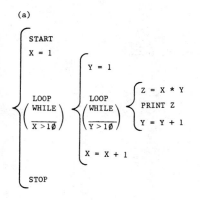

(b)

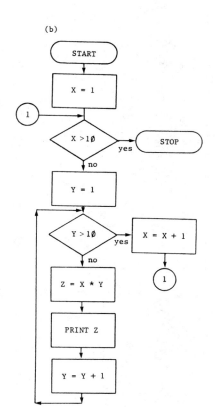

(c)

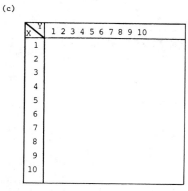

Figure 6.7 (a) Warnier diagram that includes a nested loop-while. (b) A corresponding flowchart. (c) The multiplication table that this program will complete.

Figure 6.8 describes a program comparable to that described by Figure 6.7. However, Figure 6.8 uses the loop-until rather than the loop-while.

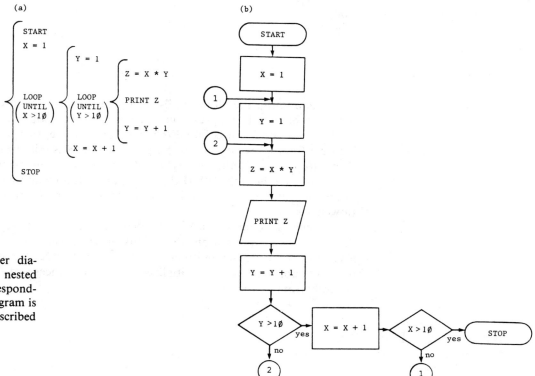

Figure 6.8 (a) Warnier diagram that includes a nested loop-until. (b) A corresponding flowchart. This program is comparable to that described in Figure 6.7.

Exercises 6.1

1. Represent the following organization chart by a Warnier diagram.

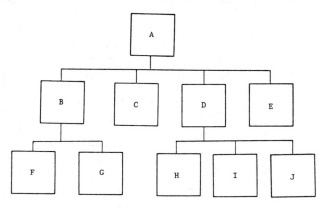

2. Represent the following Warnier diagram by a standard organization chart.

3. List the universals in the Warnier diagram given in Exercise 2. List the executables in the order of execution in the same Warnier diagram.

4. Indicate the number of times each executable statement will be executed.

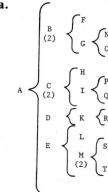

5. Indicate the order of execution, including repetition, of each executable statement.

a.   **b.**

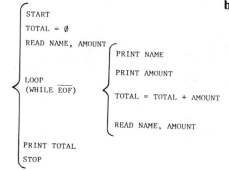

6. Represent each of the following Warnier diagrams by structured flowcharts.

a.
```
        ┌ START
        │ TOTAL = Ø
        │ READ NAME, AMOUNT    ┌ PRINT NAME
        │
A  ⟨    │                      │ PRINT AMOUNT
        │ LOOP         ⟨
        │ (WHILE EOF)          │ TOTAL = TOTAL + AMOUNT
        │
        │                      └ READ NAME, AMOUNT
        │ PRINT TOTAL
        └ STOP
```

b.
```
        ┌ START
        │ X = 1
        │ TOTAL = Ø                     ┌ Y = 1
        │                               │                    ┌ Z = X + Y
        │ LOOP           ⟨ LOOP    ⟨     │ TOTAL = TOTAL + Z
        │ (UNTIL          (UNTIL         │ PRINT Z
        │  X >1Ø)          Y > 9)        └ Y = Y + 1
        │                  X = X + 1
        │ PRINT TOTAL
        └ STOP
```

If-Then-Else and Case

If-then-else is represented by placing the symbol $\oplus$ vertically between two elements each of which is followed by a brace. The $\oplus$ indicates that the brace behind exactly one of the elements will be executed. Figure 6.9 compares representations of the same if-then-else using a Warnier diagram and a flowchart. B and C will be executed if "A" is true, and D and E will be executed if "not A" is true. (The bar over the A symbolizes "not A.") In no case will both (B and C) and (D and E) be executed.

Figure 6.9 (a) Warnier diagram that includes an if-then-else. (b) A corresponding flowchart.

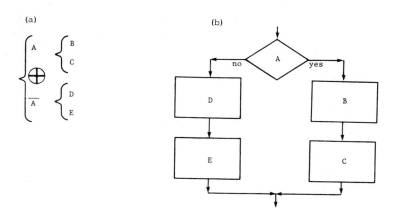

In Figure 6.9 the elements of the Warnier if-then-else are logically contradictory ("A" logically contradicts "not A"). So the elements could neither both be true nor both be false, and exactly one of the elements would be true to indicate the next processing step. When we use the Warnier if-then-else, it is not necessary that the elements be logically contradictory. However, it is necessary to ensure that, in a given program, the elements of an if-then-else will never have the same value. For example,

is permissible provided there is no possible circumstance wherein B and C could both be true or both be false when control reached this particular decision.

Warnier diagrams allow the nesting of if-then-else decisions, just as flowcharts do. Figure 6.10 compares nested if-then-else's in a Warnier diagram and a flowchart.

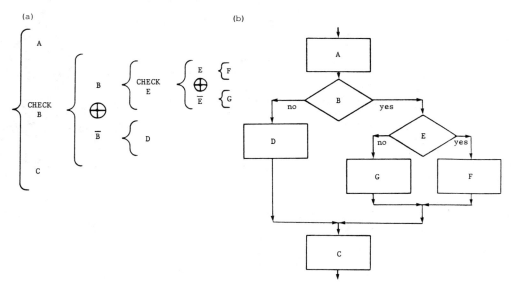

Figure 6.10 (a) Warnier diagram that includes nested if-then-else's. (b) A corresponding flowchart.

Universals (Again)

In Figure 6.10, CHECK B and CHECK E are universals and not executables. So CHECK B and CHECK E don't represent any executable statement and they are not part of the if-then-else. They only describe in general terms the processes to be completed within their braces. CHECK B and CHECK E will not be part of a coded program (except as comments or as procedure names), and they will usually not occur in flowcharts. They are purely structural elements that help us design and understand programs.

Figure 6.11 more clearly demonstrates the use of universals. It will read 10 records that contain names and ages. It will print the number of those who are over 21 and the names of those over 21 that begin with A.

Figure 6.11 (a) Warnier diagram demonstrating the use of universals. (b) A corresponding flowchart.

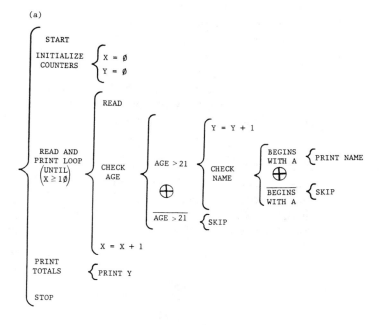

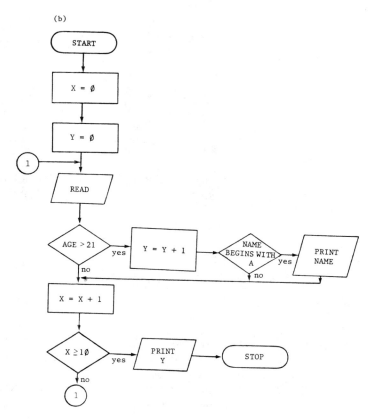

The universals describe, in general terms, the operations to be carried out within their respective braces. When such universals are provided, one can gain an understanding of the overall program structure by reading down the first brace (rather than reading the elements in the order of execution). Such a reading would show that this program will

1. Start.
2. Initialize counters.
3. Complete a read-and-print loop.
4. Print totals.
5. Stop.

Because Figure 6.11 is a simple program, it can be understood without universals. But as programs grow increasingly complex, universals that identify component structures become indispensable to program comprehension.

SKIP or NEXT

The elements of an if-then-else must always be followed by braces. Omitting one of these braces is comparable to omitting one of the flowlines from a flowchart decision. Some if-then-else decisions, however, require an action in one case but no action in the other. That is, they specify a process if, say, "A" is true, but none if "not A" is true:

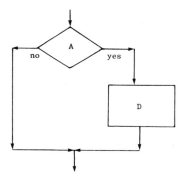

In such cases the brace behind the element that indicates no process contains the word SKIP or NEXT:

$$\left\{ \underset{\bar{A}}{\overset{A}{\oplus}} \begin{cases} B \\ \\ \text{SKIP} \end{cases} \right.$$

The effect of the SKIP or NEXT is to show that nothing is to be done for that alternative and that control is to pass to the next element. SKIP and NEXT do not indicate that anything is to be skipped or that control skips to some other part of the diagram. They simply indicate that no operation is to be performed. Figure 6.12 compares a Warnier diagram that contains SKIP to a corresponding flowchart.

(a)

(b)

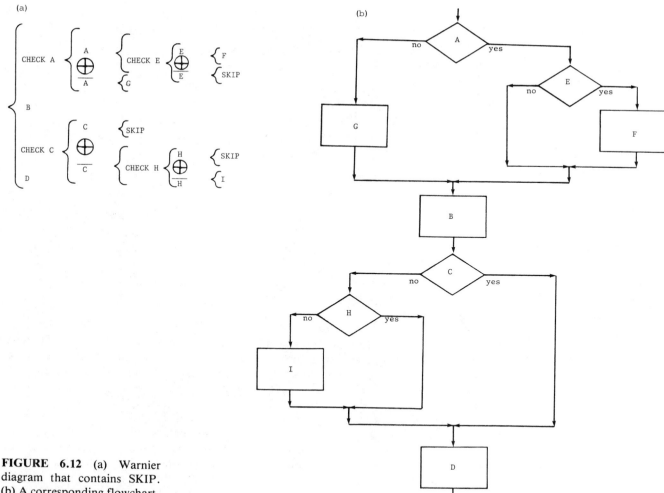

FIGURE 6.12 (a) Warnier diagram that contains SKIP. (b) A corresponding flowchart.

Case

Case is represented by a brace that contains more than a single $\oplus$. This structure indicates that exactly one of the several alternatives will be carried out. The following example compares a Warnier diagram that represents case with a flowchart representing the same structure.

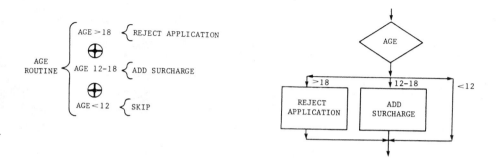

EOF

The structure of a loop that contains EOF as its exit decision varies depending on whether that loop is a do-while or a do-until. In the do-until loop, EOF is checked within the loop, to ensure that the end-of-file record is not processed, and also

6.2 EOF, Counters and Accumulators, and Indicators

Figure 6.13 (a) Warnier diagram including a do-until loop that contains EOF as its exit decision. (b) The corresponding flowchart.

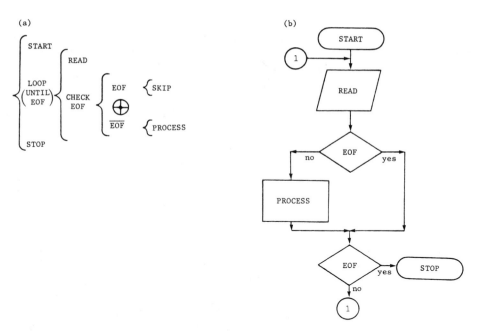

checked at the end of the loop, to exit the loop. This structure parallels exactly the design of the do-until loop in the structured flowchart. Figure 6.13 compares these two do-until loops. This program starts, loops, and stops. Within the loop, a record is read and EOF is checked. Processing of one record at a time continues until EOF is encountered. When EOF is encountered, processing is by-passed, control passes from the loop, and the program stops.

By comparison, the do-while loop checks EOF only once during each pass through the loop. However, the do-while loop requires an initial READ statement that is executed before control enters the loop. Again, the Warnier diagram mirrors the structure of the do-while flowchart, as seen in Figure 6.14. This program starts, reads, checks EOF, and then enters the brace. Within the brace, the process is done and another READ is executed. Control is then transferred to WHILE EOF, and EOF is checked. If EOF is still negative, control re-enters the brace; otherwise the program stops.

Figure 6.14 (a) Warnier diagram including a do-while loop that contains EOF as its exit decision. (b) The corresponding flowchart.

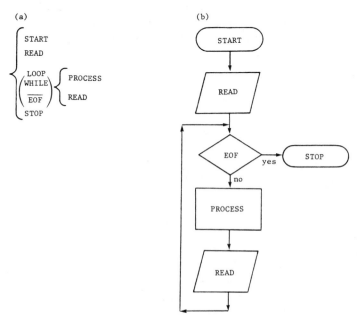

In addition to exhibiting the EOF structure, Figure 6.13 also provides a comparison between if-then-else decisions and loop exit decisions. In structured flowcharts, we informally mark this distinction by placing the negative branch at the bottom of loop exit decisions and on the left of if-then-else decisions. In Warnier diagrams the distinction is far greater. Loop exit decisions are parenthetical expressions beneath universals. If-then-else decisions use the $\oplus$ notation. In Figure 6.13, the UNTIL EOF of the Warnier diagram corresponds to the second decision of the flowchart. The if-then-else decision of the Warnier diagram corresponds to the first flowchart decision.

Counters and Accumulators

Warnier diagrams initialize counters and accumulators outside their loops and increment them within loops, just as flowcharts do. Counters and accumulators are usually initialized above and to the left of the brace in which the counting or accumulating is accomplished. Accumulators are incremented at some point within the brace. Counters are usually incremented at the bottom of the brace. The totals of both counters and accumulators are normally printed below the brace. The following Warnier diagrams demonstrate counters and accumulators.

```
        ⎧ START
        ⎪
        ⎪ X = Ø
        ⎪
        ⎪ LOOP     ⎧ PROCESS
        ⎨ (WHILE)  ⎨
        ⎪ (X < 1Ø) ⎩ X = X + 1
        ⎪
        ⎪ PRINT X
        ⎪
        ⎩ STOP
```

```
  ⎧ START
  ⎪
  ⎪ TOTAL = Ø
  ⎪
  ⎪                  ⎧ READ A    ⎧ EOF  ⎧ SKIP
  ⎪ LOOP             ⎪           ⎪      ⎨
  ⎨ (UNTIL)  ⎨       ⎪ CHECK   ⊕ ⎨
  ⎪ ( EOF )          ⎩ EOF       ⎪ ___  ⎧ TOTAL =
  ⎪                             ⎩ EOF  ⎩ TOTAL + A
  ⎪
  ⎪ PRINT TOTAL
  ⎪
  ⎩ STOP
```

Indicators

Indicators are frequently used in designing structured programs, because structured programs must have exactly one loop exit decision and many programs require that loops be exited when any of several conditions occurs. In such cases, an indicator is used in the loop exit decision and its value is controlled by conditions within the loop. When a condition requiring a loop exit occurs, the value of the indicator changes and the decision transfers control from the loop. Figure 6.15 consists of an unstructured flowchart, a structured flowchart, and a Warnier diagram. Each of them represents a program that will read records until EOF is encountered or until 10 records have been read. Note that the unstructured flowchart has two loop exits. The Warnier diagram and the structured flowchart accomplish the same task with only one loop exit by using Y as an indicator.

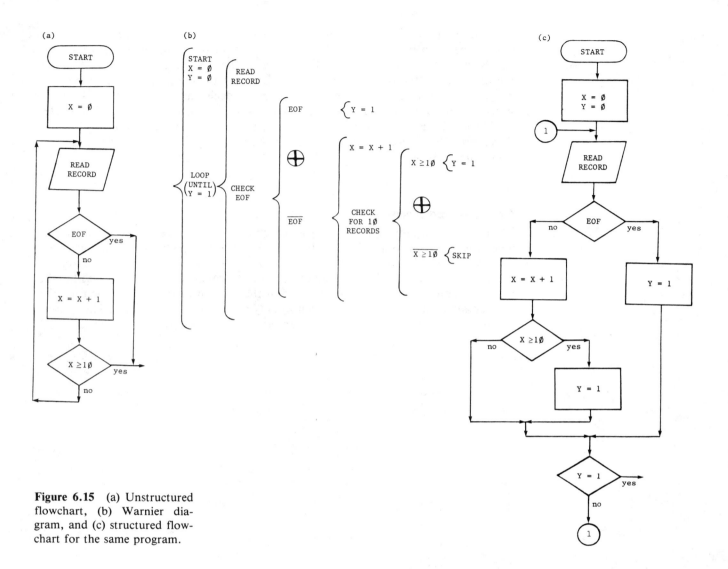

Figure 6.15 (a) Unstructured flowchart, (b) Warnier diagram, and (c) structured flowchart for the same program.

Exercises 6.2

1. Design a Warnier diagram using do-while loops for each of the following programs (from Exercises 2 and 3 on page 22).
   a. Read SALES from each record, print each sales amount, and print the total of the amounts.
   b. Read SALES from each record and print the average of the sales amounts.

2. Design a Warnier diagram using do-until loops for each of the programs described in Exercise 1 above.

3. Design a Warnier diagram using do-while loops for the following program (from Exercise 4 on page 33).

   Read names and grades. The program is to print each name and grade and to calculate and print the average of all grades. The program is to print one error message for every grade that is less than 0 and another for every grade that is over 100.

4. Design a Warnier diagram using do-until loops for the program described in Exercise 3 above.

5. Design a Warnier diagram using do-until loops for the following program (from part 5 of Exercise 1 on page 37).

Read a name and an amount from 10 or fewer records. Print each name and amount. Print an error message if fewer than 10 records were read.

6. Design Warnier diagrams using the loop indicated for programs to print, in the corresponding columns, the names of the members of the sets indicated by numerals in the following Venn diagrams (from parts (a) and (e) of Exercise 2 on page 63).

a.
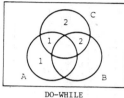

b.
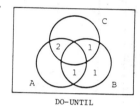

7. Design Warnier diagrams using the loop indicated for programs that will read records that contain names, division numbers, years employed, stock plan membership, and sales amounts, and that will carry out one of the following sets of directions (from parts (c), (f), (g), and (h) of the exercise on page 68).

   a. Print the number of members in the stock plan, and print the average sales of those who have been employed more than 10 years. (Assume that there will be sufficient data to avoid division by 0.) (Do-While)

   b. Determine and print whether or not everyone in Division 1 is in the stock plan. (The program is to read no more records than necessary to make the determination.) (Do-Until)

   c. Determine and print whether or not everyone in Division 1 whose sales exceed 2000 is in the stock plan. (Do-While)

   d. Print the total sales of Division 5 members who are in the stock plan. If any of those individuals' sales is negative, print ERRONEOUS DATA along with the total. (Do-Until)

6.3 Comparison Between Warnier Diagrams and Flowcharts

Flowcharts (whether structured or not) display all the features of Warnier diagrams except those that represent hierarchy. In particular, they contain all elements except universals. Conversely, Warnier diagrams are capable of representing all structured flowcharts. Figures 6.16, 6.17, and 6.18 are examples of flowcharts and their corresponding Warnier diagrams. Note that the universal statements of the Warnier diagrams (which represent only structure) are missing from the flowcharts and that the flowcharts require additional symbols to indicate repetition. Study these examples and note particularly where loops begin and end in each.

Structured flowcharts can be drawn to represent the *executable* elements of Warnier diagrams and all statements of a coded program. Except for modular flowcharts, they do not represent the purely structural elements of the Warnier diagram. For its part, the Warnier diagram can represent any structured flowchart, but it cannot represent unstructured flowcharts. One simply can't represent an unstructured flowchart with a Warnier diagram.[3] In short, the Warnier diagram can represent all good programming techniques and *only* good programming techniques.

[3] That is, one cannot do so without departing from the techniques described here.

Figure 6.16 (a) Flowchart. (b) A corresponding Warnier diagram.

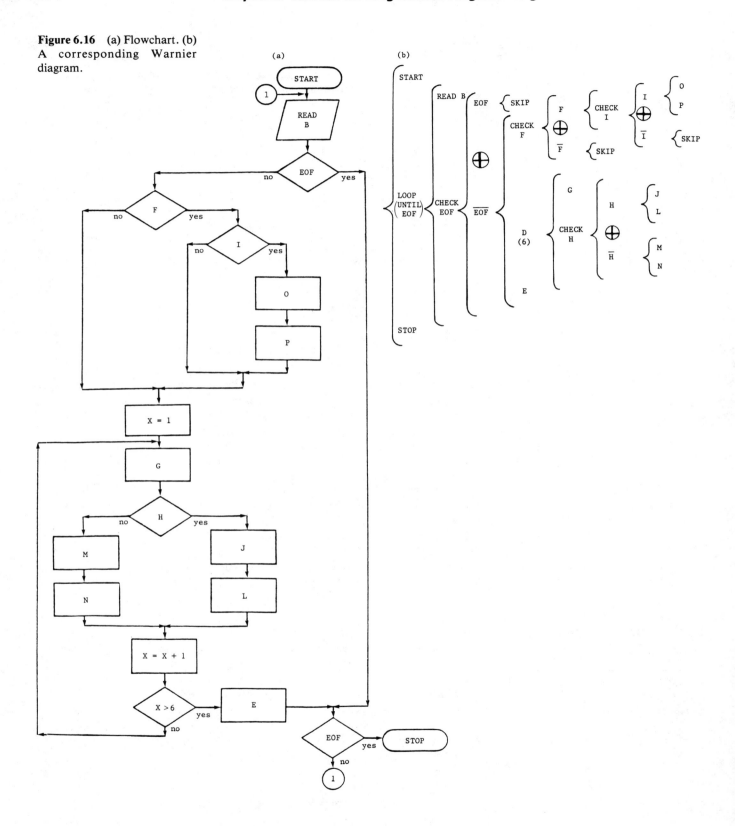

Figure 6.17 (a) Flowchart. (b) A corresponding Warnier diagram.

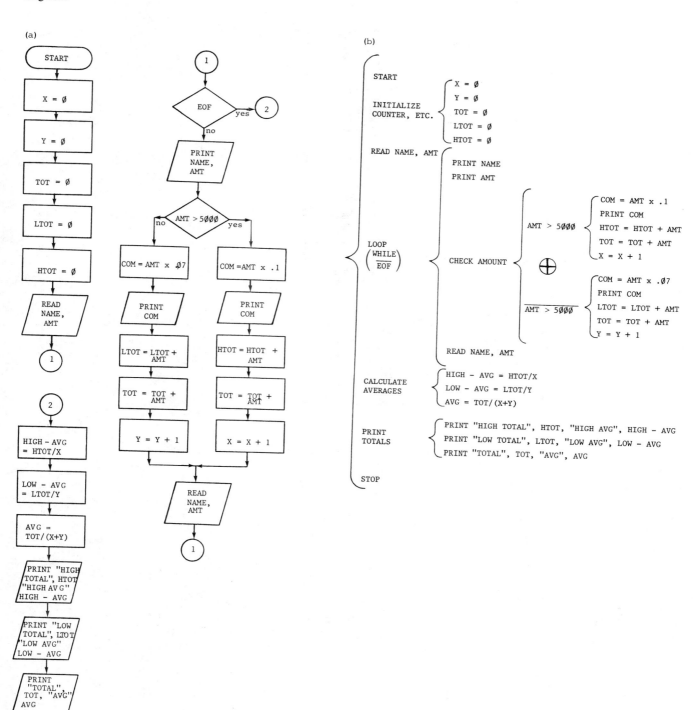

Figure 6.18   (a) Flowchart. (b) A corresponding Warnier diagram.

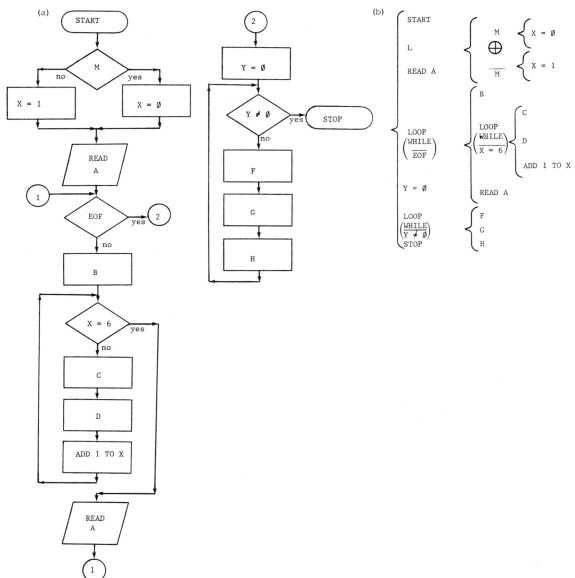

Exercises 6.3

1. Draw a structured flowchart to indicate the decisions and/or sequences that are represented by each of the following Warnier diagrams.

2. Represent the following flowcharts by Warnier diagrams.

a.

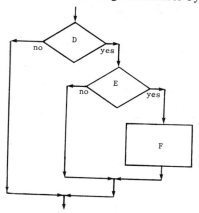

b.

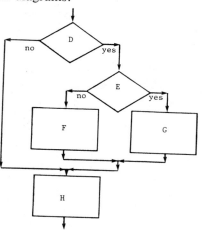

d.

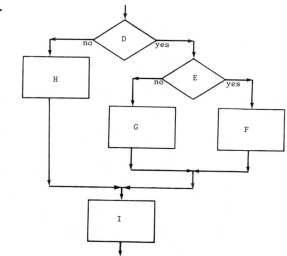

c.

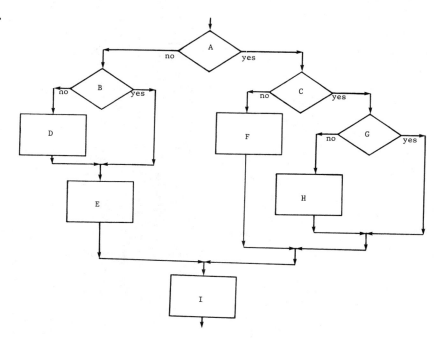

3. Represent the following flowcharts by Warnier diagrams. These flowcharts are not structured, and some redesign will be required.

a.

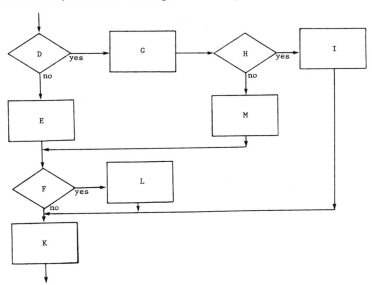

b.

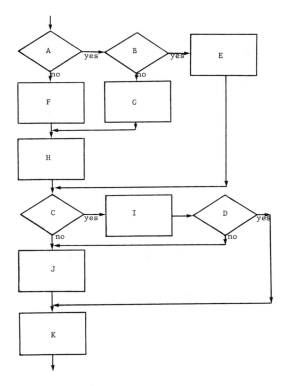

4. Design a structured flowchart to represent each of the following Warnier diagrams.

a.

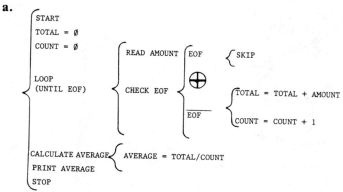

```
       ⎧ START
       ⎪ TOTAL = Ø
       ⎪ COUNT = Ø
       ⎪
       ⎪                  ⎧ READ AMOUNT   ⎧ EOF  ⎧ SKIP
       ⎪ LOOP             ⎪                ⊕
       ⎨ (UNTIL EOF)      ⎨               ⎪      ⎧ TOTAL = TOTAL + AMOUNT
       ⎪                  ⎪ CHECK EOF     ⎨ ‾‾‾‾ ⎨
       ⎪                  ⎩               ⎩ EOF  ⎩ COUNT = COUNT + 1
       ⎪
       ⎪ CALCULATE AVERAGE ⎨ AVERAGE = TOTAL/COUNT
       ⎪ PRINT AVERAGE
       ⎩ STOP
```

b.

```
        ⎧ START
        ⎪ B
        ⎪
        ⎪               ⎧ G  ⎧ L   ⎧ O
        ⎪               ⎪    ⎪ (6) ⎩ P
        ⎪     C         ⎨  ⊕ ⎨
        ⎪               ⎪    ⎩ M
        ⎪               ⎩ G̅  ⎧ SKIP
        ⎪
   A    ⎪ D
  (1)   ⎨
        ⎪               ⎧ H          ⎧ N  ⎧ Q
        ⎪     E         ⎪            ⎪  ⊕ ⎩ R
        ⎪    (2)        ⎨ I          ⎨
        ⎪               ⎩            ⎩ N̅  ⎧ SKIP
        ⎪
        ⎪     F         ⎧ J
        ⎪               ⎩ K
        ⎩ STOP
```

c.

```
            ⎧ START
            ⎪
            ⎪ X = 2
            ⎪
            ⎪ Y = 1
            ⎪
 PROGRAM    ⎪              ⎧ PRINT X
   (1)      ⎨              ⎪
            ⎪ LOOP         ⎪
            ⎪ (UNTIL       ⎨ X = X * Y
            ⎪  X > 1ØØØ)   ⎪
            ⎪              ⎪
            ⎪ STOP         ⎩ Y = Y * 2
```

d.

```
            ⎧ START
            ⎪ X = 1
            ⎪
            ⎪              ⎧ Y = 2            ⎧ Z = X + Y + 2
 PROGRAM    ⎪ LOOP         ⎪                 ⎪
   (1)      ⎨ (UNTIL       ⎨ LOOP            ⎨ PRINT Z
            ⎪  X > 7)      ⎪ (UNTIL          ⎪
            ⎪              ⎪  Y > 11)        ⎩ Y = Y + 3
            ⎪              ⎩ X = X + 2
            ⎪
            ⎩ STOP
```

4e.

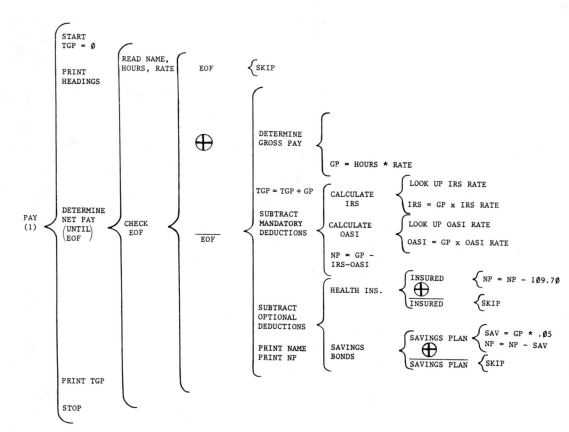

5. Design a Warnier diagram to represent each of the following flowcharts.
a.

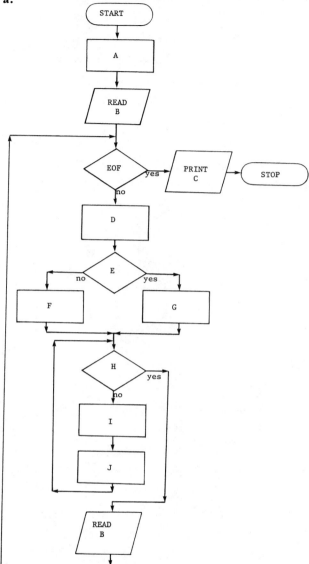

5b.

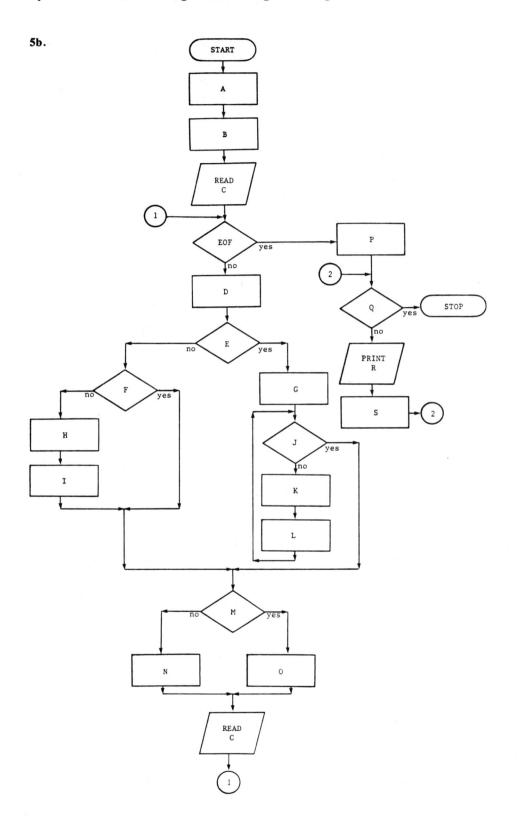

6. Design a Warnier diagram to represent each of the following flowcharts. These flowcharts are not structured, and some redesign will be required.

a.

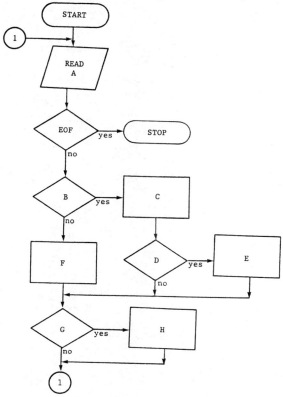

b.

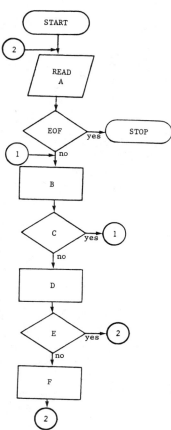

6c.

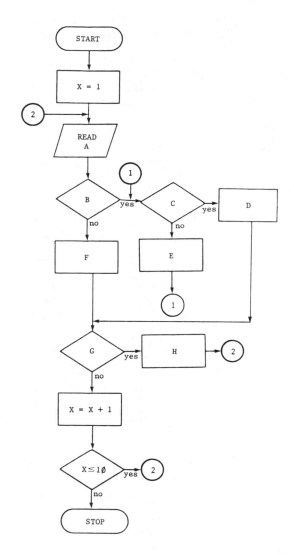

6.4 Program Design Using Warnier Diagrams

In Section 6.1 we noted that one more easily understands the program represented by a Warnier diagram if one reads down the entire left-most brace before reading any of the details to the right. This is particularly the case with Warnier diagrams for complicated programs. An understanding of the major elements of such programs precedes an understanding of the various details and their relationships. Correspondingly, the design of a complex program should begin with an outline of its major components. Using a Warnier diagram for this purpose, one completes the left-most brace from top to bottom by listing the major components. Only after the left brace is completed will the program be specified further in braces to the right. Program specification is continued by completing each brace from top to bottom before moving to the right again. The final braces to the right will contain program details, perhaps even the coded statements of the program.

An Example of Program Design

Suppose we wanted to design a program to create a sales report. The program will read a file containing records with names and totals for each agent. The report is to have a heading, including the date; it is to print each name and total; and it is to print the number of agents, a grand total, and a message that indicates whether any of the agents' totals exceed $10,000.

Such a program can be divided into an initial process, a detail process, and a final process. A Warnier diagram for such a program would begin with a large brace containing these items, along with the START and STOP. The brace is comparable to the primary flowchart of a modular flowchart (see Figure 6.19).

Figure 6.19 (a) Flowchart. (b) Warnier diagram.

Figure 6.20 Further specification of the processes given in Figure 6.19(b).

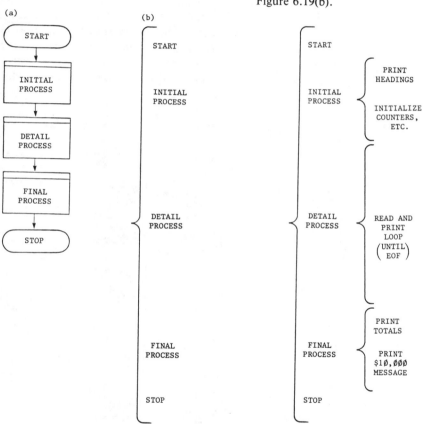

Next, each of these processes would be further specified in braces to the right. The initial process would consist of printing headings and initializing counters, accumulators, and indicators. The detail process would consist of a loop in which data was read, printed, counted, and accumulated. The final process would consist of printing totals and the $10,000 message. Each of these items is added to the Warnier diagram, as shown in Figure 6.20.

The program components that are identified by the universals in this second set of braces are then further specified by creating braces to the right. Again, each brace is completed from top to bottom before additional braces to the right are formed. The READ AND PRINT component would be specified as indicated in Figure 6.21.

Figure 6.21 Specification of the READ AND PRINT component shown in Figure 6.20.

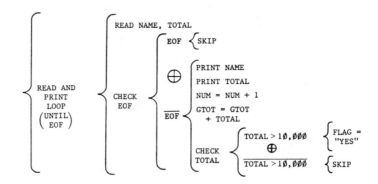

This component of the diagram would fit into the completed Warnier diagram shown in Figure 6.22. This final diagram represents the program in sufficient detail to allow its coding. The coded statements could be written directly from the executables of the Warnier diagram with only minor changes reflecting the choice of program language. The order of the coded statements would, of course, reflect the intended order of execution and not the order in which the diagram was constructed.

Figure 6.22 This Warnier diagram completes Figure 6.19(b).

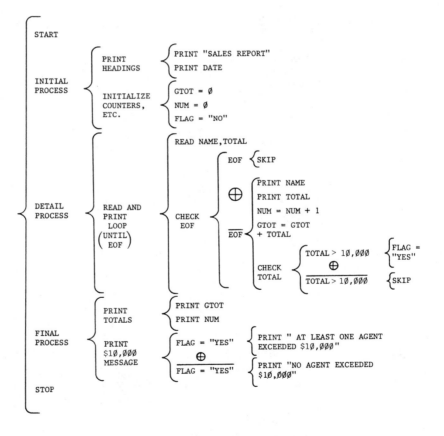

Figure 6.23 shows the step-by-step development of a Warnier diagram using a do-while loop for a program that will read amounts, keep track of the number of amounts greater than 50, print the number of amounts greater than 50, and print the total of all amounts.

Figure 6.23 Step-by-step development of a Warnier diagram.

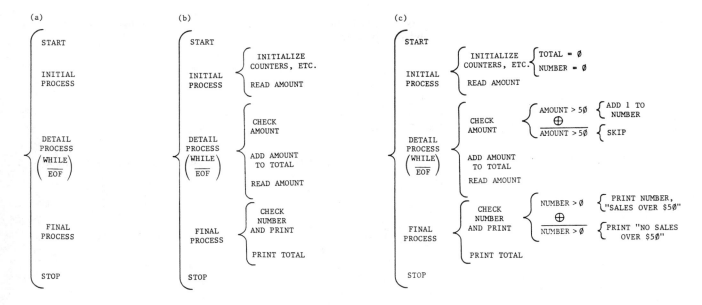

Exercises 6.4

Using the method described in Section 6.4, design Warnier diagrams for programs that meet the following requirements. (Use do-while loops for odd-numbered exercises and do-until loops for even-numbered exercises.)

1. Read records that contain names, sales amounts, and rates. Print a report that contains names, sales amounts, and commissions (commission = rate × sales amount). The report is also to contain the total of sales and commissions, and the average commission. (Assume that the file will not be empty.)

2. Read names, rates, and sales amounts from records that were sorted by name. Print each name once and each sale amount and commission (commission = rate × sale amount). Print individual sales totals and commission totals. Print a grand total of sales and commissions.

3. Read names, rates, and sales amounts. Print the name, sales amount, and commission (commission = rate × amount) from each record that has a rate greater than .07. Print the total of commissions greater than 1000 and the number of records processed.

4. Read records that contain names, sales amounts, and rates. Compute commissions as follows: commission = sales × rate, for sales less than 1000; commission = sales × rate + .02 sales, for sales from 1000 to 2000; commission = sales × rate + .05 sales, for sales greater than 2000. Print the names and commissions of all individuals whose commissions exceed 200 in column 1, and print the names and commissions of all others in column 2.

*6.5 Logical Data Structures

Data on punched cards and tapes is organized sequentially. Some types of processing require that data be organized into a hierarchy rather than a sequence. Warnier diagrams are particularly well suited for the type of hierarchial organization required.

Consider the data on the following card:

JONES   SAM   E   SALES   CLERK   Ø3   Ø5

There are many ways to organize this data, but one natural hierarchy suggests itself. That hierarchy is superimposed on the card as follows:

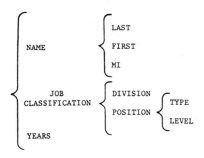

This hierarchy is represented by the following Warnier diagram, which is called a **logical data structure**.

```
        ┌         ┌ LAST
        │  NAME  <  FIRST
        │         └ MI
        │
        │                    ┌ DIVISION
       <   JOB            <             ┌ TYPE
        │  CLASSIFICATION   └ POSITION <
        │                                └ LEVEL
        │
        └  YEARS
```

Input data has no inherent structure. It lends itself to a wide variety of organization schemes. The logical data structure for a type of data may vary from program to program, and the structure to be used for a particular program is selected by the programmer or analyst on the basis of the processing to be accomplished. Without knowing other program requirements, it is impossible to determine which logical data structure is best.

Both Figure 6.24 and Figure 6.25 exhibit one possible logical data structure for the card that each represents.

Figure 6.24 (a) Punched card. (b) A logical data structure for this card.

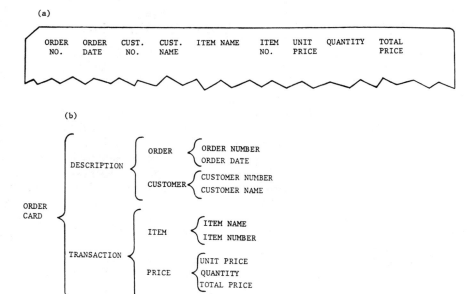

Figure 6.25 (a) Punched card. (b) A logical data structure for this card.

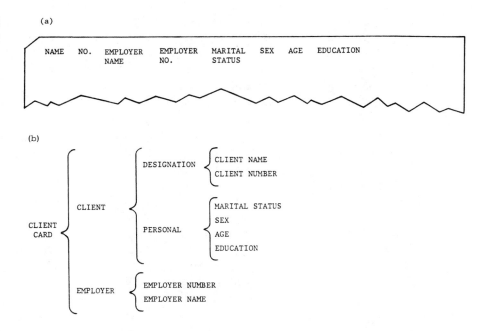

Logical Output Structure (LOS)

Logical output structures are used to represent the organization of a program's output. Often, the way in which output is organized greatly affects the ease of its use.

Compare Figure 6.26(a) and (b). The information presented in these reports is identical. But Figure 6.26(b) is more readable than Figure 6.26(a).

(a)

STORE	DEPARTMENT	EMPLOYEE	HOURS
268	GROCERY	SMITH	4Ø
268	GROCERY	JOHNSON	4Ø
268	GROCERY	HEISE	36
268	PRODUCE	JONES	4Ø
268	PRODUCE	DANIELS	4Ø
268	PRODUCE	FORD	2Ø
37Ø	GROCERY	ABBOTT	4Ø
37Ø	GROCERY	PETERS	27
37Ø	GROCERY	MARTIN	18
37Ø	PRODUCE	CURHAN	4Ø

(b)

STORE	DEPARTMENT	EMPLOYEE	HOURS
268	GROCERY	SMITH	4Ø
		JOHNSON	4Ø
		HEISE	36
	PRODUCE	JONES	4Ø
		DANIELS	4Ø
		FORD	2Ø
37Ø	GROCERY	ABBOTT	4Ø
		PETERS	27
		MARTIN	18
	PRODUCE	CURHAN	4Ø

In Figure 6.26(a), the names of the store, department, and employee are printed with each assignment of hours. The logical output structure for this report is

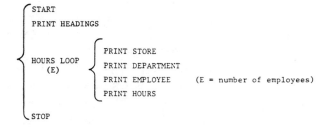

Figure 6.26 These two reports give exactly the same information, but the second is easier to read than the first.

In Figure 6.26(b), however, the different store and department names are printed only once. The logical output structure for this report is

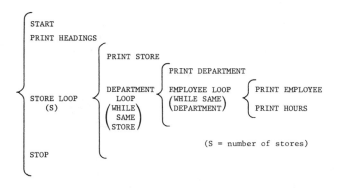

The contents of this report could easily be expanded to include totals and sub-totals and to have the appearance of Figure 6.27(a). The logical output structure for this report is given in Figure 6.27(b).

Figure 6.27 (a) This report is expanded from Figure 6.26(b). (b) The logical output structure for this expanded report.

(a)

STORE	DEPARTMENT	EMPLOYEE	HOURS
268	GROCERY	SMITH	40
		JOHNSON	40
		HEISE	36
	DEPARTMENT TOTAL		116
	PRODUCE	JONES	40
		DANIELS	40
		FORD	20
	DEPARTMENT TOTAL		100
STORE TOTAL			216
370	GROCERY	ABBOTT	40
		PETERS	27
		MARTIN	18
	DEPARTMENT TOTAL		85
	PRODUCE	CURHAN	40
	DEPARTMENT TOTAL		40
STORE TOTAL			125
GRAND TOTAL			341

(b)

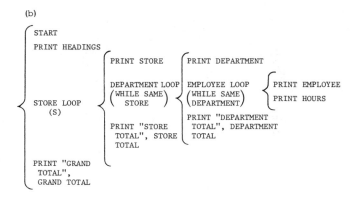

Printer Spacing Charts

Printer spacing charts are used to design the format of printed output and to provide a picture of intended output. These charts are essentially grid systems that represent all possible printing positions on the final document. They include numbers along the top and side(s) to identify both horizontal and vertical locations.

To lay out a printed document, the programmer or analyst marks spaces on the chart with X's to indicate variable output or with other symbols to indicate constant output (such as headings or editing). Only enough lines of the chart are used to indicate both vertical and horizontal spacing. The following printer spacing charts (Figures 6.28, 6.29, and 6.30) represent the reports that we have examined.

Figure 6.28 This printer spacing chart represents the report shown in Figure 6.26(a).

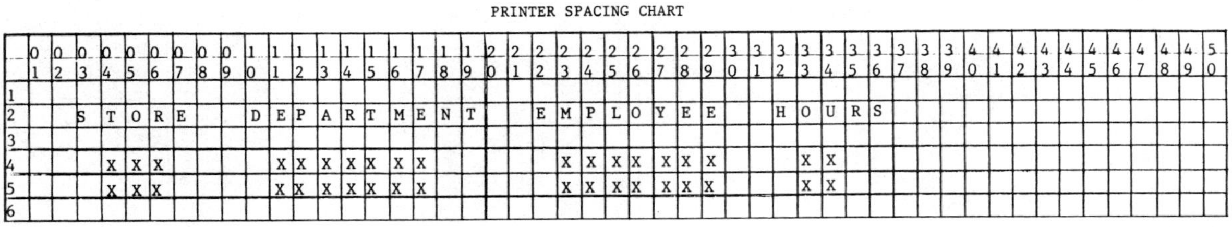

Figure 6.29 This printer spacing chart represents the report shown in Figure 6.26(b).

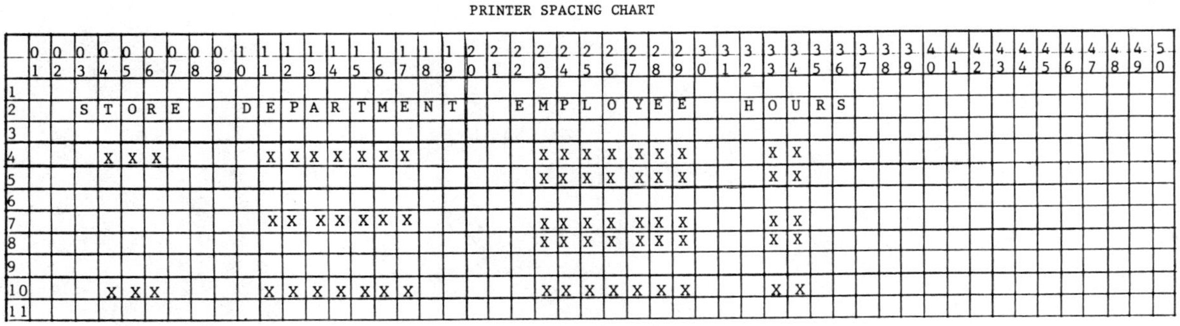

Figure 6.30 This printer spacing chart represents the report shown in Figure 6.27(a).

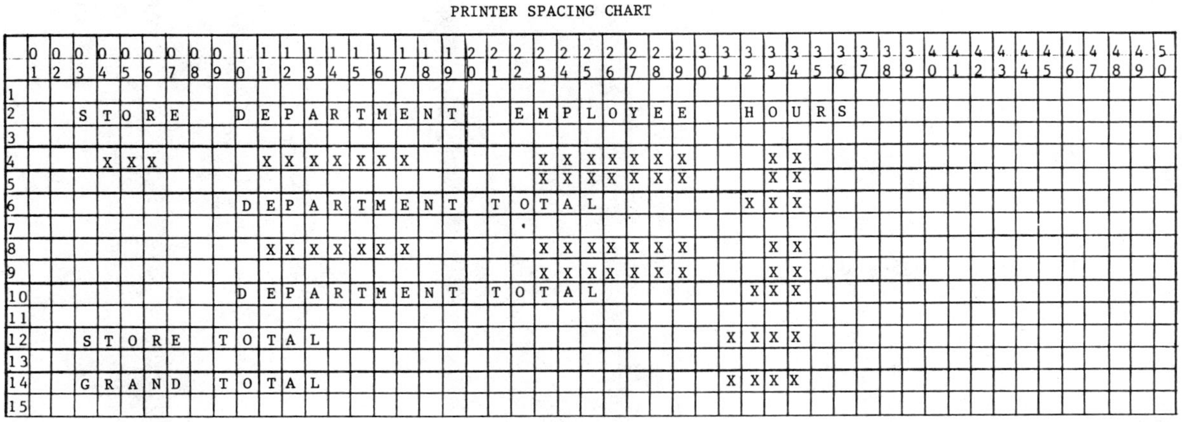

The printer spacing charts shown in Figures 6.31 and 6.32 are accompanied by appropriate logical output structures.

Figure 6.31 (a) Printer spacing chart. (b) The corresponding logical output structure.

(a)

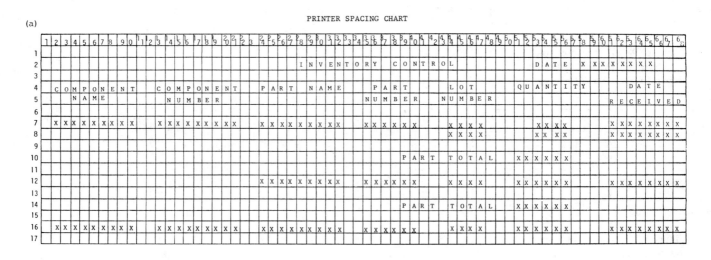

(b)

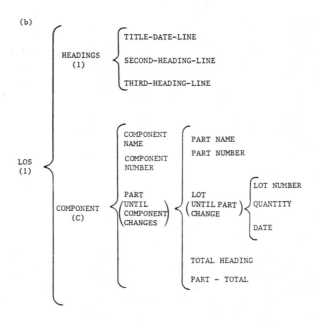

Figure 6.32 (a) Printer spacing chart.

(a)

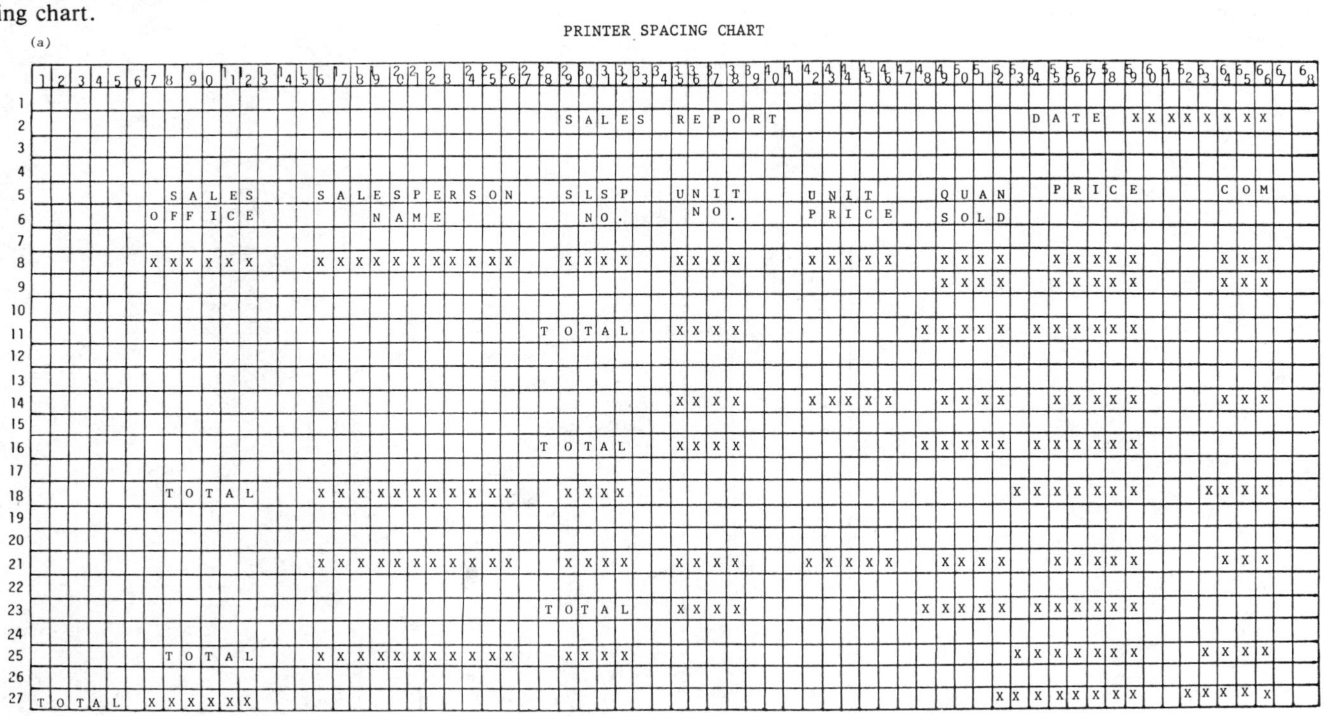
PRINTER SPACING CHART
SALES REPORT
DATE XXXXXXXX
SALES OFFICE
SALESPERSON NAME
SLSP NO.
UNIT NO.
UNIT PRICE
QUAN SOLD
PRICE
COM
XXXXXX XXXXXXXXXXX XXXX XXXX XXXXX XXXX XXXXX XXX
XXXX XXXXX XXX
TOTAL XXXX XXXXX XXXXXX
XXXX XXXXX XXXX XXXXX XXX
TOTAL XXXX XXXXX XXXXXX
TOTAL XXXXXXXXXXX XXXX XXXXXXX XXXX
XXXXXXXXXXX XXXX XXXX XXXXX XXXX XXXXX XXX
TOTAL XXXX XXXXX XXXXXX
TOTAL XXXXXXXXXXX XXXX XXXXXXX XXXX
TOTAL XXXXXX XXXXXXXX XXXXX

Figure 6.32 (b) The corresponding logical output structure.

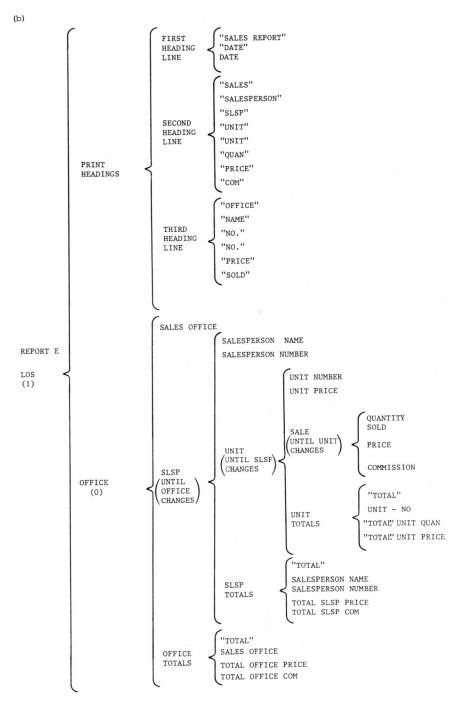

Exercises 6.5

1. Design logical data structures for each of the following cards.

a.
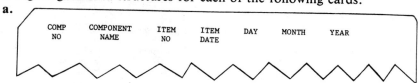

COMP NO	COMPONENT NAME	ITEM NO	ITEM DATE	DAY	MONTH	YEAR

b.
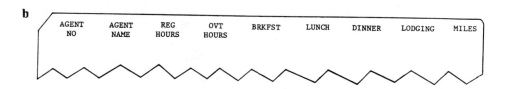

AGENT NO	AGENT NAME	REG HOURS	OVT HOURS	BRKFST	LUNCH	DINNER	LODGING	MILES

2. Design a logical output structure for each of the following reports.

a.

```
     SALES REPORT          3/17/83

AGENCY        AGENT       QUARTER        SALES

Topeka        Jones        1st             45
                           2nd             5Ø
                           3rd             25
                           4th             1Ø
              Agent Total                 13Ø

              Smith        1st             5Ø
                           2nd             6Ø
                           3rd             75
                           4th            11Ø
              Agent Total                 295

              Johnson      1st             35
                           2nd             25
                           3rd             75
                           4th             2Ø
              Agent Total                 155

Agency Total                              58Ø

Lansing       Acme         1st             1Ø
                           2nd             6Ø
                           3rd             8Ø
                           4th             3Ø
              Agent Total                 18Ø

              Brown        1st             65
                           2nd             15
                           3rd             85
                           4th             9Ø
              Agent Total                 255

Agency Total                              435

COMPANY TOTAL                            1015
```

2b.

```
                    SALES REPORT

DISTRICT    AREA    AGENCY      AGENT      SALES

  Ø7        423     Topeka      Jones       475
            423     Topeka      Smith       317
            423     Topeka      Adams       176

                            Agency Total   968

            423     Lansing     Forbes      416
            423     Lansing     Logan       1Ø5

                            Agency Total   521

            463     Jackson     Baker       219
            463     Jackson     Charles     381
            463     Jackson     Franks      116

                            Agency Total   716

                            Dist. Total   22Ø5

  Ø8        473     Lawrence    Hurd        318
            473     Lawrence    Galler      412

                            Agency Total   73Ø

                            Dist. Total    73Ø

                            Company Total 2935
```

c.

PRINTER SPACING CHART

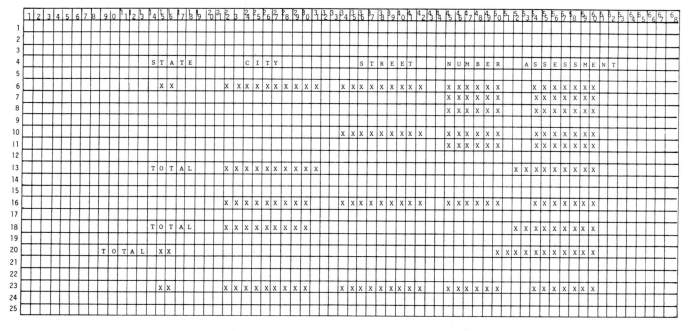

6.6 Report Programs from Logical Output Structures

Report programs are one of four basic types of business application programs. They convert data from an input file to information in the form of a printed report. These programs may or may not include extensive data manipulation, but they generally include information from every or nearly every input record. Programs of this sort were used as examples in Chapter 1 and in Chapter 4.[4] They are considered again at this point because logical output structures provide an excellent foundation for designing a Warnier diagram for a report program.

The design of a report program should begin with the program's output – that is, with the desired report. So the first step in designing a report program is constructing a printer spacing chart and then a logical output structure for that chart. The logical output structure is then converted to a Warnier diagram for the report. Printer spacing charts and logical output structures were covered in Section 6.5, so this section focuses on conversion of the logical output structure to the Warnier diagram for a report program.

Converting the logical output structure to a Warnier diagram can be accomplished in six steps by making some or all of the following additions:

1. A READ instruction inside the first brace.
2. Control break indicators.
3. Initialization of counters, accumulators, and indicators.
4. A READ and SET INDICATORS module inside innermost brace.
5. Appropriate processing inside innermost brace.
6. Changing the terminal condition on the outside loop to EOF.

A simple report program that just reads records and prints their contents would require the addition of only two READ instructions and the EOF. Figure 6.33 shows the printer spacing chart, the logical output structure, and the Warnier diagram for such a program. The program starts, prints appropriate headings, reads a first record, and then loops while it has not reached the end of the file. Within the loop, the division, department, and sale are printed and the next record read.

(a)

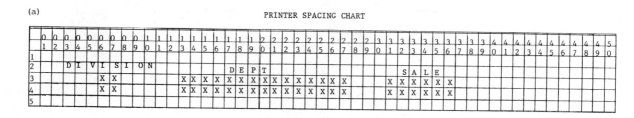

PRINTER SPACING CHART

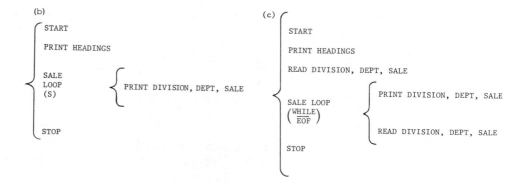

Figure 6.33 (a) Printer spacing chart. (b) Logical output structure. (c) Warnier diagram.

---

[4] Extract programs are considered in Chapters 2 and 9; edit and file maintenance programs are considered in Chapter 9.

The program represented by Figure 6.33 can easily be augmented so that it prints a total of all sales. To do this, we add an accumulator (TOTAL), as shown in Figure 6.34. TOTAL is initialized before control enters the loop, incremented within the loop, and printed after control leaves the loop. Note that this is accomplished by initializing and printing TOTAL in the same loop and by incrementing TOTAL in the next inner loop. This pattern is used for the addition of most counters and accumulators.

Figure 6.34 (a) Printer spacing chart. (b) Logical output structure. (c) Warnier diagram.

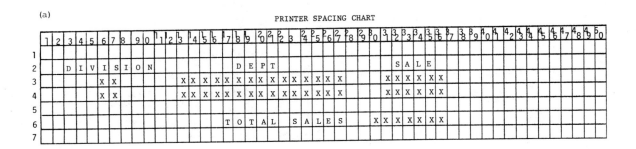

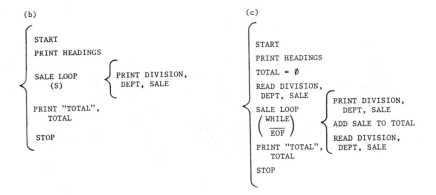

A more extensive conversion of the logical output structure is required if a control break is added to the program described by Figure 6.33. Figure 6.35 modifies Figure 6.33 so that each division name is printed only once. This modification requires the addition of a control break indicator (DIVBK) and a compare field (OLD DIV).

Figure 6.35 (a) Printer spacing chart. (b) Logical output structure. (c) Warnier diagram.

(a)

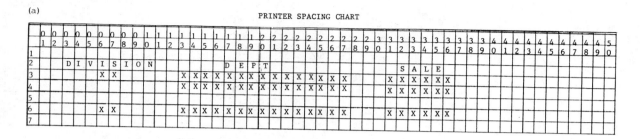

PRINTER SPACING CHART

(b)

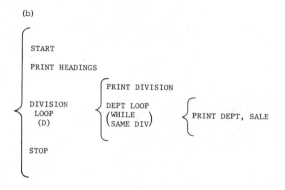

(c)

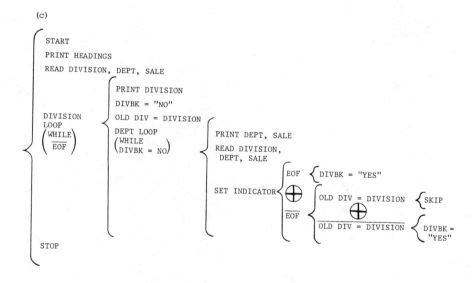

The control break indicator (DIVBK) is initialized (set to "NO") near the top of the DIVISION LOOP. DIVBK will remain "NO" until a record with a new entry in the division field is read. While DIVBK remains "NO", the DEPT LOOP will be repeated. When the DIVBK becomes "YES", control leaves the DEPT LOOP and the EOF decision is checked. If the program is not at EOF, the most recently read division is printed and stored at OLD DIV, DIVBK is reinitialized to "NO", and the department loop is entered. This processing continues until the end of the file is reached.

(a)

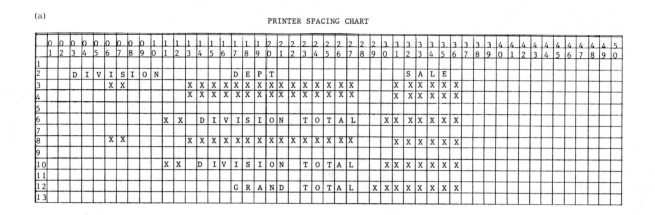

Figure 6.36 (a) Printer spacing chart. (b) Logical output structure. (c) Warnier diagram.

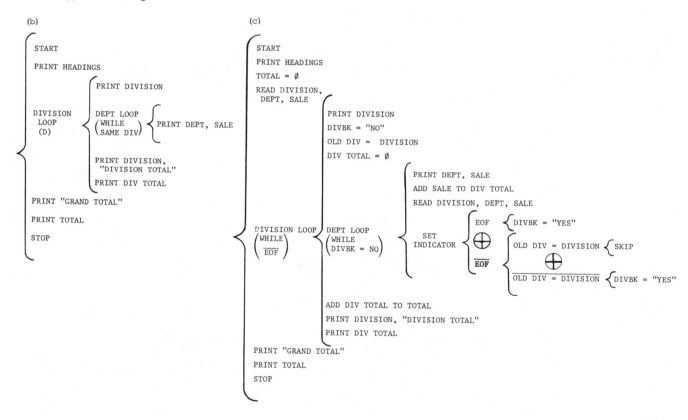

Figure 6.36 adds totals and subtotals to the program described in Figure 6.35. The addition of these totals requires the addition of a subtotal accumulator to the inner loop and a total accumulator just before each subtotal is printed.

Figure 6.37 adds to Figure 6.36 a control break and a total for each department. This creates a two-level control break program with totals.

(a)

PRINTER SPACING CHART

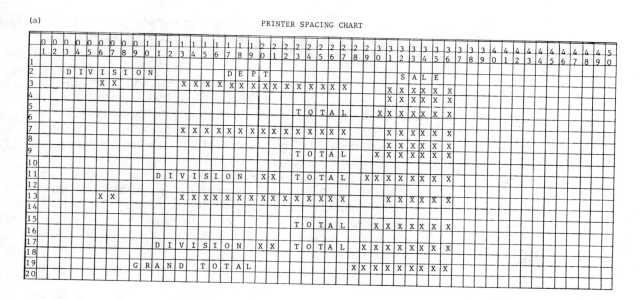

Figure 6.37 (a) Printer spacing chart. (b) Logical output structure. (c) Warnier diagram.

(b)

(c)

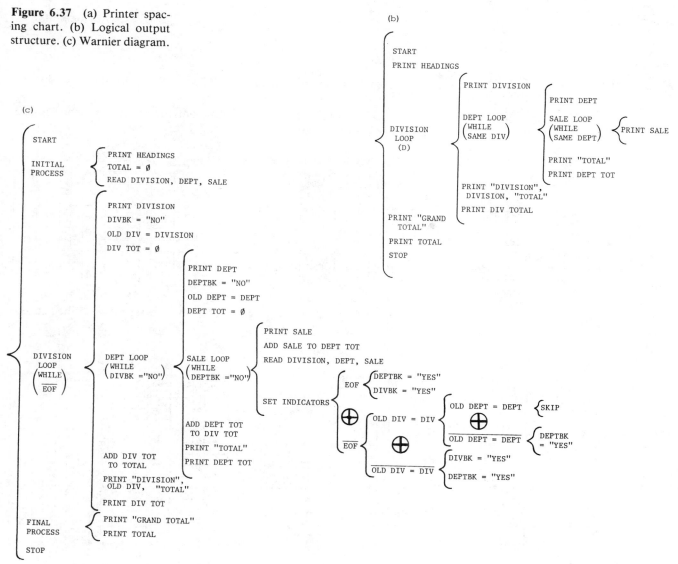

The additional control break of Figure 6.37 requires an additional control field (OLD DEPT), an additional control break indicator (DEPTBK), and a more extensive SET INDICATORS module. Department totals are also initialized, incremented, and printed.

The SET INDICATORS module of Figure 6.37 sets both DEPTBK and DIVBK to "YES" if there is a change in divisions or if EOF is encountered. In general, every control break results in the execution of all subordinate control breaks. One might think that this structure could be eliminated by checking for a division break only when there is a department break. But one must guard against the possibility of the same department occurring in two different divisions. In such a case, the division could change at a time when the department doesn't, and, in this case, control must break for both division and department. If control did not break, the sales of the Home Computer Department of the Lansing Division could be lumped together with the sales of the Home Computer Department of the Lancaster Division. Checking for a division break before checking for a department break avoids this potential problem.

Exercises 6.6

1. Design a Warnier diagram for a program to print the report shown in Figure 6.26(a).

2. Design a Warnier diagram for a program to print the report described in the following printer spacing chart.

PRINTER SPACING CHART

```
         0000000000111111111122222222223333333333444444444455
         1234567890123456789012345678901234567890123456789 0
1
2                    NAME                     AMOUNT
3        XXXXXXXXXXXXXXXXXXXX                  XXXXX
                                               XXXXX
4
5
6        XXXXXXXXXXXXXXXXXXXX                  XXXXX
                                               XXXXX
7
8
```

3. Design a Warnier diagram for a program to print the report described in the following printer spacing chart.

PRINTER SPACING CHART

```
         0000000000111111111122222222223333333333444444444455
         1234567890123456789012345678901234567890123456789 0
1
2                    NAME                     AMOUNT
3        XXXXXXXXXXXXXXXXXXXX                  XXXXX
                                               XXXXX
4
5
6              INDIVIDUAL TOTAL                XXXXXX
7
8        XXXXXXXXXXXXXXXXXXXX                  XXXXX
9
10             INDIVIDUAL TOTAL                XXXXXX
11
12       GRAND TOTAL                          XXXXXXX
13
```

4. Design a Warnier diagram for a program to print the report described in the following printer spacing chart. The program will read names and amounts and will print each name once, along with that individual's total.

PRINTER SPACING CHART

	0 0 0 0 0 0 0 0 0 1	1 1 1 1 1 1 1 1 1 2	2 2 2 2 2 2 2 2 2 3	3 3 3 3 3 3 3 3 3 4	4 4 4 4 4 4 4 4 4 5
	1 2 3 4 5 6 7 8 9 0	1 2 3 4 5 6 7 8 9 0	1 2 3 4 5 6 7 8 9 0	1 2 3 4 5 6 7 8 9 0	1 2 3 4 5 6 7 8 9 0
1					
2	N A M E	T O T A L			
3	X X X X X X X X X X X X X X X X X	T O T A L			
4	X X X X X X X X X X X X X X X X X	X X X X X X			
5					

5. Design a Warnier diagram for a program to print the report shown in Figure 6.26(b).

6. Use the following printer spacing chart to design a Warnier diagram for the program described by Figure 4.17.

PRINTER SPACING CHART

	0 0 0 0 0 0 0 0 0 1	1 1 1 1 1 1 1 1 1 2	2 2 2 2 2 2 2 2 2 3	3 3 3 3 3 3 3 3 3 4	4 4 4 4 4 4 4 4 4 5
	1 2 3 4 5 6 7 8 9 0	1 2 3 4 5 6 7 8 9 0	1 2 3 4 5 6 7 8 9 0	1 2 3 4 5 6 7 8 9 0	1 2 3 4 5 6 7 8 9 0
1					
2					
3					
4	A G E N C Y	A G E N T	S A L E		
5					
6	X X X	X X X X X X X X X X X X X	X X X X		
7			X X X X		
8					
9		A G E N T T O T A L	X X X X X		
10					
11		X X X X X X X X X X X X X	X X X X		
12			X X X X		
13					
14		A G E N T T O T A L	X X X X X		
15					
16		A G E N C Y T O T A L	X X X X X X		
17					
18	X X X	X X X X X X X X X X X X X	X X X X		
19			X X X X		
20					
21		A G E N T T O T A L	X X X X X		
22					
23		A G E N C Y T O T A L	X X X X X X		
24					
25		G R A N D T O T A L	X X X X X X X		
26					

7. Design a Warnier diagram for a program to print the report shown in Figure 6.27(a).

Review Questions

Completion

1. Warnier diagrams emphasize _____ rather than _____ .
2. Warnier diagram elements that represent structure only are called _____ .
3. _____ are used in structured programs when loops must be exited under more than one condition.
4. _____ are used to organize output into usable form.

5. In Warnier diagrams, loop exit decisions are represented by _____, by _____, or by numerals in parentheses.

6. Modular flowcharts represent universals as _____.

Discussion

1. Describe two ways of indicating a loop in Warnier diagrams.
2. How are the two EOF decisions of a do-until loop represented in a Warnier diagram?
3. How are loop exit decisions of do-while loops represented in a Warnier diagram?
4. How does a Warnier diagram represent sequence?
5. How does a Warnier diagram represent if-then-else?

True or False

1. _____ The main advantage of Warnier diagrams in program design is that they emphasize the sequence of a program rather than its hierarchy.
2. _____ Executable statements do not appear in unstructured flowcharts.
3. _____ Universals are names of general operations rather than particular tasks.
4. _____ In determining the sequence of execution that is represented by a Warnier diagram, we read all items within a brace before we read braces to the right.
5. _____ All decisions in Warnier diagrams are represented using $\oplus$.
6. _____ The elements of a decision in a Warnier diagram must be logically contradictory.
7. _____ The effect of the word SKIP is to show that nothing is to be done for a particular alternative of a decision.
8. _____ Accumulators are usually initialized at the left of or above the brace in which they are incremented.
9. _____ Totals and counters are usually printed below the brace in which they are incremented.
10. _____ There is usually a single inherent structure to input data.

7. Pseudocode and Nassi-Shneiderman Diagrams

7.1 Pseudocode

Pseudocode is a program-design technique that uses informal expressions in outline form to describe the logic of a program. Pseudocode is written in a natural language (such as English) rather than in a programming language. Pseudocode expressions are not unlike those used in flowcharts. Even though pseudocode is intended to be neutral with regard to the final programming language used, the pseudocode for a particular program is often similar in appearance to the final coded program. The chief difference is that pseudocode does not require strict adherence to the syntactical rules of a programming language. Pseudocode provides some graphic representation of a program's structure by indenting the entries of various structures.

Sequence

A sequence is represented by listing a series of instructions at the same margin, as shown in Figure 7.1.

Figure 7.1 (a) Flowchart and (b) pseudocode representing a sequence.

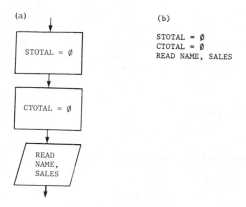

(a)

(b)

```
STOTAL = Ø
CTOTAL = Ø
READ NAME, SALES
```

Loops

Loops are represented by statements that indicate the name of the loop, the type of loop (while or until), and the loop exit decision. The operations to be performed within the loop may immediately follow the statement, and they are indented from the margin. When the operations follow the statement immediately, they are followed by the words END DO or END PERFORM. This method of representing loops is shown in Figure 7.2. The END DO is included for clarity only and does not represent any executable statement.

Loops can also be represented by using the loop statement and then defining the contents of the loop after the program STOP.

Figure 7.2 (a) Flowchart and (b) pseudocode representing a loop.

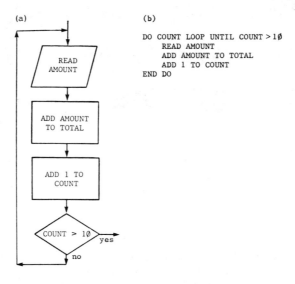

```
DO COUNT LOOP UNTIL COUNT > 1Ø
     READ AMOUNT
     ADD AMOUNT TO TOTAL
     ADD 1 TO COUNT
END DO
```

If-Then-Else

If-then-else is introduced with the word IF and a statement of the condition (such as IF COUNT > 75). The processes to take place when the condition is met are listed after the IF clause and are indented. Processes to be carried out when the condition is not met follow the word ELSE. Finally, the if-then-else is terminated with the words END IF. For a given if-then-else, the words IF, ELSE, and END all begin at the same margin, and the instructions to be carried out are indented. See Figure 7.3.

Figure 7.3 (a) Flowchart and (b) pseudocode representing an if-then-else.

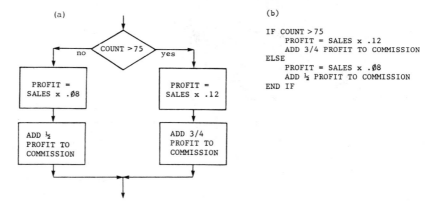

```
IF COUNT > 75
     PROFIT = SALES x .12
     ADD 3/4 PROFIT TO COMMISSION
ELSE
     PROFIT = SALES x .Ø8
     ADD ½ PROFIT TO COMMISSION
END IF
```

In the event that there is no process to be completed when the condition is not met, ELSE is omitted and END IF follows the list of processes. See Figure 7.4.

Figure 7.4 (a) Flowchart and (b) pseudocode representing an if-then.

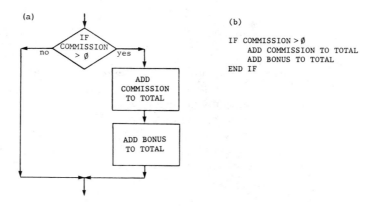

```
IF COMMISSION > Ø
     ADD COMMISSION TO TOTAL
     ADD BONUS TO TOTAL
END IF
```

If there is no process to be completed when the condition is met, the word SKIP or NEXT is used. See Figure 7.5.

Figure 7.5 (a) Flowchart and (b) pseudocode representing an if-then-else that includes SKIP.

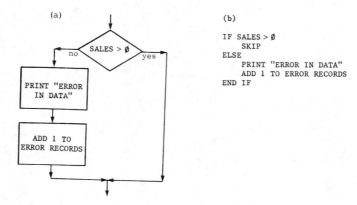

```
(b)

IF SALES > Ø
    SKIP
ELSE
    PRINT "ERROR IN DATA"
    ADD 1 TO ERROR RECORDS
END IF
```

When the if-then-else structure *contains* an if-then-else, an IF and an END or an IF, an ELSE, and an END for each if-then-else are included, and corresponding IF's, ELSE's and END's are aligned to emphasize their logical relationships. See Figure 7.6.

Figure 7.6 (a) Flowchart and (b) pseudocode representing nested if-then-else structures.

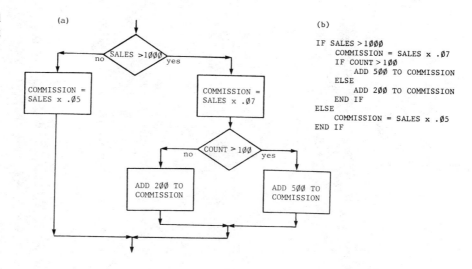

```
(b)

IF SALES > 1ØØØ
    COMMISSION = SALES x .Ø7
    IF COUNT > 1ØØ
        ADD 5ØØ TO COMMISSION
    ELSE
        ADD 2ØØ TO COMMISSION
    END IF
ELSE
    COMMISSION = SALES x .Ø5
END IF
```

The indenting and the alignment of IF, ELSE, and END are also followed when the if-then-else occurs within a loop. This indenting and alignment are shown in Figure 7.7.

Figure 7.7 (a) Flowchart and (b) pseudocode representing an if-then-else occurring within a loop.

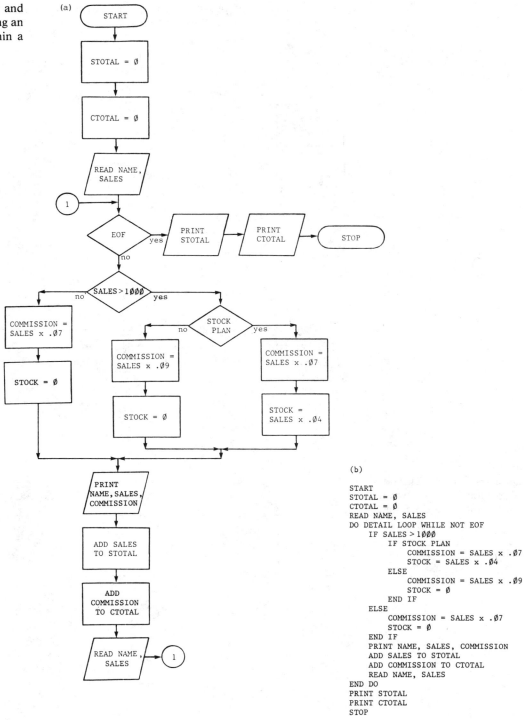

```
(b)
START
STOTAL = Ø
CTOTAL = Ø
READ NAME, SALES
DO DETAIL LOOP WHILE NOT EOF
    IF SALES > 1ØØØ
        IF STOCK PLAN
            COMMISSION = SALES x .Ø7
            STOCK = SALES x .Ø4
        ELSE
            COMMISSION = SALES x .Ø9
            STOCK = Ø
        END IF
    ELSE
        COMMISSION = SALES x .Ø7
        STOCK = Ø
    END IF
    PRINT NAME, SALES, COMMISSION
    ADD SALES TO STOTAL
    ADD COMMISSION TO CTOTAL
    READ NAME, SALES
END DO
PRINT STOTAL
PRINT CTOTAL
STOP
```

The pseudocode instructions for fairly simple programs can be written in the order in which the instructions are to be executed, as in Figure 7.7. But more complex programs are designed by modularizing the pseudocode through the use of predefined processes that are defined after the STOP instruction. The instruction DO _____ or PERFORM _____ indicates the execution of a predefined process.

Figure 7.8 is a modular version of Figure 7.7.

The modular pseudocode technique has all the advantages of the modular flowchart. In particular, modular pseudocode allows the program designer to quickly sketch the broad outlines of a program and complete the details later.

Figure 7.8 A modular version of (a) the flowchart and (b) the pseudocode given in Figure 7.7.

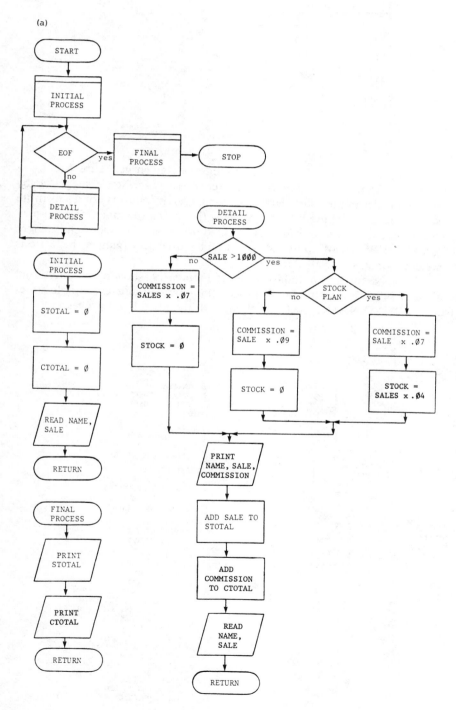

(a)

(b)

```
START
DO INITIAL PROCESS
DO DETAIL PROCESS WHILE NOT EOF
DO FINAL PROCESS
STOP

INITIAL PROCESS
    STOTAL = Ø
    CTOTAL = Ø
    READ NAME, SALES

DETAIL PROCESS
    IF SALES >1ØØØ
        IF STOCK PLAN
            COMMISSION = SALES x .Ø7
            STOCK = SALES x .Ø4
        ELSE
            COMMISSION = SALES x .Ø9
            STOCK = Ø
        END IF
    ELSE
        COMMISSION = SALES x .Ø7
        STOCK = Ø
    END IF
    PRINT NAME, SALES, COMMISSION
    ADD SALES TO STOTAL
    ADD COMMISSION TO CTOTAL
    READ NAME, SALES

FINAL PROCESS
    PRINT STOTAL
    PRINT CTOTAL
```

When pseudocode is modularized, it is frequently accompanied by hierarchy charts. These charts present a picture of a program's hierarchy and of the organization of its predefined processes. Hierarchy charts begin with a rectangle that represents a program's main module. Below this rectangle on the same horizontal line is another rectangle that represents each process mentioned in the main module. Additional levels are added below to represent the processes mentioned in subsequent modules.

Figure 7.9 A hierarchy chart for the pseudocode given in Figure 7.8.

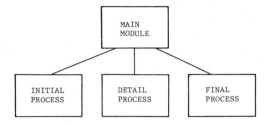

Figure 7.9 is a hierarchy chart for the pseudocode given in Figure 7.8.

The order of execution of the various predefined processes is suggested by their left-to-right order in the chart. However, the hierarchy chart is not a substitute for a flowchart, because the modules at any level (including the main module) may contain executable statements as well as predefined processes. The hierarchy chart is essentially a visual "table of contents" of modules used to organize the various pseudocode components.

Figure 7.10 is a further modularization of Figure 7.9, showing an additional level of hierarchy. Note that the detail process module contains executable statements (such as READ NAME, SALES) along with the predefined processes.

Figure 7.10 A further modularization of Figure 7.9.

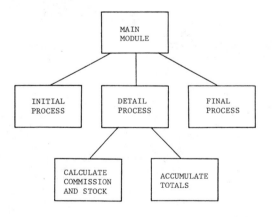

```
START
DO INITIAL PROCESS
DO DETAIL PROCESS WHILE NOT EOF
DO FINAL PROCESS
STOP

INITIAL PROCESS
    STOTAL = Ø
    CTOTAL = Ø
    READ NAME, SALES

DETAIL PROCESS
    DO CALCULATE COMMISSION AND STOCK
    PRINT NAME, SALES, COMMISSION
    DO ACCUMULATE TOTALS
    READ NAME, SALES

FINAL PROCESS
    PRINT STOTAL
    PRINT CTOTAL

CALCULATE COMMISSION AND STOCK
    IF SALES > 1ØØØ
        IF STOCK PLAN
            COMMISSION = SALES x .Ø7
            STOCK = SALES x .Ø4
        ELSE
            COMMISSION = SALES x .Ø9
            STOCK = Ø
        END IF
    ELSE
        COMMISSION = SALES x .Ø7
        STOCK = Ø
    END IF

ACCUMULATE TOTALS
    ADD SALES TO STOTAL
    ADD COMMISSION TO CTOTAL
```

Examples of Pseudocode

Examples 7.1 to 7.6 are pseudocode presentations of programs represented by structured flowcharts in Chapter 4.

Example 7.1

(from Figure 4.3)

```
START
TOTAL = 0
NUMBER = 0
READ AMOUNT
DO READ AND CALCULATE WHILE NOT EOF
    IF AMOUNT > 50
        ADD 1 TO NUMBER
    END IF
    ADD AMOUNT TO TOTAL
    READ AMOUNT
END DO
IF NUMBER > 0
    PRINT NUMBER, "SALES OVER $50."
ELSE
    PRINT "NO SALES OVER $50."
END IF
PRINT TOTAL
STOP
```

Example 7.2

(from Figure 4.4)

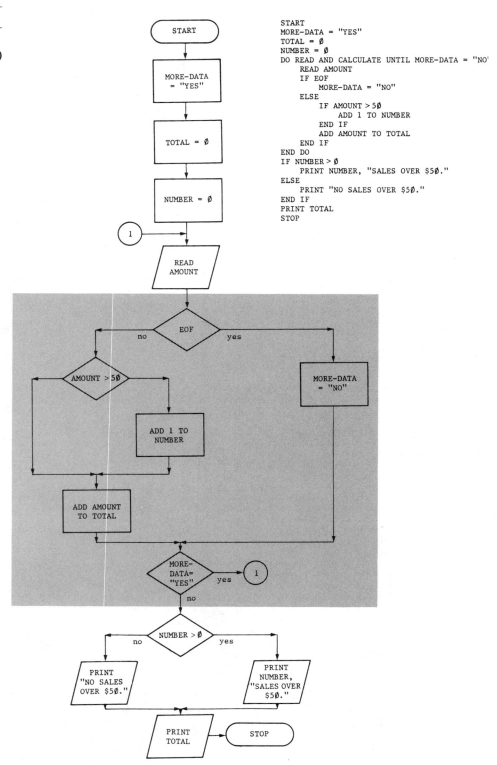

```
START
MORE-DATA = "YES"
TOTAL = Ø
NUMBER = Ø
DO READ AND CALCULATE UNTIL MORE-DATA = "NO"
    READ AMOUNT
    IF EOF
        MORE-DATA = "NO"
    ELSE
        IF AMOUNT > 5Ø
            ADD 1 TO NUMBER
        END IF
        ADD AMOUNT TO TOTAL
    END IF
END DO
IF NUMBER > Ø
    PRINT NUMBER, "SALES OVER $5Ø."
ELSE
    PRINT "NO SALES OVER $5Ø."
END IF
PRINT TOTAL
STOP
```

Example 7.3

(from Figure 4.7)

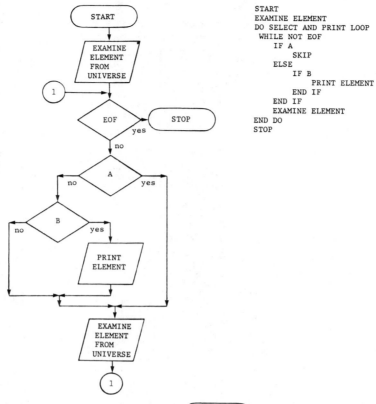

```
START
EXAMINE ELEMENT
DO SELECT AND PRINT LOOP
 WHILE NOT EOF
    IF A
        SKIP
    ELSE
        IF B
            PRINT ELEMENT
        END IF
    END IF
    EXAMINE ELEMENT
END DO
STOP
```

Example 7.4

(from Figure 4.8)

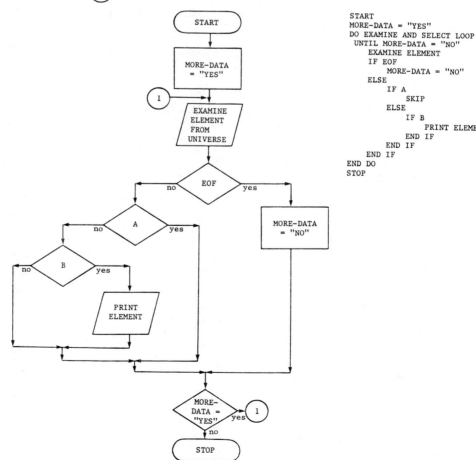

```
START
MORE-DATA = "YES"
DO EXAMINE AND SELECT LOOP
 UNTIL MORE-DATA = "NO"
    EXAMINE ELEMENT
    IF EOF
        MORE-DATA = "NO"
    ELSE
        IF A
            SKIP
        ELSE
            IF B
                PRINT ELEMENT
            END IF
        END IF
    END IF
END DO
STOP
```

Example 7.5

(from Figure 4.9)

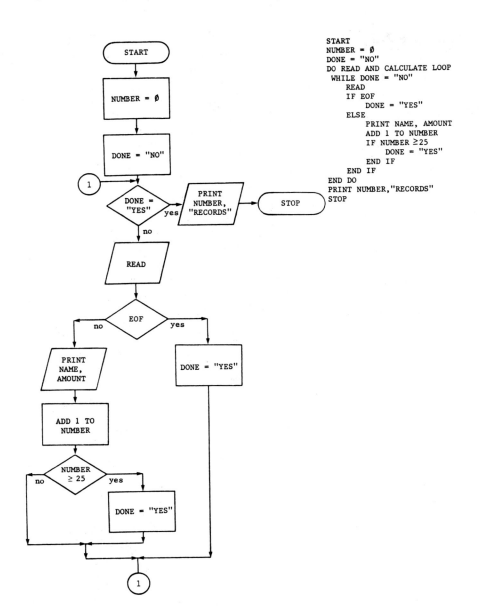

```
START
NUMBER = Ø
DONE = "NO"
DO READ AND CALCULATE LOOP
  WHILE DONE = "NO"
      READ
      IF EOF
          DONE = "YES"
      ELSE
          PRINT NAME, AMOUNT
          ADD 1 TO NUMBER
          IF NUMBER ≥25
              DONE = "YES"
          END IF
      END IF
END DO
PRINT NUMBER,"RECORDS"
STOP
```

Example 7.6

Example 7.6 is a modular version of Figure 4.16.

```
START
TOTAL = Ø
READ NAME, AMOUNT
DO DETAIL LOOP WHILE NOT EOF
PRINT TOTAL
STOP

DETAIL LOOP
    PRINT NAME
    ATOTAL = Ø
    OLDNAME = NAME
    NAMEBREAK = "NO"
    DO PROCESS AND READ WHILE NAMEBREAK = "NO"
    PRINT ATOTAL
END DETAIL LOOP

PROCESS AND READ
    ADD AMOUNT TO ATOTAL
    ADD AMOUNT TO TOTAL
    READ NAME, AMOUNT
    IF EOF
        NAMEBREAK = "YES"
    ELSE
        IF OLDNAME = NAME
            SKIP
        ELSE
            NAMEBREAK = "YES"
        END IF
    END IF
END PROCESS AND READ
```

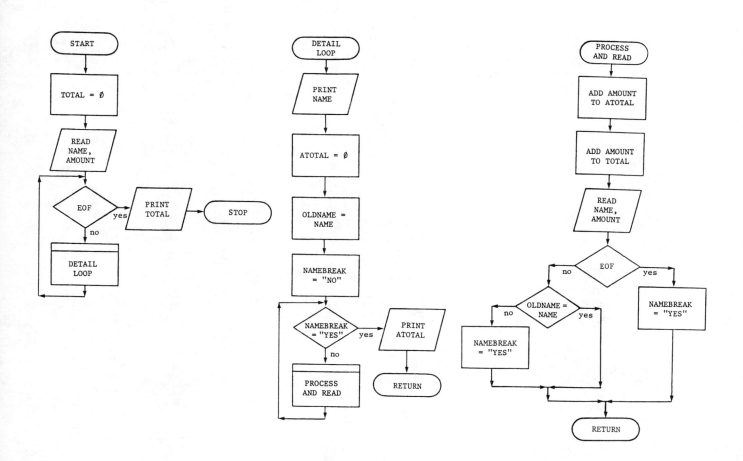

Exercises 7.1

1. Use a structured flowchart to represent each of the following examples of pseudocode.

a. START
    TOTAL = 0
    1COUNT = 0
    GTOTAL = 0
    CCOUNT = 0
    READ NAME, DIV, SALE ____
    DO DETAIL LOOP WHILE EOF
        PRINT NAME SALE
        ADD 1 TO CCOUNT
        ADD SALE TO GTOTAL
        IF DIV = 1
            ADD SALE TO TOTAL
            ADD 1 TO 1COUNT
        END IF
        READ NAME, DIV, SALE
    END DO
    PRINT "DIV 1 TOTAL", TOTAL
    PRINT "DIV 1 COUNT", 1COUNT
    PRINT "TOTAL SALES", GTOT
    PRINT "COMPANY COUNT", COUNT
    STOP

b. START
    TOTAL = 0
    X = 1
    DO ROW LOOP UNTIL X > 10
        Y = 1
        DO COLUMN LOOP UNTIL Y > 20
            Z = X + Y
            TOTAL = TOTAL + Z
            PRINT Z
            Y = Y + 1
        END DO
        X = X + 1
    END DO
    PRINT TOTAL
    STOP

c.   START
    OPEN FILES
    DO INITIAL PROCESS
    DO DETAIL PROCESS UNTIL EOF
    DO FINAL PROCESS
    CLOSE FILES
    STOP
    INITIAL PROCESS
        TOTAL = 0
        COUNT = 0
        FLAG = "NO"
    DETAIL PROCESS
        READ NAME, GRADE
        IF EOF
            SKIP
        ELSE
            PRINT NAME
            ADD GRADE TO TOTAL
            ADD 1 TO COUNT
            IF GRADE > 100
                FLAG = "YES"
            END IF
        END IF
    FINAL PROCESS
        IF COUNT > 0
            AVG = TOTAL ÷ COUNT
            PRINT AVG
            IF FLAG = "YES"
                PRINT "DATA ERROR"
            END IF
        ELSE
            PRINT "NO DATA"
        END IF

d.
```
    START
    DO INITIAL PROCESS
    DO DETAIL PROCESS WHILE NOT EOF
    DO FINAL PROCESS
    STOP

    INITIAL PROCESS
        TOTAL = 0
        ATOTAL = 0
        N = 0
        READ NAME, AMOUNT
    END INITIAL PROCESS

    DETAIL PROCESS
        DO CONTROL BREAK
        ADD AMOUNT TO TOTAL
        ADD AMOUNT TO ATOTAL
        ADD 1 TO N
        READ NAME, AMOUNT
    END DETAIL PROCESS
```

```
    FINAL PROCESS
        PRINT ATOTAL
        PRINT TOTAL
        PRINT N
    END FINAL PROCESS

    CONTROL BREAK
        IF FIRST RECORD
            PRINT NAME
            OLDNAME = NAME
        ELSE
            IF OLDNAME ≠ NAME
                DO NEW NAME PROCESS
            END IF
        END IF
    END CONTROL BREAK

    NEW NAME PROCESS
        PRINT ATOTAL
        ATOTAL = 0
        PRINT NAME
        OLDNAME = NAME
    END NEW NAME PROCESS
```

2. Represent each of the following flowcharts with pseudocode.

a.

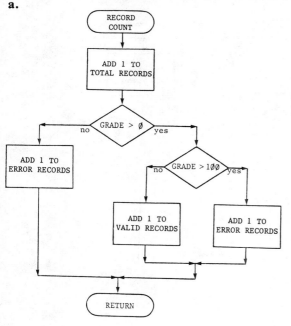

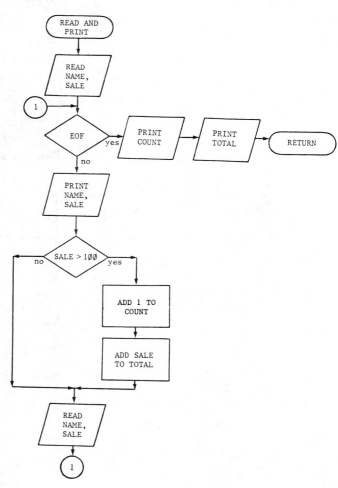

c.

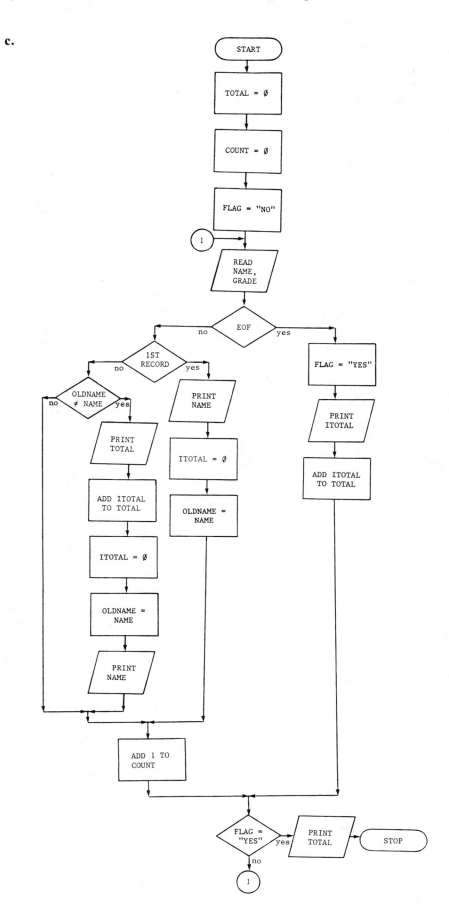

d.

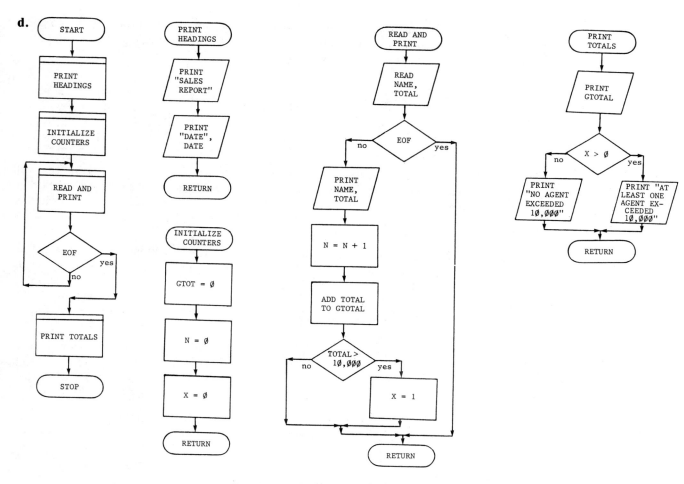

e. Provide a hierarchy chart for the pseudocode you wrote for part d.

3. Provide pseudocode specifications using do-while loops for a program that will read SALES from each record, print each sales amount, and print the total of the amounts.

4. Provide pseudocode specifications using do-until loops for a program that will read NAME and SALES from each record and print the name and sales amount from each. It is also to print the total of the amounts and a single message that indicates whether or not any amount exceeds 2000.

5. Provide pseudocode specifications using do-while loops for a program that will read names and amounts from records sorted by name. Each name is to be printed once (even though it may occur on several records). The total of the amounts and the number of different names are also to be printed.

6. Provide pseudocode specifications using do-until loops for a program that will read names and amounts from records sorted by name. Each name is to be printed once, along with the total of that individual's amounts. The total of all amounts is also to be printed.

7. Provide pseudocode specifications using do-while loops for a program that will examine a universe and print the names of the members of the sets indicated by the areas shaded in the following Venn diagrams.

a. 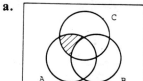 **b.** 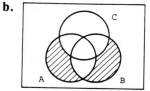 **c.**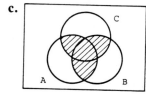

8. Provide pseudocode specifications using do-until loops for a program to print, in the corresponding columns, the names of the members of the sets indicated by numerals in the following Venn diagrams.

a.   b.   c.

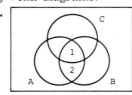

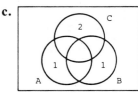

9. Provide pseudocode specifications using do-while loops for a program that will read records that contain names, division numbers, years employed, stock plan membership, and sales amounts. The program is to determine and print whether the average sales in Division 5 exceeded the average sales of those in the stock plan who have been employed more than 10 years.

10. Provide pseudocode specifications using do-while loops for a program to calculate the values and totals required to complete the following table, using the equation $z = 2x + y$.

x \ y	1	4	7	10	TOTAL
-1					
-3					
-5					
-7					
-9					
-11					

7.2

Nassi-Shneiderman Diagrams[1]

Nassi-Shneiderman diagrams are structured design tools created by dividing a page with lines and making appropriate entries in the resulting areas. Figure 7.11 is presented to provide a "picture" of a Nassi-Shneiderman diagram. Its details will be explained in subsequent paragraphs. The Nassi-Shneiderman diagram is read from top to bottom and from left to right. Figure 7.11 would be understood as follows:

1. The program starts with an initial process consisting of setting both STOTAL and CTOTAL at 0 and then executing a READ.

2. After the initial process, a detail loop is repeated while not at the end of the file. Within the detail loop:
   a. Decisions based on SALES > 1000 and STOCK PLAN determine commissions and stock to be calculated.
   b. NAME, SALES, and COMMISSION are printed.
   c. STOTAL and CTOTAL are incremented.
   d. NAME and SALES are read.

3. After the detail loop, a final process consisting of printing totals occurs.

Like other structured design tools, Nassi-Shneiderman diagrams can best be understood in terms of the way they represent sequences, loops, and if-then-else. In addition to these formal structures, Nassi-Shneiderman diagrams conveniently represent universals.

[1] Named after I. Nassi and B. Shneiderman and reported in "Flowchart Techniques for Structured Programming," *Sigplan Notices*, August 1973, pp. 12–26.

Figure 7.11 A Nassi-Shneiderman diagram.

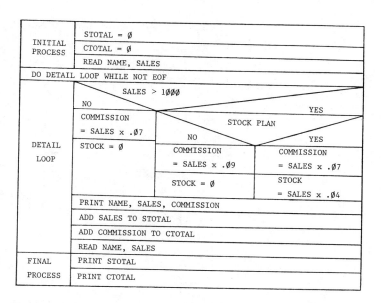

Sequence

Sequence is represented by entries separated by horizontal lines. See Figure 7.12.

Figure 7.12 (a) Flowchart, (b) Nassi-Shneiderman diagram, and (c) Warnier diagram representing sequence.

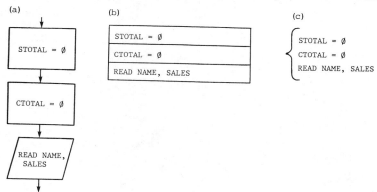

Universals

Universals are represented as marginal notations placed to the left of the process that they name. See Figure 7.13.

Figure 7.13 (a) Flowchart, (b) Nassi-Shneiderman diagram, and (c) Warnier diagram representing a universal.

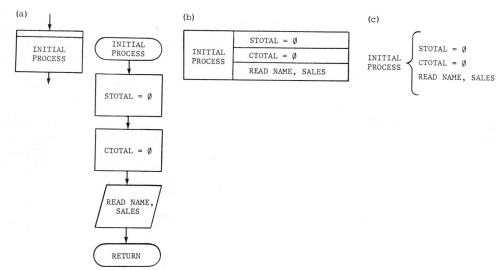

Universals can also occur within other structures. Figure 7.14 depicts a universal within a sequence.

Figure 7.14 (a) Flowchart, (b) Nassi-Shneiderman diagram, and (c) Warnier diagram representing a universal within a sequence.

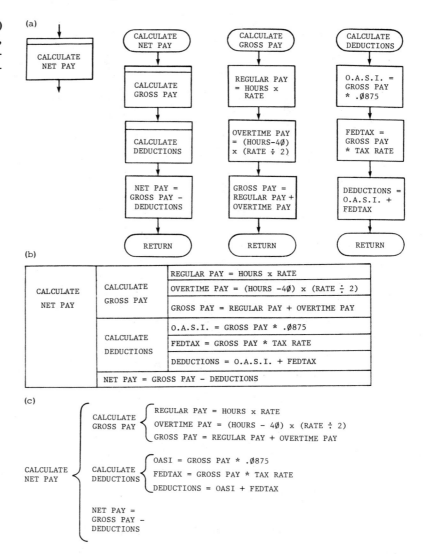

If-Then-Else

If-then-else is represented by a rectangle divided into three triangles. The top center triangle specifies the condition; the triangles on either side specify the alternatives. Rectangles below the side triangles indicate the operations to be carried out under the alternatives. See Figure 7.15.

Figure 7.15 (a) Flowchart and (b) Nassi-Shneiderman diagram representing an if-then-else.

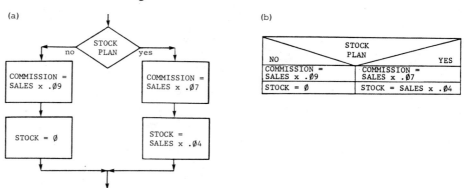

Nested Decisions

Nested decisions are written within a rectangle below an alternative of a prior decision. See Figure 7.16.

Figure 7.16 (a) Flowchart, (b) Nassi-Shneiderman diagram, and (c) Warnier diagram representing a nested if-then-else.

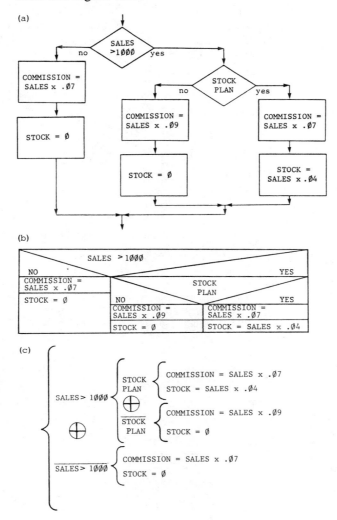

Case

Case is represented by a rectangle similar to that used for an if-then-else. Typically, one of its triangles contains all of the correct possibilities and the other contains a default condition. As with if-then-else, rectangles below the triangles indicate the operations to be completed. Figure 7.17 anticipates that the only correct codes are 1, 2, and 3. The "other" branch is added so that the program can continue in the event that erroneous data has been entered.

Figure 7.17 (a) Flowchart and (b) Nassi-Shneiderman diagram representing case.

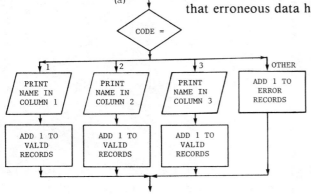

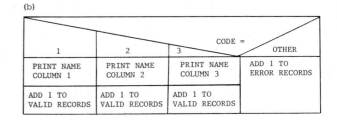

Loops

Loops are indicated in a rectangle that names the loop, indicates the type of loop, and indicates the loop exit decision. Typical expressions are DO DETAIL LOOP WHILE NOT EOF and PERFORM CALCULATE TOTALS UNTIL EOF.[2] The name and details of the loops may be specified immediately after the DO _____ or PERFORM _____ instruction, as in Figures 7.18 and 7.11, or they may be placed after the STOP, as in Figure 7.19.

Figure 7.18 (a) Flowchart, (b) Nassi-Shneiderman diagram, and (c) Warnier diagram wherein the name and details of a loop are specified immediately after the DO or PERFORM instruction.

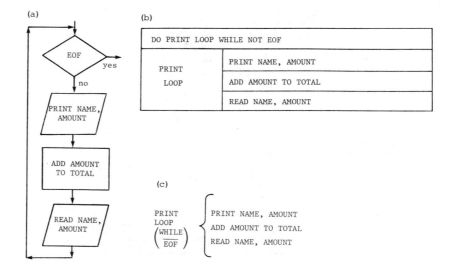

Figure 7.19 shows that any or all of a program's processes can be assigned a universal and specified after the STOP. The simple instruction DO _____ is used to indicate when each process is to be completed.

Figure 7.19 Nassi-Shneiderman diagram wherein the names and details of loops are placed after the STOP.

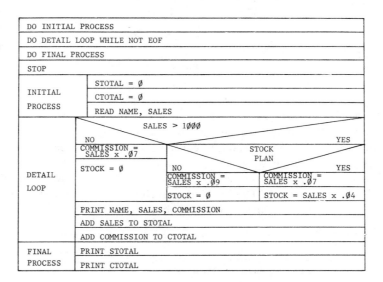

---

[2] PERFORM is often used when the intended programming language is COBOL. But the PERFORM-UNTIL instruction of COBOL is a do-while loop, not a do-until loop.

Examples of Nassi-Shneiderman Diagrams

Examples 7.7 to 7.12 are Nassi-Shneiderman diagrams of the same examples from
Chapter 4 that were used to demonstrate pseudocode. Example 7.13 is taken from
Figure 6.17.

Example 7.7

(from Figure 4.3)

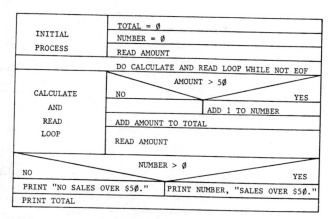

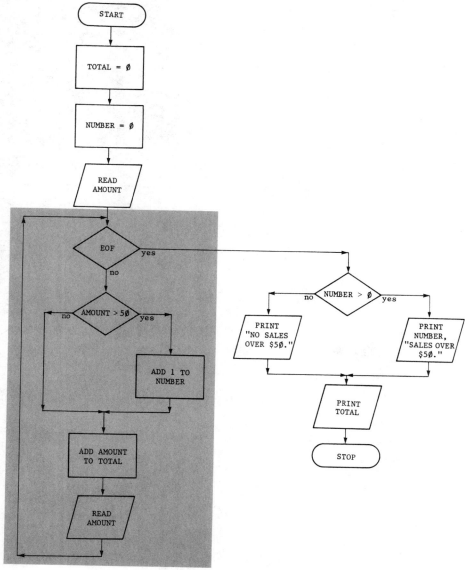

Example 7.8

(from Figure 4.4)

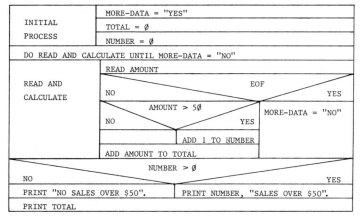

INITIAL PROCESS	MORE-DATA = "YES"		
	TOTAL = Ø		
	NUMBER = Ø		
DO READ AND CALCULATE UNTIL MORE-DATA = "NO"			
READ AND CALCULATE	READ AMOUNT		
	NO EOF YES		
	AMOUNT > 5Ø		MORE-DATA = "NO"
	NO YES		
		ADD 1 TO NUMBER	
	ADD AMOUNT TO TOTAL		
NUMBER > Ø			
NO YES			
PRINT "NO SALES OVER $50".	PRINT NUMBER, "SALES OVER $50".		
PRINT TOTAL			

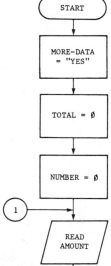

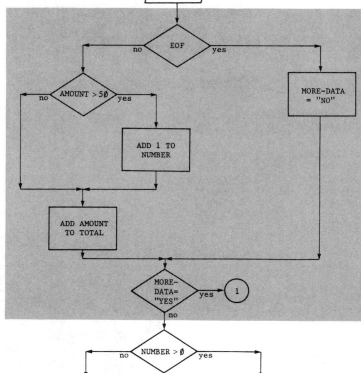

Example 7.9

(from Figure 4.7)

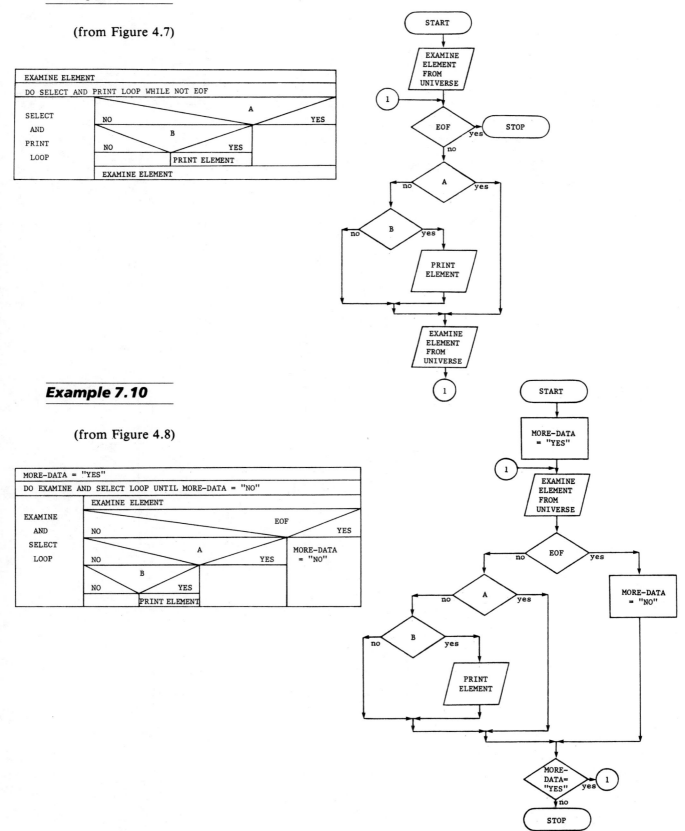

Example 7.11

(from Figure 4.9)

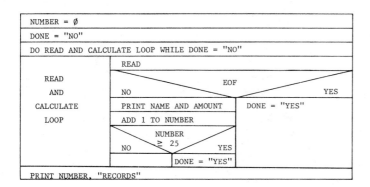

NUMBER = Ø			
DONE = "NO"			
DO READ AND CALCULATE LOOP WHILE DONE = "NO"			
READ AND CALCULATE LOOP	READ		
	NO ⟋ EOF ⟍ YES		
	PRINT NAME AND AMOUNT	DONE = "YES"	
	ADD 1 TO NUMBER		
	NO ⟋ NUMBER ≥ 25 ⟍ YES		
		DONE = "YES"	
PRINT NUMBER, "RECORDS"			

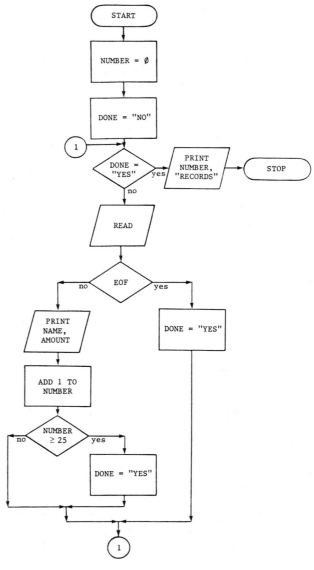

Example 7.12

Example 7.12 is a modular version of Figure 4.16.

CONTROL MODULE	TOTAL = Ø
	READ NAME, AMOUNT
	DO DETAIL LOOP WHILE NOT EOF
	PRINT TOTAL
	STOP
DETAIL LOOP	PRINT NAME
	ATOTAL = Ø
	OLDNAME = NAME
	NAMEBREAK = "NO"
	DO PROCESS AND READ WHILE NAMEBREAK = "NO"
	PRINT ATOTAL

PROCESS AND READ	ADD AMOUNT TO TOTAL			
	ADD AMOUNT TO ATOTAL			
	READ NAME, AMOUNT			
	EOF			
	NO			YES
	OLDNAME = NAME			NAMEBREAK = "YES"
	NO		YES	
	NAMEBREAK = "YES"			

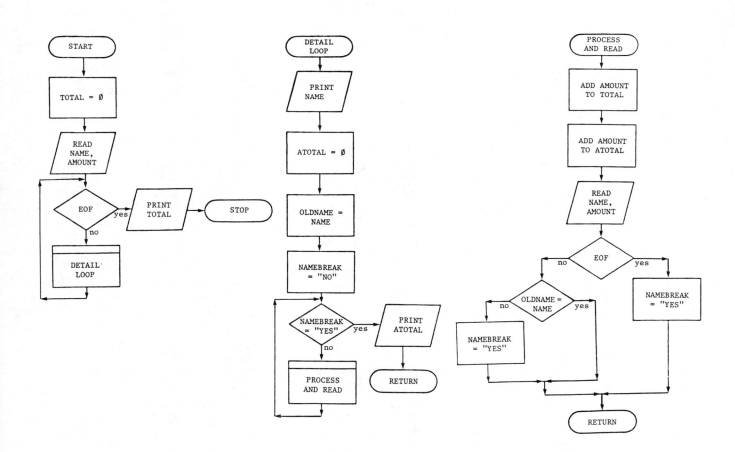

Example 7.13

INITIALIZE COUNTERS, ETC.	X = Ø	
	Y = Ø	
	TOT = Ø	
	LTOT = Ø	
	HTOT = Ø	
READ NAME, AMT		
PERFORM PRINT AND CALCULATE TOTALS WHILE E̅O̅F̅		
CALCULATE AVERAGES	HIGH-AVG = HTOT/X	
	LOW-AVG = LTOT/Y	
	AVG = TOT/(X+Y)	
PRINT TOTALS	PRINT "HIGH TOTAL", HTOT, "HIGH AVG", HIGH-AVG	
	PRINT "LOW TOTAL", LTOT, "LOW AVG", LOW-AVG	
	PRINT "TOTAL", TOT, "AVERAGE", AVERAGE	
	STOP	
PRINT AND CALCULATE TOTALS	PRINT NAME, AMT	
	AMT > 5ØØØ	
	NO	YES
	COM = AMT x .Ø7	COM = AMT x .1
	PRINT COM	PRINT COM
	LTOT = LTOT + AMT	HTOT = HTOT + AMT
	TOT = TOT + AMT	TOT = TOT + AMT
	Y = Y + 1	X = X + 1
	READ NAME, AMT	

(a)

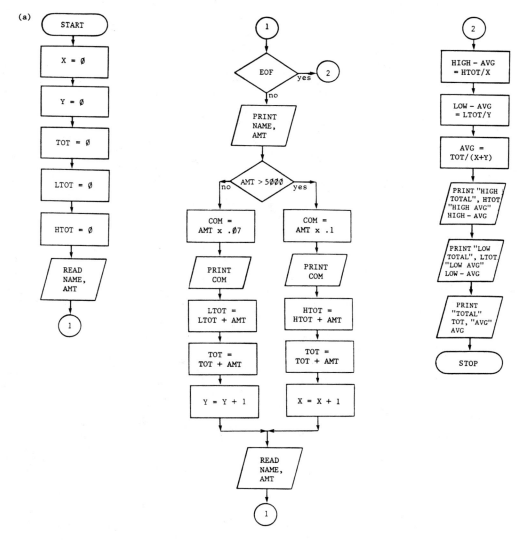

Exercises 7.2

1. Use a structured flowchart to represent each of the following Nassi-Shneiderman diagrams.

a.

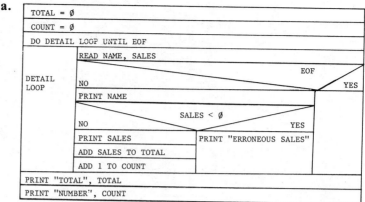

b.

c.

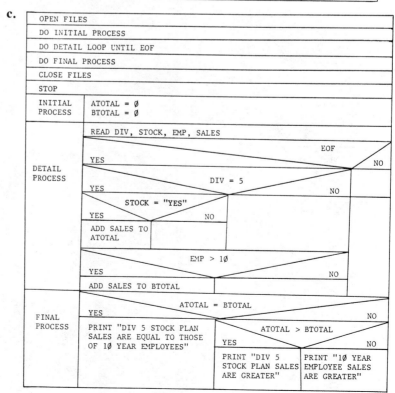

d.

INITIAL PROCESS	OPEN FILES
	READ NAME, SALES

DO DETAIL LOOP WHILE NOT EOF			

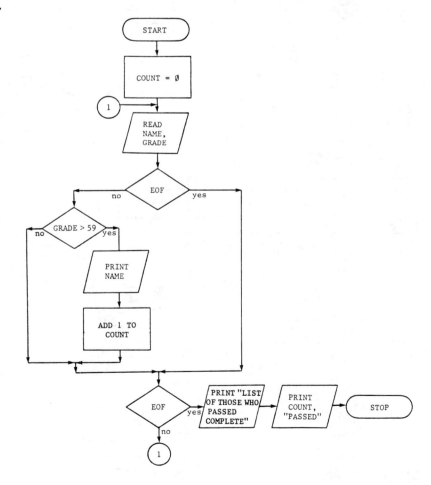

2. Design a Nassi-Shneiderman diagram for each of the following flowcharts.
   a.

b.

c.

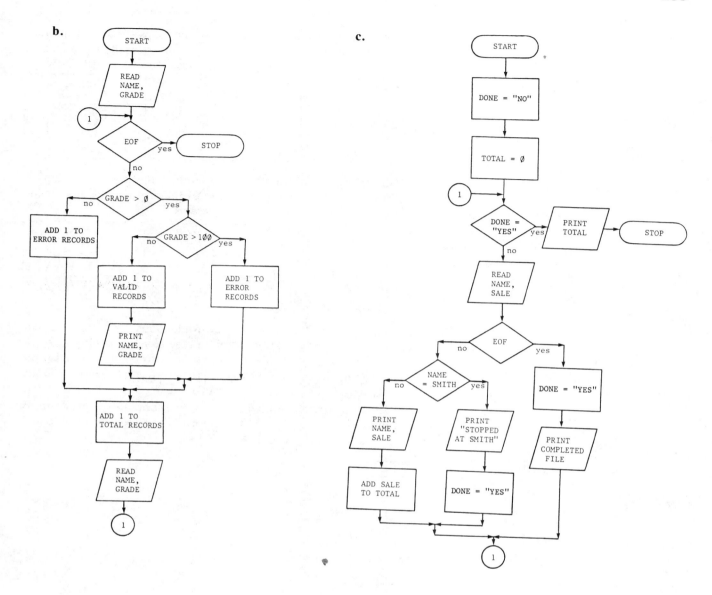

3. Provide Nassi-Shneiderman diagrams using do-while loops for a program that will read SALES from each record, print each sales amount, and print the total of the amounts.

4. Provide Nassi-Shneiderman diagrams using do-until loops for a program that will read NAME and SALES from each record and print the names and sales amounts from each. It is also to print the total of the amounts and a single message that indicates whether or not any amount exceeds 2000.

5. Provide Nassi-Shneiderman diagrams using do-while loops for a program that will read names and amounts from records sorted by name. Each name is to be printed once (even though it may occur on several records). The total of the amounts and the number of different names are also to be printed.

6. Provide Nassi-Shneiderman diagrams using do-until loops for a program that will read names and amounts from records sorted by name. Each name is to be printed once, along with the total of that individual's amounts. The total of all amounts is also to be printed.

7. Provide Nassi-Shneiderman diagrams using do-while loops for a program that will examine a universe and print the names of the members of the sets indicated by the areas shaded in the following Venn diagrams.

a. 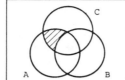   b. 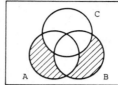   c.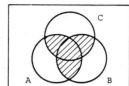

8. Provide Nassi-Shneiderman diagrams using do-until loops for a program to print, in the corresponding columns, the names of the members of the sets indicated by numerals in the following Venn diagrams.

a. 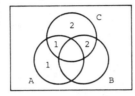   b. 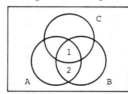   c.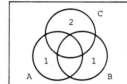

9. Provide Nassi-Shneiderman diagrams using do-while loops for a program that will read records that contain names, division numbers, years employed, stock plan membership, and sales amounts. The program is to determine and print whether the average sales in Division 5 exceeded the average sales of those in the stock plan who have been employed more than 10 years.

10. Provide Nassi-Shneiderman diagrams using do-while loops for a program to calculate the values and totals required to complete the following table, using the equation $z = 2x + y$.

x \ y	1	4	7	1Ø	TOTAL
−1					
−3					
−5					
−7					
−9					
−11					

Review Questions

Completion

1. Pseudocode is written in a _____ language rather than in a _____ language.
2. The final entry in a pseudocode do-until loop is _____ or _____.
3. Pseudocode defines predefined processes after the _____.
4. The details of a loop in a Nassi-Shneiderman diagram may be specified immediately after _____, or they may be placed after _____.

True or False

1. _____ Pseudocode is intended to be neutral with regard to the final programming language used.

2. _____ Pseudocode provides no graphic representation of a computer program.

3. _____ In pseudocode, END DO represents an executable statement.

4. _____ Pseudocode indents an ELSE more than the corresponding IF.

5. _____ In pseudocode, the end of an ELSE statement is marked by the words END ELSE.

6. _____ In pseudocode, each IF requires a corresponding ELSE.

7. _____ Nassi-Shneiderman diagrams are structured design tools.

8. _____ Nassi-Shneiderman diagrams do not permit the use of nested decisions.

8. Arrays and Array Processing

In many programs it is necessary to store a large amount of data for processing and to have that data available throughout the program. An example of such a program is one that would determine which of the sales amounts read from 100 records was greater than the average of those sales amounts. To complete this program, each sales amount would have to be used at two different times during the program: once to calculate the average and once to be compared with the average. The total and the number of sales might be calculated as the records are read, but comparison of each sale amount with the average would require that the sales amounts be stored until after that average had been calculated.

To design such a program using methods we have discussed so far, we would have to create a separate variable name for each piece of data. To process 100 items we would need 100 variable names, 100 input statements, and 100 different statements for each separate process involving those variables. Arrays provide a more efficient approach to this problem by assigning a single variable name to many different storage locations and then referring to each individual location by a numeric subscript. Such an array not only eliminates the need for separate variable names for each piece of data, but it also achieves considerable program efficiency through the use of variables as subscripts.

8.1 Fundamental Array Structures

We have thought of variables as names of locations in which values may be stored, with each location having its own name. **Arrays** differ in that they are composed of a series of locations designated by a single name; that is, one array name designates several different storage locations. Each individual location is further specified by a parenthetical numeric designation called a **subscript**. For example, COST(1), COST(2), and COST(75) would name individual storage locations within the COST( ) array. If we were designing a program to process monthly profits, we could set aside 12 locations called PROFIT( ). We would then store January's profit at PROFIT(1), February's profit at PROFIT(2), and so on (see Table 8.1). The information stored at each location is called an **array element.**

Table 8.1 A monthly profit array.

PROFIT (1)	→ → → → → → → →	2179
PROFIT (2)	→ → → → → → → →	4361
PROFIT (3)	→ → → → → → → →	8219
PROFIT (4)	→ → → → → → → →	7946
PROFIT (5)	→ → → → → → → →	9139
PROFIT (6)	→ → → → → → → →	9393
PROFIT (7)	→ → → → → → → →	9745
PROFIT (8)	→ → → → → → → →	6842
PROFIT (9)	→ → → → → → → →	8317
PROFIT (10)	→ → → → → → → →	9413
PROFIT (11)	→ → → → → → → →	8971
PROFIT (12)	→ → → → → → → →	7891
Array Element Names	Array Elements	

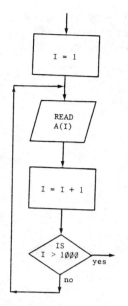

Figure 8.1 A program that loads an array with 1000 items.

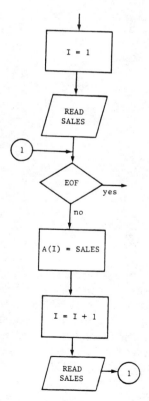

Figure 8.2 A program that loads an array while not at end of file.

PROFIT( ) is the general name for this 12-element array. The subscripts (the numerals in parentheses) indicate the various individual locations where the elements (four-digit numerals, in this example) are stored.

Array Processing

The fundamental structure used to process each element of an array is a loop in which the array subscript is identified by a variable. This variable is initialized before control enters the loop and is incremented each time through the loop. Such a loop processes different members of the array as the subscript is incremented. Figures 8.1 and 8.2 are for a program that reads a sales amount from each record and stores that information in an array. Such a program is called "loading an array."[1]

The program represented by Figure 8.1 initializes an array subscript (I), reads a first record, and stores its value at A(1). The value of the subscript is then increased by 1 so that it will be 2 when the second record is read. The value from the second record will be stored at A(2). The third value will be stored at A(3), and so on.

Figure 8.2 represents a program that uses EOF as a loop exit decision. It, too, reads records and stores values at different array locations as I is incremented. But Figure 8.2 does not load data into the array as the records are read. Instead, it temporarily stores data at a location called SALES. An individual array location is loaded only after the EOF decision is negative. When the decision is affirmative, nothing is loaded into the array. This procedure of temporarily storing the data avoids loading an array location with data from the EOF record. Loading data from the EOF record should be avoided, even if nothing but blanks would be loaded. Otherwise, throughout the program there will be one array element that should not be processed, counted, averaged, and so on.

Note that both of the examples initialize the subscript (I) before control enters their loops. Both read a record, store a value, and then increment the subscript before reading the next record. If the subscript (I) were initialized within the loop, or if it were not properly incremented, the program would store each value at A(1) and only the last value read would be retained. It is through the use of an incremented variable subscript that all of A(1), A(2), A(3). . . get used.

Figure 8.1 is less flexible than Figure 8.2, because it must read exactly 1000 records. It could be replaced by a flowchart that did not use an array and stored each sales amount under a different variable instead. But a flowchart that did not use an array (or a similar structure) would be approximately 1000 times as long as Figure 8.1. Figure 8.2 could not be replaced by a flowchart that did not use an array (or some equivalent structure).

In addition to efficiency, one of the chief advantages of arrays is that data may be stored for later use. When arrays are used, all data is often read and stored before any other processing takes place. In such cases the individual pieces of data are retained throughout processing and are available for use at any time during the program. A typical program without arrays reads one piece of data and completes processing of that piece before reading the next piece of data. Figure 1.22 is a good example of such a program. Notice that, in it, all processing is done for one value before the next value is read. Compare Figure 1.22 with Figure 8.3. Figure 8.3 loads all data (its first loop) before making any calculations. Then it retains its data throughout the program. As flowcharted, both of these programs produce the same

---

[1] Many authors use the expression "read an array." "Load an array" is used here because arrays are often loaded without the use of a READ statement.

result. But Figure 8.3 could be augmented by instructions to compare various pieces of data, whereas Figure 1.22 could not. We could, for example, add to Figure 8.3 a loop that would sort the pieces of data and print them in a numerical order. This could not be done practically by a program without arrays.

Figure 8.3 Flowchart containing both a dimension statement and a counter.

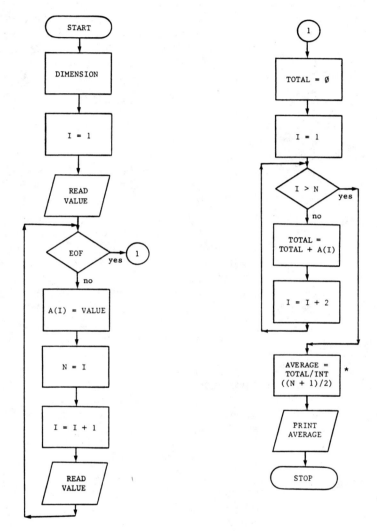

8.2 Dimension Statements and Counters

Before allowing the use of an array in a program, many languages require a dimension statement. The **dimension statement** instructs the computer to set a particular number of locations aside for a particular array. It is not necessary that all locations that are set aside actually be used. But the value of variable subscript(s) may not exceed the number of spaces set aside. We will not be concerned with how dimension statements are expressed in particular languages. Instead, we will indicate dimension statements by a processing symbol with the word DIMENSION or DIM.

---

* TOTAL is divided by the integer value of $(N + 1)/2$. Note that this will always be the number of odd-numbered values read. $INT((N - 1)/2 + .5)$ would be the number of even-numbered values read.

Counters are frequently used in loops that process arrays. Often the array subscript could serve this function. But array subscripts are frequently used to control the repetition of a loop (as in Figure 8.1). In such cases the subscript is a dependable counter within the loop, but it is not reliable when control passes from the loop.[2] That is, the variable subscript that eventually causes control to pass from a loop may not accurately record the number of times that the loop was completed. So a separate counter is used when the number of loaded elements or loop repetitions will be needed later in the program. This counter often takes the form N = I (where I is the variable subscript) and is placed after the process to be counted and before I is incremented. Such a counter also has the advantage of retaining a count of the number of items in the array while I is used as a subscript in a different loop.

Figure 8.3 includes both a dimension statement and a counter (even though I could be used as a counter).

8.3 Array Element Names Used as Variables

Array element names can be used in programs in all the ways that variables can. If, for example, we wanted to add the value stored at PROFIT(10) to TOTAL, we would simply place TOTAL = TOTAL + PROFIT(10) in a process symbol. Similarly, PROFIT(10) = PROFIT(9) placed in a decision symbol asks whether the values stored at the ninth and tenth locations of the PROFIT( ) array are equal. The instruction PROFIT(I) = M placed in a process symbol indicates that the computer is to determine the value stored at M, determine the value stored at I, use the value stored at I to determine which location of the PROFIT( ) array is being addressed, and store M's value at that PROFIT( ) location.

It is important to remember the distinction between the array subscript and a particular array element. The subscript identifies the location in the array at which the element is stored. The element is the value stored at the location designated. So the value of I in PROFIT(I) tells which location is being addressed; it does not tell what value is stored there.

Array subscripts may generally be indicated by any legitimate arithmetic expressions that designate positive integers. These subscripts are called **computed subscripts**. For example, $(J - K)$ is a computed subscript in the array element name $A(J - K)$. The expression $M = A(J - K)$ would cause the value of K to be subtracted from the value of J; the result would identify the element of array A( ) whose value would be stored at M. Figure 8.4 makes use of a computed subscript. It represents a program to read names and then print them in two side-by-side lists, one list in reverse order.

When Figure 8.4 first reaches the print symbol, I will be 1 and M will be one more than the number of items. At this point, the first and last items will be printed. The second time the print symbol is reached, I will be 2. So the second and the next-to-last items will be printed. As I increases, $M - I$ decreases so that, when I reaches N, the last item will be printed next to the first (because $M - N = 1$). Note also that $M - I$ will be a positive integer throughout the print loop.

---

[2] This is not true of every language, but we assume that our programs will eventually be written in a language of which it is true.

Figure 8.4 Flowchart that makes use of a computed subscript.

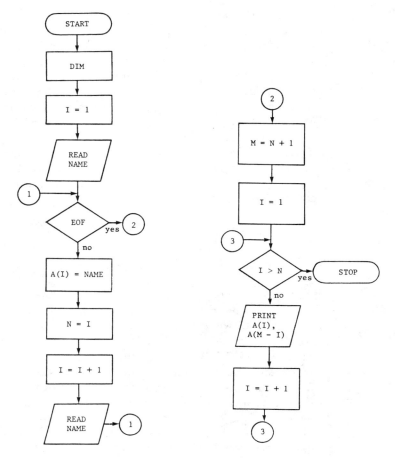

Table 8.2 represents the elements of the array PROFIT( ), together with other values. The examples following Table 8.2 show which elements are identified by various element names.

Table 8.2 Computer storage, including the array PROFIT( ).

473.61	583.27	749.13	316.79	586.24	796.18
PROFIT(1)	PROFIT(2)	PROFIT(3)	PROFIT(4)	PROFIT(5)	PROFIT(6)

1	2	4	6	3	5
I	J	K	L	M	N

Array Element Name	Array Element
PROFIT(J + K)	796.18
PROFIT(K − M)	473.61
PROFIT(K − 2)	583.27
PROFIT(L/J)	749.13
PROFIT((N + I)/J)	749.13
PROFIT(J × M)	796.18

Exercises 8.1–8.3

1. Determine which elements, if any, will be loaded in the various array locations by the following programs. Assume that the programs will read the card files presented below.

a.

START

DIM

I = 1

READ NAME

A

EOF — yes → 1

no

A(I) = NAME

I = I + 1

READ NAME

A

b.

START

DIM

I = 1

READ AMOUNT

B

I > 1Ø — yes → 2

no

A(I) = AMOUNT

I = I + 2

READ AMOUNT

B

A(1)	A(2)	A(3)	A(4)	A(5)	A(6)
A(7)	A(8)	A(9)	A(1Ø)	A(11)	A(12)

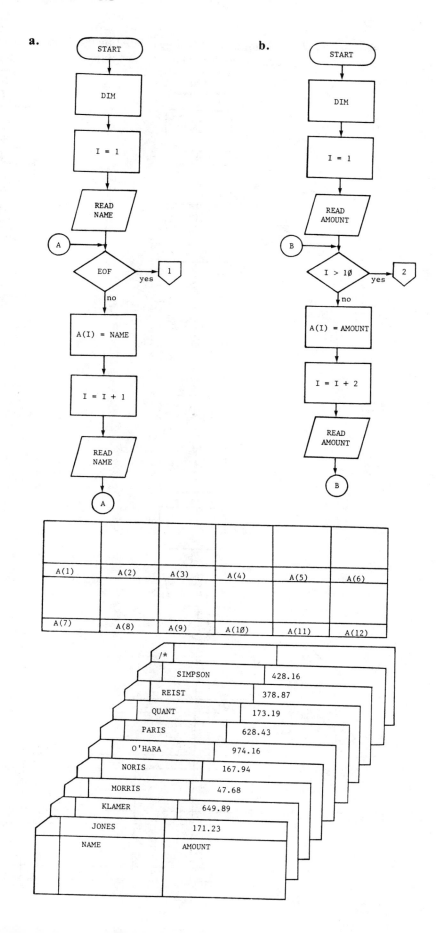

/*

SIMPSON	428.16
REIST	378.87
QUANT	173.19
PARIS	628.43
O'HARA	974.16
NORIS	167.94
MORRIS	47.68
KLAMER	649.89
JONES	171.23
NAME	AMOUNT

2. Determine what will be printed by the following programs and what elements will be in the arrays when the programs stop. Use the card file given in Exercise 1.

a.

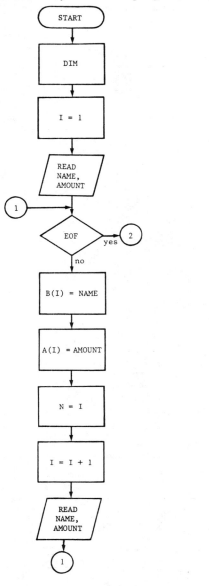

A(1)	A(2)	A(3)	A(4)	A(5)	A(6)
A(7)	A(8)	A(9)	A(10)	A(11)	A(12)
B(1)	B(2)	B(3)	B(4)	B(5)	B(6)
B(7)	B(8)	B(9)	B(1Ø)	B(11)	B(12)

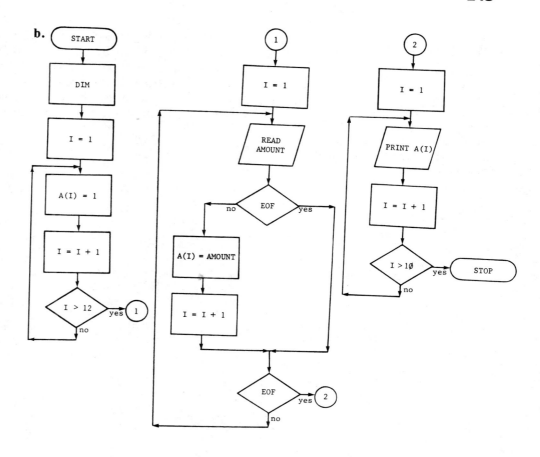

A(1)	A(2)	A(3)	A(4)	A(5)	A(6)
A(7)	A(8)	A(9)	A(10)	A(11)	A(12)

3. The following table represents the array PROFIT( ) and its elements. Indicate the array element that corresponds to each array element name.

6	3	27	9	24	15
PROFIT (1)	PROFIT (2)	PROFIT (3)	PROFIT (4)	PROFIT (5)	PROFIT (6)
2	3	1	3	4	5
I	J	K	L	M	N

a. PROFIT(J − I)

b. PROFIT(M + 2)

c. PROFIT(I × J)

d. PROFIT(PROFIT(K) − J)

e. PROFIT(PROFIT(M) − PROFIT(K))

f. PROFIT(N − (M × N) + N)

8.4 Examples of Array Processing

Figure 8.5 (a) Flowchart (do-while). (b) Warnier diagram (do-until).

The program described by Figure 8.5 loads an array with names read from records and then determines whether any of the names loaded is Samuel Jones and prints every location at which Samuel Jones is loaded. NAME( ) is the array that stores the names read for processing. In this program, NAME is a single variable used to store the name temporarily until EOF is checked. This is done so that the computer will not attempt to load data in the array from the EOF record.

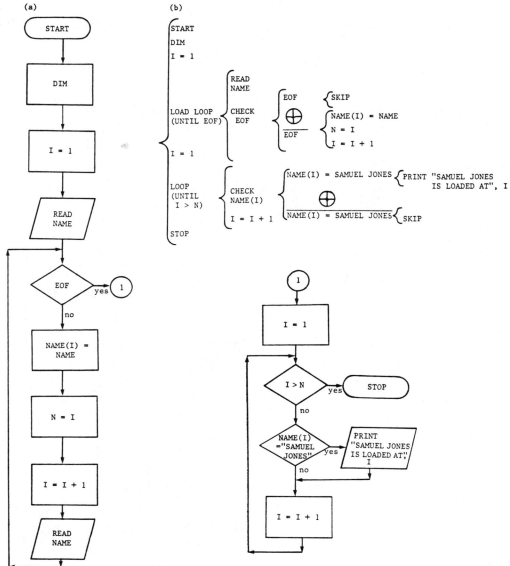

The program described by Figure 8.6 starts with an off-page connector and checks a previously loaded, N-element[3] array to determine whether it was loaded in alphabetical order. It prints a single message that indicates whether or not the array is alphabetized. The program does not rearrange the items stored in the array.

In both the flowchart and the Warnier diagram, the variable I is incremented before it is checked, and the loop stops when I = N (assuming the array was alphabetized). This is done because the program is to stop after it has compared the next-to-last element with the last element. That is, the program stops after I + 1 = N and NAME(I + 1) is the last name.

[3] Assume that the array was counted at the time it was loaded.

Figure 8.6 (a) Flowchart. (b) Warnier diagram.

(a)

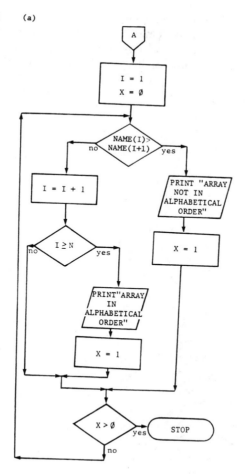

(b)

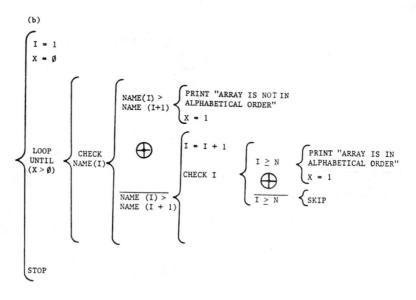

Figure 8.7 is a program that begins with an off-page connector and examines two previously loaded 50-element arrays to determine whether or not their elements are identical (and in identical positions). The program will print the elements that differ and their locations, or it will print a message that the arrays have identical elements.

Figure 8.7 (a) Flowchart. (b) Warnier diagram.

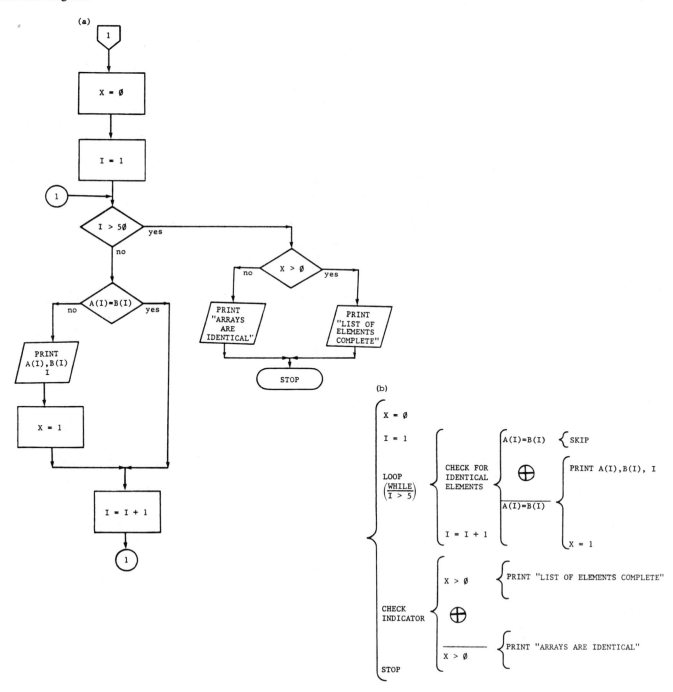

Figure 8.8 describes a program that reads a series of names, checks the series for duplicates, and prints duplicated names and the subscripts of the array elements that contain duplicated names. "Desk check" this program to see that it will work. Ensure that array subscripts will be properly initialized and incremented.

Figure 8.8 This program checks a file for duplicate names.

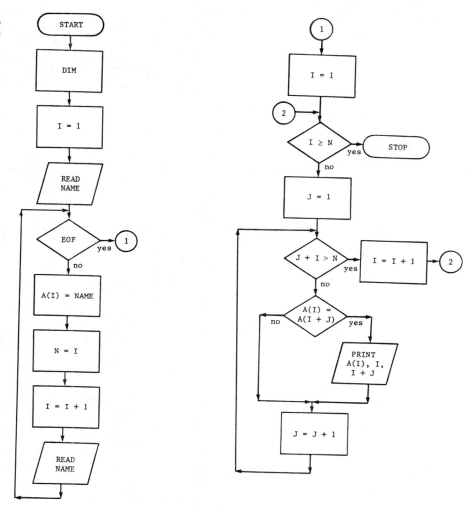

Figure 8.9 combines array processing with a control break. It is designed to accumulate the sales for each agent and store each agent's sales in a different location of the A( ) array.

Figure 8.9 This flowchart combines array processing with a control break.

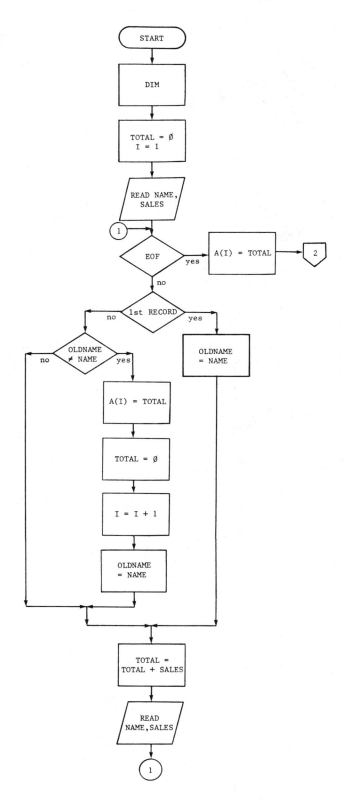

Figure 8.10 (a) Flowchart.

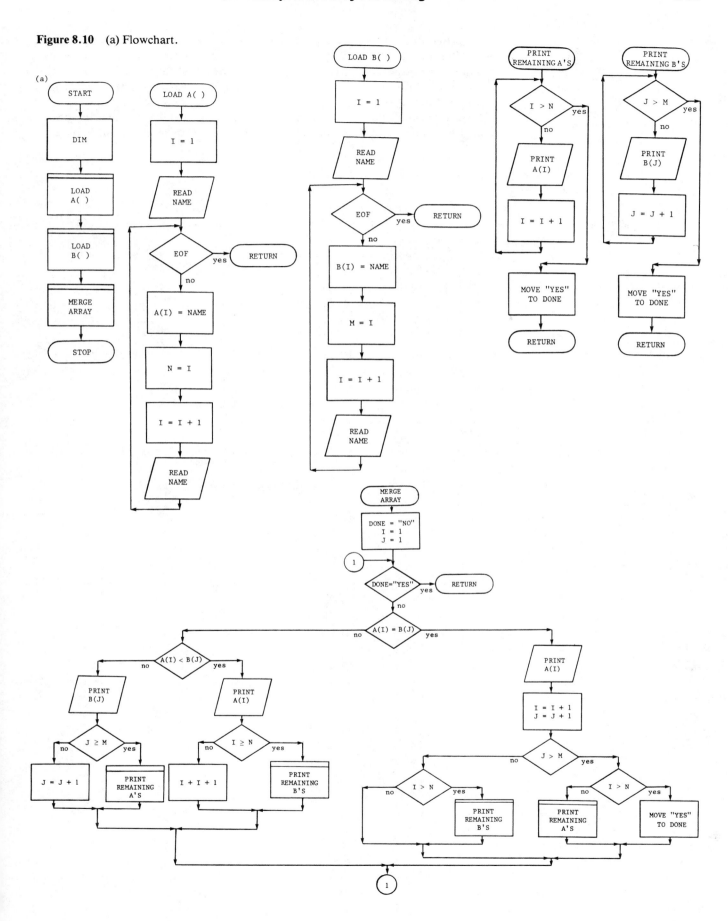

The program described by Figure 8.10 makes use of two arrays. Both arrays are loaded before other processing begins, and those values are retained throughout the program. The program is designed to read two previously alphabetized files and load them into two different arrays. It prints a single alphabetized list of names from both files, eliminating duplicates. The program starts with two loops to load the arrays. Those loops are followed by a loop to print an integrated list. In the print loop, when one list reaches its end, the members of the other list are printed out in order.

Figure 8.10 (b)
Warnier diagram.

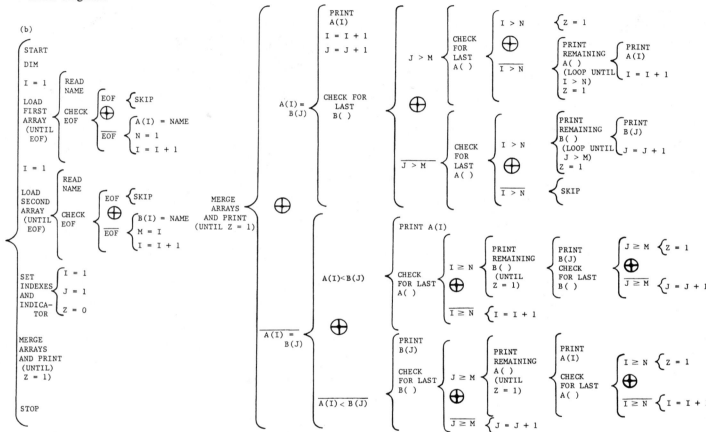

Exercises 8.4

1. "Desk check" Figure 8.10, using data under 1 below. Keep track of the counters and variable subscripts as you proceed. Determine the values that I, J, M, and N will have when "CASSEY" is printed.

1

LIST A	LIST B
ADAMS	ANDERSON
BARNET	CARLSON
CASSEY	DONALDSON
DORN	FORBES
ECKLY	FRAISER
FOSTER	

2

LIST A	LIST B
JONES	LANDON
KRAMER	SMYTH
SMITH	ZORN
ZIEGLER	

2. Repeat the foregoing procedure for the lists under 2. Determine the values that I, J, M, and N will have when "SMITH" is printed.

3. Design a structured flowchart for a program to load an array with names. The program is to transfer control to an off-page connector when either the EOF is reached or 10 names have been loaded. The program is not to load anything from the end-of-file record.

4. Design a Warnier diagram for the program described in Exercise 3.

5. Design a structured flowchart beginning with an off-page connector for a program that will examine a previously loaded 100-element array and print out each negative value and the number of the array location where that value is stored.

6. Design a Warnier diagram for the program described in Exercise 5.

7. Design a structured flowchart and a Warnier diagram for a program that will read names from exactly 10 cards and then print those names in reverse order.

8. Design a structured flowchart and a Warnier diagram to (1) read values from two files, (2) find the average of each file, and (3) divide each value in each file by the average of the values of the other file and print the result of the divisions.

8.5 User Input and User Direction

The term **user input** refers to data entered by a computer operator through a terminal (or keyboard) during the execution of a program. This form of data entry requires the computer to interrupt processing and wait for data. User input is generally slower and more expensive than is the reading of data loaded prior to program execution. But many computer tasks cannot be accomplished without user input. An example of such a task is the assignment of reservations on the basis of walk-in or call-in requests for particular seats or rooms. The desired location and customer name are not known beforehand, but the reservation should be completed before the customer leaves or hangs up the phone. Consequently, the customer's wishes can't be recorded on cards or tape and can't be batch-processed by using a READ statement. The user (reservations clerk) must be able to enter customer information as each customer comes forward and must be able to complete the reservation before that customer leaves. User input is employed for such programs. Other types of programs employ user input because that form of data entry is the most efficient way to solve a particular programming problem.

We shall abbreviate the instruction for user input as simply INPUT. INPUT COST( ) indicates that the value of the variable COST( ) will be supplied by the user at a terminal during execution of the program. The input command will cause processing to stop and the computer to wait for information from the user. After the user supplies appropriate information, the program continues.

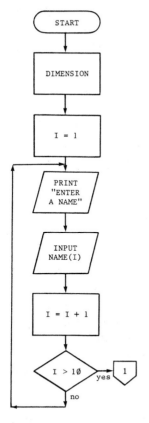

Figure 8.11 A flowchart that solicits user input via a prompter message.

Input instructions are generally preceded by print commands that contain prompter messages. These prompter messages tell the user the kind of information required. Such a message might say "Enter the name of the next salesperson." If these prompter messages are omitted, the user may not know what sort of information is required – or even realize that any information is required at all.

Input instructions and their corresponding prompter messages are often placed in loops, allowing the user to enter data repeatedly during the program. This process is described by Figure 8.11. This program requires user input to load names at the first 10 locations of array NAME(I).

User Direction

Programs that provide for user input may also provide for **user direction** of the program. They accomplish this by employing data from user input to direct further processing. A typical example of user direction occurs in programs that allow a user to enter a series of items for processing. In these programs a prompter message may be used to ask how many items will be entered or, perhaps, whether any more items are to be entered. Input commands store the user's responses, and decisions involving those responses direct processing accordingly. Figures 8.12 and 8.13 describe programs that employ these forms of user direction.

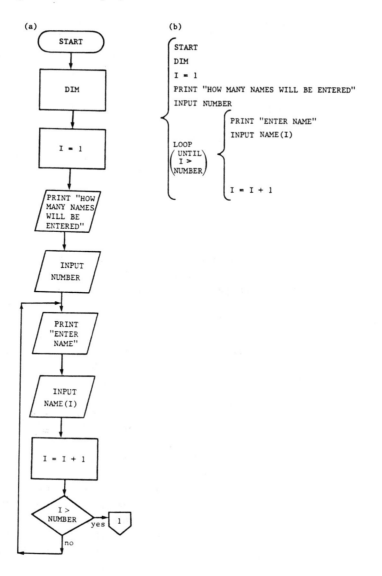

Figure 8.12   (a) Flowchart. (b) Warnier diagram.

Figure 8.13 (a) Flowchart. (b) Warnier diagram.

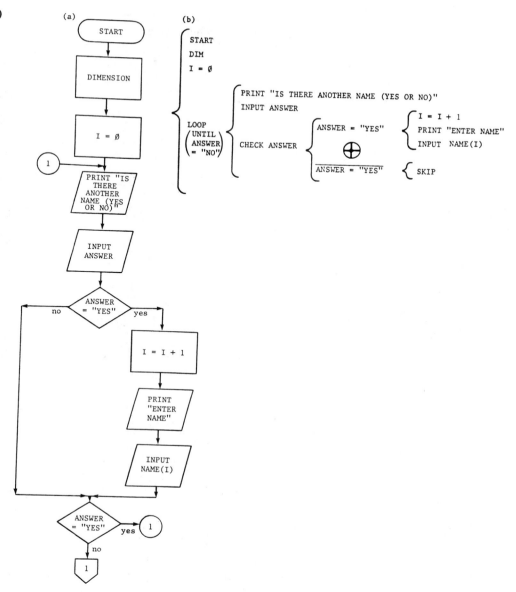

The third method of enabling a user to control the number of inputs involves designating a value (alphabetical or numeric) to be entered after the last piece of data has been entered. The designated value is entered in the same way and at the same place in the program as regular data is. But the designated value is chosen so that it could not be confused with legitimate data. The basic elements of this form of user direction are

1. A designated value to be entered after the last piece of data.
2. A decision to determine whether that value has been entered and, if so, to direct control from the loop.

Suppose a program required a user to enter a value for COST and that the designated value were 0 (assuming that nothing would be free). The input symbol would be followed by a decision to determine whether COST = 0. When COST was any other number, the input loop would continue; when COST was 0, control would be directed from the loop. The user of such a program could direct control from the loop by entering 0 whenever data was requested. Figure 8.14 is such a program.

Figure 8.14 (a) Unstructured flowchart. (b) Flowchart with a do-while loop. (c) Warnier diagram.

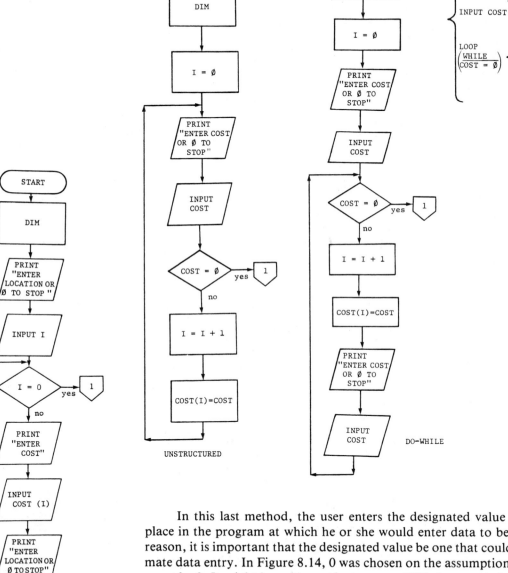

Figure 8.15 This flowchart modifies Figure 8.14 to enable the user to direct the particular location for storing each item.

In this last method, the user enters the designated value at exactly the same place in the program at which he or she would enter data to be processed. For this reason, it is important that the designated value be one that could not also be a legitimate data entry. In Figure 8.14, 0 was chosen on the assumption that the cost would never be 0. It might have been safer to use -9999, because it *is* possible for an item to be donated. When the user must enter alphabetical data (such as names), the designated value must be one that could not be a data entry. ZZZZ might be chosen when names are being entered.

Figures 8.12 to 8.14 loaded their arrays sequentially. That is, the first item was loaded in the first array location and the second item was loaded in the second array location. Programs of this sort can be expanded to enable the user to determine the location at which each item is to be stored. This is done by prompting the user to enter a location before each data item. See Figure 8.15. Because the user is to designate the storage location, the subscript (I) is neither initialized nor incremented.

As designed, this program would enable a user to load the same location repeatedly. This would result in the deletion of previously loaded information. If we wished to avoid this possibility, we could initially load each location in the array with VACANT and then allow the user to load only those locations still containing VACANT. Once a location was loaded with some other expression, it would no longer contain VACANT and could not again be loaded. Figure 8.16 makes this adjustment. (We assume a maximum of 100 elements.)

Figure 8.16 This flowchart modifies Figure 8.15 to prevent the user from loading the same location more than once.

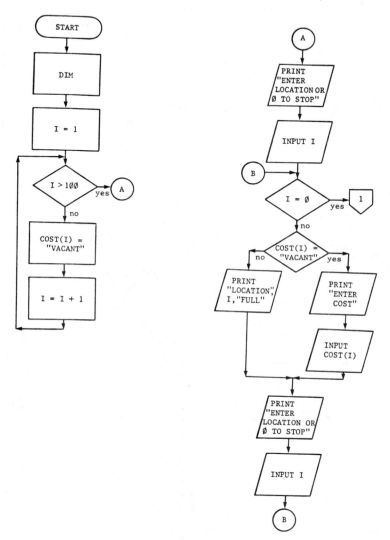

User direction need not be limited to determining the number and location of data entries. The user can also direct the processing that is to occur. This is done with a prompter message to list the user's options and an input command to record the user's choice. A decision or series of decisions then directs control appropriately.

Figure 8.17 enables the user to

1. Terminate the program,
2. Make reservations, or
3. Print a list of vacant seats.

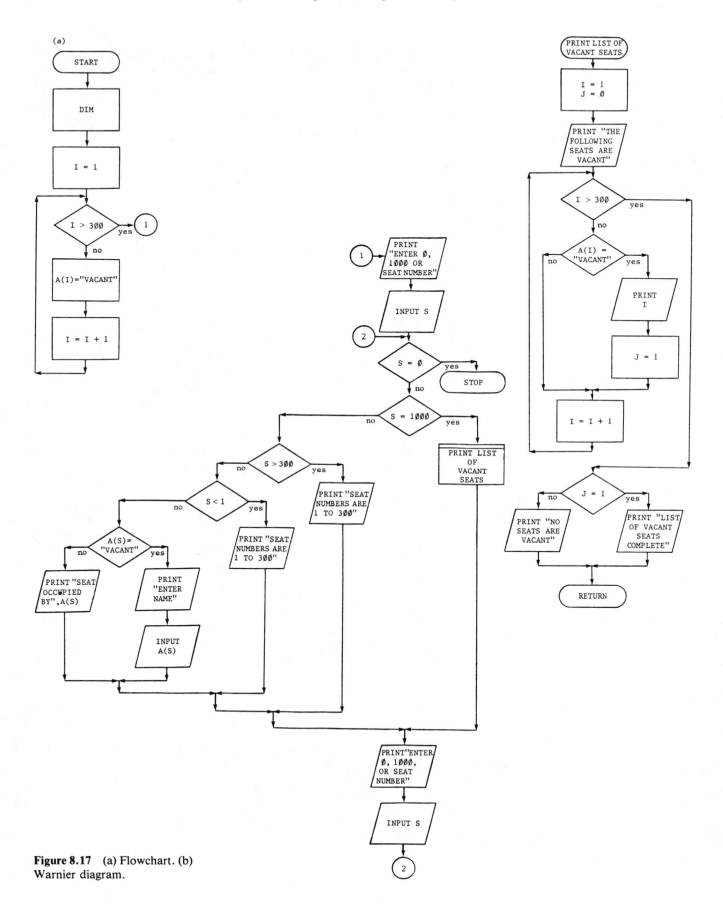

Figure 8.17 (a) Flowchart. (b) Warnier diagram.

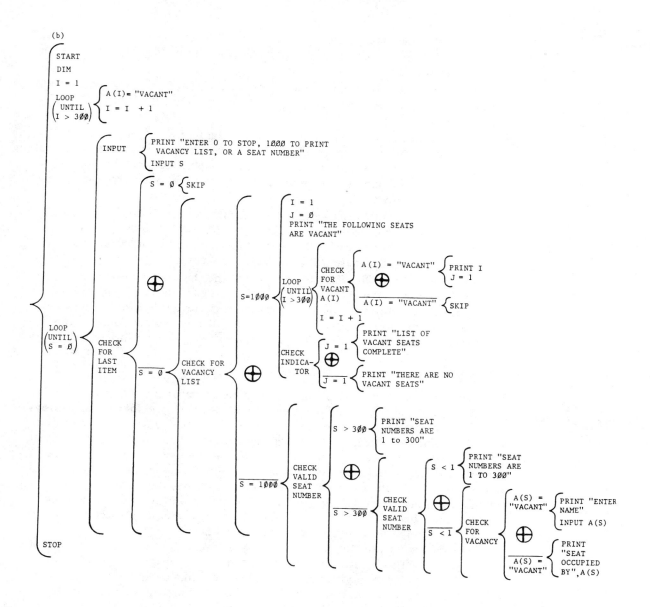

This program is designed to enable a user to make reservations for up to 300 theater seats on the basis of patron requests for particular seats. The user indicates a seat number and indicates a name if that seat is vacant. The designated values in this program are 0 and 1000. When 0 is entered, the program stops. When 1000 is entered, a list of vacant seats is printed. In "desk checking" this program, note that seats are represented by the element names of array A( ) and that the seat number becomes the array subscript for a particular seat. This program initializes each array location by loading the entire array with the word VACANT. This allows the computer subsequently to determine whether a given seat has been assigned. If an array location still has VACANT stored, the corresponding seat has not been assigned. If anything else is stored at an array location, the corresponding seat has been assigned.

If the user enters a number that is outside the expected range, the program informs the user of that fact and returns control to the user to specify a different number. Without this or a similar structure, entering a number outside the expected range would probably cause the program to stop and print an error message. And, in many situations, the user wouldn't know how to get the program going again.

Exercises 8.5

1. Design a Warnier diagram for a program that will enable a user to enter up to 100 values and then (on the basis of the user's direction) print a list of either the even-numbered or the odd-numbered items.

2. Design a structured flowchart and a Warnier diagram for a program that will receive an unspecified number of names from user input and then print those names in reverse order.

3. Design a structured flowchart and a Warnier diagram for a program that will (1) receive an unspecified number of integer (whole) numbers from user input, (2) calculate and print the integer value of the average of the inputs, (3) determine whether any of the inputs is equal to the average, and (4) print a message stating whether or not any of the inputs is equal to the average.

4. Design a structured flowchart and a Warnier diagram for a program that will (1) read agent names and sales from a series of records, presorted by agent name, (2) calculate the average of each agent's sales, and (3) print each agent's name and average. Assume that there will be at least one record.

5. Design a structured flowchart for a program that has a 100-element array, accepts user input, and will (1) allow the user to load a name in a location of his or her choice, (2) inform the user if a location was previously loaded, so that the user can make another selection, and (3) allow the user to stop the program by entering a designated value. Be sure to include all appropriate prompter messages.

8.6 Multidimensional Arrays

The arrays we have considered so far are one-dimensional arrays. Their locations are specified by a variable name followed by a single subscript. **Multidimensional arrays** differ in that locations are indicated by a variable name followed by two or more subscripts. Each different combination of array subscripts indicates a different storage location. Hence, A(1,2) would designate one array location and A(2,1) would designate a different array location. Just as is the case with one-dimensional arrays, the subscripts for two-dimensional arrays may be either variables or legitimate mathematical expressions. The number of dimensions of the array is simply the number of subscripts that follow the array name. In this section, we will be concerned only with one- and two-dimensional arrays.

The maximum value of array subscripts (and therefore the maximum size of the array) is specified by the dimension statement. When programmers talk about a 6 × 25 array (six by twenty-five array), they are speaking about a two-dimensional array whose dimension statement has limited its first subscript to 6 and its second subscript to 25. A 6 × 25 array contains 150 locations even if a program using such an array does not assign values to each location. That is, the dimension statement for a 6 × 25 array reserves 150 storage locations even though the program may not use them all.

Sometimes arrays are spoken of as though they actually had physical dimensions. A 6 × 25 array might be thought of as being rectangular. A 10 × 10 array might be called a square array. Even though array locations don't actually arrange themselves in such geometric patterns, it is sometimes convenient and/or helpful to visualize and speak of them as though they did. The storage locations of a 6 × 25 array might be thought of as 6 rows of 25 locations each or as 6 columns of 25 locations each. When using such a geometric model, we can think of one subscript as representing the row number and of the other as representing the column number. But, because this is only a model, it makes no difference which subscript we use to represent rows, as long as we are consistent within a given program.

Processing Two-Dimensional Arrays

The processing of multidimensional arrays usually requires the use of a distinct variable subscript for each dimension. This complicates processing, because each variable subscript must be initialized, checked for terminal value, and incremented.

Figure 8.18 (a) This flow-chart describes a program that loads a 6 × 25 array. (b) Warnier diagram.

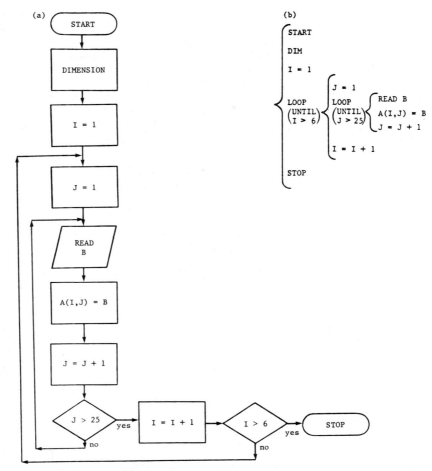

Compare Figure 8.18, which loads a 6 × 25 array, with Figure 8.1, which loads a 1000-element single-dimension array. Note the additional symbols for initializing and incrementing subscripts. Note also the order in which Figure 8.18 initializes and increments its subscripts. (The first to be initialized is the last to be incremented.)

An element of a two-dimensional array can be referred to only by an expression that contains two subscripts. But it is not necessary that those subscripts be different, even if they are variables. The program represented by Figure 8.19 uses a

Figure 8.19 (a) This flow-chart uses a single variable for both subscripts of a 10 × 10 array. (b) Warnier diagram.

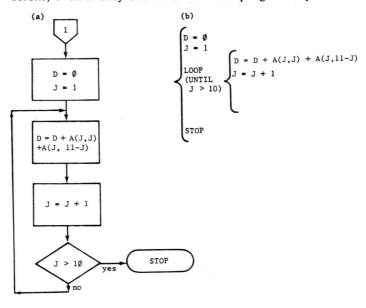

two-dimensional array – but only one variable to generate subscripts. That single variable is used in both subscripts for each array element. Only one variable is used, so only one is initialized and incremented. Figure 8.19 adds the elements of the diagonals of a 10 × 10 array. "Desk check" this program to ensure that it would work. Note how the single variable J is used in each subscript.

8.7 Examples of Programs with Two-Dimensional Arrays

The following are flowcharts and Warnier diagrams for programs that make use of two-dimensional arrays. "Desk check" these flowcharts and Warnier diagrams to ensure that their programs would work as intended.

Examples 8.1 to 8.4 represent programs that manipulate an already-loaded 10 × 10 array, A(   ). These examples assume that the first array subscript indicates the row number of this "square array"; the second array subscript indicates the column number.

Example 8.1

This flowchart and Warnier diagram represent programs that print the sums of the numbers in each of the columns.

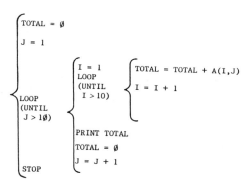

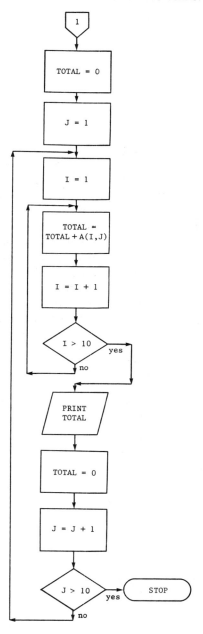

Example 8.2

This flowchart subtracts the sums of the odd-numbered rows from the sums of the even-numbered columns and prints the result.

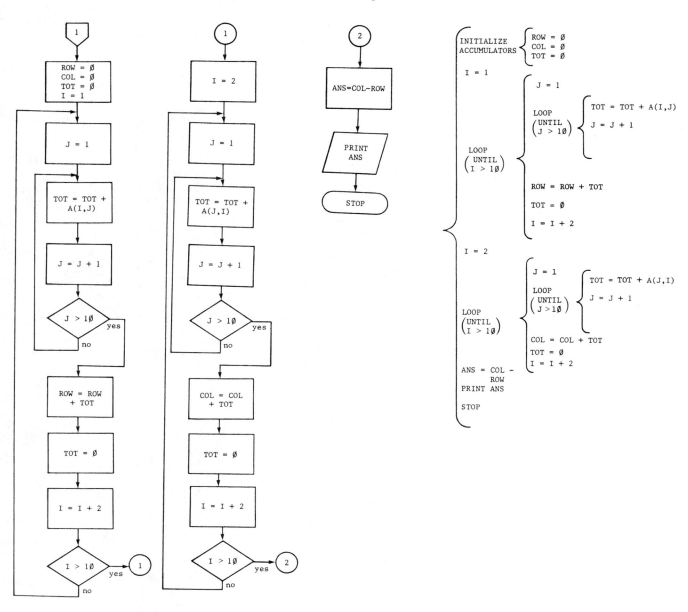

Example 8.3

This flowchart and Warnier diagram represent a program that prints the array A( ) with totals at the end of each row and at the end of each column. The array C( ) is used to accumulate the totals for each column of the array A( ). The array location C(1) accumulates totals for column 1, C(2) for column 2, and so on. After the array A( ) and its row totals are printed, the array C( ) is printed.

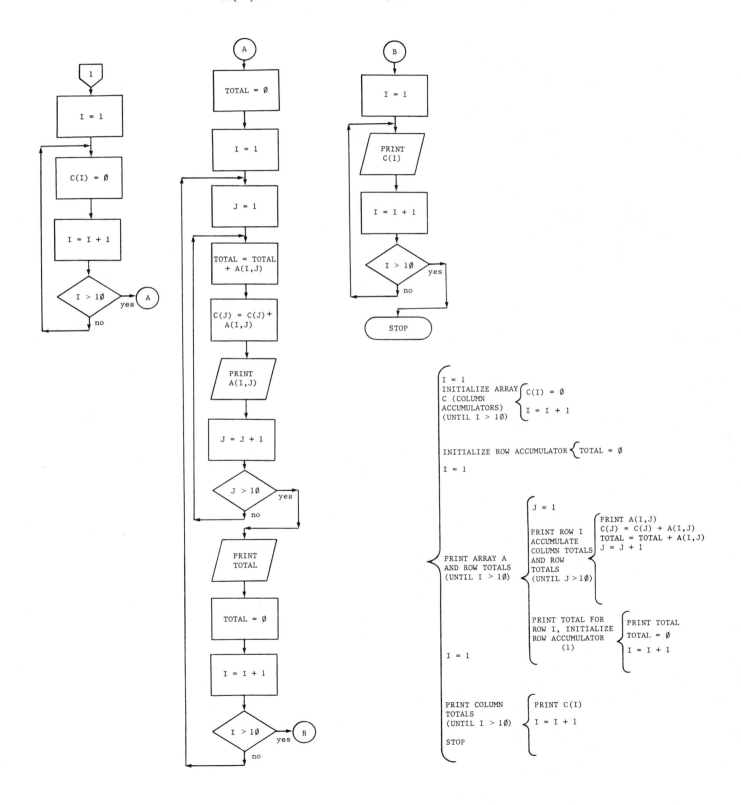

Example 8.4

This flowchart and Warnier diagram represent a program that enables a user to print either a row or a column of the 10 × 10 array. After a row or column is printed, control is returned to the user to print another row or column or to stop the program.

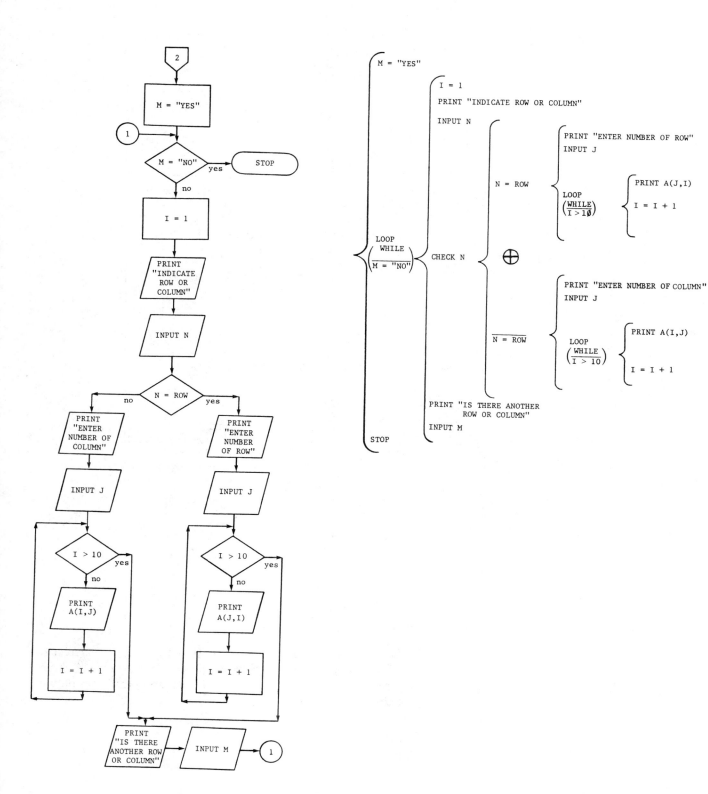

Example 8.5   This flowchart represents a program that loads a 6 × 25 array with names. EMPTY is loaded in each element for which there is no name. This program prints "ARRAY IS FULL" and stops if the array fills. It prints "OUT OF RECORDS, _____, SPACES EMPTY" and stops if the end of the file occurs before the array is full.

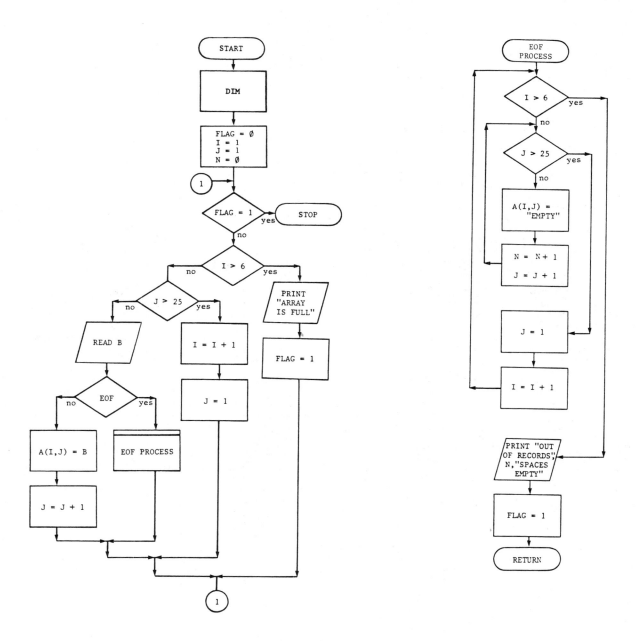

Note that, when this program reads a record, it initially stores its value at B. Only after the EOF decision is passed is that value entered into the array. This structure prevents the information on the end-of-file record from being loaded as though it were another piece of data.

Example 8.6

This flowchart and Warnier diagram represent a program that enables the user to store up to 100 names and addresses in a 100 × 2 array. The program stores this list in a second 100 × 2 array after eliminating name duplications. The list without duplications is then printed.

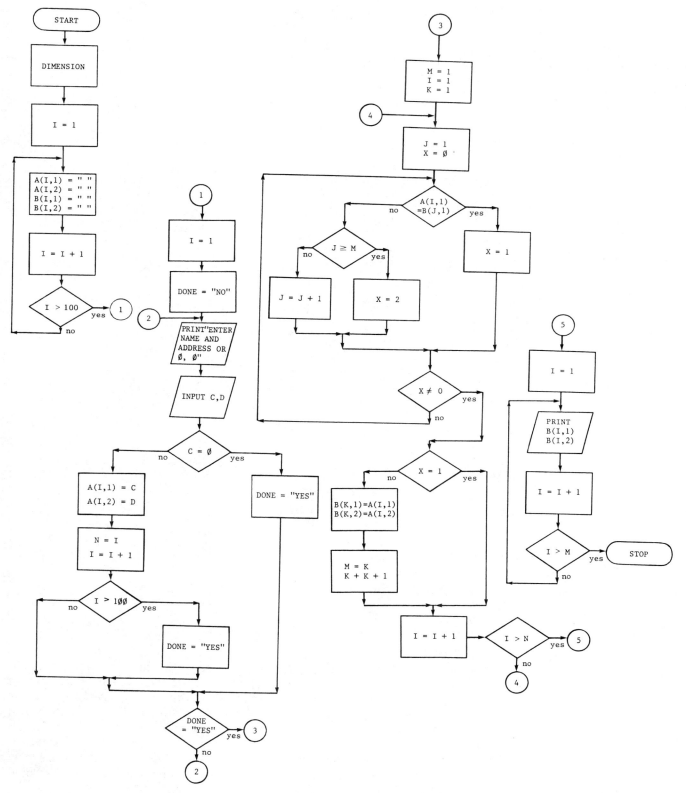

```
START
DIMENSION
I = 1

LOAD ARRAYS        ⎧ A(I,1) = " "
WITH BLANK         ⎪ A(I,2) = " "
LOOP (UNTIL        ⎨ B(I,1) = " "
I > 10Ø)           ⎪ B(I,2) = " "
                   ⎩ I = I + 1

I = 1

DONE = "NO"

                   ⎧ PRINT "ENTER NAME AND ADDRESS OR Ø,Ø TO STOP"
                   ⎪ INPUT C, D
                   ⎪
                   ⎪                      ⎧ C = Ø ⎧ DONE = "YES"
LOAD A( , ) WITH   ⎪                      ⎪       ⎨
NAMES AND          ⎪                  ⊕   ⎪       ⎧ A(I,1) = C
ADDRESSES          ⎨                      ⎪       ⎪ A(I,2) = D
LOOP (UNTIL        ⎪ CHECK FOR            ⎪ ‾‾‾‾‾ ⎪ N = I
DONE = "YES")      ⎪ END OF DATA          ⎨ C = Ø ⎨ I = I + 1               ⎧ I > 10Ø ⎧ DONE = "YES"
                   ⎪                      ⎪       ⎪ CHECK    ⊕              ⎨
                   ⎩                      ⎩       ⎩ I        ‾‾‾‾‾‾ ⎧ SKIP   ⎩ I > 10Ø ⎧ SKIP

INITIALIZE         ⎧ M = 1
COUNTERS AND       ⎨ I = 1
SUBSCRIPTS         ⎩ K = 1

                   ⎧ J = 1
                   ⎪ X = Ø
                   ⎪                          A(I,1) = B(J,1) ⎧ X = 1
                   ⎪ DETERMINE            ⊕
                   ⎪ WHETHER                  ‾‾‾‾‾‾‾‾‾‾‾‾‾‾‾     ⎧ J ≥ M ⎧ X = 2
                   ⎪ A(I,1) IS               A(I,1) = B(J,1)     ⎪       ⎨
LOAD B( , ) WITH   ⎨ LOADED IN                               ⊕  ⎨
UNIQUE LIST        ⎪ B( , ) LOOP                                ⎪ ‾‾‾‾‾ ⎧ J = J + 1
LOOP (UNTIL        ⎪ (UNTIL X ≠ Ø)                             ⎩ J ≥ M
I > N)             ⎪
                   ⎪                          X = 1 ⎧ SKIP
                   ⎪                      ⊕
                   ⎪ LOAD NEW                ‾‾‾‾‾    ⎧ B(K,1) = A(I,1)
                   ⎪ A( , ) INTO             X = 1   ⎪ B(K,2) = A(I,2)
                   ⎪ B( , )                          ⎨ M = K
                   ⎪                                 ⎩ K = K + 1
                   ⎩ I = I + 1

I = 1

PRINT THE LIST     ⎧ PRINT B(I,1)
OF NAMES AND       ⎨ PRINT B(I,2)
ADDRESSES LOOP     ⎩ I = I + 1
(UNTIL I > M)

STOP
```

Sales Report Examples

Two-dimensional arrays are particularly useful in storing and processing information that lends itself to two different organizational schemes. Examples of this type of information include sales reports that could be organized by salesperson or by month of sale. A two-dimensional array called SALES could be set up in which SALES(1,1) would be the total sales for salesperson 1 for January, SALES(1,2) would be the total sales for salesperson 1 in February, and so on. Storing information in this manner would facilitate retrieving sales information by either salesperson or month. For instance, salesperson 28's sales for the third quarter of the year would be equal to the sum of SALES(28,7), SALES(28,8) and SALES(28,9).

Example 8.7

When an array is loaded, the input is normally presorted. Either the records are from a sorted file or the data has been sorted by a sort module earlier in the program. In Example 8.7 we will assume that the data is sorted first by salesperson and then by month. With the data sorted, a control break called NAMEBK can be used to reset the "month" subscript and to increment the "salesperson" subscript. This program assumes that there will be exactly one input per salesperson per month.

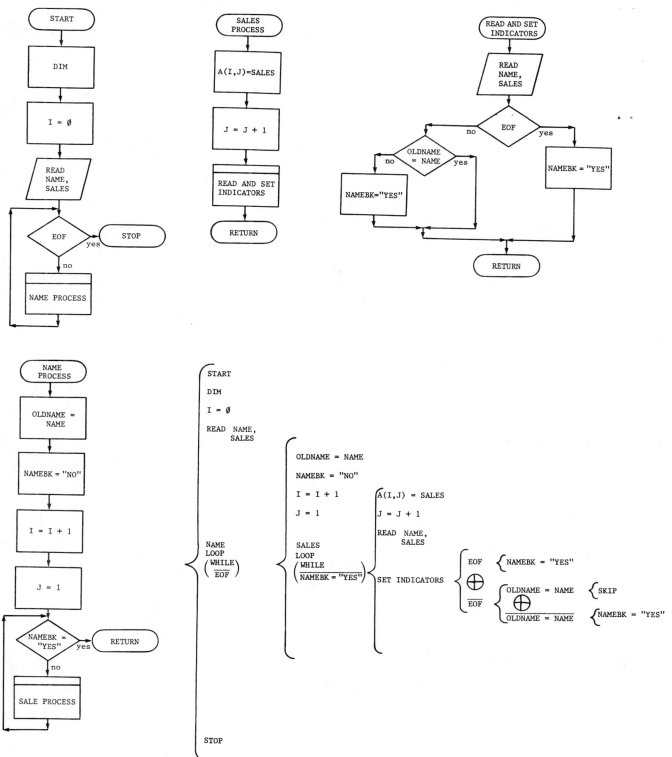

Example 8.8   A more interesting program results when there may be more than one input per month and when the array is to store the monthly totals by salesperson. The following flowchart represents such a program. One control break diverts processing so that totals for a month may be stored and the "month" subscript can be incremented. The other control break diverts processing to store a monthly total and increment both the "month" subscript and the "salesperson" subscript.

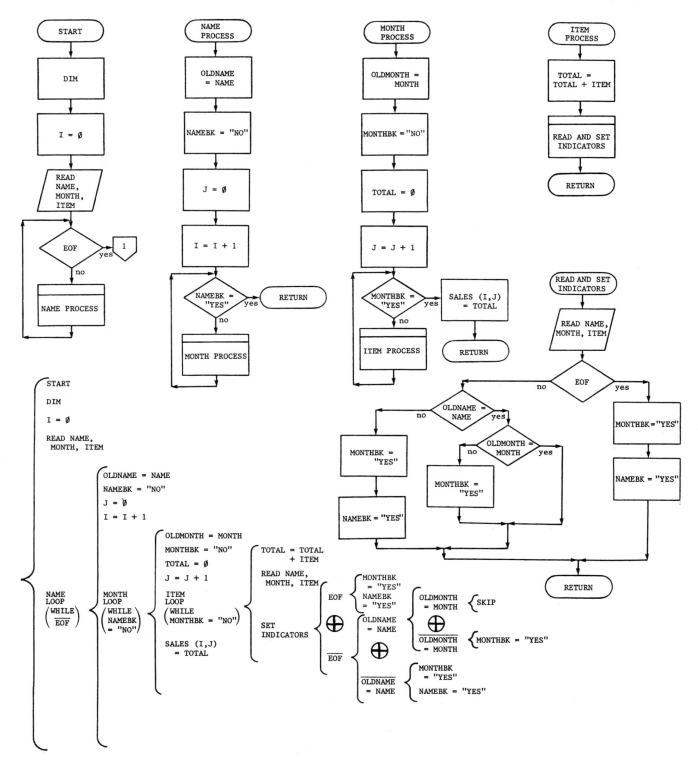

Example 8.9

Example 8.8 loads the total sales for each salesperson by month. But it does not identify those totals by salesperson's name. It identifies them only by the order in which they were entered. One could identify total sales by name by loading a second array with salespersons' names. The "name" subscript on both arrays would be identical. The following flowchart

1. Loads a one-dimensional array B( ) with names of agents,
2. Adds the sales of each agent for each month, and
3. Loads a two-dimensional array A( ) with the monthly totals by agent.

The subscript of B( ) and the first subscript of A( ) represent the agent and change with the agent. The second subscript of A( ) represents the month and changes with the month. Review this flowchart and Warnier diagram carefully to ensure that the program would store each agent's monthly total by name and by month.

Example 8.9   continued

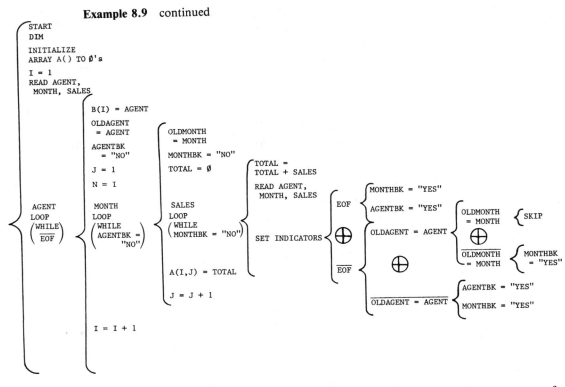

Example 8.10

The point of loading an array is to make data available for processing. Programs for processing arrays are quite similar to those for loading them. The following flowchart uses the information loaded in the previous chart to print each agent's name and total sales for the year.

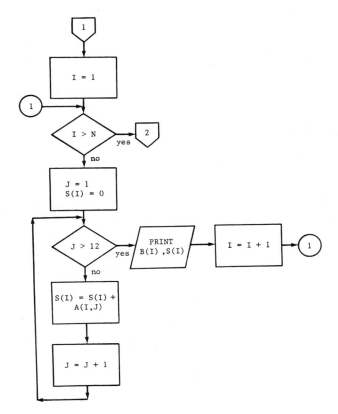

Note that the inner loop is repeated 12 times for each agent. The S( ) array functions as a series of accumulators and is incremented so that its subscript is equal in value to the "agent" subscript. Hence, S(I) is the yearly total for the agent whose name is stored in B(I). This program will process N agents.

Example 8.11

This flowchart uses the information loaded at Example 8.9 and prints the total sales by month. The array R( ) is an accumulator array that stores the totals by month. Compare this flowchart with Example 8.10. Note when each of the subscripts is incremented. "Desk check" each of these charts to ensure that Example 8.10 correctly calculates totals by agent and that Example 8.11 correctly calculates totals by month.

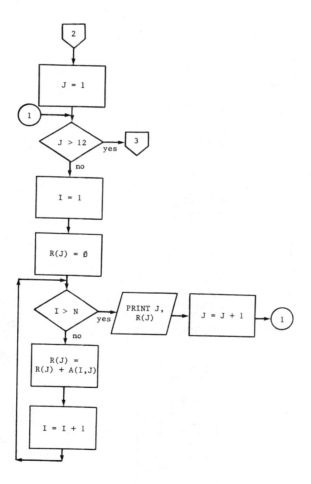

Example 8.12

This program assumes that Examples 8.9, 8.10, and 8.11 have been joined and prints the information in the arrays, including the totals. It produces the report described by the printer spacing chart that follows.

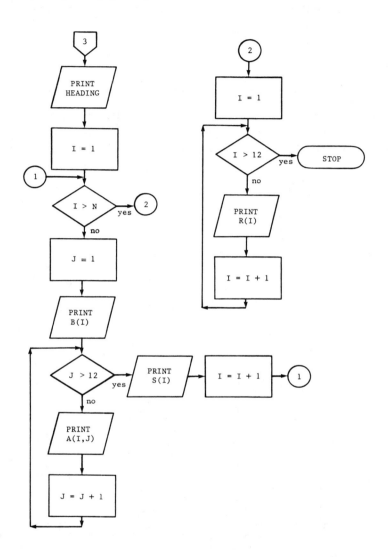

PRINTER SPACING CHART

	0	0	0	0	0	0	0	0	0	1	1	1	1	1	1	1	1	1	1	2	2	2	2	2	2	2	2	2	3	3	3	3	3	3	3	3		1	1	1	1	1	1	1	1	1	1	2
	1	2	3	4	5	6	7	8	9	0	1	2	3	4	5	6	7	8	9	0	1	2	3	4	5	6	7	8	9	0	1	2	3	4	5	6	7	8		0	1	2	3	4	5	6	7	8	9	0
1																																																		
2																										A	N	N	U	A	L		S	A	L	E			X	X	/	X	X	/	X	X		
3																																																		
4					A	G	E	N	T									J	A	N					F	E	B					M	A	R						T	O	T	A	L						
5																																																		
6	X	X	X	X	X	X	X	X	X	X	X	X	X	X	X		X	X	X	X	X	X		X	X	X	X	X	X		X	X	X	X	X		X		X	X	X	X	X	X	X	X		
7	X	X	X	X	X	X	X	X	X	X	X	X	X	X	X		X	X	X	X	X	X		X	X	X	X	X	X		X	X	X	X	X		X		X	X	X	X	X	X	X	X		
8																																																		
9															X	X	X	X	X	X	X		X	X	X	X	X	X		X	X	X	X	X	X		X										
10																																																		

Exercises 8.6–8.7

1. Use the following data to create each of the reports that would be generated by Examples 8.9 through 8.12.

Adams	Jan	$12.00	Smith	Jan	$33.00	Jones	Jan	$ 60.00
Adams	Jan	10.00	Smith	Feb	26.00	Jones	Jan	50.75
Adams	Jan	17.00	Smith	Mar	42.00	Jones	Feb	130.50
Adams	Feb	19.50	Smith	Apr	50.97	Jones	Mar	65.18
Adams	Feb	13.75	Smith	Apr	62.18	Jones	Apr	73.90
Adams	Mar	14.29	Smith	Apr	50.19	Jones	Apr	85.20
Adams	Mar	16.73	Smith	May	60.18	Jones	May	12.32
Adams	Mar	14.83	Smith	May	75.92	Jones	June	20.63
Adams	Apr	29.37	Smith	June	12.18	Jones	June	5.17
Adams	Apr	47.16	Smith	June	60.13	Jones	June	3.25
Adams	Apr	50.65	Smith	July	57.47	Jones	July	159.66
Adams	Apr	43.19	Smith	July	46.50	Jones	July	47.28
Adams	May	14.75	Smith	July	39.28	Jones	Aug	93.76
Adams	June	18.60	Smith	Aug	41.29	Jones	Aug	37.42
Adams	June	16.79	Smith	Sep	31.12	Jones	Aug	96.20
Adams	July	13.41	Smith	Sep	30.14	Jones	Sep	83.71
Adams	July	80.62	Smith	Oct	17.96	Jones	Oct	74.71
Adams	July	21.17	Smith	Nov	21.63	Jones	Oct	61.29
Adams	Aug	39.28	Smith	Nov	59.20	Jones	Oct	12.18
Adams	Aug	42.90	Smith	Dec	17.22	Jones	Nov	10.19
Adams	Sep	17.26	Smith	Dec	33.47	Jones	Dec	7.15
Adams	Oct	14.00				Jones	Dec	2.21
Adams	Oct	7.50						
Adams	Oct	9.50						
Adams	Nov	11.00						
Adams	Dec	63.00						
Adams	Dec	10.75						

2. Design a structured flowchart to assign theater seats by name from a series of records, each of which contains a name. The first person is to be assigned seat 1-1; the second, 1-2; and so on. Assume that there are 100 rows of 50 seats each. Each unassigned seat should be labeled EMPTY.

3. Design a structured flowchart to print the names of each person by row. Design a structured flowchart to print those names by seat number (by column). Refer to Exercise 2.

4. Design a structured flowchart for a program that contains two arrays and will read records, each of which contains a name and a date. The program will store the names in one array and the dates in the other. The program is then to print the names and dates in inverse order (last name and date are to be printed first).

5. Design a structured flowchart for a program with a 10 × 10 array that will read and load 100 numerals and then add the numerals on one diagonal, subtract that total from the total of the other diagonal, and print the result.

6. Design a structured flowchart and a Warnier diagram for a program that contains a 3 × 10 array. The program will provide for user input of 10 names, addresses, and telephone numbers. The program will stop when 10 names have been entered or when the user enters 0, 0, 0.

7. Design a structured flowchart and a Warnier diagram for a program using a 10 × 10 array that will enable a user to (1) enter numbers to be stored at the element of the user's choice, (2) request a print-out of the array, (3) request a total of all the values in the array, and (4) terminate the program.

8. Design a Warnier diagram for a program containing a 6 × 50 array to represent seats on a commercial aircraft with 50 rows of seats. The program will enable a user to (1) reserve empty seats by customer name on the basis of customer requests for a specific seat, (2) request a list of empty seats, and (3) stop the program when there are no more customers.

8.8 Exchange

The **exchange** is a simple structure for interchanging the values of two variables. To make this interchange without losing one of the values, a temporary storage variable is used. Figure 8.20 exchanges the values of A and B. Figure 8.21 exchanges the values of variables A(I) and B(I) in two 10-member arrays. In each case, X is the temporary storage variable.

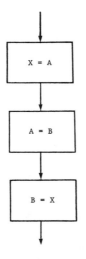

Figure 8.20   An exchange of values stored at two variables.

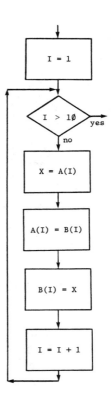

Figure 8.21   An exchange of values stored in two arrays.

8.9 Sorts

Sorting the elements of an array into alphabetical or numerical order is a routine computer task and one that often precedes other processing. The design of programs to carry out this task is complicated by the fact that computers can "see" only two pieces of data at a time. Two items can be added, subtracted, or compared. But computers generally cannot compare more than two things at once. This poses a particular problem when a set of data must be sorted. It is easy for *us* to alphabetize 10 items. We look at all 10 items and put them in order. Imagine, however, that you were asked to sort 10 items but would be allowed to see only two of the items at one time and could never remember previous items. This is the predicament of the computer. Fortunately, there are several programming solutions to this predicament. Here we will consider two of them: the **bubble sort** and the **binary sort**.[4]

---

[4] Other sorts are more efficient than the bubble and binary sorts. The bubble and binary sorts are presented here as examples whose logic is straightforward.

Both the bubble sort and the binary sort carry out a series of steps called "passes." Each of these passes rearranges the order of the items being sorted. On the first pass, one item is placed in the correct position. On each successive pass, an additional item is placed in the correct position until every item is in the correct position. Where a series to be sorted has N items, the bubble and binary sorts make N - 1 passes. The difference between the bubble and binary sorts lies in the different steps that make up each pass.

Bubble Sort

In each pass of the bubble sort:

1. The item in the first position is compared with the item in the second position. If they are out of order, they are exchanged; if they are in order, they are left alone.

2. The item now in the second position is compared with the item in the third position. If they are out of order, they are exchanged; if they are in order, they are left alone.

3. The item now in the third position is compared with the item in the fourth position. . . .

4. The steps in the pass continue until each item has been checked.

After the first complete pass, the last item will be in the correct position. After the second, the last two items will be in the correct position, and so on. After N − 1 passes, each of N items will be in the correct position (the final pass settles the position of the final *two* items).

Example 8.13

A bubble sort to sort 5 numbers in ascending order.

Original Order 4 7 3 1 6

First Pass **Result**
a. 4 is compared with 7, no exchange 47316
b. 7 is compared with 3, exchange 43716
c. 7 is compared with 1, exchange 43176
d. 7 is compared with 6, exchange 43167

Second Pass **Result**
a. 4 is compared with 3, exchange 34167
b. 4 is compared with 1, exchange 31467
c. 4 is compared with 6, no exchange 31467
d. 6 is compared with 7, no exchange[5] 31467

Third Pass **Result**
a. 3 is compared with 1, exchange 13467
b. 3 is compared with 4, no exchange 13467
c. 4 is compared with 6, no exchange[5] 13467
d. 6 is compared with 7, no exchange[5] 13467

Fourth Pass **Result**
a. 1 is compared with 3, no exchange 13467
b. 3 is compared with 4, no exchange[5] 13467
c. 4 is compared with 6, no exchange[5] 13467
d. 6 is compared with 7, no exchange[5] 13467

[5] An efficient form of the bubble sort omits these steps because the items they compare will already be in the correct order.

Example 8.14

A bubble sort of 6 letters in descending order, showing the order of items after each pass.

ORIGINAL	K	C	L	B	M	D
1st Pass	K	L	C	M	D	B
2nd Pass	L	K	M	D	C	B
3rd Pass	L	M	K	D	C	B
4th Pass	M	L	K	D	C	B
5th Pass	M	L	K	D	C	B

Binary Sort

In the first pass of the binary sort:

1. The item in the first position is compared with that in the second position. If they are out of order, they are exchanged.
2. The item now in the *first* position is compared with that in the third position. If they are out of order, they are exchanged.
3. The item now in the first position. . . .

In the second pass of the binary sort:

1. The item now in the second position is compared with the item in the third position. If they are out of order, they are exchanged.
2. The item now in the second position is compared with the item in the fourth position. If they are out of order, they are exchanged.
3. The item now in the second position is compared with the item in the fifth position. . . .

In the third pass of the binary sort:

1. The item now in the third position is compared with the item in the fourth position. . . .

Example 8.15

A binary sort of 5 items in ascending order.

Original Order   4   7   3   1   6

First Pass	**Result**
a. 4 is compared with 7, no exchange	47316
b. 4 is compared with 3, exchange	37416
c. 3 is compared with 1, exchange	17436
d. 1 is compared with 6, no exchange	17436

Second Pass	**Result**
a. 7 is compared with 4, exchange	14736
b. 4 is compared with 3, exchange	13746
c. 3 is compared with 6, no exchange	13746

Third Pass	**Result**
a. 7 is compared with 4, exchange	13476
b. 4 is compared with 6, no exchange	13476

Fourth Pass	**Result**
a. 7 is compared with 6, exchange	13467

Example 8.16   A binary sort of 6 letters in descending order.

ORIGINAL	K	C	L	B	M	D
1st Pass	M	C	K	B	L	D
2nd Pass	M	L	C	B	K	D
3rd Pass	M	L	K	B	C	D
4th Pass	M	L	K	D	B	C
5th Pass	M	L	K	D	C	B

In all these examples, only single letters and single integers were used. The sorts will also work on more extensive alphabetical and/or numerical expressions.

The obvious difference between the binary sort and the bubble sort is that the bubble sort starts each pass with the item in the first position, whereas the binary sort starts the first pass with the first item, the second pass with the second item, and so on.

Figures 8.22(a) and 8.22(b) represent a binary sort of the elements in the array A( ) in ascending order. "Desk check" these to ensure that programs based on them will work.

Figure 8.22   (a) Flowchart for a binary sort. (b) Warnier diagram.

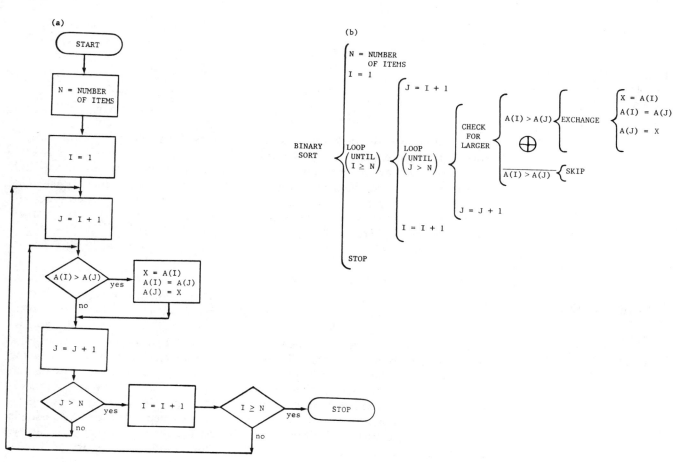

Figure 8.23 represents a bubble sort. It avoids the unnecessary comparisons mentioned in the footnote on page 275.

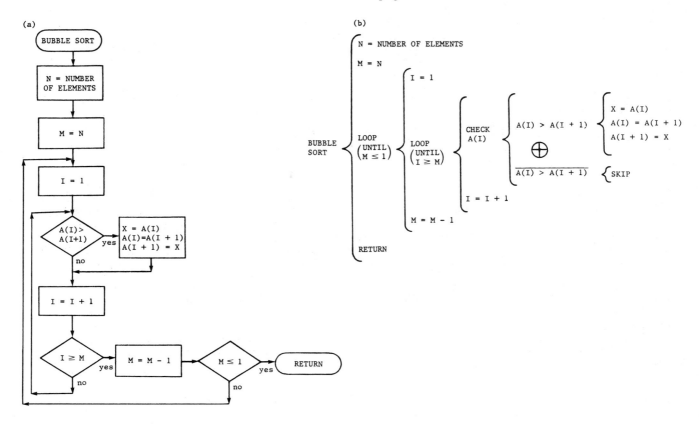

Figure 8.23 (a) Flowchart for a bubble sort. (b) Warnier diagram.

The bubble sort makes at least one exchange on each pass until the array is sorted. In the event that a 100-element array was sorted after only one pass, the bubble sort we have described would continue with another 98 passes even though no values would be exchanged. The efficiency of the bubble sort can be increased by including an indicator to determine whether any exchanges were made on a given pass. This indicator can then be used to terminate the sort after the first "extra" pass, as shown in Figure 8.24.

8.10

Miscellaneous

Array

Manipulations

Find the Largest (Smallest) Element

Finding the largest or the smallest element of an array could be accomplished by sorting the array and then printing the first or the last element. It could also be accomplished by using a single pass of either the bubble or the binary sort. But both of these methods rearrange the elements within the array, and in some situations their rearrangement is not desirable. There is a much shorter method of finding the largest (smallest) element of an array without rearranging its elements. This method sets a temporary storage variable equal to the first element. This variable is compared in turn with each of the other elements, and, if that element is larger (smaller), the storage variable takes on the value of the array element. At the end of a single pass, the storage variable is equal to the largest (smallest) element of the array. Figures 8.25 and 8.26 represent such programs for one-dimensional arrays.

Figure 8.24 This bubble sort includes an indicator to eliminate unnecessary passes.

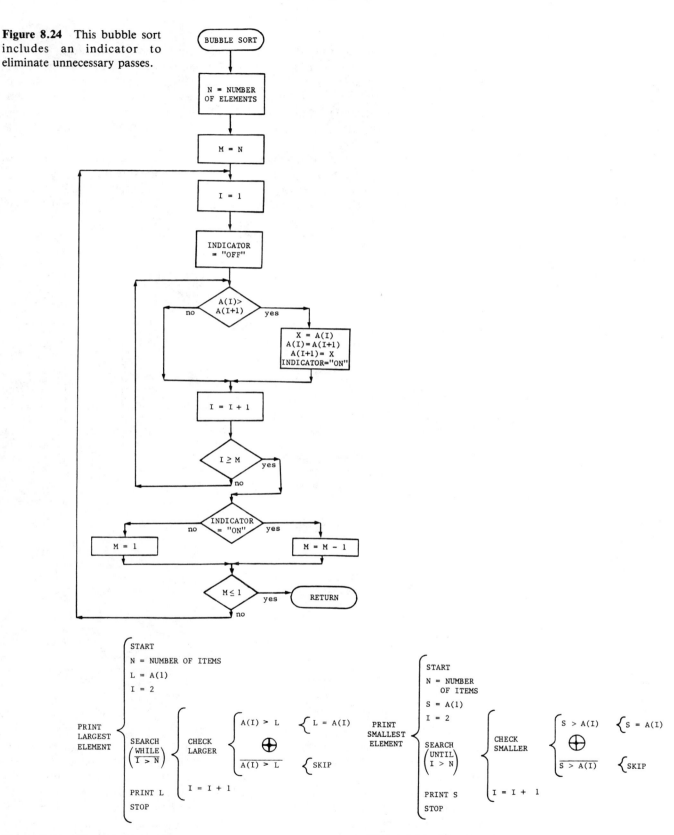

Figure 8.25 Warnier diagram for finding and printing the largest element of an array.

Figure 8.26 Warnier diagram for finding and printing the smallest element of an array.

Search

If an array has been carefully designed, retrieving information from that array is relatively straightforward. For example, suppose we wanted to look up a student's name from an array called A( ), using his or her student number. Our task would be greatly simplified if the names were placed in the array by student number — that is, if the name of the student whose number is 1 were stored in A(1) and that of the student whose number is 2 were stored in A(2). Figure 8.27 is a flowchart for a simple look-up program.

Of course, the trick to such an easy search procedure is the design of the array. Multidimensional array search is no more difficult than one-dimensional array search, provided that those arrays are well planned. Suppose sales data are stored by salesperson number (first subscript) and month (second subscript). Figure 8.28 describes a program to look up a particular sales amount.

Figure 8.27 Flowchart for a simple look-up program.

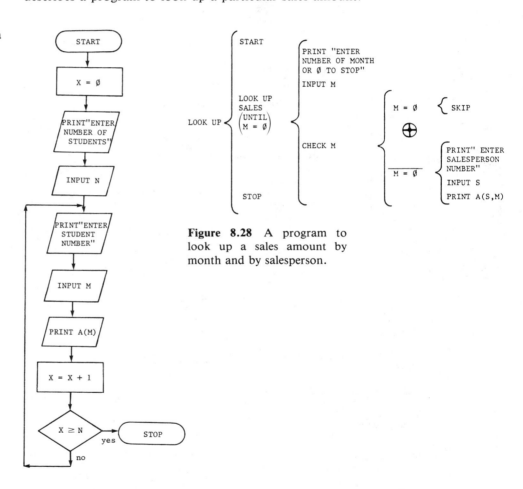

Figure 8.28 A program to look up a sales amount by month and by salesperson.

Sequential Search

The search procedure is more complicated when the array to be searched is not designed for that particular search. Consider our examples with student numbers. Suppose we wanted to look up a student number using the name as input. We would have to compare the name with all the names in the array and print the item number when a match was found. Two standard search methods that carry out this process are the sequential search and the binary search. The **sequential search** compares the item to be searched with each array element, in sequence, beginning with the first element. When a match is found or the end of the array is reached, the search stops and prints an appropriate message. Figure 8.29 describes a sequential search.

Figure 8.29 Warnier diagram describing a sequential search.

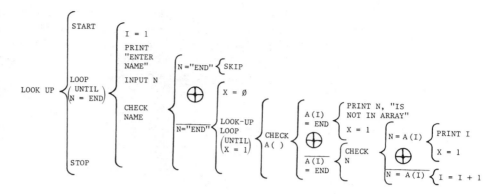

Figure 8.29 assumes that END is the last element of the array and also that the user will enter END after the last number is looked up. It also assumes that a name will occur only once in the array, because it will print only the first number for any particular name. If the second occurrence of X = 1 were deleted, the program would print every number for a particular name. (The NOT IN ARRAY message would be printed at the end of each set of numbers, unless additional provisions were made.)

Binary Search

The logic of the **binary search** is more complicated than that of the sequential search, and the binary search requires that the array to be searched be presorted. (The sequential search does not require that an array be presorted.) But the binary search itself is far more efficient than the sequential search.

The binary search makes its first comparison at the midpoint of the array and, if a match is not found, moves to the midpoint of the half in which a match must be found (if there is a match). This procedure of dividing the remaining part in half is continued until a match is found or until the possibility of a match is eliminated. Figure 8.30 describes a binary search.

Figure 8.30 Warnier diagram describing a binary search.

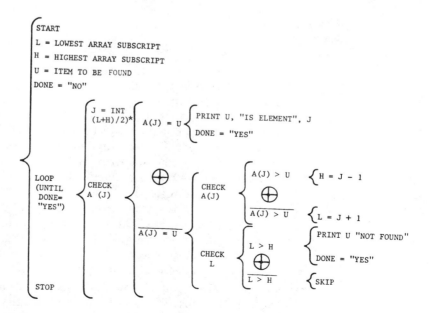

* J equals the integer value of the quotient when L + H is divided by 2.

The binary search shown in Figure 8.30 is easily augmented to allow a designated section of the array to be searched. This is accomplished by initializing L with a value greater than 1 and H with a value less than the total number in the array. Figure 8.31 describes a program that enables a user to control a binary search by entering a name and search boundaries.

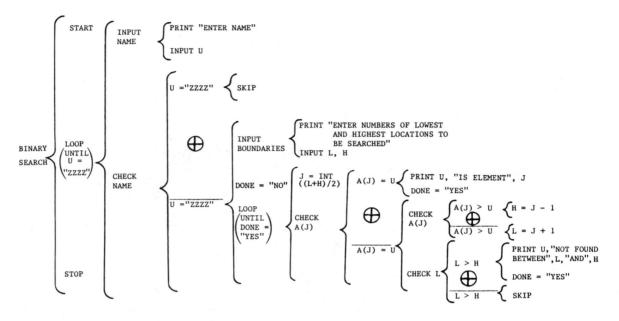

Figure 8.31 This program searches between limits entered by a user.

Coordinated Arrays

In many computer languages, it is not possible to store both alphabetical and numerical data in the same array. Other languages do allow both numerical and alphabetical data to be stored in the same array, but, when this is done, the numbers are often treated as though they were letters. This means that the numbers could be read and printed but could not be used in arithmetic operations. Hence numerical data is often stored in one array, while alphabetical data is stored in another. Corresponding data in the two arrays is coordinated by the array index. For example, if array element NAME(1) contains ''Jones,'' then array element NUMBER(1) contains numerical information concerning Jones.

Figure 8.32 describes a program that will read a name and a sales amount. It will store the names in NAME( ) and the amounts in SALES( ). The subscript of the array location for a particular name is the same as the subscript for the location of a corresponding amount.

Figure 8.33 makes use of the array loaded by Figure 8.32 and enables a user to look up a sales amount by entering a name. The program first searches for the name and uses the subscript of its location to identify the location of the sales amount. Then it prints the name and sales amount.

Figure 8.32 This program loads names into one array and sales into another so that corresponding elements have the same subscript.

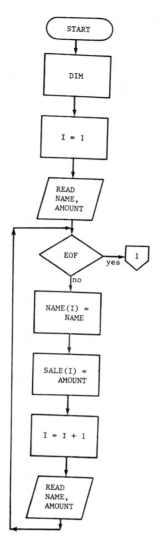

Figure 8.33 This program looks up a name in the NAME( ) array and then prints it and a corresponding sale from the SALE( ) array.

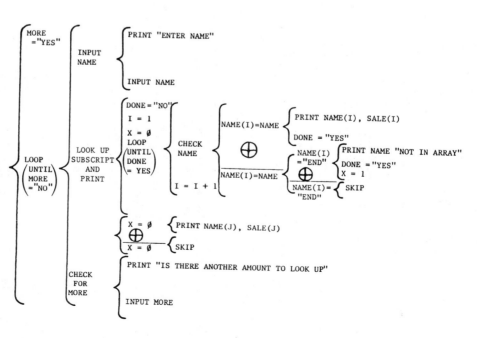

Figure 8.34 describes a program that uses previously loaded arrays A( ) and S( ). Array A( ) lists agent names by agent numbers. Array S( ), a two-dimensional array, lists monthly sales by agent number and by month. The program prints the first-quarter sales of various agents. It reads a series of records containing agent names, uses a sequential search to look up an agent number from array A, and prints out first-quarter sales from array S.

Figure 8.34 This program stores names in the B( ) array, searches for them in the A( ) array, and then prints corresponding first-quarter sales based on calculations from the S( ) array.

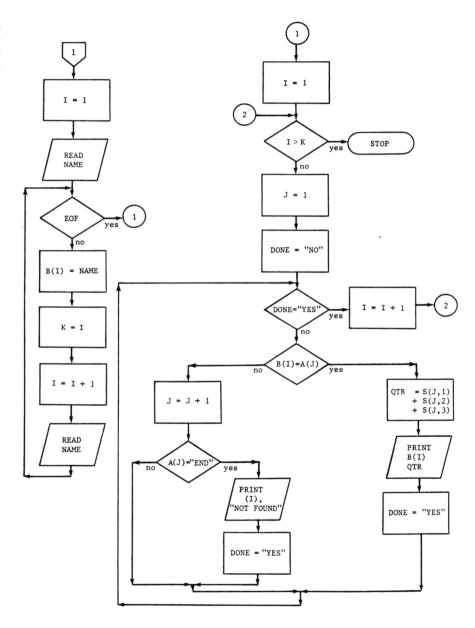

Exercises 8.8–8.10

1. Explain what will happen if the temporary storage variable is not included in the exchange routine. Explain why the temporary storage variable need not be subscripted even though the variables exchanged are subscripted.

2. Sort each of the following sets of numbers in the order indicated, using the sort indicated.

BUBBLE ASCENDING								
ORIGINAL	4	2	7	1	6	8	3	5
1st Pass								
2nd Pass								
3rd Pass								
4th Pass								
5th Pass								
6th Pass								
7th Pass								

BINARY ASCENDING								
ORIGINAL	4	2	7	1	6	8	3	5
1st Pass								
2nd Pass								
3rd Pass								
4th Pass								
5th Pass								
6th Pass								
7th Pass								

BUBBLE DESCENDING								
ORIGINAL	4	2	7	1	6	8	3	5
1st Pass								
2nd Pass								
3rd Pass								
4th Pass								
5th Pass								
6th Pass								
7th Pass								

BINARY DESCENDING							
ORIGINAL	4	2	7	1	6	8	3	5
1st Pass								
2nd Pass								
3rd Pass								
4th Pass								
5th Pass								
6th Pass								
7th Pass								

3. Construct a Warnier diagram and a flowchart for a program that will read a list of names and print the list in alphabetical order, using:
   a. A bubble sort (ascending).
   b. A bubble sort (descending).
   c. A binary sort (descending).

4. Design a structured flowchart for a program to print the smallest element in a one-dimensional array. Assume that the array was previously loaded and that END is the last element.

5. Design a Warnier diagram for a program to print the smallest element in a 50 × 100 array. Assume that the array was previously loaded.

6. Design a structured flowchart for the program described in Exercise 5.

7. Design a structured flowchart for a program that will receive one name at a time from user input, look up that name in a one-dimensional array A( ), and print the array subscript of that name if the name is found or print "NAME NOT IN ARRAY" if the name is not found. The user is to be able to look up names until a designated value is entered. Assume that there are 20 entries in the array.

8. Design structured flowcharts to represent the Warnier diagrams given in Figures 8.25, 8.26, 8.28, and 8.29.

9. Design Warnier diagrams to represent Figures 8.27 and 8.34.

*10. Load a 25 × 30 two-dimensional array with names read from unsorted records. When the array is full or EOF is reached, the names in the array are to be sorted and then printed in alphabetical order.

Review Questions

Completion

1. The fundamental structure for array processing is a _____ .

2. The _____ instructs the computer to set a particular number of locations aside for a particular array.

3. The _____ identifies the locations in the array at which an element is stored.

4. The term *user input* refers to data entered by _____ through a terminal during the _____ of the program.

5. Input instructions are generally preceded by _____ .
6. The number of dimensions of an array is the number of _____ .
7. The processing of multidimensional arrays generally requires the use of a distinct _____ for each dimension.
8. After the first complete pass of a bubble sort, the _____ item is in the correct position.
9. After the first complete pass of a binary sort, the _____ item is in the correct position.
10. A _____ search requires that the array to be searched be presorted.

Discussion

1. What is an array?
2. What is the difference between a one-dimensional array and a two-dimensional array?
3. What is a dimension statement?
4. Explain why Figure 8.2 uses the instruction READ SALES rather than the instruction READ A(I).
5. Describe what takes place when the instruction INPUT SALE is executed.
6. Explain the function of prompter messages.
7. Describe three methods of enabling a user to control the number of items entered.
8. Describe the pass of a bubble sort.
9. Describe the pass of a binary sort.

True or False

1. _____ The fundamental structure used to process each element of an array is the nested if-then-else structure.
2. _____ The instruction READ COST(I) is used to obtain a value that was previously stored in an array.
3. _____ All locations that are set aside by the dimension statement must be used in the program.
4. _____ Array subscripts may usually be indicated by any legitimate arithmetic expressions that designate positive integers.
5. _____ User input is generally faster than the reading of records.
6. _____ Prompt messages usually follow input instructions.
7. _____ The processing of a two-dimensional array always requires the use of a distinct variable subscript for each dimension.
8. _____ An element of a two-dimensional array can be referred to only by an expression that contains two subscripts.
9. _____ The bubble sort and the binary sort are very efficient sort routines.
10. _____ After the first pass of a binary sort, the first of the items to be sorted is in the correct position.

9. Edit and File-Processing Programs

9.1 Edit Programs

Edit programs are designed to review data files before regular processing occurs. They validate data within individual records, ensuring that only formally correct records are processed. An edit program does not detect every error in the data, but it checks for certain types of data that could not possibly be correct. For example, an edit program would not detect the fact that an age of 48 was entered for an individual who was only 47. It could, however, determine that an age of 248 or an age of −7 was an error. It could also detect the fact that alphabetic characters were entered or that no entry at all was made. In short, the edit program makes certain that the individual data records are reasonable.

A typical edit program processes one or more input files and produces an output file and an exception report. The output file contains records that are ready for processing. The exception report contains a list of all records or all error records printed exactly as they were entered,[1] a statement that indicates the nature of each error, and tallies of correct, incorrect, and total records.

Figure 9.1 is an example of an input file, an output disk file, and an exception report for the input records for a payroll program.

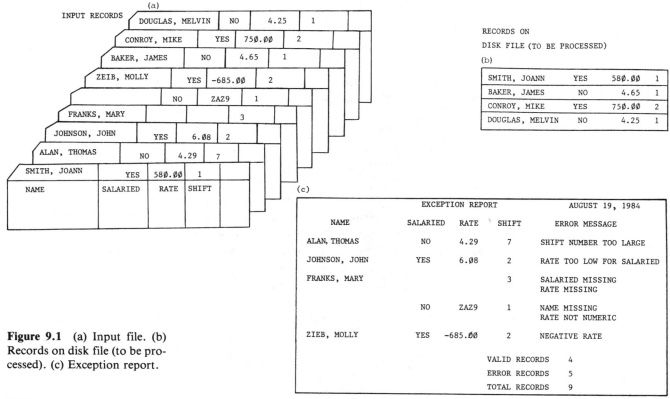

Figure 9.1 (a) Input file. (b) Records on disk file (to be processed). (c) Exception report.

[1] An output record that precisely duplicates an input record is called a *record image*.

Edit programs check the various fields of input records for anticipated errors. Typically, they make several of the following types of checks:

Check	Determines
1. Presence check	Whether field is blank.
2. Class check	Whether field is numeric, alphanumeric, or alphabetic.
3. Sign check	Whether numeric field is positive, negative, or zero.
4. Actual code check	Whether field is equal to one of several predetermined values.
5. Limit check	Whether field is within certain limits.
6. Consistency check	Whether a value in one field is reasonable, given values in other fields.

Figure 9.2 is a simple edit program that checks a payroll file to determine that an hours-worked field is not blank (presence check), that the entry is a number (class check), and that the entry is positive (sign check). This program produces an exception report that includes each record image and error messages for incorrect records. Note the natural progression of edit checks. Each subsequent decision is encountered only after a correct condition at previous decisions. (It makes no sense to ask whether hours are greater than or equal to zero if the hours are not numeric.)

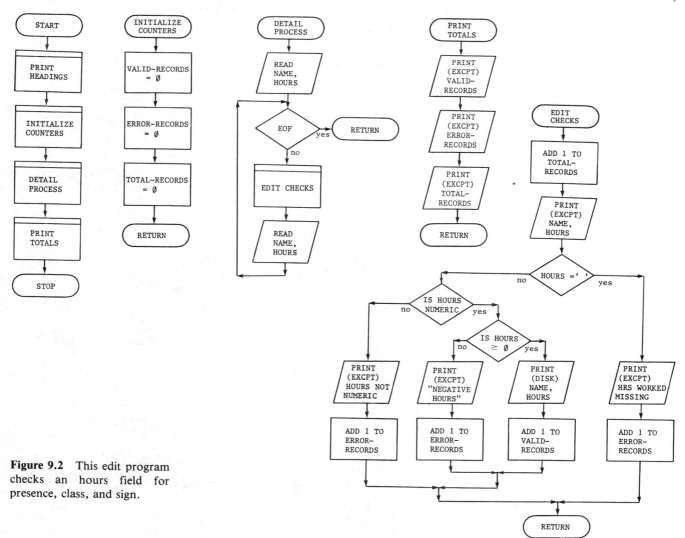

Figure 9.2 This edit program checks an hours field for presence, class, and sign.

Edit programs become more difficult when more than one field is to be checked. An indicator is used to identify errors so that a record will be written on the disk and counted as correct only if all of its fields pass all checks. Figure 9.3 processes the same file as Figure 9.2, but Figure 9.3 contains a presence check for the name field and a class check for the hours field.

Note that the indicator (ERROR) is set to NO just before each record is checked. It remains NO as long as no errors are found.

Figure 9.3 This edit program contains a presence check for the name field and a class check for the hours field.

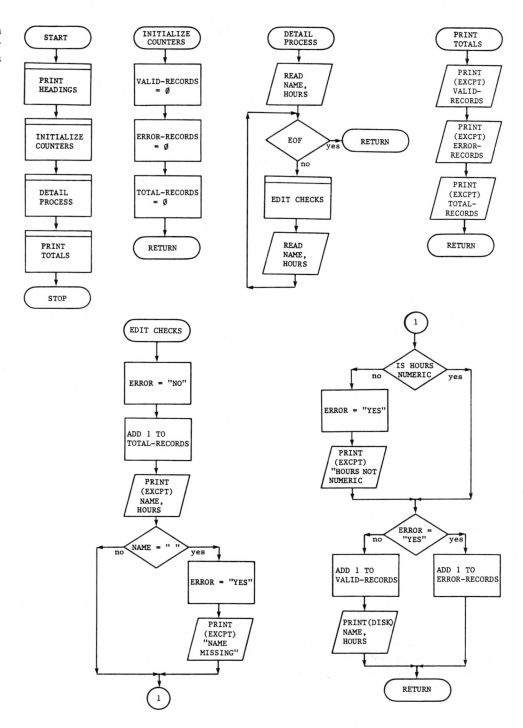

Figure 9.4(a) produces the exception report shown in Figure 9.4(b), which lists the record image of erroneous records only. It uses the ERROR indicator to print the record image only once, with the first error message for that record. The ERROR indicator is checked before printing the error message for all errors except a missing name. This ensures that the record image will be printed for the first error encountered and not for subsequent errors within the same record. (Flowcharts INITIALIZE COUNTERS, DETAIL PROCESS, and PRINT TOTALS are identical to those for Figure 9.2.)

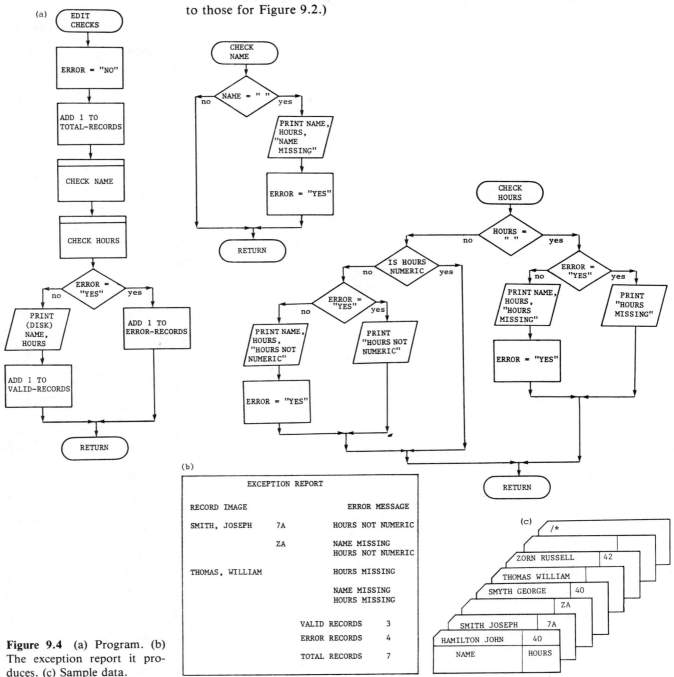

Figure 9.4 (a) Program. (b) The exception report it produces. (c) Sample data.

Figures 9.2 to 9.4 are good functional models for simple edit programs. Figure 9.4 can easily be expanded to handle many more fields by adding modules to the EDIT CHECKS segment. Figure 9.5 provides an alternative strategy for the edit program. In order to facilitate program maintenance, it places all print statements at the end of the program and uses individual indicators for each type of error. Such

Figure 9.5 This program checks a payroll record to ensure that the NAME and HOURS fields are present and that the HOURS field is numeric.

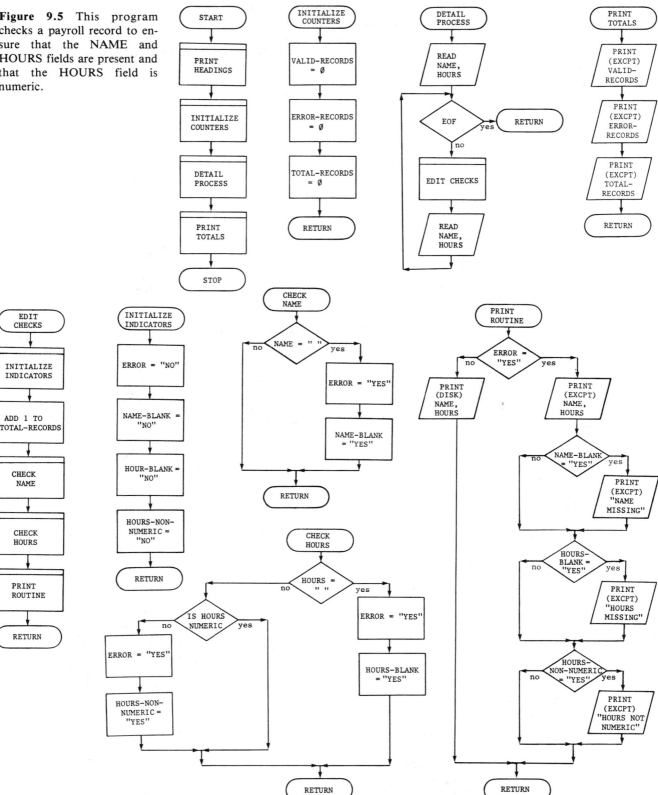

programs check desired fields for appropriate characteristics, set specific indicators for each different error, and then print error messages on the basis of which indicators were set.

Figure 9.5 is less efficient than Figure 9.4, but in many instances it is easier to maintain. We could easily make Figure 9.5 accommodate more sophisticated requirements by simply adding to its set of indicators, checks, and print decisions.

Exercises 9.1

1. Design a structured flowchart for an edit program that will read ITEM and COST and will check the COST field for presence, create a new file of correct records, and print an exception report that contains only error records and totals.

2. Design a structured flowchart for an edit program that will read ITEM and COST and will check a COST field for presence and for a positive value. A new file of correct records is to be created, and an exception report that contains all records is to be printed.

3. Design a structured flowchart for an edit program that will make an actual code check on a CODE field for an entry of ADD, CHG, or DEL. The program is also to check a NAME field for presence. A new file of correct records and an exception report are to be created. The exception report is to print the record image only once per erroneous record. Correct record images are not to appear on the exception report.

4. Design a Warnier diagram for the program described in Exercise 2.

5. Design a Warnier diagram for the program described in Exercise 3.

9.2 Sequential File Processing

Many of the programs described in earlier chapters included a READ statement. Each of these programs processed a sequential file. The first models considered employee card files with each record on a separate card. Such files are organized and must be processed sequentially. That is, the first record must be read first and either processed or discarded before the next record is read. No record can be read out of order.

Sequential files stored on electronic media such as tapes or disks are organized in this same manner. Each record is stored on a separate segment of the tape or disk and cannot be read or processed before all previous records have been read or processed. So all of the programs in earlier chapters could be used with a sequential disk or tape file.

Each record of a sequential file contains various fields, such as name, address, age, and so on. When these records are read, these fields are stored at various locations. Sequential files frequently contain a field designated as the **record key**. This field may simply be one of the regular record fields (such as customer number or policy number), or it may be a field whose only function is to be the record key.

Individual records are stored in sequential files in the order (usually ascending) of their record keys. Access to a particular record may be gained by reading the records in the file and comparing their record keys with a given value. When the record with the correct record key is encountered, that record is processed.

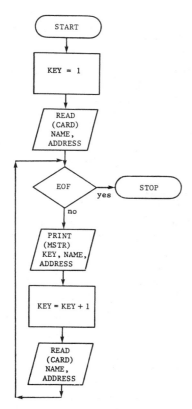

Figure 9.6 A file-creation program.

Various programming languages handle the tasks of reading records from files and creating records on files in various ways. Here we shall simply use the instructions READ and PRINT. The instruction READ MSTRKEY, MSTRNAME reads the next record on file and stores the first field at a location called MSTRKEY and a second at a location called MSTRNAME. The instruction PRINT MSTRKEY, MSTRNAME prints the information stored at MSTRKEY and MSTRNAME in the first two fields of the next record. When more than one file is being used in a given program, we will use a parenthetical expression to indicate the appropriate file. The instruction READ (MSTR) MSTRKEY, MSTRNAME reads the master file and stores the first two fields as indicated.

Sequential processing can be divided into three types of programs: file creation, file extraction, and file maintenance. Each of these is considered in the pages that follow. A sequential file is created by reading records or accepting data from user input and writing those records on some recording device. The key number of each record may be supplied by the program and simply reflect the numerical order in which the records were received, or (assuming that the records have been presorted) it may be part of the record.

Figure 9.6 represents a file-creation program. The result of running this program would be a file of records each of which contained a record key, a name, and an address. We shall assume that an appropriate EOF marker for the file will be supplied without specific directions.

Once a file is created, processing usually involves both the file to be processed, which is called the **master file**, and another file called the **transaction file**. Records in the transaction file contain record keys that indicate which of the records from the master file are to be processed. The transaction records may also include other fields that indicate the nature of the processing desired. The transaction file is a sequential file whose records are in the same order as those of the master file.

9.3 Extract Program (Sequential Files)

Extract programs read files, select particular records, and create new files or reports from the selected records. Records can be selected on the basis of the information they contain (such as age, smoking habits, or department), or they can be selected on the basis of their record key. Chapter 2 dealt with selection of the first type. Here we will consider selection from sequential files on the basis of record key.

Extract programs (on the basis of record key) for sequential files use a transaction file and a master file. The records of the transaction file need contain only a record key (TRNSKEY) that corresponds to the record key (MSTRKEY) of a record in the master file. The record keys of the transaction file indicate which records of the master file are to be printed. In this program both files are read, their keys are compared, and a master is printed when the keys are equal. The most difficult logical problem with this program is reading the correct file at the correct time. Figure 9.7(a) simplifies the problem somewhat by assuming that the transaction file contains no erroneous records. That is, we assume that each TRNSKEY will match one MSTRKEY. Given this assumption, the following considerations help produce the decision table shown in Figure 9.7(b).

1. When TRNSKEY equals MSTRKEY, the master is to be printed. Both the master file and the transaction file are read to seek another match.
2. When TRNSKEY does not equal MSTRKEY, the program has not yet reached the master record that is indicated by the current transaction record. So a new master record is read.

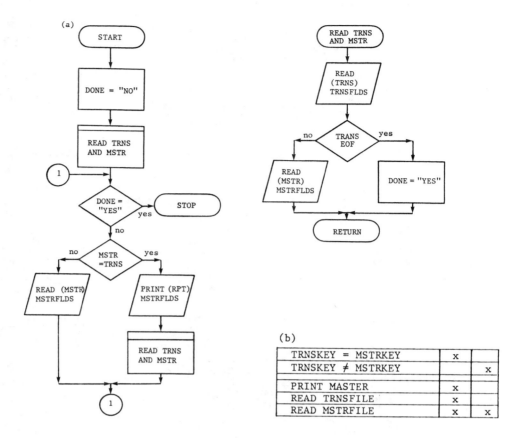

Figure 9.7 (a) An extract program based on record key. (b) Decision table.

TRNSKEY = MSTRKEY	x	
TRNSKEY ≠ MSTRKEY		x
PRINT MASTER	x	
READ TRNSFILE	x	
READ MSTRFILE	x	x

In Figure 9.7 a record is read from both files, and the record keys are compared. When the keys are equal, the record is printed and both files are again read. When the keys are not equal, only the master is read. Figure 9.7 contains an EOF for only the transaction file, because each TRNSKEY matches a MSTRKEY. In this situation the master file cannot be exhausted before the transaction file, so processing can continue until the transaction file reaches its end. Note that the master file will not be read after the transaction file reaches its end.

Ordinarily it is not prudent to assume that the record keys in a transaction file are without error. Besides the obvious errors due to erroneous data entry for the transaction file, the master file itself presents a problem. A master file that has been updated since its creation frequently has gaps in its record keys due to the deletion of various records. Hence the fact that keys on master records ranged from 0001 to 9999 would not guarantee the presence of, say, a master record key 768. The problem of erroneous record keys could be overcome by an edit program for the transaction file. But a program that would ensure a correct file of transaction keys would require nearly as much processing as the contemplated extract program. So it is generally more efficient to handle the error records within the extract program itself.

Figures 9.8 and 9.9 handle transaction files with erroneous records and, in addition to printing extract reports, print exception reports that list erroneous transaction records. Figure 9.8(a) is somewhat simplified by the omission of EOF considerations. The following considerations determine the decision table shown in Figure 9.8(b).

1. When MSTRKEY = TRNSKEY, a master record has been identified for printing. The master is printed on the extract report, and the next records in both the transaction file and the master file are read.

2. When MSTRKEY < TRNSKEY,[2] the program has not yet reached the master record (if any) that is indicated by the current TRNSKEY. Another master record is to be read.

3. When MSTRKEY > TRNSKEY, the program has passed all potential matching master records.

   a. No previous master record matched the current transaction record. (If there had been such a match, a new transaction record would have been read.)

   b. No subsequent master record will match, because the record keys of all subsequent master records will be greater than that of the current master record. So the current transaction record is an error, and an exception report line is printed and a new transaction record is read.

Figure 9.8 (a) An extract program that provides for erroneous transaction records. (b) Decision table.

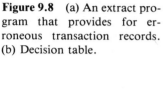

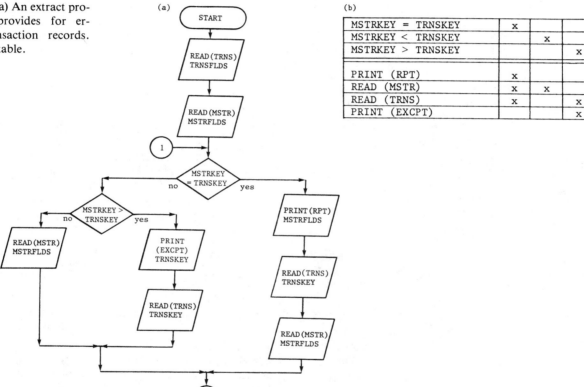

(b)

	x		
MSTRKEY = TRNSKEY	x		
MSTRKEY < TRNSKEY		x	
MSTRKEY > TRNSKEY			x
PRINT (RPT)	x		
READ (MSTR)	x	x	
READ (TRNS)	x		x
PRINT (EXCPT)			x

Figure 9.9 corrects the endless loop of Figure 9.8 by adding appropriate EOF processing. There are two files, either of which could reach its end first, so there are two EOF structures. When the transaction file EOF is reached, the program is completed, because there will be no more records from the master file to be printed. But in the event that the master file reaches its end first, all remaining records in the transaction file are erroneous and will be noted on the exception report. Hence this extract program will be completed only when the transaction file is at its end.

Note that, when the MSTR EOF occurs, a value called HIGH VALUES is stored at MSTRKEY. HIGH VALUES is a value that is greater than any anticipated value in either the master file or the transaction file.[3] Storing a high value in

---

[2] This example, like subsequent examples, assumes that both the master file and the transaction file are in ascending order.

[3] In COBOL, "HIGH-VALUES" designates the highest possible value for a given computer.

MSTRKEY causes all subsequent TRNSKEYs to be less than the MSTRKEY and all subsequent transaction records to be recorded as error records.

Figure 9.9 would generate the following sales report and the following exception report from the files described.

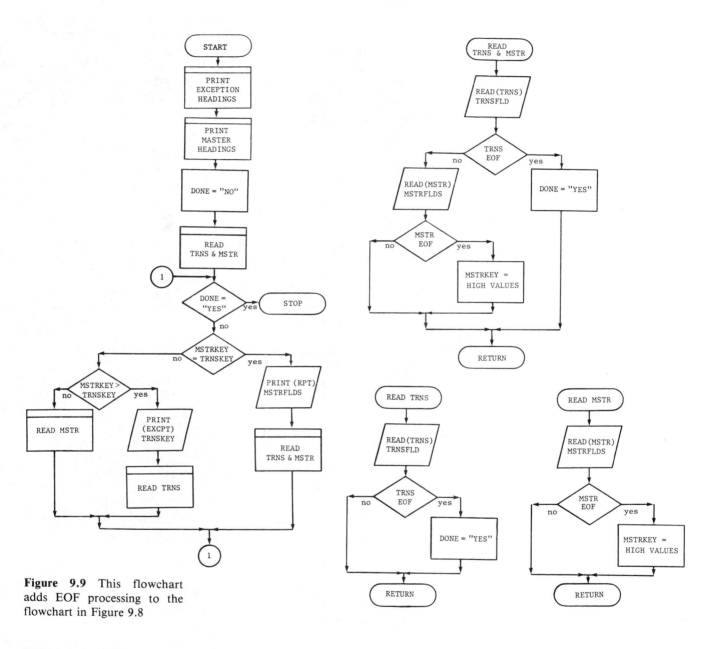

Figure 9.9 This flowchart adds EOF processing to the flowchart in Figure 9.8

MASTER FILE		
KEY	NAME	SALES
ØØ1	Smith JoAnn	1467.93
ØØ2	Alan Thomas	6314.16
ØØ4	Johnson John	4596.71
ØØ7	Franks Mary	3164.27
ØØ8	Fisher James	4968.46
Ø1Ø	Zeib Molly	3964.27
Ø11	Baker James	5697.48
Ø13	Conroy Mike	2614.79
Ø15	Douglas Melvin	8631.28

TRNS FILE
KEY
ØØ2
ØØ3
ØØ4
ØØ5
ØØ7
ØØ8
Ø11
Ø15
Ø16
Ø17

SALES REPORT		
EMPLOYEE NUMBER	EMPLOYEE NAME	SALES
ØØ2	Alan Thomas	6314.16
ØØ4	Johnson John	4596.71
ØØ7	Franks Mary	3164.27
ØØ8	Fisher James	4968.46
Ø11	Baker James	5697.48
Ø15	Douglas Melvin	8631.28

EXCEPTION REPORT ERRONEOUS TRANSACTIONS
ØØ3
ØØ5
Ø16
Ø17

Exercises
9.2–9.3

1. Design a structured flowchart for a program that will create a transaction file of record keys from user input. The file is to be in ascending order, and the program is not to accept a record that is out of order. Be sure to include appropriate prompter messages.

2. Design a structured flowchart for an extract program that will create a file of records from a master file on the basis of matching record keys in a transaction file. Print a report that contains all keys from the transaction file. Along with each key, either print the master fields of matching master records or print the word "invalid". Do *not* assume that all TRNSKEYs will match MSTRKEYs. (Assume that both the master file and the transaction file are in ascending order.)

3. Design a Warnier diagram for the program described in Exercise 1.

4. Design a Warnier diagram for the program described in Exercise 2.

9.4 Sequential File Maintenance

Sequential file maintenance programs are used to update a master file by adding records, deleting records, and/or changing records. Actually this description is somewhat misleading, because no alterations are made to the master file. Instead a new master file is created from an existing master file and the transaction file. Just as was the case with the extract program, the master file and the transaction file are read, their keys are compared, and (depending on conditions) an entry is made on the new master. When such a program is finished, the transaction file and the old master file remain as they were and a new master file reflects all changes. The new master becomes the master file for subsequent operations, and the old master is retained as a back-up.

Sequential file maintenance programs are considerably more complex than extract programs, because they must perform three distinct functions. They must add

OLD MASTER	
KEY	CITY
01	Topeka
05	Wichita
06	Lansing
08	St. Marys
10	Dodge City
11	Fort Scott
13	Emporia
14	Goodland

TRANSACTION FILE		
KEY	CODE	CITY
01	C	Lawrence
02	A	Hays
04	C	Topeka
05	D	
06	A	Independence
09	A	Ottawa
10	C	Kansas City
11	D	
12	D	
14	C	Hutchinson
15	A	Garden City

NEW MASTER	
KEY	CITY
01	Lawrence
02	Hays
06	Lansing
08	St. Marys
09	Ottawa
10	Kansas City
13	Emporia
14	Hutchinson
15	Garden City

	TRANSACTION REPORT			
RECORD KEY	OLD MASTER	TRANSACTION	NEW MASTER	ERROR
01	Topeka	Change	Lawrence	
02		Add	Hays	
04		None		Change with no Master
05	Wichita	Delete		
06		None		Add with Existing Master
09		Add	Ottawa	
10	Dodge City	Change	Kansas City	
11	Fort Scott	Delete		
12		None		Delete with no Master
14	Goodland	Change	Hutchinson	
15		Add	Garden City	

Valid Records 8
Error Records 3
Total Records 11

new records, delete old records, and change existing records. Each transaction record contains a record code that indicates which of the three functions is to occur. **Add records** contain the record code, a record key, and a complete set of fields for the new record. **Change records** contain a record code, a record key, and the fields to be changed (what the master is to be changed to). **Delete records** need contain only the record code and the key of the record to be deleted. The following charts indicate how an old master, a transaction file, a new master, and a transaction report might look.

Establishing the decision table for the file maintenance program involves much of the same reasoning as was used in the extract example. It will, of course, be more complex in order to reflect the three types of transactions.

The program assumes that both the master file and the transaction file are in ascending order. The program will not allow any alteration (changes or deletions) of newly added records. That is, no change or delete records may follow an add record with the same record key. The program *does* provide for multiple changes of the same record and for deletion of a changed record.[4]

Error conditions are perhaps the most obvious. Each of the following conditions indicates an erroneous transaction record.

1. An add record whose key matches that of the master is an error, because a given key can appear only once on the new master.
2. A delete record whose key is less than the key of the current master is an error, because any matching record, if present, would have been processed. (Same reasoning as in extract program.)
3. A change record whose key is less than the key of the current master is an error, because any matching record, if present, would have been processed. (Same reasoning in extract program.)

In any of these cases, an error entry is made on the transaction report, the error counter is incremented, and the next record is read from the transaction file. These considerations are recorded in columns 1, 5, and 6 of Table 9.1.

A second step in completing the decision table is the determination of conditions that require the new master to be printed.

1. When MSTRKEY $\geq$ TRNSKEY, it is possible for a subsequent change record or delete record to match the master record key, so the new master cannot yet be printed.
2. When MSTRKEY $<$ TRNSKEY, all transactions that apply to that master record have occurred, the new master record is printed, and the old master file is read.
3. When the old master is read, its fields are stored at locations called old master fields. Immediately after this occurs, that information is moved to (duplicated in) fields called new master fields. This double set of fields is required to handle both changes and deletions.

These directions are recorded in columns 7, 8, and 9 of Table 9.1.

The final considerations are the valid add, change, and delete conditions.

1. The add record is effective when the TRNSKEY $<$ MSTRKEY. This situation arises when a master with a higher key has just been read but not yet processed. If the previous MSTRKEY had been equal to TRNSKEY, an error message would have been printed and a new transaction record read. So all

---

[4] Other file maintenance programs may make different provisions.

previous MSTRKEYs were lower than the TRNSKEY, and the record to be added has a higher key than any previously processed record and a lower key than the master currently awaiting processing. No change record or delete record with this key number may follow, so the add record should be printed on the new master. Column 4 of Table 9.1 indicates the operations that must occur.

2. The change record is effective when TRNSKEY = MSTRKEY. On this condition, the fields present in the transaction record are moved to (duplicated in) the new master fields. No printing occurs at this time, because a subsequent record may indicate an additional change or even a deletion of the same master record. Column 2 of Table 9.1 indicates the operations that must occur.

3. The delete record is effective when TRNSKEY = MSTRKEY. To delete a record, the program simply fails to print the old master record on the new master file and proceeds to read both another old master record and a transaction record. We assume that no add record or change record will follow a deletion with the same record key. This could easily be ensured by a simple edit program. Column 3 of Table 9.1 represents the processing that is to occur.

Table 9.1   Decision table.

		1	2	3	4	5	6	7	8	9
KEY CONDITION	MSTR = TRNS	X	X	X						
	MSTR > TRNS				X	X	X			
	MSTR < TRNS							X	X	X
RECORD TYPE	ADD	X			X			X		
	CHANGE		X			X			X	
	DELETE			X			X			X
PRINT ERROR MESSAGE		X				X	X			
READ TRANSACTION FILE		X	X	X	X	X	X			
PRINT NEW MASTER							X	X	X	X
READ OLD MASTER				X				X	X	X
MOVE OLD MSTR TO NEW MSTR				X	X			X	X	X
MOVE TRNS TO NEW MSTR			X		X					
PRINT TRANSACTION LINE			X	X	X					
INCREMENT ERROR COUNTER		X				X	X			
INCREMENT VALID COUNTER			X	X	X					
INCREMENT TOTAL COUNTER		X	X	X	X	X	X			

Figures 9.10 and 9.11 represent a file maintenance program. Figure 9.10 is presented without counters and EOF considerations (and contains, of course, an endless loop). Figure 9.11 includes both EOF processing and counters. Both the master file and the transaction file set their key fields to HIGH VALUES at EOF. When the master file reaches its end and MSTRKEY = HIGH VALUES, remaining add records continue to be added and all remaining changes and deletions are recorded as errors on the exception report. When the transaction file reaches EOF and TRNSKEY = HIGH VALUES, all remaining master records are printed on the new master.

Figure 9.10 File maintenance program without counters and EOF considerations.

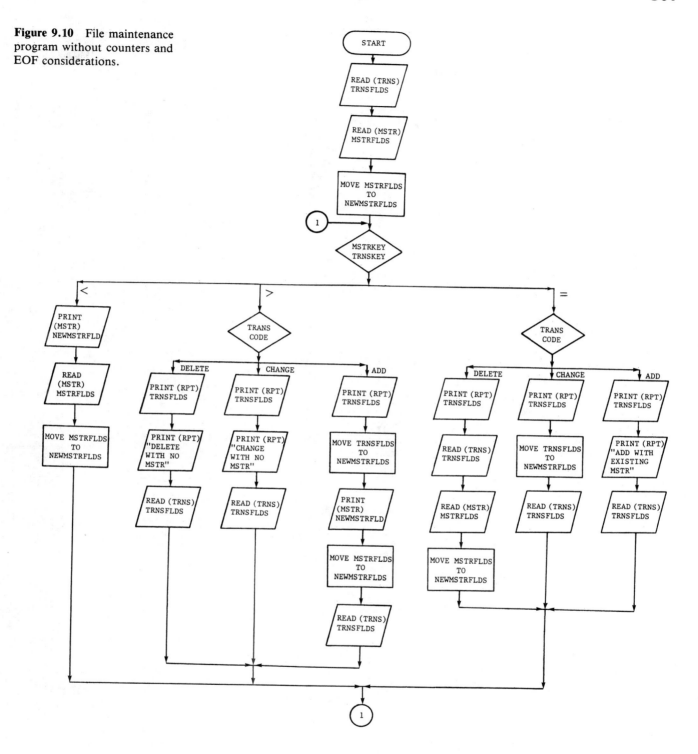

Figure 9.11 File maintenance program that includes both counters and EOF processing.

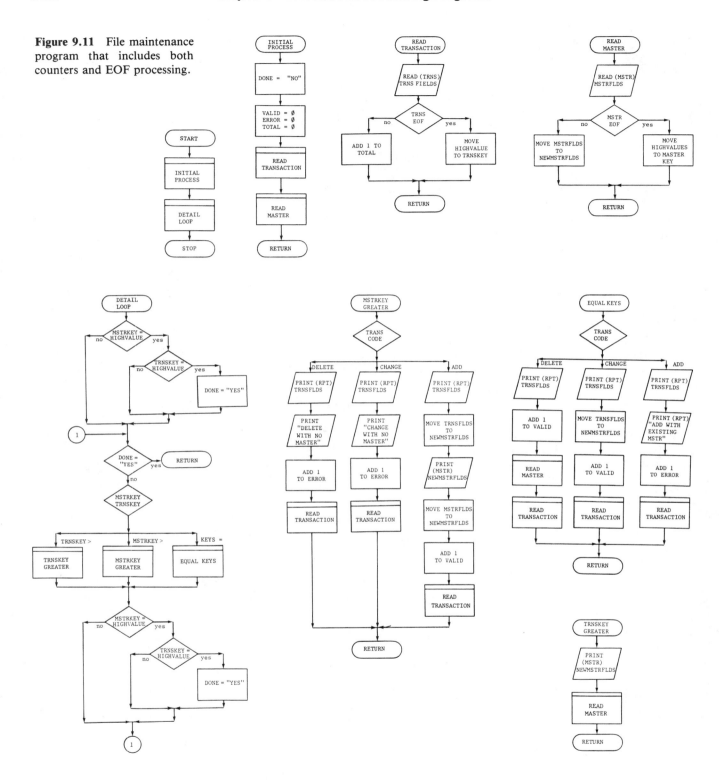

9.5 Random File Processing

Random file processing is non-sequential file processing. Random file processing allows records to be read and printed in any order without reading previous records. It would, for example, allow a program to read the 14th, the 87th, and the 256th records without reading any other records. Random processing is potentially more efficient than sequential processing, because only records that are to be processed are read. Random processing is also potentially *less* efficient than sequential processing, because it requires more steps to read individual records. Sequential file processing is the most efficient form of processing when transaction items are batched in sequential order and a high percentage of the master file is to be used. However, when items are to be processed one at a time (through user input, perhaps) or when only a small percentage of the master file is to be processed, non-sequential or random processing is more efficient.

Non-sequential processing can be divided into ISAM file processing and direct file processing. Both of these forms of processing make use of the fact that records on a disk or drum have designated locations or addresses and that these addresses can be used to read individual records. Random processing uses the record key of the desired record to determine its address within its file. The difference between ISAM processing and direct processing lies in the way those addresses are determined. ISAM files use an index to match the record key with an address. Direct processing uses a mathematical formula to convert the record key into a record address.

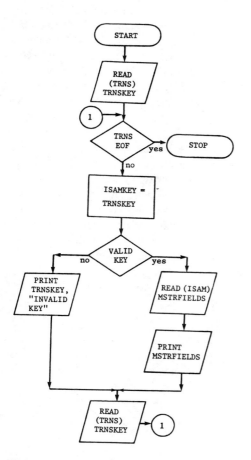

Figure 9.12 An extract program for an ISAM file.

ISAM Processing

ISAM (Indexed Sequential Access Method) **processing** makes use of an index to find a particular record on the basis of that record's key field. When an ISAM file is created and when records are added, an index for that file is also created. The index relates each record's key field to its location. Later, when a record key is supplied to the computer, the computer uses the index to access the record at the correct location. The details of building the index and of using the index to look up an item are handled by the computer and are not designed by the programmer.

Because records are read at random, the program must supply the record key of the record to be read, and the ISAM file must be checked to determine whether the key is valid (that is, whether the file contains a record with that key). Figure 9.12 describes an extract program for an ISAM file. It supplies a record key from a transaction file and tests for a valid key prior to reading an ISAM record.

The program begins by reading a transaction record and checking for EOF. The value of TRNSKEY is then assigned to ISAMKEY, providing a record key for the record to be read. The ISAM file is checked for a record with a key equal to ISAMKEY. If the ISAM file contains a record with that key, it is read and its fields are printed. If the ISAM file contains no record with that key, nothing is read and the error message is printed. In either case, the next transaction record is read.

The only ISAM file records to be read are those that match the key of the transaction record, so there is no need to compare record keys as in sequential processing. And, because the ISAM records are not read in any particular order, we are not concerned with an EOF for the ISAM file.

ISAM File Maintenance

Unlike sequential file maintenance, ISAM file maintenance programs actually change the ISAM file. They do not simply create an updated file, leaving the old master as it was; they add, change, and delete records from a single ISAM file. The systems flowcharts shown in Figures 9.13 and 9.14 compare these sequential and ISAM maintenance programs.

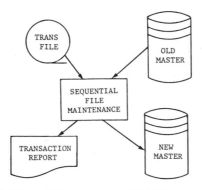

Figure 9.13 A sequential file maintenance program.

Figure 9.14 An ISAM file maintenance program.

ISAM maintenance programs add, change, and delete records by using the instructions PRINT, REPRINT, and DELETE. PRINT inserts a record where there is none, REPRINT prints a new record in place of an existing record, and DELETE eliminates an existing record. These instructions are similar to the READ instructions in that each requires that a record key be provided and that the file be checked for a valid key (the presence of a record with that key). In the case of PRINT, which is used to add a record, a key is valid only if there is not already a record with that key. REPRINT, which is used to change a record, and DELETE, which is used to delete a record, have valid keys only when there is a current record with the key indicated.

An ISAM maintenance program reads a transaction record, sets the value of an ISAMKEY equal to the value of the TRNSKEY, prints the fields of the transaction record, and then determines whether the record is an add, a change, or a delete. For an add record, the program checks for a valid key and then prints the new record on the file or prints an error message. For a change record, it checks for a valid key. If the key is valid, then a record is read, the transaction fields are moved to the master fields, and the record is reprinted. If an invalid key is encountered, an error message is printed. For a delete record, the program checks for a valid key and either deletes the record or prints an error message. Appropriate counts are made of valid, error, and total records, and a transaction report is printed. The decision table given in Table 9.2 summarizes these requirements.

Table 9.2 Decision table for ISAM file update program.

RECORD TYPE	ADD	X	X				
	CHANGE			X	X		
	DELETE					X	X
KEY CONDITION	VALID KEY	X		X		X	
	INVALID KEY		X		X		X
READ MASTER RECORD				X			
MOVE TRANSACTION FIELDS TO MASTERFIELDS		X		X			
PRINT MASTER		X					
REPRINT MASTER				X			
DELETE RECORD						X	
PRINT ERROR MESSAGE			X		X		X
INCREMENT VALID RECORDS		X		X		X	
INCREMENT ERROR RECORDS			X		X		X

Figure 9.15 describes the ISAM file maintenance program.

Figure 9.15 An ISAM file maintenance program.

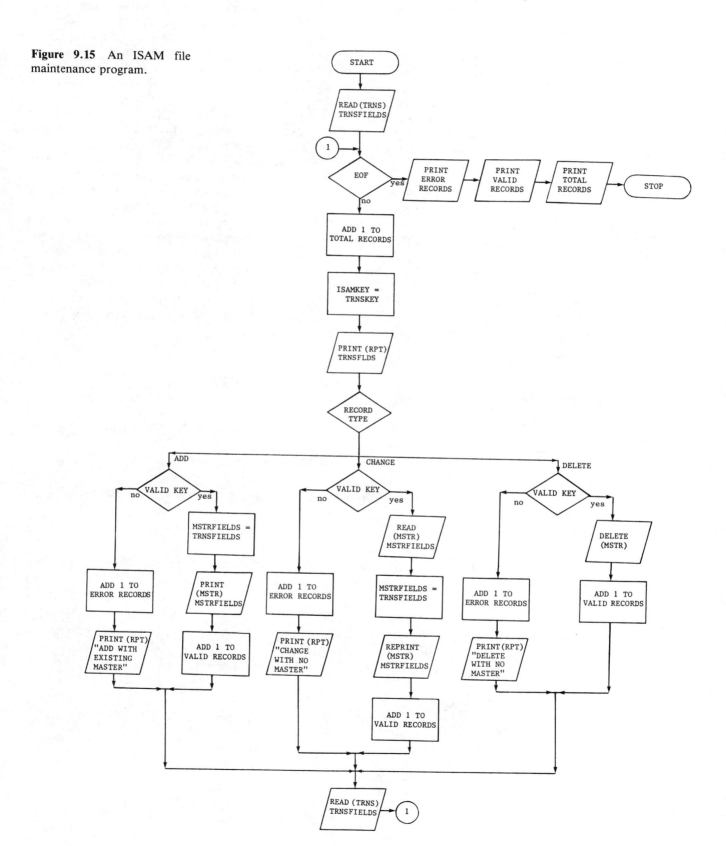

Direct File Processing

Direct file processing differs from ISAM file processing primarily in the way the record key is used to look up a record. In ISAM processing, looking up a record involves an index that is used by the computer; the programmer has only to provide the record key. In direct file processing, the programmer must provide one or more mathematical functions (called **hashing functions**) that convert the record key of each record to its location in the file. The programmer must also code the details of the look-up procedure.

Hashing functions and look-up procedures are usually very complicated to design. A typical problem in designing a workable hashing function and storage-and-retrieval process arises when one anticipates filing 8000 records in a 10,000-record file, using the Social Security number as a key. There will be plenty of room for the 8000 records, but there will not be an available location for each of the 999,999,999 different possible Social Security numbers. No matter what hashing function is used, there will be 10,000 Social Security numbers for each location. Provision must be made to store a second, third, etc., record with the same computed location and to recover those records on demand. These problems are not unsolvable, but their solutions and the resulting programs are very complicated. Except for the design of the hashing function and look-up procedure, the logic of direct file processing is essentially the same as that of ISAM file processing. Even though direct file processing is generally faster than ISAM processing, the difficulties in coding programs, especially working out hashing functions, make direct files less attractive than ISAM files and much less common.

Review Questions

Completion

1. _____ programs are designed to review data files before regular processing occurs.
2. Sequential files store individual records in the order of their _____ .
3. _____ is a value that is greater than any anticipated value.
4. The three types of transaction records in a sequential file update program are _____ , _____ , and _____ .
5. In a sequential file update, transaction file update records must contain a record key and a _____ .
6. A _____ uses a hashing function to convert record keys into file addresses.
7. A _____ uses an index to locate particular records.
8. ISAM is an acronym for _____ .
9. _____ file processing is the most efficient form of file processing when transaction records are sorted and batch-processed and a high percentage of the master file records are to be used.
10. _____ is the most efficient form of random processing.

Discussion

1. What is meant by each of the following terms?
   a. Presence check
   b. Class check
   c. Sign check
   d. Actual code check
   e. Limit check
   f. Consistency check
2. What is an exception report?

3. What is a record image?
4. For a file update program, what fields must be included in the transaction records for each of the following?
   a. An add
   b. A change
   c. A delete
5. Why is direct file processing less popular than ISAM file processing?
6. Explain what the reprint instruction is and why it is necessary in ISAM processing.

True or False

1. _____ Edit programs are designed to detect every error in a set of data.
2. _____ Edit programs are used before regular processing occurs.
3. _____ Before a particular record of a sequential file can be read, all previous records of that file must be read first.
4. _____ Transaction file records seldom contain record keys.
5. _____ There can be no gaps in record key numbers in a sequential file.
6. _____ In sequential file processing, both the master file and the transaction file must be in the same order.
7. _____ A sequential file update program changes the original master file.
8. _____ ISAM processing requires a comparison between the transaction record key and the master record key.
9. _____ An ISAM file update program changes the original master file.
10. _____ In direct file processing, both the master file and the transaction file must be in the same order.

Appendix
A. Documentation

Programs are seldom written for a programmer's own use. Generally they are written for other people (called users) who may be accountants, managers, or auditors within or outside of the programmer's company. Once the program is completed and tested, it is usually turned over to an operations department to be run at the user's request. As long as the program functions correctly, the programmer does not see it again. Even if adjustments to the program (called program maintenance) are required, the chances are that changes will be made by a different programmer. Thus, once a program is complete, a number of people other than the programmer use it or work with it in some way. Each of them will require information about the program. A collection of this information is called **documentation**. Documentation designed for *users* includes a description, in lay terms, of what the program does, including what data is required and what information will be generated. Documentation for *operators* includes designation of the CPU to be used and the specific tapes, disks, or card files to be loaded. It includes other directions necessary for running the program — perhaps even who may authorize a run and where the output is to be delivered. Documentation for the *maintenance programmer* includes detailed information concerning the program's logic.

Documentation standards vary greatly among installations. Minimal documentation usually includes the following items:

1. A program narrative
2. A system flowchart
3. An operations run sheet
4. A printer spacing chart
5. Detailed program logic
6. A program listing

The requirements for each of these items are usually specified in some detail, and preprinted forms have been designed for many of them.

The **program narrative** describes the program in terms that are understandable to the program's intended users; technical programming terminology is avoided. The narrative includes a description of a program's input requirements, its major components (including methods of calculation and data manipulation), and its intended output. The narrative should be thorough enough to allow a potential user to determine whether or not the program will carry out a task that he or she wants done.

The **system flowchart** is a graphic representation of the system that includes the program. It indicates the type of input/output media and identifies the other programs belonging to that system.

Operations run sheets are usually prepared on standard forms to provide operators with specific instructions for running the program. Run sheets describe the hardware to be used, including the specific CPU and I/O devices. They identify the files or data to be loaded and perhaps the final destination of output. They may include a list of persons who can authorize a program run and the name of the person to call in case of a problem. Run sheets may also include recovery procedures to be followed in the event that problems that could be anticipated arise.

Printer spacing charts are preprinted forms that indicate the way printed results are to appear.

Detailed program logic is provided by any of a number of program-design tools, including flowcharts, Warnier diagrams, Nassi-Shneiderman diagrams, and pseudocode. The detailed logic, together with the program listing, is used by the maintenance programmer to update the program.

A **program listing** is a print-out of the actual program as it has been entered into the computer.

In addition to these items, one or more of the following are frequently included in program documentation:

1. Tape, disk, and card layouts
2. Record descriptions
3. Run log
4. Test data and test methods used
5. Project history
6. Program evaluation

Tape, disk, and card layouts use standard forms to describe the position of each field with a record and the positions of the various records within a file. They are used by data-entry personnel.

Record descriptions use standard forms to describe records used by a program. Record descriptions identify each field, give its location within a record, and specify whether the field is to contain alphabetic or numeric data and what decimal positions are assumed or indicated. The record descriptions also indicate any editing that is to occur within the field.

The **run log** provides a record of each time a program was run. It may include items such as the operator's name and the name of the person or the department who authorized the run. The run log includes a comments section that describes any problems incurred regarding a particular run.

Test data and methods of testing show how the program was tested before it was put into operation.

The **project history** is a file of all communications regarding the program — from the original work request or preliminary inquiries to the present date. All telephone communications and interviews are reduced to notes, and these notes are included in the project history. The project history also includes all previous program modifications and a record of who has accessed the program.

The **project evaluation** is a narrative account as required by the installation. Items frequently included are an assessment of audit information produced by the program and an assessment of the program's and the system's security.

Figures A.1 to A.10 comprise a sample documentation package for the program represented by Figure 6.37(c). (This program is also used as an example in Appendix B.)

Figure A.1 Program narrative.

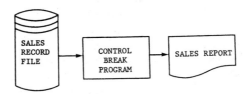

This program is an example of a control-break program [Figure 6.37(c)]. Data for the program consists of records that contain a division number, a department name, and a sales amount. Department totals are calculated by adding sales amounts; division totals are calculated by adding department totals. Each sale, department total, and division total is printed.

Figure A.2 System flowchart.

SALES RECORD FILE → CONTROL BREAK PROGRAM → SALES REPORT

Figure A.3 (a) Side 1 of operations run sheet. (b) Side 2.

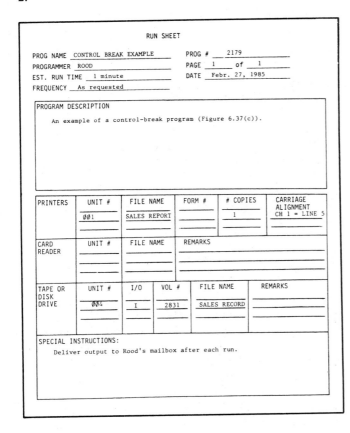

RUN SHEET

PROG NAME CONTROL BREAK EXAMPLE   PROG #   2179
PROGRAMMER ROOD   PAGE   1   of   1
EST. RUN TIME   1 minute   DATE   Febr. 27, 1985
FREQUENCY   As requested

PROGRAM DESCRIPTION

   An example of a control-break program (Figure 6.37(c)).

PRINTERS	UNIT #	FILE NAME	FORM #	# COPIES	CARRIAGE ALIGNMENT
	ØØ1	SALES REPORT		1	CH 1 = LINE 5

CARD READER	UNIT #	FILE NAME	REMARKS

TAPE OR DISK DRIVE	UNIT #	I/O	VOL #	FILE NAME	REMARKS
	ØØ4	I	2831	SALES RECORD	

SPECIAL INSTRUCTIONS:
   Deliver output to Rood's mailbox after each run.

RECOVERY PROCEDURES	
MESSAGE	ACTION TO BE TAKEN
PRINTS ONLY HEADING	(1) CHECK FOR CORRECT INPUT FILE
	(2) CHECK FOR DATA IN INPUT FILE
NOTHING PRINTED	LEAVE NOTE IN ROOD'S MAILBOX
	(DO NOT CALL)

CONTROLS
   NONE

Figure A.4 Printer spacing
chart.

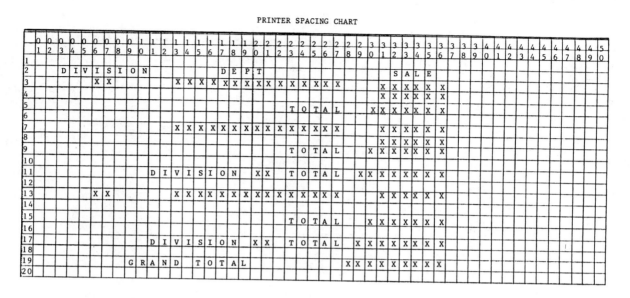

Figure A.5 Detailed program
logic.

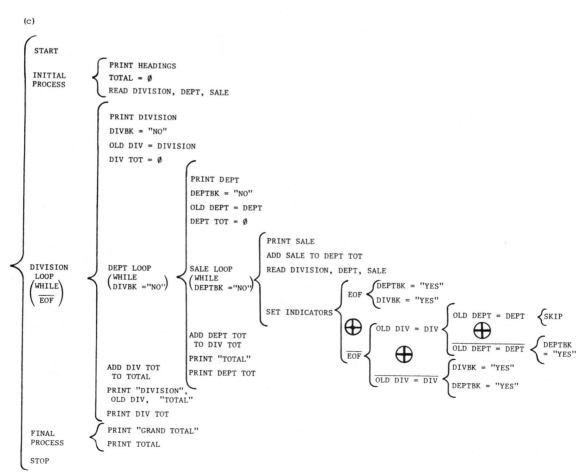

Figure A.6 (a) Program listing. (b) Output.

(a)
```
IDENTIFICATION DIVISION.
PROGRAM-ID.    CONTROL-BREAK-EXAMPLE.
AUTHOR.        ROOD.
*DATE-WRITTEN. FEB 1985.
*DATE-COMPILED FEB 1985.
*
********************************************************************
*                                                                *
* THIS CONTROL BREAK PROGRAM PROVIDES AN EXAMPLE OF CODING A      *
* PROGRAM FROM A WARNIER DIAGRAM.                                 *
*                                                                *
********************************************************************
*
ENVIRONMENT DIVISION.
*
*
CONFIGURATION SECTION.
*
    SOURCE-COMPUTER.   HJR 1900.
    OBJECT-COMPUTER.   HJR 1900.
*
*
INPUT-OUTPUT SECTION.
*
    FILE-CONTROL.
        SELECT SALES-RECORD-FILE
            ASSIGN TO PFMS.
        SELECT SALES-REPORT-FILE
            ASSIGN TO PFMS.
*
*
*
DATA DIVISION.
*
*
FILE SECTION.
*
FD  SALES-RECORD-FILE
    RECORD CONTAINS 80 CHARACTERS
    LABEL RECORDS ARE STANDARD
    DATA RECORD IS SALES-RECORD.
*
01  SALES-RECORD.
    05  SR-DIVISION             PIC XX.
    05  SR-DEPARTMENT           PIC X(15).
    05  SR-SALE                 PIC 9(3)V99.
    05  FILLER                  PIC X(58).
*
FD  SALES-REPORT-FILE
    RECORD CONTAINS 80 CHARACTERS
    LABEL RECORDS ARE STANDARD
    DATA RECORD IS REPORT-LINE.
*
01  REPORT-LINE                 PIC X(80).
*


*
WORKING-STORAGE SECTION.
*
01  PROGRAM-INDICATORS.
    05  END-OF-FILE             PIC X(3)  VALUE 'NO'.
        88 THERE-ARE-NO-MORE-RECORDS      VALUE 'YES'.
    05  DIVBK                   PIC X(3).
    05  DEPTBK                  PIC X(3).
*
01  WORK-AREAS.
    05  WS-DIVISION-TOTAL       PIC 99999V99.
    05  WS-DEPARTMENT-TOTAL     PIC 9999V99.
    05  WS-GRAND-TOTAL          PIC 999999V99.
    05  WS-OLD-DIVISION         PIC X(2).
    05  WS-OLD-DEPT             PIC X(15).
*
01  PRINTER-CONTROLS.
    05  PROPER-SPACING          PIC 9.
    05  ONE-LINE                PIC 9     VALUE 1.
    05  TWO-LINES               PIC 9     VALUE 2.
*
01  DETAIL-LINE.
    05  CARRIAGE-CONTROL        PIC X.
    05  FILLER                  PIC X(5)  VALUE SPACES.
    05  DL-DIVISION             PIC XX.
    05  FILLER                  PIC X(5)  VALUE SPACES.
    05  DL-DEPARTMENT           PIC X(15).
    05  FILLER                  PIC X(3)  VALUE SPACES.
    05  DL-SALE                 PIC 999.99.
    05  FILLER                  PIC X(43) VALUE SPACES.
```

Figure A.6 continued

```
*
01  HEADING-LINE
    05  CARRIAGE-CONTROL              PIC X.
    05  FILLER                        PIC XX      VALUE SPACES.
    05  FILLER                        PIC X(8)    VALUE 'DIVISION'.
    05  FILLER                        PIC X(6)    VALUE SPACES.
    05  FILLER                        PIC X(4)    VALUE 'DEPT'.
    05  FILLER                        PIC X(11)   VALUE SPACES.
    05  FILLER                        PIC X(4)    VALUE 'SALE'.
    05  FILLER                        PIC X(44)   VALUE SPACES.
*
01  DEPARTMENT-TOTAL-LINE.
    05  CARRIAGE-CONTROL              PIC X.
    05  FILLER                        PIC X(22)   VALUE SPACES.
    05  FILLER                        PIC X(5)    VALUE 'TOTAL'.
    05  FILLER                        PIC X(2)    VALUE SPACES.
    05  DEPARTMENT-TOTAL              PIC 9999.99.
    05  FILLER                        PIC X(43)   VALUE SPACES.
*
01  DIVISION-TOTAL-LINE.
    05  CARRIAGE-CONTROL              PIC X.
    05  FILLER                        PIC X(10)   VALUE SPACES.
    05  FILLER                        PIC X(8)    VALUE 'DIVISION'.
    05  FILLER                        PIC X       VALUE SPACE.
    05  DT-DIVISION                   PIC XX.
    05  FILLER                        PIC X       VALUE SPACE.
    05  FILLER                        PIC X(5)    VALUE 'TOTAL'.
    05  FILLER                        PIC X       VALUE SPACE.
    05  DIVISION-TOTAL                PIC 99999.99.
    05  FILLER                        PIC X(43)   VALUE SPACES.
*
01  GRAND-TOTAL-LINE.
    05  CARRIAGE-CONTROL              PIC X.
    05  FILLER                        PIC X(8)    VALUE SPACES.
    05  FILLER                        PIC X(6)    VALUE 'GRAND'.
    05  FILLER                        PIC X(5)    VALUE 'TOTAL'.
    05  FILLER                        PIC X(8)    VALUE SPACES.
    05  GRAND-TOTAL                   PIC 999999.99.
    05  FILLER                        PIC X(45)   VALUE SPACES.
*
*
*
PROCEDURE DIVISION.
*
100-MAIN-LINE
    PERFORM 220-INITIAL-PROCESS.
    PERFORM 240-DIVISION-LOOP
        UNTIL THERE-ARE-NO-MORE-RECORDS.
    PERFORM 260-FINAL-PROCESS.
    STOP RUN.
*
220-INITIAL-PROCESS.
    OPEN INPUT SALES-RECORD-FILE.
    OPEN OUTPUT SALES-RECORD-FILE.
    MOVE SPACES TO REPORT-LINE.
    WRITE REPORT-LINE FROM HEADING-LINE
        AFTER ADVANCING PAGE.
    MOVE ONE-LINE TO PROPER-SPACING.
    MOVE ZERO TO WS-GRAND-TOTAL.
    READ SALES-RECORD-FILE
        AT END MOVE 'YES' TO END-OF-FILE.
*
240-DIVISION-LOOP.
    MOVE SR-DIVISION TO DL-DIVISION.
    MOVE 'NO' TO DIVBK.
    MOVE SR-DIVISION TO WS-OLD-DIVISION.
    MOVE ZERO TO WS-DIVISION-TOTAL.
    PERFORM 340-DEPT-LOOP
        UNTIL DIVBK NOT EQUAL TO 'NO'.
    ADD WS-DIVISION-TOTAL TO WS-GRAND-TOTAL.
    MOVE WS-OLD-DIVISION TO DT-DIVISION.
    MOVE WS-DIVISION-TOTAL TO DIVISION-TOTAL.
    WRITE REPORT-LINE FROM DIVISION-TOTAL-LINE
        AFTER ADVANCING PROPER-SPACING.
    MOVE TWO-LINES TO PROPER-SPACING.
*
260-FINAL-PROCESS.
    MOVE WS-GRAND-TOTAL TO GRAND-TOTAL.
    WRITE REPORT-LINE FROM GRAND-TOTAL-LINE
        AFTER ADVANCING PROPER-SPACING.
    CLOSE SALES-RECORD-FILE.
    CLOSE SALES-REPORT-FILE.
```

Figure A.6 continued

```
*
340-DEPT-LOOP.
    MOVE SR-DEPARTMENT TO DL-DEPARTMENT.
    MOVE 'NO' TO DEPTBK.
    MOVE SR-DEPARTMENT TO WS-OLD-DEPT.
    MOVE ZERO TO WS-DEPARTMENT-TOTAL.
    PERFORM 440-SALE-LOOP
        UNTIL DEPTBK = 'YES'.
    ADD WS-DEPARTMENT-TOTAL TO WS-DIVISION-TOTAL.
    MOVE WS-DEPARTMENT-TOTAL TO DEPARTMENT-TOTAL.
    WRITE REPORT-LINE FROM DEPARTMENT-TOTAL-LINE
        AFTER ADVANCING PROPER-SPACING.
    MOVE TWO-LINES TO PROPER-SPACING.
*
440-SALE-LOOP.
    MOVE SR-SALE TO DL-SALE.
    ADD SR-SALE TO WS-DEPARTMENT-TOTAL.
    WRITE REPORT-LINE FROM DETAIL-LINE
        AFTER ADVANCING PROPER-SPACING.
    MOVE ONE-LINE TO PROPER-SPACING.
    MOVE SPACES TO DETAIL-LINE.
    READ SALES-RECORD-FILE
        AT END MOVE 'YES' TO END-OF-FILE.
    PERFORM 540-SET-INDICATORS.
*
540-SET-INDICATORS.
    IF THERE-ARE-NO-MORE-RECORDS
        MOVE 'YES' TO DEPTBK
        MOVE 'YES' TO DIVBK
    ELSE
        IF WS-OLD-DIVISION = SR-DIVISION
            IF WS-OLD-DEPT = SR-DEPARTMENT
                NEXT SENTENCE
            ELSE
                MOVE 'YES' TO DEPTBK
        ELSE
            MOVE 'YES' TO DIVBK
            MOVE 'YES' TO DEPTBK.
```

(b)

```
DIVISION       DEPT           SALE

   12       AUTOMOTIVE       436.18
                            364.39
                            714.61
                    TOTAL   1515.18

            HOME REPAIR      016.12
                            874.93
                            469.61
                            941.36
                    TOTAL   2302.02

        DIVISION 12 TOTAL  03817.20

   14       HOME REPAIR      436.24
                            717.31
                    TOTAL   1153.55

            FARM EQUIPMENT   472.16
                            716.94
                            584.12
                    TOTAL   1773.22

            MISCELLANEOUS    816.25
                            921.66
                    TOTAL   1737.91

        DIVISION 14 TOTAL  04664.68

   18       HOME REPAIR      462.51
                            761.39
                            864.20
                            952.16
                    TOTAL   3040.26

            FARM EQUIPMENT   643.79
                            714.28
                            688.44
                            771.76
                    TOTAL   2818.27

            MISCELLANEOUS
                    TOTAL   0942.18

        DIVISION 18 TOTAL  06800.71

        GRAND TOTAL       015282.59
```

Figure A.7 Record layout.

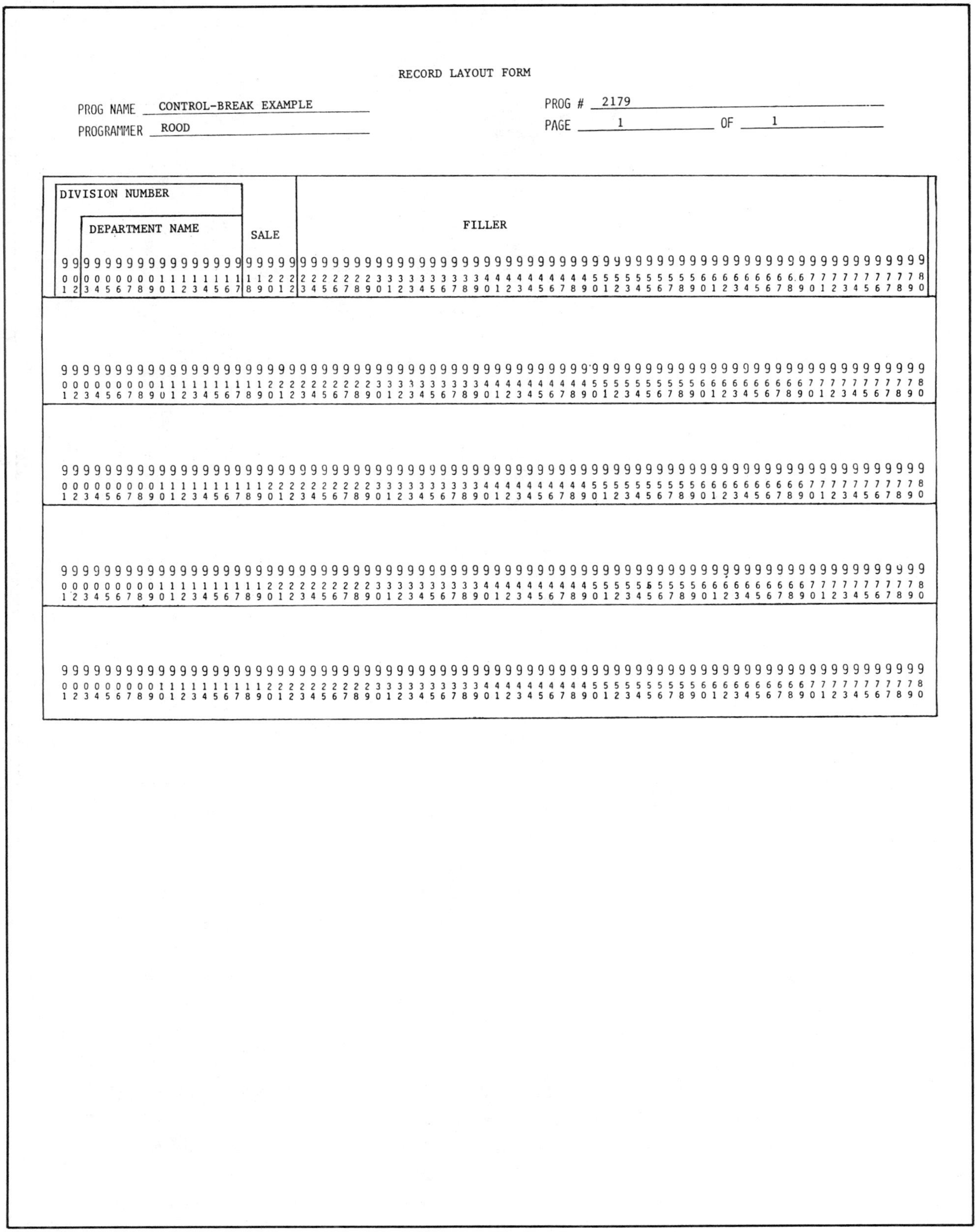

RECORD LAYOUT FORM

PROG NAME   CONTROL-BREAK EXAMPLE   PROG #   2179

PROGRAMMER   ROOD   PAGE   1   OF   1

DIVISION NUMBER

DEPARTMENT NAME   SALE   FILLER

```
9 9 9 9 9 9 9 9 9 9 9 9 9 9 9 9 9 9 9 9 9 9 9 9 9 9 9 9 9 9 9 9 9 9 9 9 9 9 9 9 9 9 9 9 9 9 9 9 9 9 9 9 9 9 9 9 9 9 9 9 9 9 9 9 9 9 9 9 9 9 9 9 9 9 9 9 9 9 9 9
0 0 0 0 0 0 0 0 0 0 1 1 1 1 1 1 1 1 1 1 2 2 2 2 2 2 2 2 2 2 3 3 3 3 3 3 3 3 3 3 4 4 4 4 4 4 4 4 4 4 5 5 5 5 5 5 5 5 5 5 6 6 6 6 6 6 6 6 6 6 7 7 7 7 7 7 7 7 7 8
1 2 3 4 5 6 7 8 9 0 1 2 3 4 5 6 7 8 9 0 1 2 3 4 5 6 7 8 9 0 1 2 3 4 5 6 7 8 9 0 1 2 3 4 5 6 7 8 9 0 1 2 3 4 5 6 7 8 9 0 1 2 3 4 5 6 7 8 9 0 1 2 3 4 5 6 7 8 9 0
```

```
9 9 9 9 9 9 9 9 9 9 9 9 9 9 9 9 9 9 9 9 9 9 9 9 9 9 9 9 9 9 9 9 9 9 9 9 9 9 9 9 9 9 9 9 9 9 9 9 9 9 9 9 9 9 9 9 9 9 9 9 9 9 9 9 9 9 9 9 9 9 9 9 9 9 9 9 9 9 9 9
0 0 0 0 0 0 0 0 0 0 1 1 1 1 1 1 1 1 1 1 2 2 2 2 2 2 2 2 2 2 3 3 3 3 3 3 3 3 3 3 4 4 4 4 4 4 4 4 4 4 5 5 5 5 5 5 5 5 5 5 6 6 6 6 6 6 6 6 6 6 7 7 7 7 7 7 7 7 7 8
1 2 3 4 5 6 7 8 9 0 1 2 3 4 5 6 7 8 9 0 1 2 3 4 5 6 7 8 9 0 1 2 3 4 5 6 7 8 9 0 1 2 3 4 5 6 7 8 9 0 1 2 3 4 5 6 7 8 9 0 1 2 3 4 5 6 7 8 9 0 1 2 3 4 5 6 7 8 9 0
```

```
9 9 9 9 9 9 9 9 9 9 9 9 9 9 9 9 9 9 9 9 9 9 9 9 9 9 9 9 9 9 9 9 9 9 9 9 9 9 9 9 9 9 9 9 9 9 9 9 9 9 9 9 9 9 9 9 9 9 9 9 9 9 9 9 9 9 9 9 9 9 9 9 9 9 9 9 9 9 9 9
0 0 0 0 0 0 0 0 0 0 1 1 1 1 1 1 1 1 1 1 2 2 2 2 2 2 2 2 2 2 3 3 3 3 3 3 3 3 3 3 4 4 4 4 4 4 4 4 4 4 5 5 5 5 5 5 5 5 5 5 6 6 6 6 6 6 6 6 6 6 7 7 7 7 7 7 7 7 7 8
1 2 3 4 5 6 7 8 9 0 1 2 3 4 5 6 7 8 9 0 1 2 3 4 5 6 7 8 9 0 1 2 3 4 5 6 7 8 9 0 1 2 3 4 5 6 7 8 9 0 1 2 3 4 5 6 7 8 9 0 1 2 3 4 5 6 7 8 9 0 1 2 3 4 5 6 7 8 9 0
```

```
9 9 9 9 9 9 9 9 9 9 9 9 9 9 9 9 9 9 9 9 9 9 9 9 9 9 9 9 9 9 9 9 9 9 9 9 9 9 9 9 9 9 9 9 9 9 9 9 9 9 9 9 9 9 9 9 9 9 9 9 9 9 9 9 9 9 9 9 9 9 9 9 9 9 9 9 9 9 9 9
0 0 0 0 0 0 0 0 0 0 1 1 1 1 1 1 1 1 1 1 2 2 2 2 2 2 2 2 2 2 3 3 3 3 3 3 3 3 3 3 4 4 4 4 4 4 4 4 4 4 5 5 5 5 5 5 5 5 5 5 6 6 6 6 6 6 6 6 6 6 7 7 7 7 7 7 7 7 7 8
1 2 3 4 5 6 7 8 9 0 1 2 3 4 5 6 7 8 9 0 1 2 3 4 5 6 7 8 9 0 1 2 3 4 5 6 7 8 9 0 1 2 3 4 5 6 7 8 9 0 1 2 3 4 5 6 7 8 9 0 1 2 3 4 5 6 7 8 9 0 1 2 3 4 5 6 7 8 9 0
```

```
9 9 9 9 9 9 9 9 9 9 9 9 9 9 9 9 9 9 9 9 9 9 9 9 9 9 9 9 9 9 9 9 9 9 9 9 9 9 9 9 9 9 9 9 9 9 9 9 9 9 9 9 9 9 9 9 9 9 9 9 9 9 9 9 9 9 9 9 9 9 9 9 9 9 9 9 9 9 9 9
0 0 0 0 0 0 0 0 0 0 1 1 1 1 1 1 1 1 1 1 2 2 2 2 2 2 2 2 2 2 3 3 3 3 3 3 3 3 3 3 4 4 4 4 4 4 4 4 4 4 5 5 5 5 5 5 5 5 5 5 6 6 6 6 6 6 6 6 6 6 7 7 7 7 7 7 7 7 7 8
1 2 3 4 5 6 7 8 9 0 1 2 3 4 5 6 7 8 9 0 1 2 3 4 5 6 7 8 9 0 1 2 3 4 5 6 7 8 9 0 1 2 3 4 5 6 7 8 9 0 1 2 3 4 5 6 7 8 9 0 1 2 3 4 5 6 7 8 9 0 1 2 3 4 5 6 7 8 9 0
```

Figure A.8 Record description.

FILE/RECORD DESCRIPTION

PROG NAME   CONTROL-BREAK EXAMPLE   PROG #   2179

PROGRAMMER ROOD   PAGE   1   of   1

FILE NAME   SALES - RECORD FILE

FILE TYPE	RECORD LENGTH 8Ø	BLOCKING FACTOR NONE	COMMENTS
I			

OUTPUT FROM	DATA ENTRY

INPUT TO	CONTROL BREAK PROGRAM

COLUMNS FROM	TO	FIELD NAME	FORMAT (PICTURE)	LENGTH	EXPLANATION
1	2	SR-DIVISION	XX	2	DIVISION NUMBER
3	17	SR-DEPARTMENT	X(15)	15	DIVISION NAME
19	22	SR-SALE	9(3)V99	5	SALE AMOUNT
23	8Ø	FILLER	X(58)	58	

TOTAL CHARACTERS   80

Figure A.9 Run log.

RUN LOG

PROG NAME   CONTROL-BREAK EXAMPLE   PROG #   2179
PROGRAMMER   ROOD   PAGE   1   of   1

RUN/DATE	RUN #	USER	OPERATOR	COMMENTS
Feb. 15, 85	1	ROOD	GEORGE	HEADINGS ONLY – NO DATA
Feb. 17, 85	2	ROOD	SMITH	OK

Figure A.10 Test data.

```
12AUTOMOTIVE          43618
12AUTOMOTIVE          36439
12AUTOMOTIVE          71461
12HOME REPAIR         01612
12HOME REPAIR         87493
12HOME REPAIR         46961
12HOME REPAIR         94136
14HOME REPAIR         43624
14HOME REPAIR         71731
14FARM EQUIPMENT      47216
14FARM EQUIPMENT      71694
14FARM EQUIPMENT      58412
14MISCELLANEOUS       81625
14MISCELLANEOUS       92166
18HOME REPAIR         46251
18HOME REPAIR         76139
18HOME REPAIR         86420
18HOME REPAIR         95216
18FARM EQUIPMENT      64379
18FARM EQUIPMENT      71428
18FARM EQUIPMENT      68844
18FARM EQUIPMENT      77176
18MISCELLANEOUS       94218
```

Appendix

B. COBOL Coding from a Warnier Diagram

Transition from a completed Warnier diagram to a coded COBOL program is a routine matter, especially if the intended language was known to the designer of the Warnier diagram. Figure B.1 compares a Warnier diagram with the procedure division of a corresponding COBOL program.

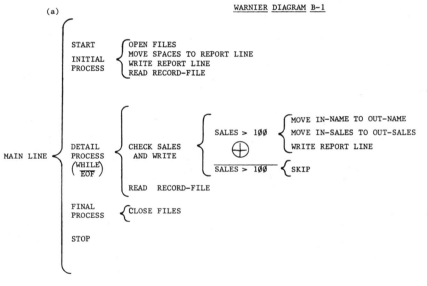

(a)

WARNIER DIAGRAM B-1

(b)
```
      PROCEDURE DIVISION.
*
      100-MAIN-LINE.
          PERFORM 220-INITIAL-PROCESS.
          PERFORM 240-DETAIL-PROCESS
              UNTIL END-OF-FILE EQUALS 'YES'.
          PERFORM 260-FINAL-PROCESS.
          STOP RUN.
*
      220-INITIAL-PROCESS.
          OPEN INPUT RECORD-FILE
              OUTPUT REPORT-FILE.
          MOVE SPACES TO REPORT-LINE.
          WRITE REPORT-LINE
              AFTER ADVANCING TO-TOP-OF-THE-PAGE.
          READ RECORD-FILE
              AT END MOVE 'YES' TO END-OF-FILE.
*
      240-DETAIL-PROCESS.
          PERFORM 340-CHECK-SALES-AND-WRITE.
          READ RECORD-FILE
              AT END MOVE 'YES' TO END-OF-FILE.
*
      260-FINAL-PROCESS.
          CLOSE RECORD-FILE
              REPORT-FILE.
*
      340-CHECK-SALES-AND-WRITE.
          IF IN-SALES > 100
              MOVE IN-NAME TO OUT-NAME
              MOVE IN-SALES TO OUT-SALES
              WRITE REPORT-LINE
                  AFTER ADVANCING-ONE-LINE.
```

Figure B.1 (a) Warnier diagram. (b) The procedure division of a corresponding COBOL program.

Each brace (other than braces for decisions) represents a paragraph. Each universal represents a paragraph name. The content of each brace is transferred from top to bottom, observing the syntactical requirements of COBOL. The leftmost brace becomes the main-line or control module. Braces to the right become submodules and are coded below the main-line module. Because Figure B.1(a) was designed with COBOL in mind, expressions such as MOVE and WRITE are included, and READ instructions specify files rather than fields.

Coding in COBOL from Warnier diagrams that were not specifically designed for COBOL requires a bit more conversion. COBOL programs print entire records rather than single fields, so Warnier diagram instructions to print fields are coded as MOVE statements in the program. Several MOVE statements are followed by a WRITE statement. Directions to print literals are absent, because literals are included when output areas are printed.

Instructions to read fields are converted to read files, and MOVE instructions replace many equations as storage instructions.

Figure B.2 results from coding Figure 6.37(c) in COBOL.

Figure B.2 COBOL program that results from coding Figure 6.37(c).

```
*
*
*
*
  PROCEDURE DIVISION.
*
  100-MAIN-LINE.
      PERFORM 220-INITIAL-PROCESS.
      PERFORM 240-DIVISION-LOOP
          UNTIL THERE-ARE-NO-MORE-RECORDS.
      PERFORM 260-FINAL-PROCESS.
      STOP RUN.
*
  220-INITIAL-PROCESS.
      OPEN INPUT SALES-RECORD-FILE.
      OPEN OUTPUT SALES-RECORD-FILE.
      MOVE SPACES TO REPORT-LINE.
      WRITE REPORT-LINE FROM HEADING-LINE
          AFTER ADVANCING PAGE.
      MOVE ONE-LINE TO PROPER-SPACING.
      MOVE ZERO TO WS-GRAND-TOTAL.
      READ SALES-RECORD-FILE
          AT END MOVE 'YES' TO END-OF-FILE.
*
  240-DIVISION-LOOP.
      MOVE SR-DIVISION TO DL-DIVISION.
      MOVE 'NO' TO DIVBK.
      MOVE SR-DIVISION TO WS-OLD-DIVISION.
      MOVE ZERO TO WS-DIVISION-TOTAL.
      PERFORM 340-DEPT-LOOP
          UNTIL DIVBK NOT EQUAL TO 'NO'.
      ADD WS-DIVISION-TOTAL TO WS-GRAND-TOTAL.
      MOVE WS-OLD-DIVISION TO DT-DIVISION.
      MOVE WS-DIVISION-TOTAL TO DIVISION-TOTAL.
      WRITE REPORT-LINE FROM DIVISION-TOTAL-LINE
          AFTER ADVANCING PROPER-SPACING.
      MOVE TWO-LINES TO PROPER-SPACING.
*
  260-FINAL-PROCESS.
      MOVE WS-GRAND-TOTAL TO GRAND-TOTAL.
      WRITE REPORT-LINE FROM GRAND-TOTAL-LINE
          AFTER ADVANCING PROPER-SPACING.

          CLOSE SALES-RECORD-FILE.
          CLOSE SALES-REPORT-FILE.
*
  340-DEPT-LOOP.
      MOVE SR-DEPARTMENT TO DL-DEPARTMENT.
      MOVE 'NO' TO DEPTBK.
      MOVE SR-DEPARTMENT TO WS-OLD-DEPT.
      MOVE ZERO TO WS-DEPARTMENT-TOTAL.
      PERFORM 440-SALE-LOOP
          UNTIL DEPTBK = 'YES'.
      ADD WS-DEPARTMENT-TOTAL TO WS-DIVISION-TOTAL.
      MOVE WS-DEPARTMENT-TOTAL TO DEPARTMENT-TOTAL.
      WRITE REPORT-LINE FROM DETAIL-LINE
          AFTER ADVANCING PROPER-SPACING.
      MOVE TWO-LINES TO PROPER-SPACING.
*
  440-SALE-LOOP.
      MOVE SR-SALE TO DL-SALE.
      ADD SR-SALE TO WS-DEPARTMENT-TOTAL.
      WRITE REPORT-LINE FROM DETAIL-LINE
          AFTER ADVANCING PROPER-SPACING.
      MOVE ONE-LINE TO PROPER-SPACING.
      MOVE SPACES TO DETAIL-LINE.
      READ SALES-RECORD-FILE
          AT END MOVE 'YES' TO END-OF-FILE.
      PERFORM 540-SET-INDICATORS.
*
  540-SET-INDICATORS.
      IF THERE-ARE-NO-MORE-RECORDS
          MOVE 'YES' TO DEPTBK
          MOVE 'YES' TO DIVBK
      ELSE
          IF WS-OLD-DIVISION = SR-DIVISION
              IF WS-OLD-DEPT = SR-DEPARTMENT
                  NEXT SENTENCE
              ELSE
                  MOVE 'YES' TO DEPTBK
          ELSE
              MOVE 'YES' TO DIVBK
              MOVE 'YES' TO DEPTBK.
```

Answers to Selected Exercises

Exercises 1.1-1.3 (page 6)

1. a. 0, 2, 4   **b.** 5, 5   **c.** 5

TABLE OF VALUES

Y	X	PRINT Y	2ND DECISION
Ø	1	Ø	1
1	2	2	2
2	3	4	3
3	3		4
4	4		5
5	5		
	5		

Exercises 1.4-1.5 (page 22)

1.

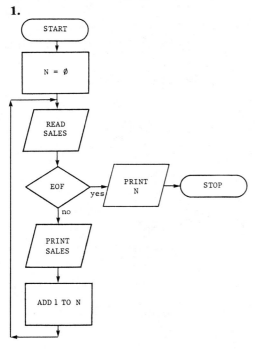

3.

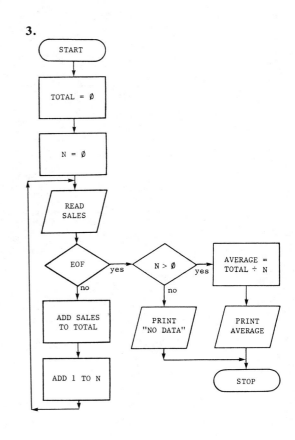

Exercises 1.6 (page 27)

1.

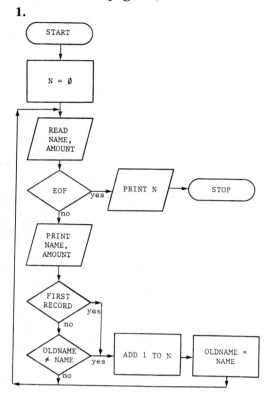

4.

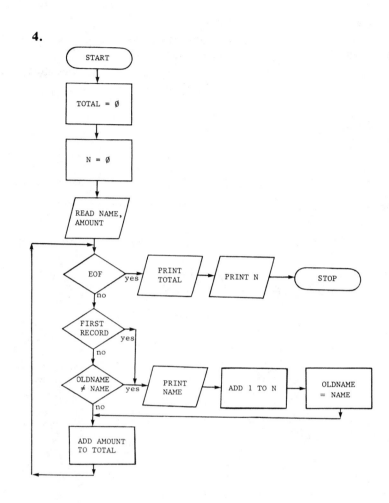

Exercises 1.7-1.8 (page 31)

1. Loops don't include decisions leading to stop; so, loop 1 is a continuous loop. No directions are given to be carried out after PRINT.

2. Program has no stop. No first record decision; accumulator is initialized within the loop; counter is initialized within loop.

3. 0, 0, 0, 10, 2

4.

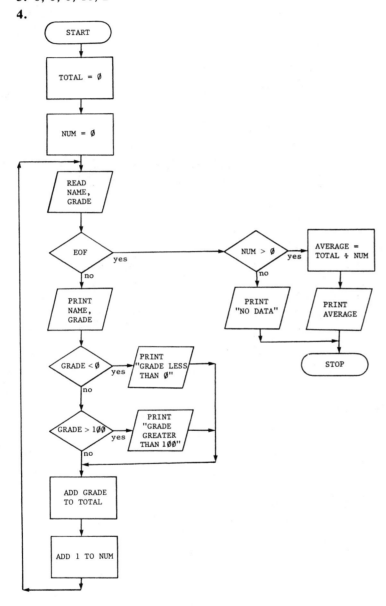

6.

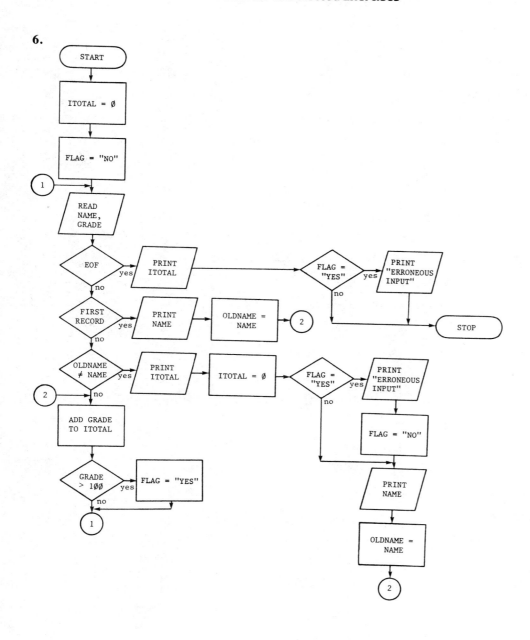

Exercises 1.9 (page 37)

1.

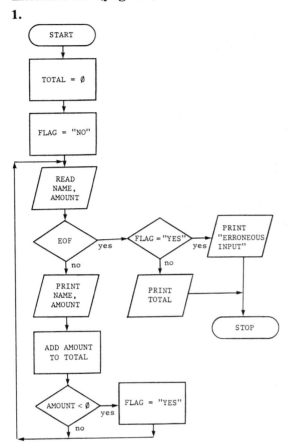

2.

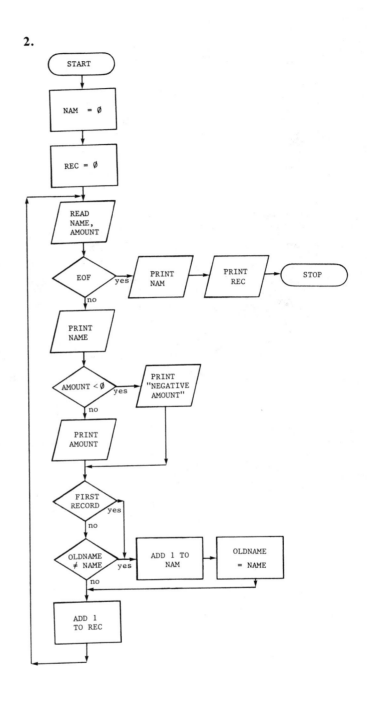

5.

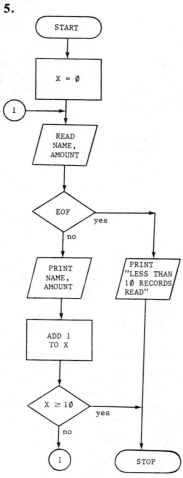

Exercises 1.10 (page 40)
2.

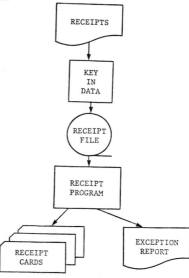

Exercises 2.1-2.4 (page 48)
1. a. {a, c}   **(d)** {d}   **g.** {a, b, c, d, f}
2. a.   **b.**   **e.**

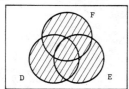 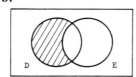 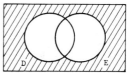

3. a. (A ∩ B)   **d.** ((A ∩ B′) ∪ (B ∩ A′))   **f.** (B′ ∪ A)

Exercises 2.5-2.6 (page 53)
1. a. F′   **d.** (R ∪ F)′   **e.** ((O ∩ R) ∪ T)
  g. ((L ∩ T) ∪ (O ∩ F))   **h.** L ∩ (F ∪ T)′
2. b.   **d.**   **f.**

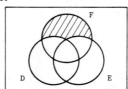 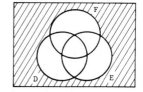 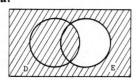

Exercises 2.5-2.6 continued

3. a. $((A \cap C) \cap B')$ **c.** $(C \cap B')$ **e.** $((A \cup B) \cup C)'$
   g. $((B \cap C) \cup (A \cap (B \cup C)'))$ **j** $((A \cap C) \cup (B \cap C))$
   m. $((B \cap C') \cup (C \cap B'))$

4. a. new components under warranty
   d. new components and components under warranty
   g. components that are not in service and not under warranty
   j. components that are neither in service nor under warranty

Exercises 2.7 (page 63)

1. a.

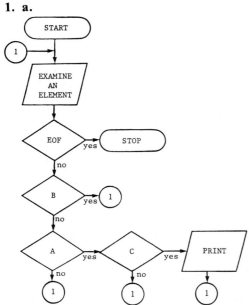

c.

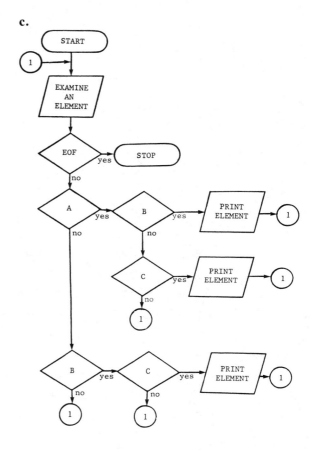

2. a.

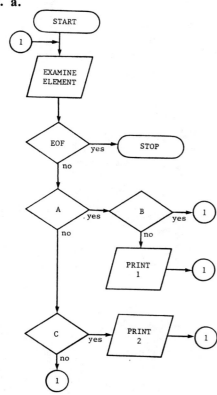

d.

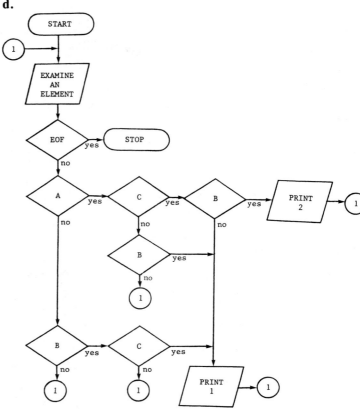

3. a.

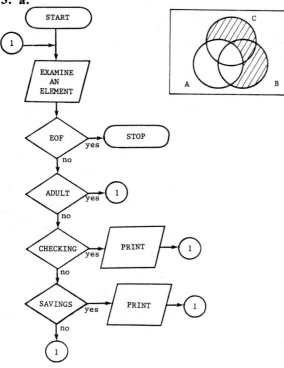

d.

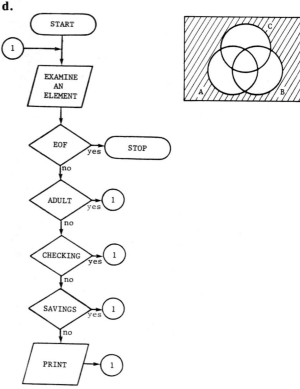

Exercises 2.8 (page 68)

1. a.

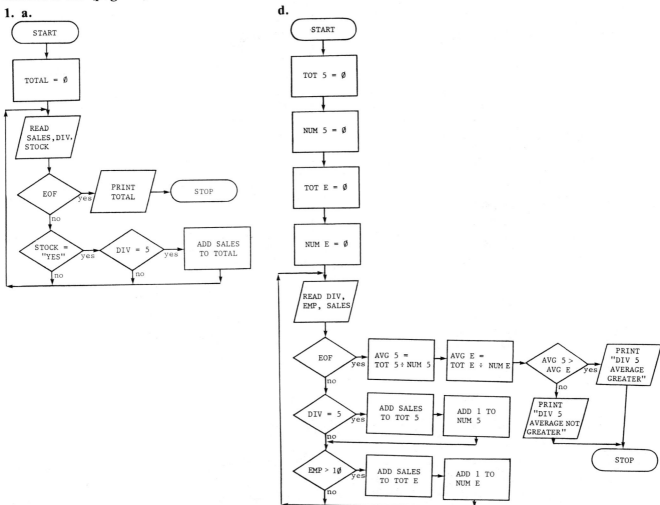

d.

f.

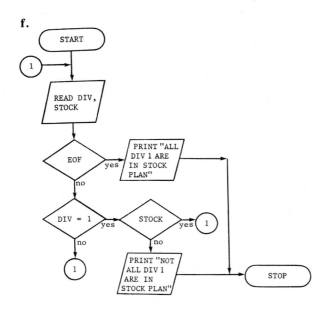

1. i.

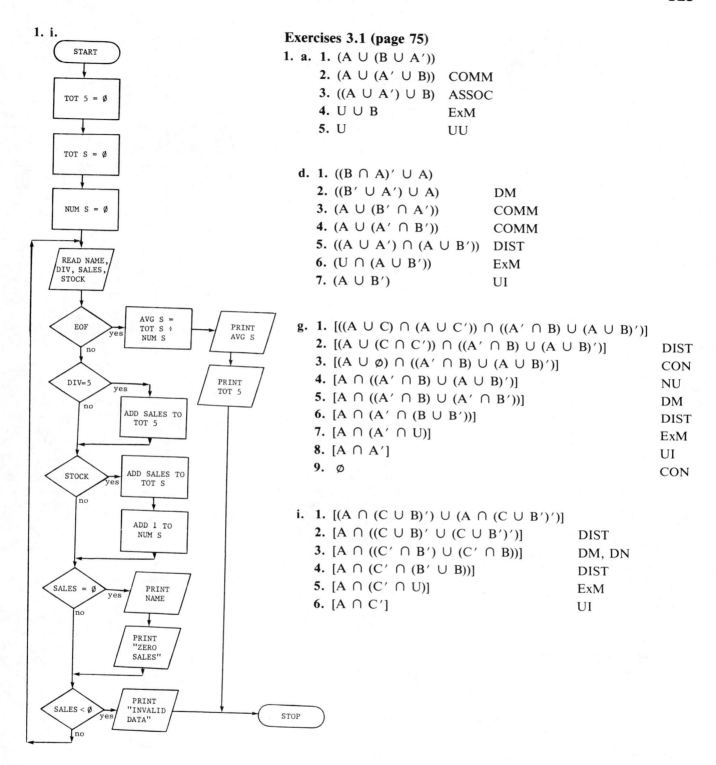

Exercises 3.1 (page 75)

1. a.
1. $(A \cup (B \cup A'))$
2. $(A \cup (A' \cup B))$ COMM
3. $((A \cup A') \cup B)$ ASSOC
4. $U \cup B$ ExM
5. U UU

d.
1. $((B \cap A)' \cup A)$
2. $((B' \cup A') \cup A)$ DM
3. $(A \cup (B' \cap A'))$ COMM
4. $(A \cup (A' \cap B'))$ COMM
5. $((A \cup A') \cap (A \cup B'))$ DIST
6. $(U \cap (A \cup B'))$ ExM
7. $(A \cup B')$ UI

g.
1. $[((A \cup C) \cap (A \cup C')) \cap ((A' \cap B) \cup (A \cup B)')]$
2. $[(A \cup (C \cap C')) \cap ((A' \cap B) \cup (A \cup B)')]$ DIST
3. $[(A \cup \emptyset) \cap ((A' \cap B) \cup (A \cup B)')]$ CON
4. $[A \cap ((A' \cap B) \cup (A \cup B)')]$ NU
5. $[A \cap ((A' \cap B) \cup (A' \cap B'))]$ DM
6. $[A \cap (A' \cap (B \cup B'))]$ DIST
7. $[A \cap (A' \cap U)]$ ExM
8. $[A \cap A']$ UI
9. $\emptyset$ CON

i.
1. $[(A \cap (C \cup B)') \cup (A \cap (C \cup B')')]$
2. $[A \cap ((C \cup B)' \cup (C \cup B')')]$ DIST
3. $[A \cap ((C' \cap B') \cup (C' \cap B))]$ DM, DN
4. $[A \cap (C' \cap (B' \cup B))]$ DIST
5. $[A \cap (C' \cap U)]$ ExM
6. $[A \cap C']$ UI

Exercises 3.2 (page 77)

1.

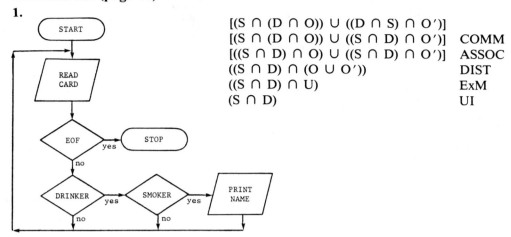

$[(S \cap (D \cap O)) \cup ((D \cap S) \cap O')]$
$[(S \cap (D \cap O)) \cup ((S \cap D) \cap O')]$ COMM
$[((S \cap D) \cap O) \cup ((S \cap D) \cap O')]$ ASSOC
$((S \cap D) \cap (O \cup O'))$ DIST
$((S \cap D) \cap U)$ ExM
$(S \cap D)$ UI

2.

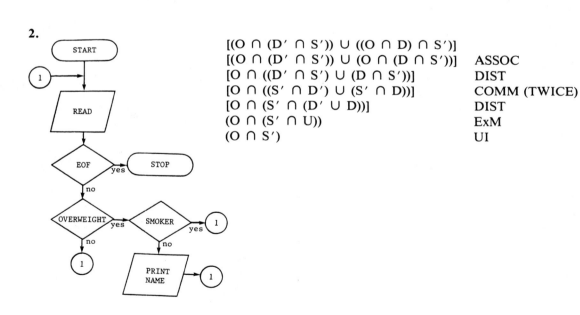

$[(O \cap (D' \cap S')) \cup ((O \cap D) \cap S')]$
$[(O \cap (D' \cap S')) \cup (O \cap (D \cap S'))]$ ASSOC
$[O \cap ((D' \cap S') \cup (D \cap S'))]$ DIST
$[O \cap ((S' \cap D') \cup (S' \cap D))]$ COMM (TWICE)
$[O \cap (S' \cap (D' \cup D))]$ DIST
$(O \cap (S' \cap U))$ ExM
$(O \cap S')$ UI

Exercises 3.3-3.4 (page 83)

1. a. True **d.** False **g.** True **j.** False
2. a. True **d.** True **g.** True **j.** False
3. a.

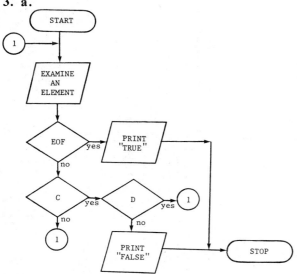

d.

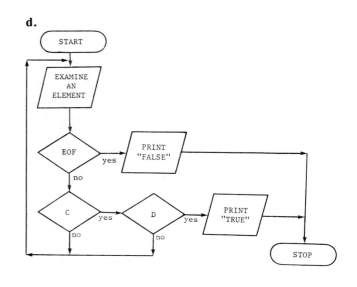

g.

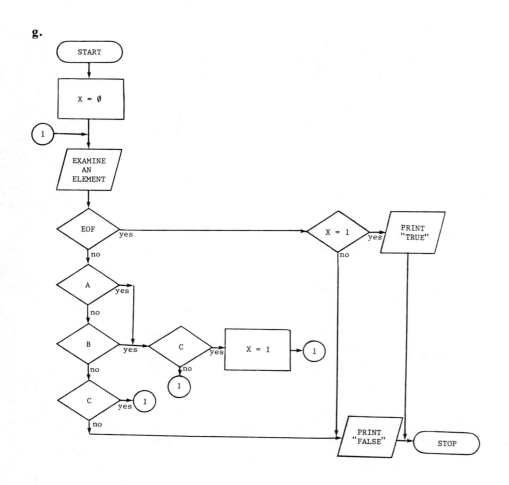

Exercises 3.3-3.4 continued

3. **j.**

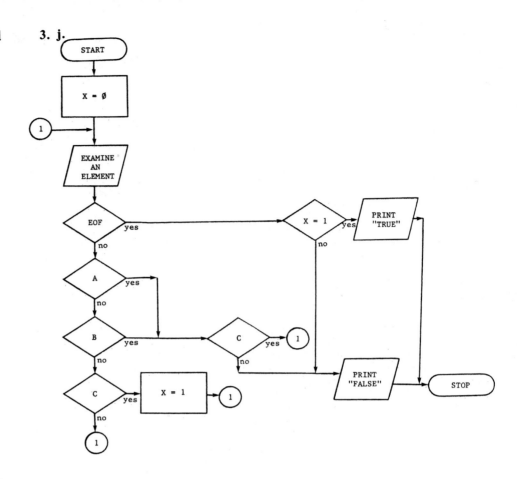

Exercises 3.5-3.6 (page 87)

1. a. $F \subseteq E$ **d.** $(F \cap E') \neq \emptyset$ **g.** $(J \cap (S \cap F)) = \emptyset$
   j. $(J \cup S) \subseteq E$ **m.** $((S \cap E) \cap F') \neq \emptyset$

2. a. $((S \cap F) \subseteq M)$

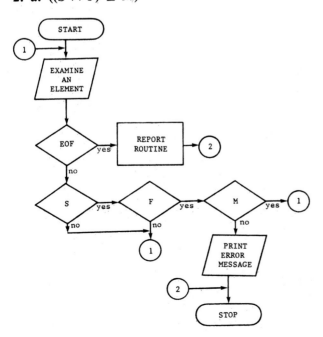

d.

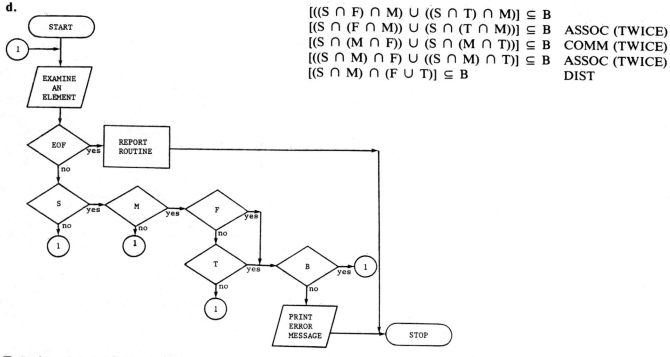

$$[((S \cap F) \cap M) \cup ((S \cap T) \cap M)] \subseteq B$$
$$[(S \cap (F \cap M)) \cup (S \cap (T \cap M))] \subseteq B \quad \text{ASSOC (TWICE)}$$
$$[(S \cap (M \cap F)) \cup (S \cap (M \cap T))] \subseteq B \quad \text{COMM (TWICE)}$$
$$[((S \cap M) \cap F) \cup ((S \cap M) \cap T)] \subseteq B \quad \text{ASSOC (TWICE)}$$
$$[(S \cap M) \cap (F \cup T)] \subseteq B \quad \text{DIST}$$

Exercises 4.1-4.3 (page 102)

1. **a.** Sequence, do-until loop that contains two if-then-else's.
   c. Sequence that contains an if-then-else. The if-then-else contains a sequence consisting of an input/output and a do-while loop. The do-while loop contains an if-then-else and an input/output.

2. **a.**   3. **a.**

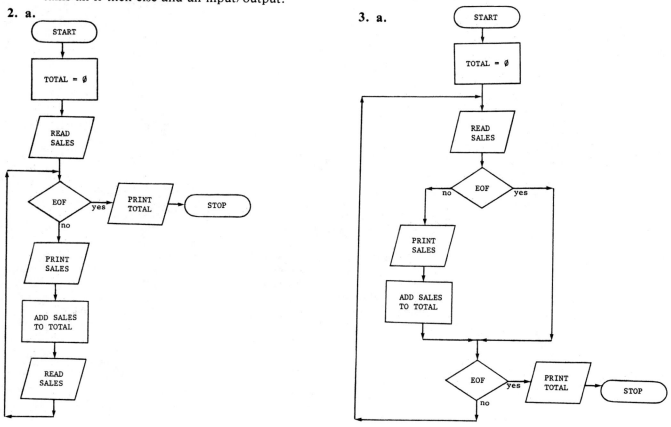

Exercises 4.1-4.3 continued **5.** **7. a.**

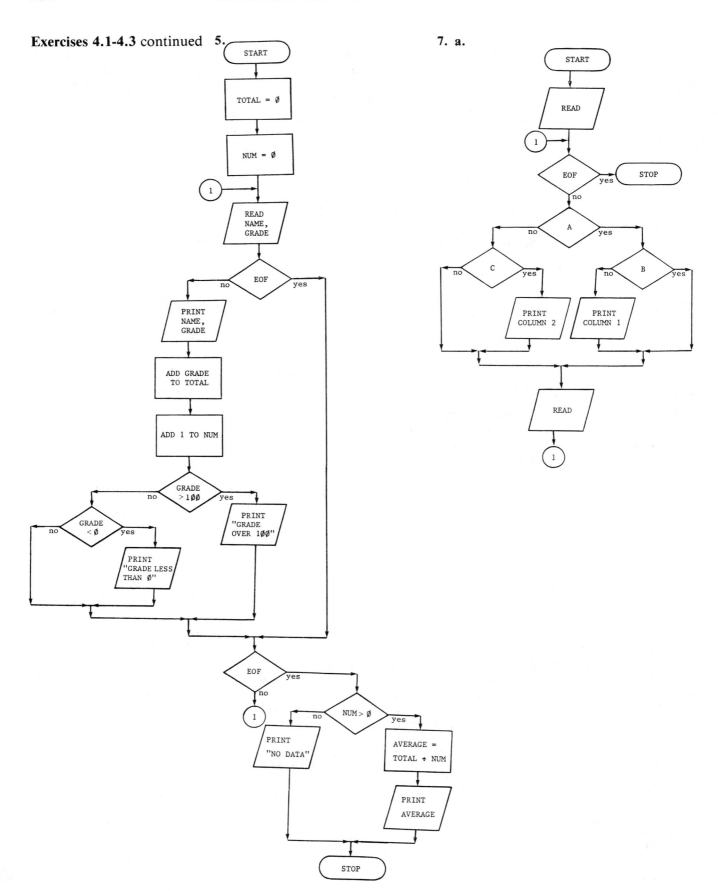

8. b.

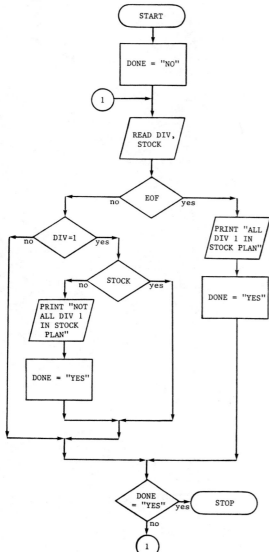

Exercises 4.4 (page 107)

1.

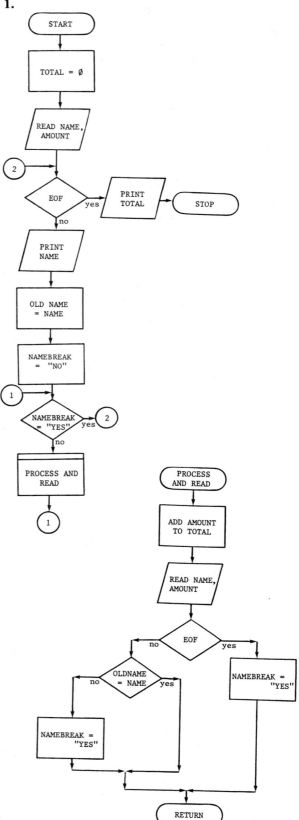

Exercises 4.5 (page 116)

1. a.

2. a.

5.

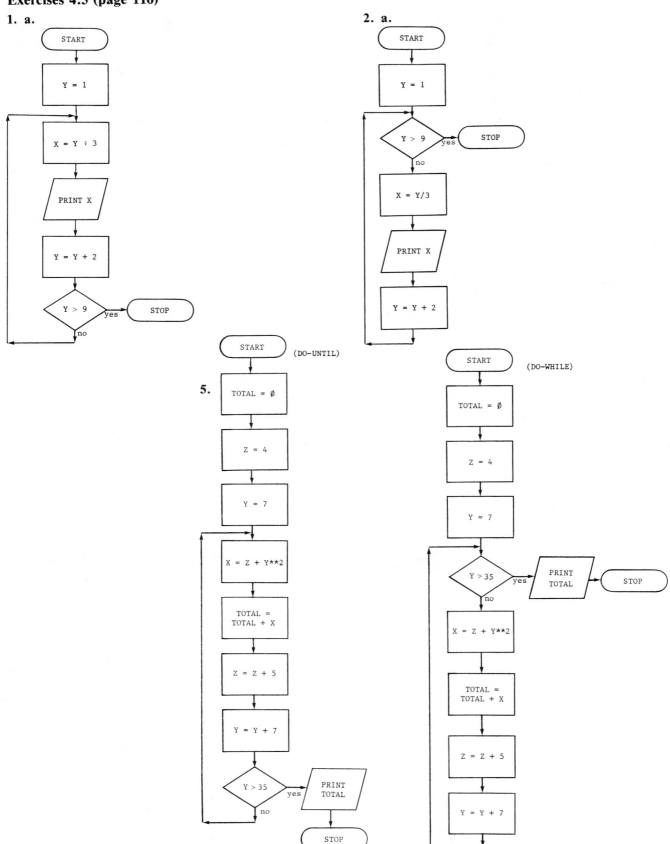

Exercises 5.1 (page 120)

1. [not A and B]   False
   F T F F

4. [not (not A and not B) and C]   True
   T   F T F   T F   T T

Exercises 5.2-5.3 (page 123)

1. a. (C ∧ A)   **d.** (A ∨ B)   **g.** (~A ∨ B)   **j.** (~A ∨ C)
  m. (~(A ∧ B) ∧ (A ∨ B))

2. a. False   **d.** True   **g.** False   **j.** False   **m.** True

Exercises 5.4-5.5 (page 126)

1. a.

A	B	~(A ∧ B)	(~A ∨ ~B)	
T	T	F T T T	F T F F T	
T	F	T T F F	F T T T F	
F	T	T F F T	T F T F T	
F	F	T F F F	T F T T F	EQUIVALENT

d.

A	B	C	(A ∨ (B ∨ C))	((A ∨ B) ∨ (A ∨ C))	
T	T	T	T T T T T	T T T T T T T	
T	T	F	T T T T F	T T T T T T F	
T	F	T	T T F T T	T T F T T T T	
T	F	F	T T F F F	T T F T T T F	EQUIVALENT
F	T	T	F T T T T	F T T T F T T	
F	T	F	F T T T F	F T T T F F F	
F	F	T	F T F T T	F F F T F T T	
F	F	F	F F F F F	F F F F F F F	

2. a.

A	B	((A ∨ B) ∧ ~A)	
T	T	T T T F F T	
T	F	T T F F F T	
F	T	F T T T T F	CONTINGENT
F	F	F F F F T F	

d.

A	B	((A ∨ B) ∧ ~B)	
T	T	T T T F F T	
T	F	T T F T T F	
F	T	F T T F F T	CONTINGENT
F	F	F F F F T F	

3. a.

C	P	((C ∨ P) ∧ (C ∧ ~P))	
T	T	T T T F T F F T	
T	F	T T F T T T T F	
F	T	F T T F F F F T	CONTINGENT
F	F	F F F F F F T F	

d.

C	P	((C ∨ P) ∧ ~(C ∧ P))	
T	T	T T T F F T T T	
T	F	T T F T T T F F	
F	T	F T T T T F F T	CONTINGENT
F	F	F F F F T F F F	

Exercises 5.6 (page 129)

1. $(T \rightarrow F)$ **4.** $(R \rightarrow F)$ **7.** $\sim(0 \vee L)$ **10.** $(\sim T \vee M)$

13. $(T \wedge \sim R)$ **19.** $(T \rightarrow E)$ **22.** $(\sim P \vee E)$

Exercises 5.7 (page 137)

1. a. (Do-While)   **c.** (Do-Until)

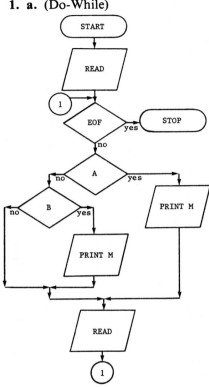

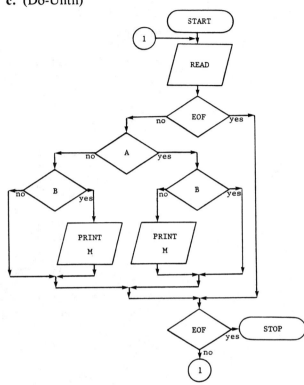

1. g. (Do-Until)

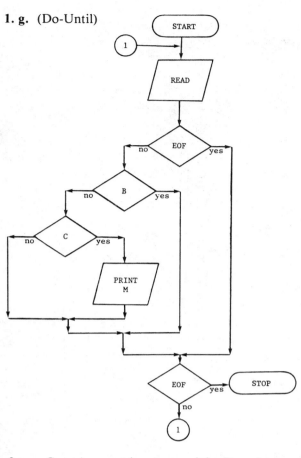

h. (Do-While)

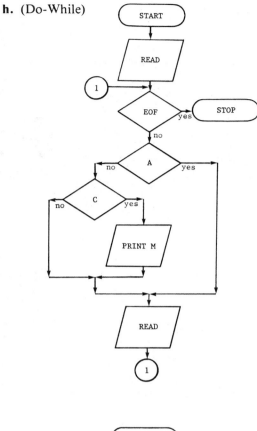

2. a. C = Account is commercial   P = Account has a past due balance
B = Account has a current balance due

C	B	P	$((\sim C \land (B \lor P)) \lor (C \land P))$
T	T	T	F T F T T T T T T T (Do-While)
T	T	F	F T F T T F F T F F
T	F	T	F T F F T T T T T T
T	F	F	F T F F F F F T F F
F	T	T	T F T T T T T F F T
F	T	F	T F T T T F T F F F
F	F	T	T F T F T T T F F T
F	F	F	T F F F F F F F F F

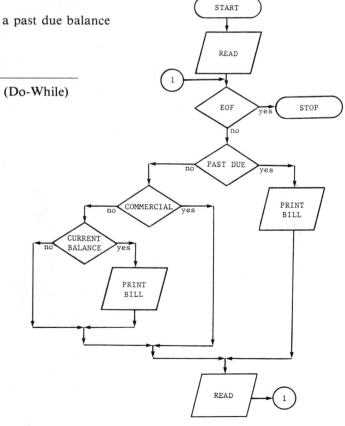

Exercise 5.7 continued

2.c.

C	B	P	((C ∧ (B ∨ ~P)) ∨ (B ∨ (C ∧ P)))	
T	T	T	T T T T F T T T T T T T	(Do-Until)
T	T	F	T T T T T F T T T T F F	
T	F	T	T F F F F T T F T T T T	
T	F	F	T T F T T F T F F T F F	
F	T	T	F F T T F T T T T F F T	
F	T	F	F F T T T F T T T F F F	
F	F	T	F F F F F T F F F F F T	
F	F	F	F F F T T F F F F F F F	

3. a.

R	P	B	((R ∨ P) ∨ (P ∨ B))
T	T	T	T T T T T T T
T	T	F	T T T T T T F
T	F	T	T T F T F T T
T	F	F	T T F T F F F
F	T	T	F T T T T T T
F	T	F	F T T T T T F
F	F	T	F F F T F T T
F	F	F	F F F F F F F

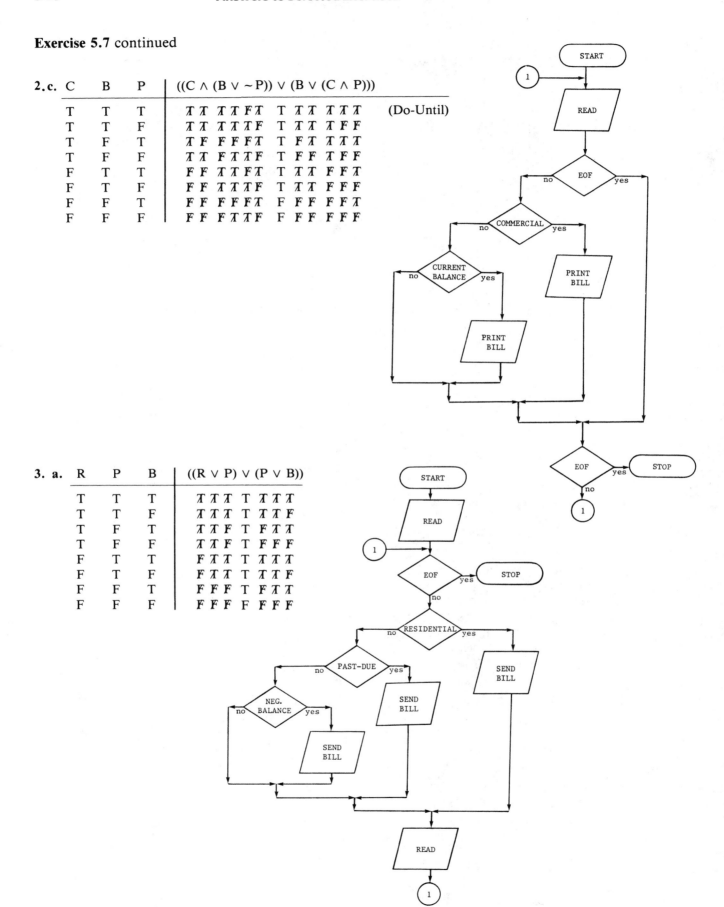

c.

R	C	P	(~(R ∨ C) ∨ ((~P ∧ R) ∨ (C ∧ P)))
T	T	T	F T T T T F T F T T T T T
T	T	F	F T T T T T F T T T T F F
T	F	T	F T T F F F T F T F F F T
T	F	F	F T T F T T F T T T F F F
F	T	T	F F T T T F T F F T T T T
F	T	F	F F T T F T F F F F T F F
F	F	T	T F F F T F T F F F F F T
F	F	F	T F F F T T F F F F F F F

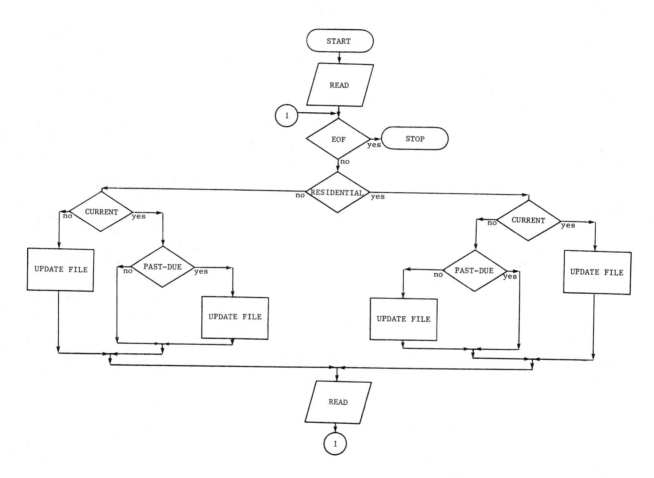

Exercises 5.8 (page 142)

1.

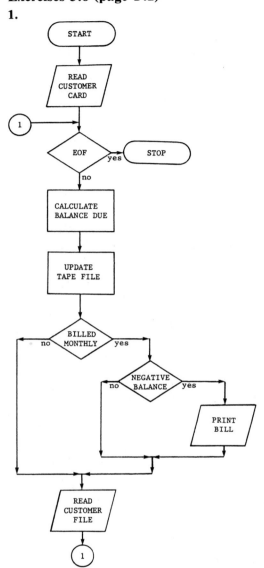

4.

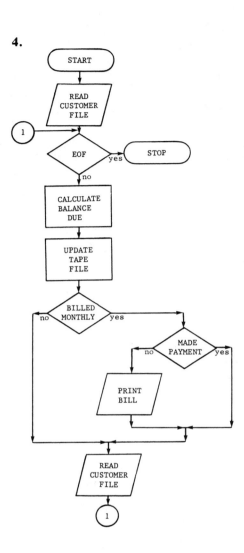

Exercises 5.9 (page 144)

1. Not Equivalent	**4.** DM	**7.** Not Equivalent	**10.** DM
13. Not Equivalent	**16.** Not Equivalent	**19.** COMM	
22. Not Equivalent	**25.** DIST		

Exercises 5.10 (page 147)

1. a.
  1. $(A \lor (\sim B \lor C))$
  2. $((A \lor \sim B) \lor C)$ ASSOC
  3. $((\sim A \to \sim B) \lor C)$ IMP

d.
  1. $(\sim C \to (\sim A \lor \sim B))$
  2. $(\sim C \to \sim (A \land B))$ DM
  3. $((A \land B) \to C)$ CONTR

g.
  1. $(C \to A)$
  2. $\sim C \lor A$ IMP
  3. $\sim (\sim \sim C \land \sim A)$ DM
  4. $\sim (C \land \sim A)$ DN
  5. $\sim (\sim A \land C)$ COMM

j.
  1. $\sim (A \lor (B \land \sim C))$
  2. $(\sim A \land \sim (B \land \sim C))$ DM
  3. $(\sim A \land (\sim B \lor \sim \sim C))$ DM
  4. $(\sim A \land (B \to \sim \sim C))$ IMP
  5. $(\sim A \land (B \to C))$ DN
  6. $(\sim A \land (\sim C \to \sim B))$ CONTR

2. a.
  1. $\sim [(C \lor B) \lor (\sim B \lor \sim (A \land \sim A))]$
  2. $\sim [(C \lor B) \lor (\sim B \lor \sim \perp)]$ CON
  3. $\sim [(C \lor B) \lor (\sim B \lor T)]$ NC
  4. $\sim [(C \lor B) \lor T]$ TD
  5. $\sim T$ TD
  6. $\perp$ NT

d.
  1. $[(B \land (C \land A)) \lor ((C \land \sim B) \land A)]$
  2. $[((B \land C) \land A) \lor ((C \land \sim B) \land A)]$ ASSOC
  3. $[(A \land (B \land C)) \lor ((C \land \sim B) \land A)]$ COMM
  4. $[(A \land (B \land C)) \lor (A \land (C \land \sim B))]$ COMM
  5. $[A \land ((B \land C) \lor (C \land \sim B))]$ DIST
  6. $[A \land ((C \land B) \lor (C \land \sim B))]$ COMM
  7. $[A \land (C \land (B \lor \sim B))]$ DIST
  8. $[A \land (C \land T)]$ TAUT
  9. $[A \land C]$ TC

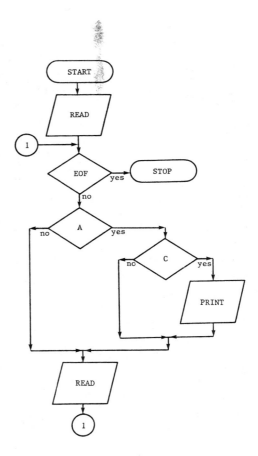

Exercises 5.11-5.12 (page 154)

1.

ACCIDENTS	yes	x	x		
	no			x	x
MOVING VIOLATIONS	yes	x		x	
	no		x		x
RISK A		x			
RISK B			x	x	
NO RISK					x
SURCHARGE		x	x		

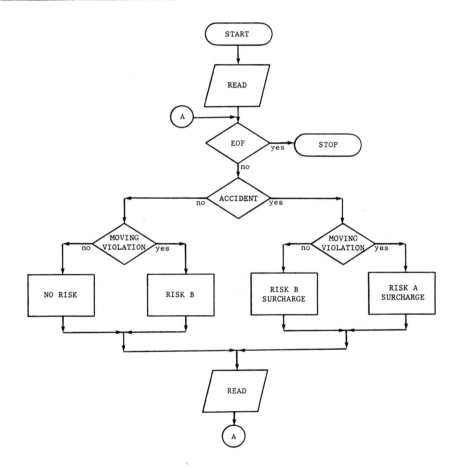

2.

AGE	UNDER 21	X	X	X	X							
	21 TO 24					X	X	X	X			
	OVER 24									X	X	X	X
SEX	MALE	X	X			X	X			X	X		
	FEMALE			X	X			X	X			X	X
MARITAL STATUS	MARRIED	X		X		X		X		X		X	
	SINGLE		X		X		X		X		X		X
RISK A			X	X	X		X	X	X				
RISK B		X				X					X		
NO RISK										X		X	X
SURCHARGE		X	X	X	X								

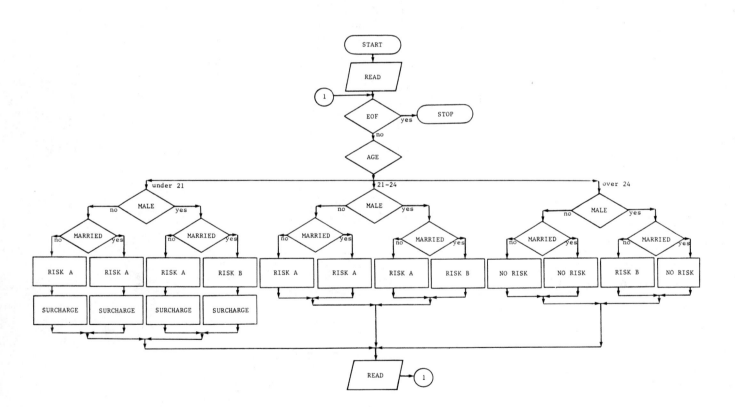

Exercises 6.1 (page 164)

1. UNIVERSALS: A, C, E, F, H, J, K, O, R
   EXECUTABLES (IN ORDER): B, P, Q, L, G, M, N, D, I, T, S

5. **a.** F, N, O, F, N, O, H, P, Q, H, P, Q, R, L, S, T, S, T

6. **a.**

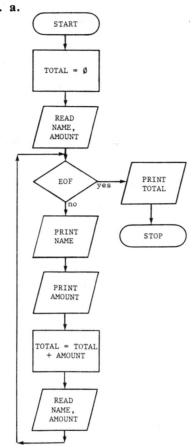

Exercises 6.2 (page 172)

1. b.

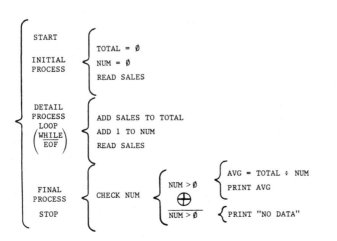

2. b.

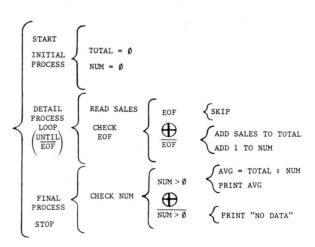

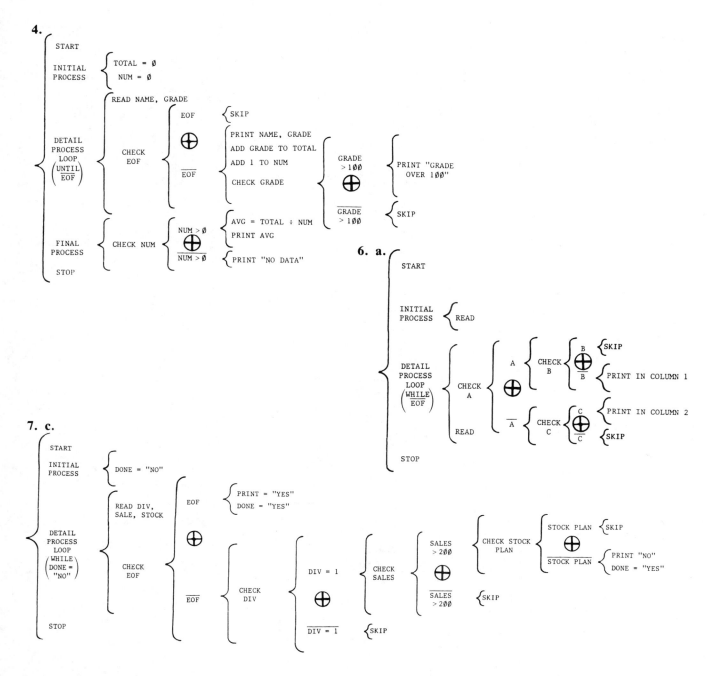

4.

```
START
INITIAL      ⎰ TOTAL = Ø
PROCESS      ⎱ NUM = Ø

DETAIL       READ NAME, GRADE
PROCESS
LOOP                              EOF   ⎰ SKIP
(UNTIL       CHECK      ⊕
 EOF)        EOF              ___       PRINT NAME, GRADE
                              EOF       ADD GRADE TO TOTAL      GRADE    PRINT "GRADE
                                        ADD 1 TO NUM            >1ØØ     OVER 1ØØ"
                                        CHECK GRADE      ⊕
                                                           _____       SKIP
                                                           GRADE
                                                           >1ØØ

FINAL                     NUM > Ø    AVG = TOTAL ÷ NUM
PROCESS      CHECK NUM  ⊕            PRINT AVG
                          _____
STOP                      NUM > Ø    PRINT "NO DATA"
```

6. a.

```
START
INITIAL      READ
PROCESS
DETAIL                                       A            B    SKIP
PROCESS                             CHECK   ⊕   CHECK     ___
LOOP         CHECK   ⊕              A            B        B    PRINT IN COLUMN 1
(WHILE       A
 EOF)                                        __           C    PRINT IN COLUMN 2
             READ                   A   CHECK            ⊕
STOP                                    C                __    SKIP
                                                         C
```

7. c.

```
START
INITIAL
PROCESS      DONE = "NO"

DETAIL       READ DIV,
PROCESS      SALE, STOCK                EOF    PRINT = "YES"
LOOP                            ⊕              DONE = "YES"
(WHILE       CHECK
 DONE =      EOF                 ___                        SALES
 "NO")                           EOF   CHECK      DIV = 1   > 2ØØ   CHECK STOCK   STOCK PLAN   SKIP
                                       DIV  ⊕     CHECK   ⊕ PLAN   ⊕
STOP                                             SALES                _____    PRINT "NO"
                                       ____      _____              STOCK PLAN   DONE = "YES"
                                       DIV = 1   SALES
                                         SKIP    > 2ØØ   SKIP
```

Exercises 6.3 (page 176)

1. a.

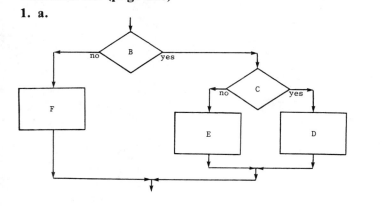

2. a.

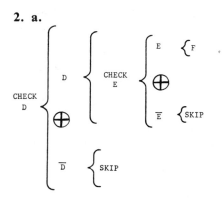

```
                        D        CHECK     E    F
CHECK       ⊕           E      ⊕
D                                __   SKIP
                                 E
            __
            D    SKIP
```

Exercises **6.3** continued

2. d.

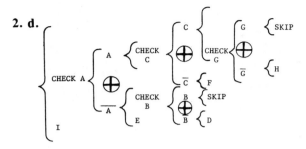

3. a.

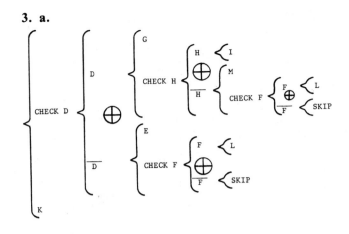

4. a.

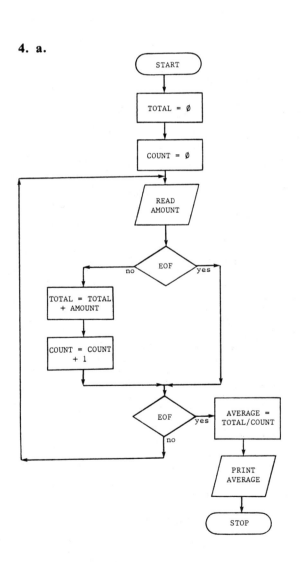

d.

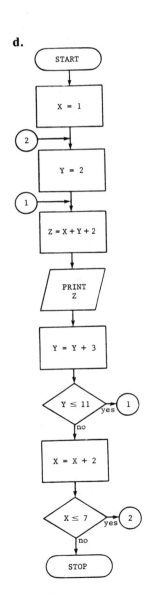

5. a.

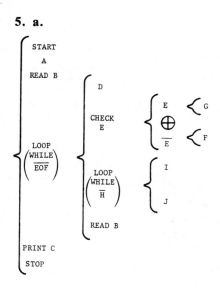

```
START
A
READ B
LOOP      D
(WHILE    CHECK     E  <  G
 ‾‾‾       E         ⊕
 EOF)                E̅  <  F

          LOOP       I
          (WHILE
           H̅  )      J

          READ B
PRINT C
STOP
```

6. a.

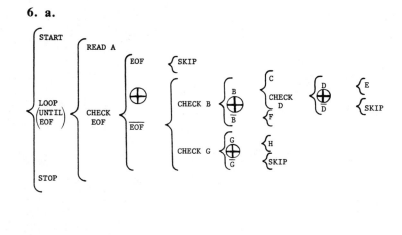

```
START          READ A
LOOP                   EOF  <  SKIP
(UNTIL  CHECK   ⊕                        B
 EOF)   EOF            CHECK B  ⊕   C    CHECK   D   <  E
                       E̅OF       B̅   <  D    D̅        D̅  <  SKIP
                                         F
STOP                   CHECK G  ⊕   G   <  H
                                    G̅      SKIP
```

Exercises 6.4 (page 187)

1.

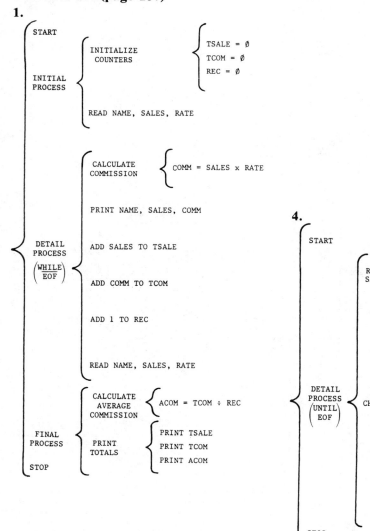

```
START
INITIAL    INITIALIZE      TSALE = 0
PROCESS    COUNTERS        TCOM = 0
                           REC = 0

           READ NAME, SALES, RATE

DETAIL     CALCULATE        COMM = SALES x RATE
PROCESS    COMMISSION
(WHILE
 E̅O̅F)      PRINT NAME, SALES, COMM
           ADD SALES TO TSALE
           ADD COMM TO TCOM
           ADD 1 TO REC
           READ NAME, SALES, RATE

FINAL      CALCULATE
PROCESS    AVERAGE         ACOM = TCOM ÷ REC
           COMMISSION
STOP                        PRINT TSALE
           PRINT           PRINT TCOM
           TOTALS          PRINT ACOM
```

4.

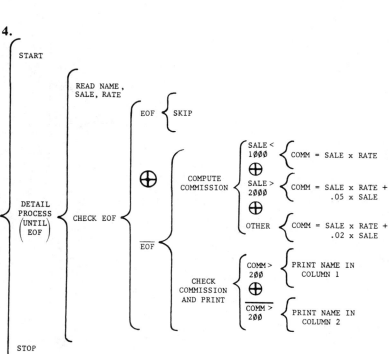

```
START
                READ NAME,
                SALE, RATE
                              EOF  <  SKIP
DETAIL
PROCESS  CHECK EOF   ⊕                  SALE <
(UNTIL                       COMPUTE    1000    <  COMM = SALE x RATE
 EOF)                        COMMISSION  ⊕
                E̅OF                     SALE >     COMM = SALE x RATE +
                                        2000    <  .05 x SALE
                                         ⊕
                                        OTHER   <  COMM = SALE x RATE +
                                                   .02 x SALE

                             CHECK       COMM >     PRINT NAME IN
                             COMMISSION   200    <  COLUMN 1
                             AND PRINT    ⊕
                                         C̅O̅M̅M̅ >    PRINT NAME IN
STOP                                      200    <  COLUMN 2
```

Exercises 6.5 (page 195)

1. a.

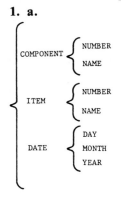

2. a.

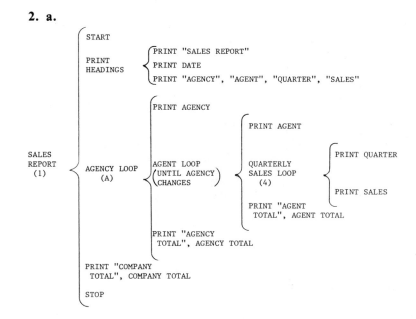

c.

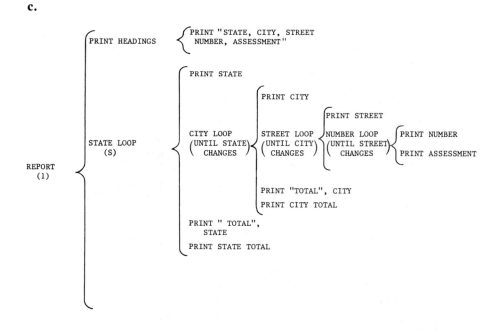

Exercises 6.6 (page 202)

2.

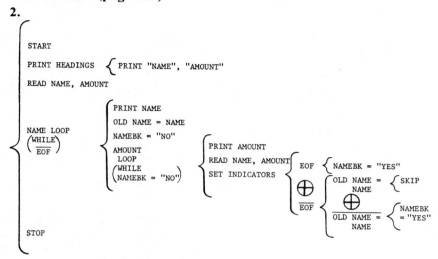

4.

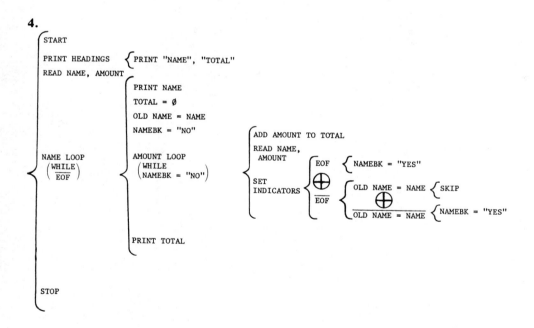

Exercise 6.6 continued

6.

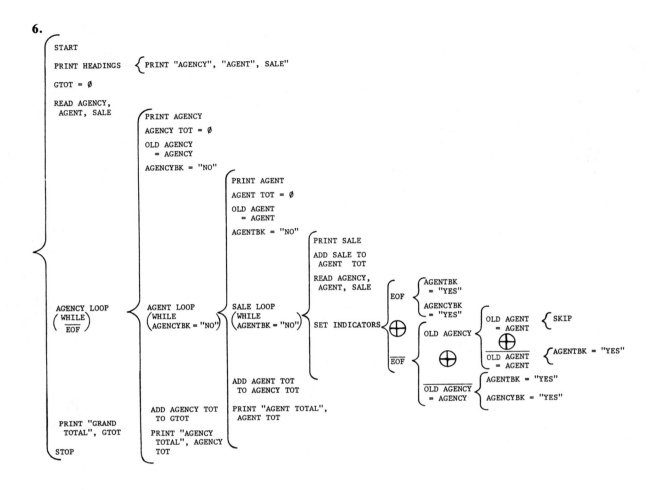

Exercises 7.1 (page 216)

1. a.

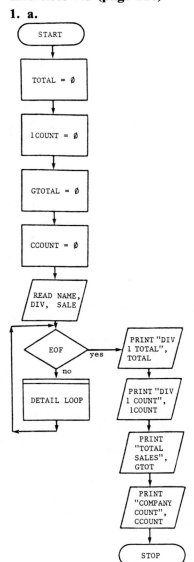

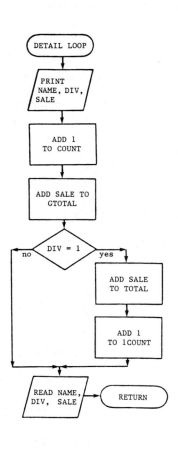

2. a.

```
RECORD COUNT
    ADD 1 TO TOTAL RECORDS
    IF GRADE > 0
        IF GRADE > 100
            ADD 1 TO ERROR RECORDS
        ELSE
            ADD 1 TO VALID RECORDS
        END IF
    ELSE
        ADD 1 TO ERROR RECORDS
    END IF
END RECORD COUNT
```

Exercises 7.1 continued

2. d.
START
DO PRINT HEADINGS
DO INITIALIZE COUNTERS
DO READ AND PRINT UNTIL EOF
DO PRINT TOTALS
STOP

PRINT HEADINGS
    PRINT "SALES REPORT"
    PRINT "DATE", DATE
END PRINT HEADINGS

INITIALIZE COUNTERS
    GTOT = 0
    N = 0
    X = 0
END INITIALIZE COUNTERS

READ AND PRINT
    READ NAME, TOTAL
    IF EOF
        SKIP
    ELSE
        PRINT NAME, TOTAL
        N = N + 1
        ADD TOTAL TO GTOTAL
        IF TOTAL > 10,000
            X = 1
        END IF
    END IF
END READ AND PRINT

PRINT TOTALS
    PRINT GTOTAL
    IF X > 0
        PRINT "AT LEAST ONE
           AGENT EXCEEDED 10,000"
    ELSE
        PRINT "NO AGENT EXCEEDED
           10,000"
    END IF
END PRINT TOTALS

4.
```
START
TOTAL = 0
FLAG = "NO"
DO DETAIL LOOP UNTIL EOF
    READ NAME, SALES
    IF EOF
        SKIP
    ELSE
        PRINT NAME, SALES
        ADD SALES TO TOTAL
        IF SALES > 2000
            FLAG = "YES"
        END IF
    END IF
END DO
PRINT TOTAL
IF FLAG = "YES"
    PRINT "AT LEAST ONE EXCEEDED 2000"
ELSE
    PRINT "NONE EXCEEDED 2000"
END IF
STOP
```

8. a.
```
START
DO DETAIL LOOP UNTIL EOF
    READ RECORD
    IF EOF
        SKIP
    ELSE
        IF A
            IF B
                SKIP
            ELSE
                PRINT 1
            END IF
        ELSE
            IF C
                PRINT 2
            END IF
        END IF
    END IF
END DO
STOP
```

Exercise 7.1 continued

10.
```
START
X = −1
DO OUTER LOOP WHILE X ≥ −11
    Y = 1
    TOTAL = 0
    DO INNER LOOP WHILE Y ≤ 10
        Z = 2 × X + Y
        PRINT Z
        ADD Z TO TOTAL
        Y = Y + 3
    END DO
    PRINT TOTAL
    X = X − 2
END DO
STOP
```

Exercises 7.2 (page 231)

1. b.

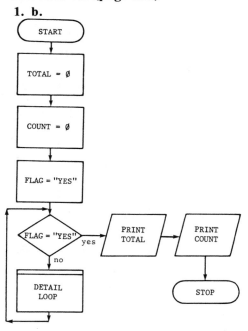

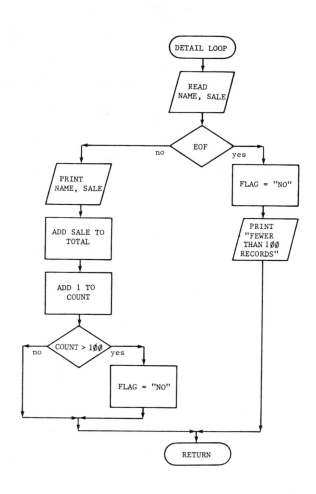

2. b.

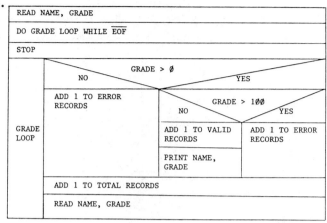

```
READ NAME, GRADE

DO GRADE LOOP WHILE EOF

STOP

GRADE          GRADE > Ø
LOOP      NO                        YES
        ADD 1 TO ERROR        GRADE > 100
        RECORDS           NO              YES
                     ADD 1 TO VALID    ADD 1 TO ERROR
                     RECORDS           RECORDS
                     PRINT NAME,
                     GRADE
        ADD 1 TO TOTAL RECORDS
        READ NAME, GRADE
```

5.

```
INITIALIZE    TOTAL = Ø
              NAM = Ø

READ NAME, AMOUNT

DO DETAIL LOOP WHILE EOF

PRINT TOTAL

PRINT NAM

STOP

                              FIRST RECORD
              NO                               YES
                  OLDNAME              OLDNAME = NAME
                  = NAME
              NO          YES          PRINT NAME
DETAIL    PRINT NAME                   ADD 1 TO NAM
LOOP      ADD 1 TO NAM
          OLDNAME = NAME
          ADD AMOUNT TO TOTAL
          READ NAME, AMOUNT
```

7.

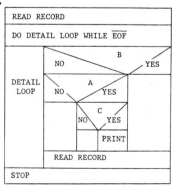

```
READ RECORD

DO DETAIL LOOP WHILE EOF

                        B
            NO              YES
DETAIL          A
LOOP    NO          YES
            C
        NO      YES
                PRINT
        READ RECORD

STOP
```

10.

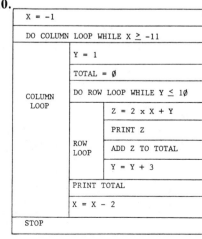

```
X = -1

DO COLUMN LOOP WHILE X ≥ -11

              Y = 1
              TOTAL = Ø
              DO ROW LOOP WHILE Y ≤ 10
COLUMN                  Z = 2 x X + Y
LOOP                    PRINT Z
              ROW       ADD Z TO TOTAL
              LOOP      Y = Y + 3
              PRINT TOTAL
              X = X - 2

STOP
```

Exercises 8.1-8.3 (page 240)

1. a. A(1) Jones; A(2) Klamer; A(3) Morris; A(4) Noris; A(5) O'Hara;
A(6) Paris; A(7) Quant; A(8) Reist; A(9) Simpson

2. a.

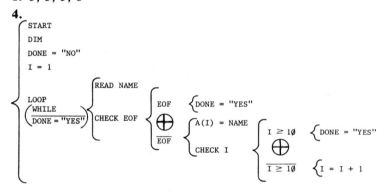

171.23	649.89	47.68	167.94	974.16	628.43
A(1)	A(2)	A(3)	A(4)	A(5)	A(6)
173.19	378.87	428.16			
A(7)	A(8)	A(9)	A(10)	A(11)	A(12)
Jones	Klamer	Morris	Noris	O'Hara	Paris
B(1)	B(2)	B(3)	B(4)	B(5)	B(6)
Quant	Reist	Simpson			
B(7)	B(8)	B(9)	B(10)	B(11)	B(12)

Jones	428.16
Klamer	378.87
Morris	173.19
Noris	628.43
O'Hara	974.16
Paris	167.94
Quant	47.68
Reist	649.89
Simpson	171.23

Exercises 8.4 (page 251)

1. 3, 3, 5, 6

4.

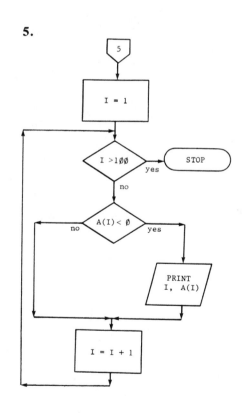

5.

8.

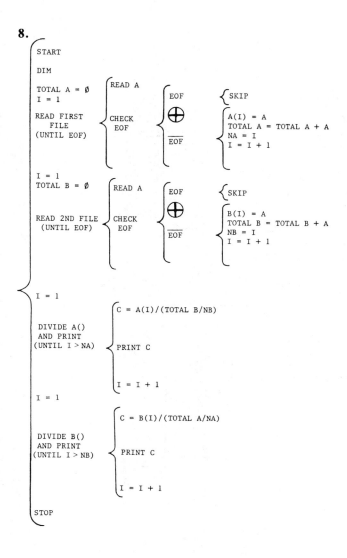

```
START

DIM

TOTAL A = Ø              READ A              EOF         SKIP
I = 1
                                                        A(I) = A
READ FIRST    CHECK                                     TOTAL A = TOTAL A + A
    FILE      EOF                           ───         NA = I
(UNTIL EOF)                                 EOF         I = I + 1


I = 1
TOTAL B = Ø              READ A              EOF         SKIP

                                                        B(I) = A
READ 2ND FILE  CHECK                                    TOTAL B = TOTAL B + A
  (UNTIL EOF)   EOF                         ───         NB = I
                                            EOF         I = I + 1



I = 1
                        C = A(I)/(TOTAL B/NB)

DIVIDE A()
AND PRINT
(UNTIL I > NA)          PRINT C


                        I = I + 1
I = 1
                        C = B(I)/(TOTAL A/NA)

DIVIDE B()
AND PRINT
(UNTIL I > NB)          PRINT C


                        I = I + 1

STOP
```

Exercises 8.5 (page 258)

2.

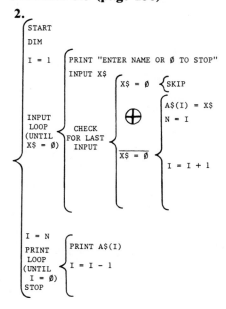

```
START
DIM
I = 1          PRINT "ENTER NAME OR Ø TO STOP"
               INPUT X$
                                    X$ = Ø    ⎧SKIP
INPUT                                         ⎨
LOOP           CHECK        ⊕                  A$(I) = X$
(UNTIL         FOR LAST                        N = I
X$ = Ø)        INPUT
                                    ‾X$‾=‾Ø‾   I = I + 1

I = N          PRINT A$(I)
PRINT
LOOP           I = I - 1
(UNTIL
 I = Ø)
STOP
```

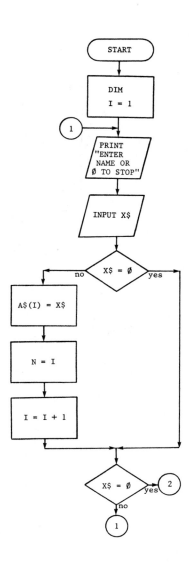

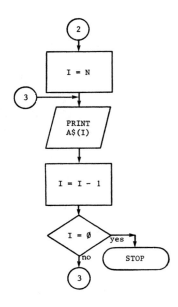

4.

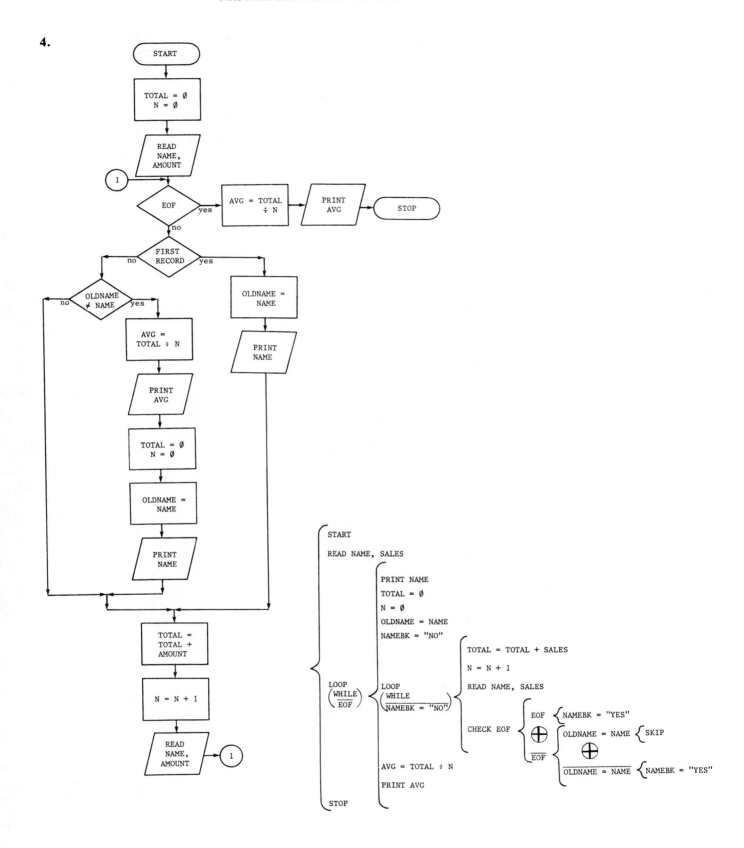

Exercises 8.6-8.7 (page 273)

1.

SALES REPORT

Name	Jan	Feb	Mar	Apr	May	June	July	Aug	Sep	Oct	Nov	Dec	Total
Adams	39.00	33.25	45.85	170.37	14.75	35.39	115.20	82.18	17.26	31.00	11.00	73.65	668.90
Smith	33.00	26.00	42.00	163.34	136.10	72.31	143.25	41.29	61.26	17.96	80.83	50.69	868.03
Jones	110.75	130.50	65.18	159.10	12.32	29.05	206.94	227.38	83.71	148.18	10.19	9.36	1192.66
Totals	182.75	189.75	153.03	492.81	163.17	136.75	465.39	350.85	162.23	197.14	102.02	133.70	

3.

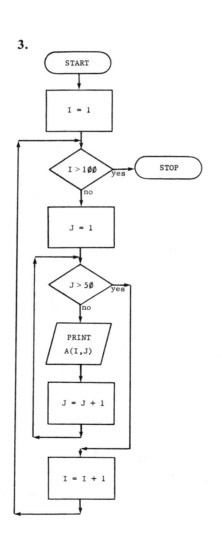

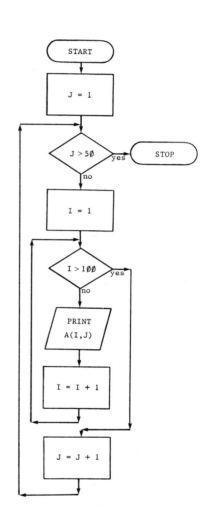

6.

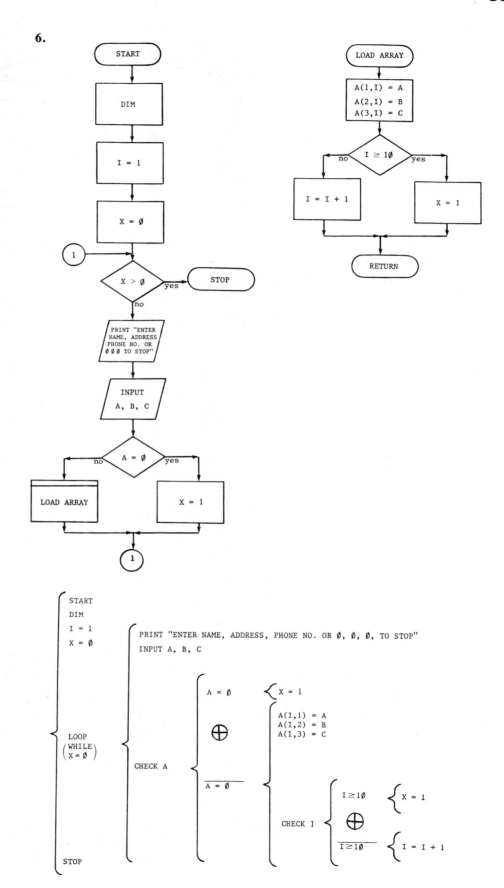

Exercises 8.8-8.10 (page 285)

3. a.

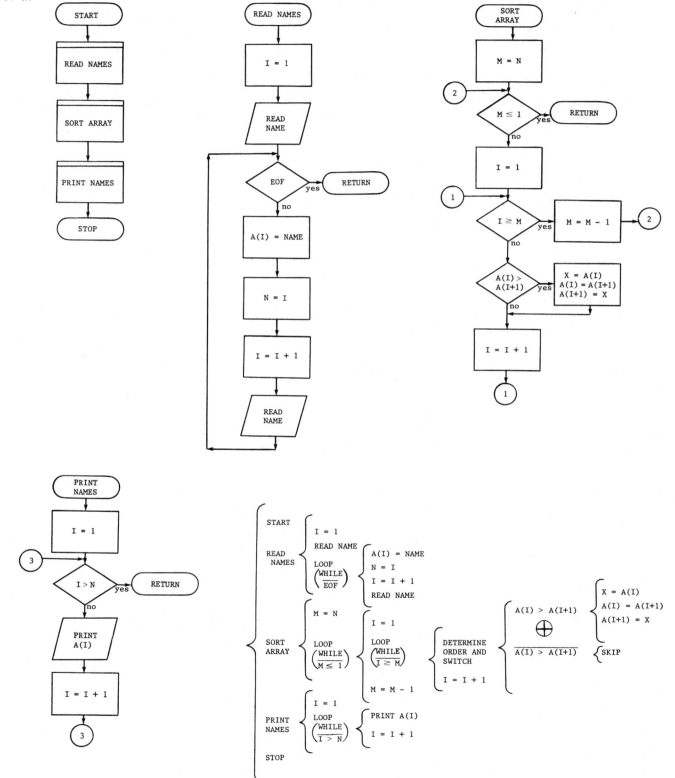

3. c.

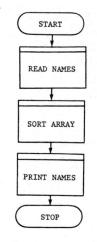

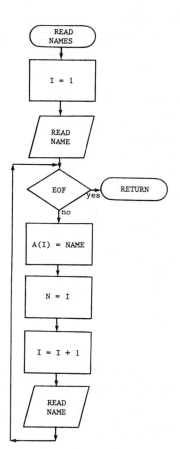

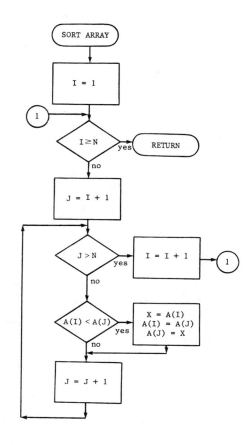

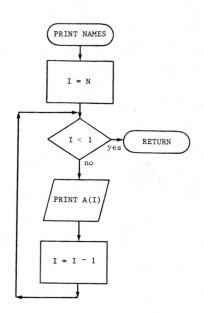

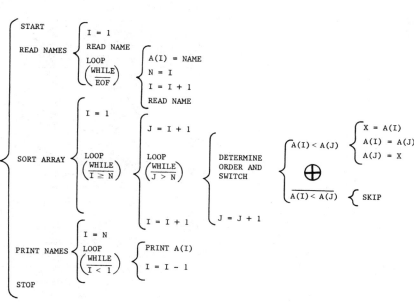

Exercises 9.1 (page 293)

2.

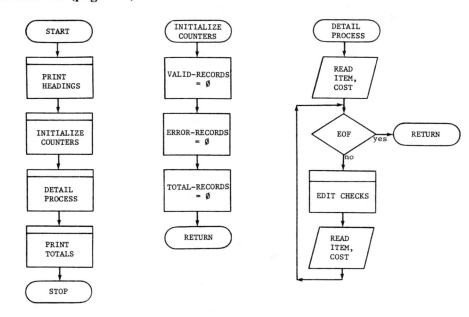

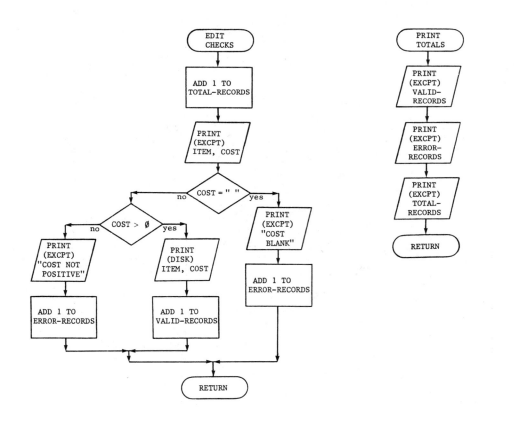

Exercises 9.2-9.3 (page 298)

2.

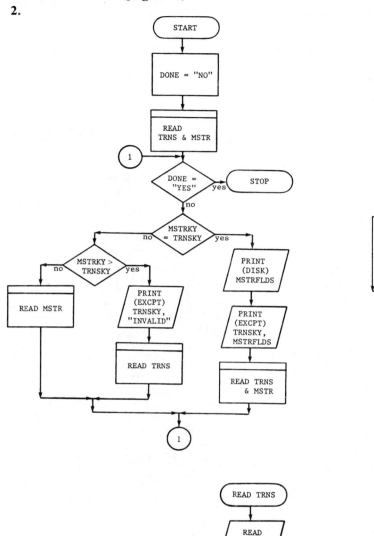

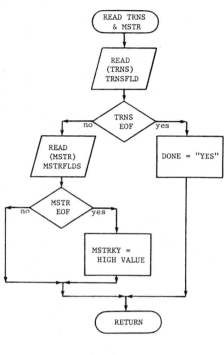

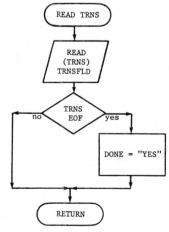

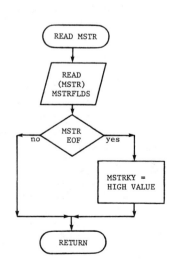

Index

0325
9